Asia's emerging regional order

Publication of this book was made possible with the support of the Japan Foundation, Asia Centre.

Asia's emerging regional order: Reconciling traditional and human security

Edited by William T. Tow, Ramesh Thakur, and In-Taek Hyun

United Nations University Press

TOKYO · NEW YORK · PARIS

The views expressed in this publication are those of the authors and
do not necessarily reflect the views of the United Nations University.

United Nations University Press
The United Nations University, 53-70, Jingumae 5-chome,
Shibuya-ku, Tokyo, 150-8925, Japan
Tel: +81-3-3499-2811   Fax: +81-3-3406-7345
E-mail: sales@hq.unu.edu
http://www.unu.edu

United Nations University Office in North America
2 United Nations Plaza, Room DC2-1462-70, New York, NY 10017, USA
Tel: +1-212-963-6387   Fax: +1-212-371-9454
E-mail: unuona@igc.apc.org

United Nations University Press is the publishing division of the United Nations
University.

Cover design by Andrew Corbett

Printed in the United States of America

UNUP-1046
ISBN 92-808-1046-4

Library of Congress Cataloging-in-Publication Data
Asia's emerging regional order : reconciling traditional and human security /
edited by William T. Tow, Ramesh Thakur, and In-Taek Hyun.
    p.   cm.
  Includes bibliographical references and index.
  ISBN 92-808-1046-4
  1. Quality of life-Asia. 2. Economic security-Asia. 3. National security-
Asia. I. Tow, William T. II. Thakur, Ramesh. III. Hyun, In-Taek.
  HN652.7.A75   2000
  306'.095—dc21   00-009584

Acknowledgements

As is usually the case with such projects, space limitations preclude the editors from thanking every individual and organization that played a role in making this publication possible. Without the efforts of both those listed below and a number of others who must be thanked anonymously, the quality of discussion and exchange which transpired during the project workshop and subsequently throughout this project's duration would not have been as strong as turned out to be the case.

We would like to thank the staff members of the Australian Defence Studies Centre for arranging and hosting the Canberra workshop component. In particular, the efforts of its Director, Associate Professor Anthony Bergin, and its Centre Manager, Kim Hogan, should be acknowledged. The Brisbane leg of the project was largely coordinated by Ulrika Bjorken, administrative coordinator for Griffith University's Centre for the Study of Australia-Asia Relations (CSAAR). She was ably assisted by Linda Buckham and Karen LaRocca, both on the administrative staff of the University of Queensland's Department of Government and its International Relations and Asian Politics Research Unit (IRAPRU). Sue Lochran from that Department was a key contributor to this book's production by typing and editing several manuscript drafts. The editors are also indebted to David Dellitt for extensive manuscript editing. CSAAR and IRAPRU were the project's two major research units but they were well supported by three other centres: Chulalongkorn University's Institute of Asian Studies, Korea University's Ilmin International Relations Institute and the University of Sydney's Research Institute for the Asia-Pacific (RIAP). Dr. Withaya Sucharithanarugse, Associate Professor In-Taek Hyun, and Dr. Rikki Kirsten represented these three centres at the workshop and all made substantial contributions to its success. The Australian Members Board of the Council for Security Cooperation in the Asia Pacific (AUS-CSCAP) was another project co-sponsor and a number of its personnel contributed papers or served as discussants to the Canberra programme.

The Japan Foundation's Asia Centre deserves special thanks for providing critical financial support for the project. We were honoured to have Samantha Johnson, the Japan Cultural Centre's (JCC's) project manager in Sydney, attend the Brisbane proceedings where she made a genuine contribution to the dialogue there. Kathryn Thomas, also of the JCC, was very helpful on a number of logistical issues. Australia's Department of Foreign Affairs and Trade (DFAT) contributed financial support and, as importantly, contributed through several of its key officials attending various workshop segments in both Canberra and Brisbane. DFAT also hosted the Asian workshop participants for special policy briefing and interchange on regional security in Canberra. Dr. Alan Thomas, First Assistant Secretary, North Asia Division, Dr. Richard Rigby, Assistant Secretary, East Asia Branch, and Mr. Frank Ingruber, Director, Korea Section, were all extremely helpful and instrumental in facilitating official participation and support from the Australian side.

We would like to thank Manfred F. Boemeke, Head of the UNU Press, Janet Boileau, the UNU Press Managing Editor, and the capable UNU staff for their collective efforts in seeing this project through to its final stages. Without their patience and continued support for the project, we would not have achieved its culmination. In particular, the two anonymous referees they engaged to review the original draft of the manuscript provided a number of incisive comments and useful suggestions.

Finally, the editors would like to thank their partners and children for their continued support and understanding for those of us who expend most of our professional and personal energies on generating academic analysis, all too often at the expense of their own priorities and schedules. We hope that this book might provide enough insight to justify our all too frequent absences and late hours.

Introduction

William T. Tow

At the start of a new century, the problem of how to conceptualize and achieve international security remains as elusive as ever. Many would argue that traditional, state-centric thinking is becoming increasingly outmoded by the frequency and diversity of episodes that directly threaten the safety and welfare of people throughout different regions and societies but that seem beyond the power of national governments to resolve.

Recent developments in south-eastern Europe, Indonesia, the Middle East, and sub-Saharan Africa, encompassing seemingly intractable ethnic and religious hostilities, appear to reinforce the dire warning embodied in the "clash of civilizations" thesis that one's future security will hinge not so much on where you are but who you are.[1] Intensified trends of "globalization," rendering all of us more economically and technologically interdependent than at any other point in history, have diluted the state's capacity to exercise coercive power in every instance when its interests or values are challenged. However, the ravages of international anarchy have not been curbed because consensus about how international law should be applied or how international human rights should be interpreted is still highly elusive. What Seyom Brown describes as the "widening gap" between the emergent realities of interdependence in civil society, public order, economics, ecology, culture, and human rights on one hand, and the legal/political structure of the nation-state system on the other, has not yielded a new security paradigm that can be applied

1

effectively and universally to generate an international consensus on order, security, and justice.[2]

The idea of "human security" is commanding increased attention as an alternative approach to conceptualizing and meeting such challenges. This concept is hardly new.[3] It has assumed particular salience, however, in the aftermath of the Cold War. As Canadian Foreign Minister Lloyd Axworthy recently observed, human security issues are those that "strike directly home to the individual ... largely ignor[ing] state boundaries" and requiring "action and co-operation at different levels – global, regional and local – if they are to be tackled effectively."[4] Human security thus transcends the traditional "levels of analysis" problem which has confronted international relations policy-makers and analysts. It endeavours to link the processes and problems of globalization to the community and the individual that it is supposed to serve. It is intended to allow each citizen, regardless of sovereign origins, to be in touch with their world in ways which make that environment less forbidding and more palatable. It also holds separate states accountable, however, to the norms of international humanitarian law: "to civilize warfare and to aid its victims." Or, put in slightly different terms, "to save lives and reduce the suffering of individuals during armed conflict."[5]

This concept appears to be especially relevant to the Asia-Pacific region, which is experiencing immense structural changes. The region's recent economic crisis imposed widespread economic disparity and immense socio-political hardship on the people of a region that had previously been living apart in what was the world's most unqualified economic success story. Overvalued currencies, falling foreign exchange reserves, and high levels of short-term foreign debt in such countries as Indonesia, Malaysia, South Korea, and Thailand all led to panic by foreign creditors and to the ruination of national economies. Unemployment rates grew several-fold in most affected countries.[6]

Yet rescue packages structured by the International Monetary Fund (IMF) were condemned by many of their intended Asian beneficiaries as unreasonable demands by the United States and other Western industrialized states to force through social and political reforms alien to their own culture and values. Although the economic crisis was bottoming out by mid-1999, it still imposed severe and long-lasting social ramifications for large proportions of Asia's population: a sizeable percentage dipped below the poverty line, increasing numbers of young people dropped out of school, and confidence in existing political systems declined sharply. Falling real incomes, destabilizing migration flows, food shortages and malnutrition, declining public health and education, and intensifying crime rates are all now confronting Asia's incumbent leaderships. Indonesia's political turmoil leading to the fall of the Suharto government in May 1999 was the most graphic illustration of how such frustrations can generate wholesale instability. Many Asian governments continue to face similar pressures, which may well prove to be beyond their capacity to resolve or contain if they continue to adhere to more traditional security focuses and approaches.

The human security approach may have a different conceptual focus than its traditional security counterpart, but the obstacles confronting its implementation are no less complex and are often overlapping. The East Timor crisis exploded into genocidal warfare after an indigenous population exercised its democratic right to opt for self-determination by use of the ballot box in late summer 1999. The quick and forceful response of the international community to forge a "coalition of the willing" to check the pro-Indonesian militia groups' rampant killing sprees on that island underscored the increased role of humanitarian intervention in facing contemporary human security crises. Yet the convergence of interests that allowed for most Asian states to contribute to that coalition contrasts markedly with the conflict of interests that currently shapes nuclear weapons politics in the Asia-Pacific. China, North Korea, India, and Pakistan all view their nuclear forces as instruments of just war, developed and deployed to protect their current political systems and their populations-at-large from hegemonic threats posed by each other or by extra-regional powers. Even the two nuclear superpowers, the United States and Russia, are becoming less able to view each other's conduct in this policy area as reflecting their mutual determination to liberate the world's peoples from the spectre of nuclear war. This is particularly true as the United States embraces new defensive technologies that promise radically to transform thinking about deterrence and other components of the traditional security paradigm. It is clear that the various divisions and configurations that rendered traditional security politics so uncertain during the Cold War will be no less complicated concerning human security issues in the region as they emerge in a post–Cold War context.

Yet the very complexity of these challenges defies their resolution through traditional and exclusive state-centric approaches. The economic crisis, for example, was reflective of a larger paradigm shift in international security politics from a predominantly military emphasis to a broader focus on non-military challenges to human survival and welfare.[7] As Japanese Prime Minister Obuchi argued before a conference on human security convened in Tokyo in 1998, these problems cannot be solved by deploying military forces or relying on international diplomats to fashion traditional power balances along state-centric lines. They must instead be resolved through cooperative intellectual interaction leading to transnational knowledge and "epistemic communities." Most fundamentally, governments must initiate and sustain more direct ties with those over whom they presume to rule.[8]

Acknowledging the potential importance of human security in shaping the Asia-Pacific's geopolitical and economic destinies, several Australian research centres convened a workshop in August/September 1998 to consider its dimensions. Discussions were conducted in Canberra and Brisbane over four days, involving both Asian and Australian participants. Some of these were chosen because their research embodies various aspects of the human security problem. Others were selected as established authorities in various traditional approaches to security studies. It was hoped that they could provide useful checks and balances in a workshop dedicated to exploring alternative approaches to human security. The overall intent underscoring participant selection was to bring together a diverse and stimulating group of analysts that could enrich our understanding of how human security politics relates to the dynamics of the contemporary international environment.

Some preliminary conclusions about the human security concept were reached and additional questions were generated. Among the questions were the following:

- What levels of activity and/or what interest groups can best facilitate human security politics; what future role, if any, can traditional nation-states play in either advancing or impeding human security?
- Who will lead a human security approach to regional security and how will it be organized?
- How would structural concerns be overcome in organizing human security? and
- To what extent could Asia-Pacific "middle powers" such as Korea and Australia work together to affect great power interest and political behaviour in ways that could facilitate a new and more individually oriented regional security order?

It became clear as the workshop's discussions intensified that a consensus on how to answer these questions would not be achieved rapidly or easily. States can threaten their own populaces as easily and frequently as they support them. Different and very diverse interest groups may be involved in future efforts to implement the concept. Regional implementation of human security will be complicated by the reality that it is likely to be driven by "bottom–up" rather than "top–down" forces and processes, with grass-roots movements pressuring otherwise indifferent or insensitive élites to incorporate their agendas into policy-making initiatives.

The question of who will – or should – exercise the human security franchise will be integral to shaping its overall impact and effectiveness.

This relates directly to the question of who is the target audience for this volume. There is no single target group but it is our intent to stimulate debate about the human security problem among those who may be most willing to accept the challenge of developing and implementing this approach into tangible policy strategies. This process may occur at either the state-centric or non-state levels of operation. It may involve established government policy-makers, non-governmental organizations (NGOs) promoting a particular dimension of human security covered in this study, or independent analysts concerned with strengthening its analytical utility. It matters less from which professional or social sector human security "practitioners" may originate than that the concept be debated within a sufficiently wide and diverse audience to consider its merits and shortcomings. This book is intended to provide a catalyst for such a debate.

The workshop discussions particularly focused on structural concerns. Is human security pursued within an exclusively multilateral security environment or can bilateral ties facilitate its advancement? Is human security more "holistic" in nature (as implied by Prime Minister Obuchi), with increasingly universal ideas of "civil society" and "interdependence" rendering traditional demarcations between "domestic" and "international" security less relevant? A case can be made that states remain critical agents in implementing and enforcing standards and mechanisms designed to overcome functional challenges to human prosperity and welfare such as narcotics traffic, environmental degradation, and terrorism. States (and especially so-called "middle powers," which are less beholden to traditional security postulates such as power balancing or strategic deterrence) are presumably best able to identify niche policy areas and to direct resources toward fulfilling them.

It can be counter-argued, however, that sovereignty and human security are basically incompatible ideas, as the security referent shifts from the state to the individual. Indeed, states in the Asia-Pacific and elsewhere are often governed by élites whose legitimacy is contested and whose policies threaten their own polities more than any external threat. The idea of "failed states" is often ignored or downplayed by traditional security approaches that emphasize state-centric power balances and treat the concept of "state" as a single and undifferentiated unit of analysis.[9] In this context, non-governmental organizations may be destined to play a greater role as conduits between the concerns and priorities of individuals and the state's willingness and ability to respond.

This book is organized into four major sections. Initially, it identifies and evaluates some key theoretical propositions that underlie the idea of human security from Australian and "Asian" vantagepoints, respectively. Chapter 1, co-authored by William Tow and Russell Trood, and Chapter

2, written by Woosang Kim and In-Taek Hyun, apply somewhat different analytical frameworks to assess how the traditional and human security approaches might be reconciled. Both chapters, however, conclude that existing institutions such as the United Nations or regional security organizations such as the Regional Forum of the Association of South East Asian Nations (ARF) have not yet successfully linked individual safety as it is embodied in human security with the broader parameters of stability and order that underwrite most traditional security approaches. Tow and Trood call for the forging of more compatible agendas between the two schools of thought, whereas Kim and Hyun advocate greater use of middle power diplomacy and independent groups of experts or "epistemic communities" to reconcile the two camp's agendas.

Part 2 of this volume is concerned with relating the human security ethos to a specific Asia-Pacific context. Withaya Sucharithanarugse argues that it must move beyond the common referents of human rights and humanitarian intervention if it is to make a lasting impression with Asian élites and populaces. He also makes a case that the concept must not restrict its mandate to one of ensuring survival but also entail the pursuit of dignity, an objective all too often ignored by state-centric actors and authorities. Indonesia constitutes a particularly important case study of how the application of human security could "make a difference" in the region. Ikrar Nusa Bhakti forwards a relatively optimistic portrayal of Indonesia's recent political liberalization and concludes that its development of a recognizable civil society and effective epistemic communities leading up to the Suharto government's demise bodes well for the future of human security in what is arguably South-East Asia's most critical polity. Carl Ungerer applies the middle power diplomacy model initially introduced by Kim and Hyun in chapter 2 to Australia's efforts to promote various arms control issues related to the overall human security agenda. The "Asian dimension" of this diplomatic style is highly instructive as Australian officials took care to initiate special dialogues with their regional counterparts concerning the banning of chemical weapons and landmines. Most Asian states were able to close ranks with the Australians in pressing for the implementation of the two relevant conventions under review, exemplifying how state-centric and non-state objectives could be integrated on specific issues by a well-coordinated diplomatic campaign.

Part 3 of the book delves more specifically into human security's relevance to key issue areas. Chapter 6, written by Hyun-Seok Yu, weighs how human security's postulates interrelate with the so-called "Asian values" debate. Yu adopts a reasonably critical approach to the issues raised by the Asian values discourse and concludes that human security facilitates a proper "social distance" between the individual and the state.

Part 1

Human security: Developing the concept

1

Linkages between traditional security and human security

William T. Tow and Russell Trood

Security is a contested concept, with controversies surrounding its meaning being especially pronounced during times of historical change. The end of the Cold War has prompted a particularly lively debate over the meaning of security and security studies as a field of enquiry. Set against a traditional view of security, with its emphasis on postulates, such as confronting anarchy and achieving national security through the use of military power, more contemporary approaches take a broader perspective, often incorporating economic, societal, and environmental dimensions into their agenda. In recent years, "human security" has attracted increasing attention as a fresh variant of the latter approach. As defined by the United Nations *Human Development Report 1994*, "human security" includes "safety from chronic threats such as hunger, disease, and repression, as well as protection from sudden and harmful disruptions in the patterns of daily life."[1] In more recent scholarship and as employed by some policy-makers, the concept has been expanded to include economic, health, and environmental concerns, as well as the physical security of the individual.[2] So conceived, human security represents a radically different approach to security from that presented by the traditional security paradigm.

The debate between traditional and human security advocates is, as the editors of one recent text evaluating it have argued, healthy for the field.[3] There is a danger, however, that the controversy may generate little more than intellectual chaos in an already confused and crowded field and default security policy to the scholarly supporters and enthusiastic advocates of the traditional approach. Certainly there continues to be a large number of both writers and practitioners for whom the key elements of the traditional security paradigm are as relevant today as they were at the height of the Cold War.[4] In these circumstances, the challenge for the advocates of human security is to define and present their concept with rigour and clarity and to demonstrate how it might be operationalized in an international environment not readily conducive to radical reinterpretations of security.

Those who inhabit the two broad intellectual camps under review here tend to defend their respective views zealously, not readily conceding the merits of the other side's position. Human security advocates often tend to be dismissive of the "old geopolitics" and its tendency to declare fault lines around individual nation-states.[5] The need to confront and resolve the challenges created by the changing nature of the states system leaves them little room to indulge traditionalist preoccupations with armed conflict, power balancing, and anarchy. They are visionary by predisposition and believe their normative horizons wider than the narrow prejudices of the realist. Traditionalists, likewise, have little patience with those who would dilute the established field of security studies by overloading it with an ambitious agenda of problems and issues that would compromise the analytical power of their critical ideas. They remain overwhelmingly positivist and instrumental. Human security advocates are cast as offering the promise of a new, more cooperational, but perhaps unattainable and unrealistic international order. Traditional security proponents are forced to defend the old, and discredited, international order, unable to transcend the static limitations of their thinking.

Overcoming this mutual intellectual disdain will be no easy task and we cannot presume to undertake it here. Rather, we can seek to identify some areas of congruity in the two sides' thinking and explore them (briefly) in a specific regional (Asian) context. Before examining these "linkages," however, it may be useful to define and discuss the two concepts more fully and to suggest their importance to the flourishing debate about the character of international security. In this context, a key question is "security for whom?" because traditional and human security paradigms usually answer this question in fundamentally different ways. Although this makes the issue of "linkage" especially problematic, it is no less compelling. Without achieving at least some reconciliation between traditional and human security, the theoretical and policy tensions between them will not be resolved and security studies will be little more than a proliferation of incompatible approaches and concepts seen through different and conflicting prisms.

Traditional security

Several distinct concepts set "traditionalists" in security studies apart from their more "radical" human security counterparts.[6] First, to traditionalists, the state is the central unit of analysis. Security is commensurate with national survival within a world that is inherently contentious and anarchical. Accordingly, much of what passed for security studies prior to 1991 was most concerned with how *national security* was managed in a "self-reliant" world.

Second, understanding force postures and capabilities is a key tenet of traditional security. Justified by their sovereign prerogatives, states develop military doctrines; weapons systems serve their defence, but may also intensify inter-state tensions and fuel security dilemmas. This is an ineluctable consequence of the fact that states perceive each other's military postures and systems to be offensive and threatening to their own, which they regard as defensive and benign.[7]

Third, the major preoccupation of traditionalists is state survival. Since force capabilities are the ultimate means by which a state's will can be imposed upon those who might oppose or contest it, modern security studies, as Steven Walt has argued, have evolved around seeking "cumulative knowledge" about the role of military force.[8] This conforms with the general positivist orientation embraced by much of the traditional security literature. The traditionalists' operative paradigm secures legitimacy on the basis of realist principles that are declared to be immutable to collective human behaviour. Competition for power and relative gains within an international states system are regarded as natural conditions within any "states system."

Several variants of the traditional approach have emerged over the past decade as the predominance of state "schisms" has become increasingly questioned. Among the most important traditional security variants are: the theory of hegemonic competition; the "clash of civilizations" thesis; the "democratic peace" thesis; and complex interdependence.

Hegemonic competition predicts that new forms of state polarity and power balancing will replace the Soviet–American competition that dominated the last half of the twentieth century, perhaps with three or four major powers vying with the United States for global pre-eminence.[9] It is most compatible with the traditional security paradigm because it is state-centric in its assumptions about the nature of international competition and the (meaningful) distribution of power. By way of contrast, however, Samuel Huntington contends that schisms and conflicts will be less state-centric and based more on cultural identity. Ethno-nationalists and civilizations, he claims, can be just as ruthless in pursuing their survival as sovereign states, even if their physical boundaries are less precise.[10] Contests for power between these civilizations will define the international politics of the coming era. The "democratic peace" thesis anticipates that liberal democracies will be less prone to conflict than a heterogeneous states system because they cultivate and sustain common values.[11] Finally, complex interdependence contests the traditional maxims of self-help and relative gains, arguing that anarchy can be overcome through pursuing mutual dependence through cooperation. Although the state is a penetrated entity in the interdependence model, it retains its traditional nomenclature since it prescribes alternative means to attain the same end – greater stability and a higher probability of states surviving in an anarchical world.[12]

There is now a large and growing literature presenting a range of different approaches to the traditional security paradigm. Many of these newer perspectives pre-date the end of the Cold War, but the proliferation of approaches has certainly since gained momentum. Those dissatisfied with traditional or "realist" explanations of security politics discount the above variants and call for a broadening of the entire security paradigm. Pressure has thus intensified to revise the World War II "strategic studies" legacy that underscored much of security politics and that assigned primacy to the interrelationship between military means and political ends. Against this background, a growing number of scholars and analysts have called for a more comprehensive and systematic approach to security, one that moves beyond the narrow preoccupation with the state and examines more general threats to human existence and ways to overcome them.[13]

These approaches have translated into the development of the concept of "human security." But although the concept has been taken up in the security studies literature, it has not necessarily been embraced by states' policy-makers. For the most part, they continue to concentrate on what they view as their primary mission: pursuing national security interests and state survival. The positivist and competitive orientations of traditional security are thus reinforced, and broader concerns about the quality of life, community-building, and other problems outside the realm of traditional geo-strategy are relegated to a less urgent agenda to be managed by others. Indeed, advocates of broadening the security paradigm acknowledge that traditional strategic dimensions of international security remain important. As Booth and Herring have noted, "there will be wars ... defence ministries will devise strategies ... and people will be killed."[14] Until the policy sanctity of "the national interest" and *realpolitik* concepts – particularly conspicuous among Asian policy élites – is overcome or modified, however, prospects are slight that policy-makers' preference for state-centric referents will be supplanted by, or even complemented with, more "humanistic" calculations.

Human security

The intellectual roots of the human security movement precede the Cold War's demise by nearly a quarter century. Writing shortly before his death in the mid-1960s, Canadian psychologist W. E. Blatz derived a theory of "individual security" based on his observations of human learning processes and how they interrelate with society and authority. Blatz's main premise was that security is "all inclusive and all pervasive," encompassing social relations, belonging to groups and communities, and compensating for self-perceived vulnerabilities or insecurities by accepting particular types of authority – a state of "mature dependent security."[15] His theory departed from that later developed as part of "orthodox" human security, however, insofar as he insisted that a secure state of mind does not equate with the feeling of "safety"; secure people become their own agents who hardly need the "protective armour of an agent."[16] In the end, Blatz espoused the gospel of self-sufficiency. Agents within a community could best facilitate their own "independent security" rather than seeking their individual "emancipation" through primary dependence upon others' goodwill.

Another dimension of the foundations of human security can be found in the theories of international development and particularly in the concept of "world system."[17] According to these ideas, developed "cores" of socio-economic élite groups and underdeveloped and marginalized groups living in the world's "peripheries" interact in ways that condemn the latter to a permanent condition of economic and social exploitation. "Structural violence" is thus ingrained in the international system and belies the notion of complex interdependence. Decision-making is regulated by highly mechanistic and rigid regimes that reinforce this process of exploitation. This cycle of oppression is best alleviated, world system theorists have concluded, by changing the "teleologies" (systemic purposes) of the paradigm that justifies it. Peace and security need to be refocused away from states that are in the core and aspire to ensuring their "security" through war or containment and toward human rights and greater equality in resources, health, and environment.

The end of the Cold War has served as the backdrop for a more comprehensive exploration of these ideas. In this context, this historical benchmark was noteworthy less for the clarity of structural or systemic change than for precipitating debate over an unprecedented array of complex issues previously subordinated by ideological competition between the superpowers. The United Nations was a natural focal point for organizing agendas on problems of socio-economic inequality, environmental degradation, and humanitarian concerns. Its annual *Human Development Reports* have reflected this orientation. Since early 1996, the UN Security Council has worked with a selected group of non-governmental organizations (NGOs) to advance human security through the Global Policy Forum (GPF). The GPF includes such groups as Oxfam, Amnesty International, and the Cooperative for Assistance and Relief Everywhere, with, overall, more than 30 organizations being represented and consulting regularly with UN ambassadors to explore ways of integrating human security initiatives into the Security Council agenda. Particular concerns include the effects of Security Council sanctions on the lives of innocent civilians, women's rights, humanitarian relief, and global disarmament.[18]

"Human security" analysts have thus argued that there are compelling and urgent reasons for revising traditional security approaches. First, it is argued that national security approaches are insufficiently sensitive toward cultural differences, and thus ignore many states' decisions to use or apply military force.[19] Indeed, state fragmentation is intensifying along socio-ethnic lines in a number of geographic locales, including Eastern Europe and various parts of Africa and Central Asia, and other nationalities such as the Kurds and the Karins in Myanmar are clamouring for sovereign autonomy. Increasingly, "societal security" – the study of social organization along ethnic lines – is vying with traditional national security concerns for policy-makers' attention.[20]

A second consideration in assigning greater priority to human security relates to the recent increase in complex humanitarian emergencies that defy traditional deference to the principle of "non interference in sovereign affairs." Humanitarian interventions in Kosovo and East Timor by "coalitions of the willing" have reflected this trend. Conflicts in today's world are increasingly about defending ethnic and religious groups from each other or salvaging the remnants of civilized life that remain after natural disasters. These types of operations have thus become the international community's ultimate human security endeavours. Intervention in inter-state disputes with peace-keeping or peace enforcement contingents is still important but relatively less so. Yet the agents of humanitarian intervention remain cautious and discriminate over what specific episodes of ethnic strife or natural disasters merit their involvement and resource expenditures.[21]

A third issue is predictability: not only did traditional security approaches fail to anticipate the end of the Cold War, their applicability in its aftermath is increasingly questionable. International politics, it is contended, is increasingly conducted at diverse levels of international society, not exclusively by the state.[22] Placing the state at the centre of the security paradigm accords less and less with the reality of the states' role in the international system. Approaching the issue from a somewhat different perspective, observers of a "constructivist" persuasion question the fundamental existence of anarchy, a proposition that underlies state-centric assumptions about self-reliance. They contend that this condition is "learned" rather than intrinsic to international politics and can be obviated by behavioural change.[23]

Perhaps the most basic challenge to traditional security, however, emanates from the "globalist" school of thought, from which many of the postulates of "human security" are derived. Globalists argue that an "international society" is emerging that integrates communications, cultures, and economics in ways that transcend state-centric relations. Global social movements are fostered often through the creation and applications of NGOs to specific causes and through the development of an international "civil society." Yet the complexity of this process also generates a wide array of new problems related to the security and welfare of humanity, which are often beyond the capabilities of individual states to control. "Globalization" has thus precipitated threats to traditional institutions such as the nuclear family, religious groups, and labour unions. The effects are far greater, however, in developing societies where governments are often overwhelmed by the costs, technological barriers, and social cleavages impeding their ability to provide even the most basic necessities to their populaces. A radical transformation of international security politics and the formation of more comprehensive security regimes and communities are thus required to meet these challenges.[24]

Human security's specific contribution to the globalist argument has thus been its focus on the *individual* as the object of security. Canadian Foreign Minister Lloyd Axworthy, perhaps the developed world's most conspicuous diplomatic proponent of human security, has listed safety for people from both violent and non-violent threats and taking measures to reduce vulnerability or remedial action where prevention fails as core preconditions.[25] More specifically, as George MacLean has observed, it "recognises that an individual's personal protection and preservation comes not just from the safeguarding of the state as a political unit, but also from access to individual welfare and the quality of life."[26]

A further distinguishing feature of the human security approach is its concern with "structural violence" emanating from non-territorial (as opposed to state-centric) security threats. This flows from the world systems theory legacy described above and targets attention on environmental degradation, food shortages, uncontrolled refugee flows, or various pandemics.[27] Scarcity of environmental resources, for example, is regarded as a direct cause of aggravated stresses within peripheral areas. These, in turn, destabilize economic relations, provoke migrations and, ultimately, can precipitate conflict and war. Further, rapid population growth in developing areas could lead to the collapse of some of the world's fundamental physical and biological systems halfway into the twenty-first century.[28] According to human security analysts, the basic struggle between the world's core and periphery or "North–South" sectors continues to intensify.

Yet another component of human security entails addressing threats to citizens originating from *within* states. Human rights violations, inter-group hostility and violence, and class stratification exemplify this dimension of the human security problem, one that, again, is not integral to the way sovereign boundaries are drawn. MacLean again captures the essence of the differences between the traditional and human security paradigms in this area of policy concern:

[J]ust as traditional notions of territorial security involve the structured violence manifest in state warfare, human security also attends to the issue of unstructured violence. Human security, in short, involves the security of the individual in their personal surroundings, their community, and in their environment.[29]

Although not intended to be comprehensive, table 1.1 presents a comparative exploration of different dimensions of traditional and human security approaches.

By viewing the individual's identity as a problem of "societal security" or "communitarian security" rather than "national security," the framework of state-centric levels of analysis employed by the traditional security paradigm becomes contestable. Underscoring human security's determi-

Table 1.1 Traditional and human security: Comparative aspects

Traditional security	Human security
Territorially sovereign	Not necessarily spatially oriented
State	Community and individual
Diplomatic and military	Socio-political, socio-economic, environmental
Institutionalized	Non-institutionalized
Formal (political)	Informal (intuitive)
Structured violence	Unstructured violence
Diplomatic and military; unilateral	Scientific, technological; multilateral governance

Source: Extracted from George MacLean, "The United Nations and the New Security Agenda" at http://www.unac.org/canada/security/maclean.html.

nation to disaggregate the state and focus on the security of the individual, the watchword for human security's orientation is interconnectedness, with good governance the key to its realization. Various NGOs have emerged to become active in the United Nations and in other policy settings in overcoming the dominance of state-centric security politics, and this process has generated some visible successes – including the December 1997 landmine treaty and several major covenants on global warming.[30]

Good governance – sometimes labelled "humane governance" – recognizes that all individuals are stakeholders in security, not on the basis of sovereign affiliation but as "members of a transcendent human community with common global concerns." In many cases, however, individuals' "citizenship" works against their security, enabling élites and institutions to impose constraints on political opposition and to rationalize the use of violence on the basis of reinforcing "us" versus "them."[31]

To be more specific, traditional security forces in many of the states in the Asia-Pacific region have often been just as concerned with the "enemy within" as with a real or imagined external foe. "Internal" enemies have often been opposed to the government rather than to the state and/ or regime – although they have sometimes opposed the latter and sought to overthrow them as well. For example, secessionist movements are generally opposed to the state, and usually seek to set up a sovereign state of their own. But movements for democratization (e.g. in South Korea during the 1980s, in the Philippines under Marcos, in Indonesia under Suharto, and in Myanmar under the State Law and Order Restoration Council) are usually opposed to the regime, not necessarily to the state. They seek to establish a new or at least reformed constitutional order.

Political opposition movements, however, often simply oppose the government within a liberal political framework. This is the case in most Western democracies where governments change but the state remains intact. However, in a number of Asian states, these kinds of opposition movements are viewed as a threat to the ruling party – which often sees itself as synonymous with the state – and thus are seen to be internal security threats. This had led to a separation between liberalism and democracy (people vote for their leaders but their genuine choice is limited to the authorities in power). It has also led to internal political repression and to the prioritizing of the maintenance of political power. The resultant neglect of other problems that affect the general citizenry's safety and welfare thus leads to some of the very problems of human security weighed by this volume's collection of articles. It should be noted that the "internal security" problem (as perceived by state élites) cannot really fit the "traditional" security paradigm, focused as it is on state-centric or external threats. It does relate to human security if ensconced regional élites remain largely unaccountable to their electorates for addressing issues related to an individual's quality of life. If the root problems of conflict are approached by treating people as "citizens" accountable to state interests, rather than as the unique individuals they are, the issue of "whose security" is to be promoted is resolved in favour of the self-appointed guardians of state sovereignty.

Potential linkages

Are we at a historical crossroads where non-military factors have so transformed security politics that to downplay them will only intensify our collective peril? Or are we destined to become embroiled in "more of the same": international security competition mainly fuelled by "wars that matter" between contending great powers in response to perceived aggression or hegemonic opportunism? Are there components within the two contending international security paradigms outlined above that can be integrated or linked to derive a more unified and useful approach to the *security problematique*?

One linkage can be found in the field of conflict prevention. Traditional security has been as much about preventing conflict as about waging it, insofar as states prefer to realize interests through more cost-effective means than war (i.e. bargaining, coercion, or deterrence). Those who argue that various factors in contemporary international relations encourage states' sensitivity to other states' interests point to various episodes of cooperative security overcoming states' usual preoccupations with their own self-interest. Arms control agreements, concert behaviour, and regional integration movements are all illustrative.[32]

A second linkage relates to the need to reduce the vulnerability of the security subject. Traditional security approaches have employed such concepts as the state, territorial sovereignty, and social contract as organizing principles to derive order in an anarchical world. "Order" has usually been a transcending concept, a means to other, separate political ends that relate to the status and welfare of those individuals whom it addresses.[33] Human security also emphasizes "welfare goals," but views the state as only one agent among several or many that, collectively, constitute an international security environment. Magna Carta, the Treaty of Westphalia, and the League of Nations Covenant all in some way addressed the issue of welfare for those subjects who were destined to live under their guidelines. The Universal Declaration of Human Rights, the Lomé Convention, and various global warming covenants all promote norms or values that envisage adherence to specific values and the need to be accountable to them. They may be legally less binding than traditional diplomatic treaties or security alliances, but their intended purview and effects are no less significant. The important point is that both types of instruments employ cooperative security ideas to foreclose deviational behaviour, which could threaten states, groups of states, or the subjects residing within the state concerned. Both traditional and human security thus "seek to guarantee or guard against some deprivation felt by either the individual or the community."[34]

A third linkage between traditional and human security evolves around the problem of who is to be governed and who is to be secured. The Toda Institute's ongoing project on Human Security and Global Governance, for example, is intended to "foster an inter-civilizational dialogue" on personal, social, economic, political, and military security problems. The perspectives of "a variety of civilisations" are to be taken into account. By acknowledging that human security is a civilizational problem, the Institute is at least indirectly acknowledging that fault lines do exist between peoples and that these need to be understood and overcome if an international security community is to be realized. This is not very different from Huntington's premise, or those of various feminist scholars, who have argued that security will be increasingly predicated on "who you are" as much as "where you are at." States will reorient their own identities toward assimilating or addressing socio-cultural dynamics but so, too, will NGOs, communities (at the local, state, and international levels), and movements. A truly "global" civilization must be based "on unity in diversity [and] hinges upon the resolution of ... contradictions and conflicts" between democratic and hegemonic forms of globalization.[35] Succinctly put, by reconciling civilizations, they can be humanized and gradually transformed into human communities, capable of addressing and managing the broadest global threats.

A final linkage relates to the ongoing crisis of collective security in both a regional and international context. As mentioned previously, rallying coalitions of the willing in response to human security crises has become increasingly difficult as Western policy-makers become more casualty adverse and as public demands for greater accountability on how they expend national resources intensify. Regional organizations such as the Association of South East Asian Nations (ASEAN), moreover, still have difficulties talking openly about each other's national problems, much less acting collectively to prevent them from "spilling over" into a broader regional context. By way of illustration, Indonesia's financial and political instability precluded it from acting more forcefully to quell intensifying atrocities in East Timor in late 1999. But Jakarta's ASEAN affiliates proved no more capable of interceding as part of a peace-keeping contingent without strong Australian leadership and belated American pressure.

That these challenges are taken seriously by increasing numbers of security analysts reflects their increased propensity to contemplate the implications of recent and monumental structural change within international relations. Conflicts still rage in our time, but they have little resemblance to the wars we had been preparing to fight over the past half-century and relate less to state interests or ideologies than to people's identities, histories, and resources. Contemporary turmoil (and the reporting of it) appears to be generated more by overpopulation, famine, uncontrolled migration, ethnic cleansing, pandemics, terrorism, and emotional stress than by outright military invasions or by the costs of avoiding them. International anarchy may still be present, but it is more ambiguous in its patterns, processes, and effects. A new "discourse" or frame of reference does seem to be emerging as the language of international security and not merely among academic analysts. Over the past decade, as the work of the United Nations testifies, practitioners and policy-makers have begun to recast the foundations upon which international security rested for much of the second half of the twentieth century. To be sure, states still can – and do – conduct nuclear tests, weigh the deployment of theatre missile defence systems, and maintain vast land armies close to hostile borders. Yet the forging of new security communities and regimes to manage the imperatives of conflict avoidance, to reduce states' vulnerability, and perhaps even to reconcile rival civilizations seems as applicable to both sets of threats.

Caveats

If a realist such as E. H. Carr were resurrected to witness the beginning of the new millennium, he might find disconcerting parallels between the language of human security and that employed by the utopianists or universalists of his own time.[36] Human nature is more complex and diverse than any abstract image of "what a person ought to be" and this is particularly the case when human beings must interact in a collective sense.

This consideration poses a major problem for human security advocates. Specific social, cultural, and historical contexts underwrite human existence and to deny that this unmistakable factor of difference or "otherness" influences security perceptions and behaviour is intellectually dishonest and culturally naive. Indeed, the so-called "third wave" or "strategic culture" literature now appearing in the international security field's most respected scholarly venues attests to a growing recognition that security is often about the way statist imperatives are shaped and redirected through cultural experiences.[37] A sense of identity invariably breeds a sense of obligation or responsibility – and thus a sense of social contract. This, in turn, reintroduces the problem of organizing principles – i.e. if not into a state, into what? As Krause and Williams have observed, "[i]t makes the move from individuals to states seemingly unavoidable, and one is caught again in the traditional dualisms of universal and particular orders."[38] Moreover, the identity question as it relates to security cannot be separated very easily from the claims of the group or collective with which the individual identifies. If a group declares it is capable of governing itself, it is claiming nothing less than sovereignty – the state's classic barometer of legitimacy.[39]

A second concern engendered by the human security agenda relates to the problem of prematurely interpreting history. A representative interpretation of the emerging global security environment is that offered by Canadian human security proponent Jorge Nef. Arguing that problems of strategic deterrence and power balancing have now been superseded by high technology and "regional polycentrism," Nef concludes that "the kind of Cold War 'realism' that has permeated much of the international relations and security studies literature is now rendered meaningless." Any return to classic systemic multipolarity, anticipated by realists, is also improbable.[40]

Yet drawing such sweeping conclusions may be premature. Although the Cold War probably marked the end of one historical era (that of Soviet–American bipolar superpower competition), it is far from certain that a globalist-driven international security agenda is about to replace it. Most contemporary policy élites have been conditioned to conduct state-centric politics and may well have difficulty in adjusting their "traditionalist" analytical frameworks, cultivated over the previous half-century. More fundamentally, however, some of the world's most powerful states continue to adhere to very realist foreign policy agendas, rejecting much of the globalist agenda, which they view as pre-empting their own, justifiable national interests. Russia spurns expansionism by the North Atlantic Treaty Organisation (advertised by its proponents as a step toward achieving democratic peace throughout Europe) as a threat to its own historical sphere of influence. Nor is it certain that a post-Yeltsin Russia will not once more become a communist state with a very strong anti-Western and anti-globalist orientation. China remains adamantly opposed to Western human rights initiatives directed toward itself and, along with India, has remained sceptical of international initiatives to control the levels and quality of its nuclear forces and energy emissions processes. Even France is rallying its European neighbours against what it sees as an emerging *pax Americana* in a post–Cold War world.[41] It is far from certain that NGOs, grass-roots movements, or other common forms of human security advocacy will accrue the necessary influence to have their way merely on the basis of what they may deem to be self-evident logic and preferred values against such powerful resistance.

The Asian dimension

A sense of "otherness" and nationalism thus represent potent challenges to the human security agenda. Asia constitutes one of the most interesting tests for that agenda's future relevance, precisely because these two characteristics are so prominently ingrained there.[42] The region's legacy is largely hierarchical, thanks to the Sinic world order's – and thus Confucianism's – predominance over much of it for nearly three millennia.[43] Tributary relationships, "heavenly mandates," and wars of state (dynastic) unification are all integral parts of that legacy; the idea of social contract and the primacy of the individual are not. The West's presence in and interactions with the region are viewed as much as colonial incursions (still hierarchical) as a period of regional modernization. The "Asian values" debate may be decried by certain Asian leaders such as South Korea's President Kim Dae Jung.[44] However, the tradition of a strong central authority acting on behalf of the collective polity and the extension of this into strategies of international power politics remain very strong among the Asia-Pacific's great powers and throughout the entire region.[45] China, in particular, safeguards its sovereign prerogatives and may be, as one observer recently characterized it, "the high church of realpolitik in the post–Cold War world."[46]

This is all the more frustrating to human security advocates because Asia has been the world's major success story for development and modernization over the past three decades. It is likely to continue in this vein, notwithstanding its recent financial crisis. It has more people (half of the earth's population will live there by the mid-twenty-first century), higher growth rates of foreign direct investment, and the world's most numerous military forces. Human rights issues in China, Myanmar, and elsewhere throughout South-East Asia continue to make international headlines, while the region's refugee flows have intensified as regional economies deteriorate. Various Asian regimes have recently tended to emphasize self-constructed cultural differentiation from their Western counterparts as justification for intimidating domestic political opponents and ethnic minorities (similar to their seizing upon idealistic threats during the Cold War to achieve the same ends). The extent to which this practice reflects a genuine difference in values compared with more democratic states, however, is debatable. If Asian cultures, for example, tend to favour communitarianism over individualism, this may be reflected in Sino-Confucian societies' reverence for family and kinship.[47] Yet the forces of modernization and globalization have clearly affected the perceptions and behaviour of the region's younger generation and have reoriented their priorities toward greater materialism and self-fulfilment. This may well have less to do with the effects of democracy and human rights than with the introduction of forces for irreversible social change, generated by new technologies and global communications.[48]

Asia is by no means the only testing ground for comparing the future relevance of traditional and human security approaches to regional security politics. It is, however, a fascinating and dynamic laboratory for evaluating how the gospel of individual worth will fare as the challenges of most concern to human security proponents close in on incumbent Asian élites. For how long can China increase its defence budget while its unemployment problem intensifies, its basic service sector is strained to new limits, and its pollution problems stifle its huge populace? To what degree can the Malay states in South-East Asia maintain their precarious balance between secular authority and Islamic fundamentalism? Islamic fundamentalism rejects what it views as the materialism inherent in the secular authorities' policies. It has had little to say, however, about how to deal with haze, to restock depleted fisheries, or to overcome malnutrition. To what extent can élites in India and Pakistan resist the religious nationalism that has fuelled a nuclear arms race on the subcontinent and disdain for outsiders attempting to control it? The extent to which traditional or human security postulates can be applied to confront such monumental "problems" will reveal much about the creativity and adaptability of those who are currently debating their relative utility.

Conclusion

Locating the world's "fault lines" is less important than identifying the sources of such divisions and applying solutions to alleviate them. The security dilemmas generated by contending national interests are still very much with us. It is undeniable that various states constitute the most serious threats to their subjects through the neglect or outright violation of their safety and welfare. To debate which paradigm is more relevant in these times, however, seems superfluous and misdirected. To examine how both might simultaneously improve the prospects for international stability and individual safety seems a more productive enquiry.

If survival is the cardinal precondition for security, the initial and very hard question to be asked is how many of us can reasonably be expected to survive, given the challenges of the international environment with which we are now confronted? Famine is becoming more common in many developing areas (the northern part of the Korean peninsula and portions of East Africa have been most publicized, but many other parts of the world are facing a crisis in producing and distributing adequate foodstuffs). Pandemics are ever-present concerns as new viruses are proving to be more robust and less vulnerable to standard medical defences. The extent to which traditional national security resources can be adapted to alleviate suffering in their own sovereignties or for others who have asked for help (rather than adhere to means of "self-help") has not been fully explored. But how human security approaches employing less organized and less resourced NGOs or grass-roots movements can be relatively more effective in such contingencies also needs more objective and hard analysis.

If the human security "agenda" were the only variable to be confronted in the new century, the magnitude of contemporary security threats might seem less daunting. Unfortunately, we cannot presume that the world's humanitarians will be left alone to implement their bold agenda unencumbered by the affairs of state. The coordination of strategies and resources needed to advance security on a global basis cannot be achieved by relying solely, or even primarily, on the present assortment of universalist organizations and regimes. The United Nations and its special agencies are fully dependent upon the collective assent of their member states to implement policy. It is most unlikely that the forces of nationalism and sovereignty will assent to such a wholesale cession of their own authority. More importantly, events may justify a reversion to the very type of classical state power balancing that most proponents of human security and globalism claim has passed into history. Time will be the ultimate arbiter of how continued structural changes in international relations will evolve; until then, it is unlikely that any one non-military threat will become so pervasive as to shake the resolve of traditionalist forces in high places.

In the interim, the best that may be accomplished is to sharpen and refine both agendas in ways that they may complement each other more effectively. This is not a self-evident observation. Strategic reassurance and other positive approaches to the traditional security paradigm are regarded as more esoteric and abstract than traditional habits of containment, deterrence, and power balancing. Accordingly, "the acceptance of the idea that security is a matter of mutual concern and cooperative action is experiencing great difficulty."[49] Yet adopting regional confidence-building measures would seem to have much in common with human security's emphasis on individual safety. It could contribute to the equally difficult quest of broadening the concept of security to encompass the growing problems of human security. In Asia, "second track" organizations such as the Council for Security Cooperation in the Asia Pacific might serve as effective conduits between grass-roots movements and official policy-making circles for exploring how strategic reassurance and human security can be integrated more innovatively to achieve regional stability and individual welfare. Eventually, such an arrangement might be linked systematically to similar networks in other regions and/or to selected global forums.

Perhaps the most important precondition for achieving tangible success in such ventures is that both the traditionalists and human security proponents must be prepared to concede that they need each other's support and expertise if their common objective of a better and more stable world is to be realized. Without winning this initial struggle, the prospects of overcoming emerging threats to international security, in whatever form, will be far more elusive.

Notes

1. United Nations, *Human Development Report 1994*, as cited in the Report of the Commission on Global Governance, *Our Global Neighbourhood* (Oxford: Oxford University Press, 1995), reprinted on the Internet at http://www.cgg.ch/chap3.htm. Astri Suhrke has argued that by the 1990s "human-centered development" with an emphasis on equity and on the need to reduce the numbers of losers in the development process had become the core element of human security. But this emphasis obfuscates the distinction between "development" and "security" – with the former focusing on long-term structural change and the latter on sudden crisis-like disruptions. See Astri Suhrke, "Human Security and the Interest of States," *Security Dialogue* 30, no. 3 (September 1999), p. 271.
2. For an inventory, see the International Human Development Program Research Project on Global Environmental Change and Human Security synopsis on "What is 'Human Security'?" on the Internet at http://ibm.rhrz.uni-bonn.de/ihdp/gechs.htm.
3. Michael C. Williams and Keith Krause, "Preface" in Keith Krause and Michael C. Williams, eds., *Critical Security Studies: Concepts and Cases* (Minneapolis: University of Minnesota Press, 1997), p. vii.
4. The premier realist critique remains John Mearsheimer's "The False Promise of International Institutions," *International Security* 19, no. 3 (Winter 1994/95), pp. 5–49.
5. Note, for example, the observations of Seyom Brown. Acknowledging that realists have made "contributions" to state-centric analysis and understanding the distribution of international coercive power, he concludes that such focuses tend to be "self-confirming" and that the "contemporary world system departs considerably from the traditional picture of sovereign nation-states interacting warily with each other only at the margins of their existence." Hence, Brown concludes, the traditionalist or realist model has become "largely irrelevant to policy analysis because of its failure to comprehend some of the most serious predicaments of contemporary society." Brown, "World Interests and the Changing Dimensions of Security" in Michael T. Klare and Yogesh Chandrani, eds., *World Security: Challenges for a New Century*, 3rd edn (New York: St. Martin's Press, 1998), pp. 1–3. A similar assessment is offered by Michael T. Klare, "Redefining Security: The New Global Schisms," *Current History* 95, no. 604 (November 1996), pp.

353–358. To a greater extent than Brown, Klare acknowledges a continued role for traditionalist outlooks in world security affairs, although, he argues, they may still not explain the central components of international security as it is presently evolving (p. 355).

6. A particularly useful article setting out the relevant perspectives is John Baylis, "International Security in the post–Cold War Era," in John Baylis and Steve Smith, eds., *The Globalization of World Politics* (Oxford: Oxford University Press, 1997), pp. 193–211.

7. The concept of the "security dilemma" is assessed in depth by Robert Jervis, "Cooperation under the Security Dilemma," *World Politics* 30, no. 2 (January 1978), pp. 167–214, and Glenn H. Snyder, "The Security Dilemma in Alliance Politics," *World Politics* 36, no. 4 (July 1984), pp. 461–496.

8. Stephen M. Walt, "The Renaissance of Security Studies," *International Studies Quarterly* 35, no. 2 (June 1991), pp. 211–239.

9. Two of the most representative articles positing this argument are by Kenneth Waltz, "The Emerging Structure of International Politics," *International Security* 18, no. 2 (Fall 1993), pp. 44–79, and Christopher Layne, "Unipolar Illusion: Why Great Powers Will Rise," *International Security* 17, no. 4 (Spring 1993), pp. 5–51.

10. Samuel Huntington, "The Clash of Civilizations?" *Foreign Affairs* 72, no. 3 (Summer 1993), pp. 22–49.

11. Michael Doyle, "On the Democratic Peace," *International Security* 19, no. 4 (Spring 1995), pp. 180–184, and Bruce Russett, *Grasping the Democratic Peace: Principles for a post–Cold War World* (Princeton, NJ: Princeton University Press, 1993).

12. Robert O. Keohane and Joseph S. Nye, Jr., *Transnational Relations and World Politics* (Cambridge, MA: Harvard University Press, 1972).

13. Among the most notable are Barry Buzan, *People, States and Fear* (New York: Harvester Wheatsheaf, 1983); Colin S. Gray, *Strategic Studies: A Critical Assessment* (London: Aldwych, 1982); Edward Kolodziej, "What Is Security and Security Studies? Lessons from the Cold War," *Arms Control* 13, no. 1 (1992), pp. 1–31; and Krause and Williams, *Critical Security Studies*.

14. Kenneth Booth and Eric Herring, *Keyguide to Information Sources in Strategic Studies* (London: Mansell, 1994), p. 131.

15. W. E. Blatz, *Human Security: Some Reflections* (Toronto: University of Toronto Press, 1966), pp. 112–116.

16. Ibid., p. 63.

17. Robert Cox, "Social Forces, States and World Orders: Beyond International Relations Theory," *Millennium* 10, no. 2 (Summer 1981), pp. 126–155; Johann Galtung, "A Structural Theory of Imperialism," *Journal of Peace Research* 8, no. 1 (1971), pp. 81–117; and Immanuel Wallerstein, *The Modern World System: I, Capitalist Agriculture and the Origins of the European World-Economy in the Sixteenth Century* (San Diego: Academic Press, 1974). For an effort to relate world system theory more directly to the human security question, see Jorge Nef, *Human Security and Mutual Vulnerability* (Toronto: IDRC, 1995), chap. 1, pp. 1–2, as reprinted on the Internet at http://www.idrc.ca/books/focus/795/795.html.

18. See *Global Policy Forum 1998 Year-end Report: Security Council Programme – Promoting Human Security*, as reprinted on the Internet at http://www.igc.apc.org/globalpolicy/visitctr/ann-rep4-htm.

19. Buzan, *People, States and Fear*, pp. 211–242.

20. Ole Waever, Barry Buzan, Morton Kelstrup, and Pierre Lemaitre, *Identity, Migration and the New Security Agenda in Europe* (London: Pinter, 1993).

21. For two authoritative American perspectives on this point, see Charles William Maynes, "America's Fading Commitments," *World Policy Journal* 16, no. 2 (Summer 1999), especially pp. 12–16, and Sarah B. Sewall, "Peace Operations: A Department of Defense

Perspective," *SAIS Review* 15, no. 1 (Winter/Spring 1995), pp. 113–133. Also see Susan L. Woodward, "Should We Think Before We Leap? A Rejoinder," *Security Dialogue* 30, no. 3 (September 1999), pp. 277–281, who argues that judging the adequacy of the human security concept cannot be divorced from the (negative) consequences of NATO's military intervention in Kosovo. Geopolitics, Woodward argues, prevailed over genuine humanitarianism, and the operation actually increased south-east European élites' feelings of vulnerability by intensifying regional security dilemmas.

22. Waever et al., *Identity, Migration and the New Security Agenda, passim*, and Brown, "World Interests and the Changing Dimensions of Security," pp. 3–10.

23. Alexander Wendt, "Anarchy Is What States Make of It: The Social Construction of Power Politics," *International Organization* 46, no. 2 (1992), pp. 391–425.

24. Anthony Giddens, *The Consequences of Modernity: Self and Society in the Late Modern Age* (Cambridge/Stanford: Polity Press/Stanford University Press, 1990); and Martin Shaw, *Global Society and International Relations* (Cambridge: Polity Press, 1994).

25. Lloyd Axworthy, "Human Security: Safety for People in a Changing World," a concept paper, April 1999. On the Internet at http://www.dfait-maeci.gc.ca/foreignp/Human Security/secur-e.htm#3.

26. George MacLean, "The United Nations and the New Security Agenda," conference paper on the Internet at http://www.unac.org/canada/security/maclean.html. Also see Keith Krause and Michael C. Williams, "From Strategy to Security: Foundations of Critical Security Studies," in Krause and Williams, *Critical Security Studies*, p. 43.

27. For detailed analysis, see Michael Renner, *Fighting for Survival: Environmental Decline, Social Conflict and the New Age of Insecurity* (New York and London: W. W. Norton, 1996).

28. Janet Welsh Brown, "Population, Consumption and the Path to Sustainability," *Current History* 95, no. 604 (November 1996), pp. 366–371, and Jessica Tuchman Matthews, "Redefining Security," *Foreign Affairs* 68, no. 2 (Spring 1989), pp. 162–177.

29. MacLean, "The United Nations and the New Security Agenda."

30. Renner, *Fighting for Survival*, pp. 136–137.

31. Richard Falk, *On Humane Governance: Toward a New Global Politics* (Cambridge: Polity, 1995), pp. 40–41; and Krause and Williams, "From Strategy to Security," p. 45.

32. On "contingent realism," see Charles Glaser, "Realists as Optimists: Cooperation as Self-Help," *International Security* 19, no. 3 (Winter 1994/95), pp. 50–90; on "mature anarchy," see Buzan, *People, States and Fear*, p. 208; on security communities, see Karl W. Deutsch, et al., *Political Community and the North Atlantic Area* (Princeton, NJ: Princeton University Press, 1957); and on security regimes, see Robert Jervis, "Security Regimes," *International Organization* 36, no. 2 (1982), pp. 357–378.

33. The classic statement on order in international relations remains Hedley Bull's *The Anarchical Society: A Study of Order in World Politics* (New York/London/Melbourne: Macmillan, 1977).

34. MacLean, "The United Nations and the New Security Agenda," p. 2.

35. Toda Institute for Peace and Policy Research, "Human Security and Global Governance: Prospectus for an International Collaborative Research Project 1996–2000," on the Internet at http://www.toda.org/hugg_prospectus.html.

36. Edward Hallett Carr, *The Twenty Years' Crisis 1919–1939*, 2nd edn (London: Macmillan, 1946).

37. Prime examples include Alistair Ian Johnston, "Thinking about Strategic Culture," *International Security* 19, no. 4 (Spring 1995), pp. 32–64; Elizabeth Kier, "Culture and Military Doctrine," *International Security* 19, no. 4 (Spring 1995), pp. 65–93; and Chris Rues-Smit, "The Constitutional Structure of International Society and Nature of Fundamental Institutions," *International Organization* 51, no. 4 (Autumn 1997), pp. 555–

589. For a specific examination of strategic culture in the Asia-Pacific, see Ken Booth and Russell Trood, eds., *Strategic Cultures in the Asia-Pacific Region* (London: Macmillan, 1999).

38. Krause and Williams, "From Strategy to Security," p. 46.

39. Ibid., p. 47.

40. Nef, *Human Security and Mutual Vulnerability*, Introduction, p. 4.

41. For in-depth analysis on this point, see William Pfaff, "France Airs Its Slant on America," *International Herald Tribune*, 8 February 1999, p. 8.

42. For a general discussion of the challenges to developing a "peace culture in Asia-Pacific," see Russell Trood and Ken Booth, "Strategic Culture and Conflict Management in the Asia-Pacific," in Booth and Trood, *Strategic Cultures in the Asia-Pacific Region*, pp. 339–361.

43. For background, consult John K. Fairbank, "The Early Treaty System in the Chinese World Order," in John K. Fairbank, ed., *The Chinese World Order: Traditional China's Foreign Relations* (Cambridge, MA: Harvard University Press, 1968), pp. 257–275.

44. Kim Dae Jung, "Is Culture Destiny? The Myth of Asia's Anti-Democratic Values," *Foreign Affairs* 73, no. 6 (November–December 1994), pp. 189–194.

45. Muthiah Alagappa, "International Politics in Asia: The Historical Context," in Alagappa, ed., *Asian Security Practice: Material and Ideational Influences* (Stanford, CA: Stanford University Press, 1998), pp. 110–111.

46. Thomas Christensen, "Chinese Realpolitik," *Foreign Affairs* 75, no. 5 (September/October 1996), p. 37.

47. Alan Dupont, "Is There an 'Asian Way'?" *Survival* 38, no. 2 (Summer 1996), p. 24.

48. Kenneth Christie, "Regime Security and Human Rights in Southeast Asia," *Political Studies* 43, Special Issue (1995), p. 211.

49. Benjamin Rivlin, "Boutros Ghali's Ordeal: Leading the UN in an Age of Uncertainty," in Dimitris Bourantonis and Marios Evriviades, eds., *A United Nations for the Twenty-First Century: Peace, Security and Development* (The Hague/London/Boston: Kluwer Law International, 1996), p. 135.

2

Toward a new concept of security: Human security in world politics

Woosang Kim and In-Taek Hyun

Introduction

Among the rapid international political changes unfolding in the 1980s and 1990s, the demise of repressive regimes and ideologies was prominent. The collapse of the Soviet empire in 1989 and the demise of the Soviet Union in 1991 were representative of similar moves towards liberalization and democratization in many parts of the world. Such political changes, along with other fluctuations in the global balance of military and economic power, have led to a great deal of discussion about a "new world order." As the Cold War recedes into history, many analysts have called for the reconceptualization of the term "security" and a reevaluation of the definition of "security studies." Some of them have participated in discourses on comprehensive security, covering environmental, economic, societal, political, communal, and ecological issues. Others have broadened the dialogue to include human rights and human security issues.[1] Although the "Westphalian" international order is still in effect, we are beginning to witness a major conceptual shift in security thinking – from a focus on national security, with its emphasis on the military defence of the state, to an emphasis on comprehensive security and human security issues, underscoring the need to ensure the tranquillity and welfare of individuals who live in the state.

In this chapter, we will summarize the theoretical perspectives that are currently being brought to bear on the concept of security. As part of this

33

process we will introduce the concept of "human security" as it currently exists and we will then make an effort to redefine it in such a way as to make the concept more useful. We will also suggest several ideas designed to promote the discussion of human security, including the objects or referents, the instruments, and the probable costs involved in achieving it.

Theoretical perspectives on the concept of security

To begin this discussion our attention must turn initially to the "realist" view of national security based on the Westphalian system. For realists, each state is struggling for power and the principal goal of a state must be to protect its own national interests and security while seeking to expand its power in a "self-help" international system. Realists consider nation-states to be the most important actors in international politics. They also assume that states are rational, unitary actors pursuing the same goals (that is, national interests, by carefully calculating costs of alternative courses of action and seeking to maximize their expected returns) regardless of particular forms of government or economy. They all seek power – both the ability to influence others and resources that can be used to exercise influence – and they calculate their interests in terms of power, whether as ends or as necessary means to a variety of other ends.[2]

According to the realists' view, the international system is an anarchic system, that is, a system without a ruling authority. Nations in the international system interact or compete with each other to pursue individual advantage. There is no appeal to a higher authority to settle disputes among nations. The realists' view of world politics is dominated by "the struggle for power," the struggle by individual nation-states to maximize their own power.[3] Because states always face security dilemmas, they are a natural object or referent in the discussion of security (and it is important to note that national security, from the realist perspective, is achieved mainly by military means).

Kenneth Waltz, an early advocate of "neo-realism," suggests, on the other hand, that the structure of the international system, rather than the struggle for power by individual nation-states, determines the foreign policy choices of national leaders. Anarchy and the absence of central institutions characterize the structure of the system. States, especially the great powers, are the primary actors, and they seek power to ensure their own national survival. For Waltz, capabilities define the relative position of states within the system, and the distribution of capabilities defines the structure of the system. So, changes in the distribution of capabilities stimulate changes in the structure of the system. Balance of power emerges more or less automatically from the instinct for survival.[4]

Neo-realists further argue that, in a self-help world, an increase in interaction between states actually promotes conflict. This view is based on an assessment that problems associated with cheating and making relative gains have placed a distinct limitation on the possibilities for cooperation among states. States are sensitive to their relative position in the distribution of power. They fear that they may become too dependent on others for their own well-being and that others may cheat on any agreements reached and thus attempt to gain advantages over them.[5] Cooperation is also limited because states tend to be concerned with relative gains rather than absolute gains.[6] So, for neo-realists (as well as realists), nation-states attempt to maximize their gains in a competitive, devious, and uncertain international system. Consequently, cooperation among them will be very difficult to achieve.

"Liberals" and "neoliberal institutionalists" perceive matters somewhat differently. They do not fully accept the dominance of the Westphalian order, with its emphasis on the sovereignty and territoriality of nation-states. They instead argue that the state is not the only important actor in the international system but that multinational corporations, human rights activists, and even terrorist groups have a major influence in how international security relations unfold. For liberals, security studies can be understood best by focusing on the individual level of analysis.

Indeed, this school of thought believes that human nature is essentially good and peace loving. It argues that "bad" human behaviour such as war is the product of "bad" institutions and structural arrangements. War is not inevitable and eradicating the structural and behavioural characteristics that precipitate it can reduce the risk of war. Liberals suggest that collective efforts are the best way to solve international conflicts.

The perceptions of "neoliberal institutionalists" differ from those of "liberals" in several key theoretical areas. To begin with, their perspective conforms largely to the realist framework. That is, they subscribe to the assumptions that states are the most important actors in the international system, that they act rationally, and that the international system is anarchic. However, they part company with the realists by suggesting that transnational actors such as international institutions, multinational corporations, and non-governmental organizations (NGOs) are important actors in the system and that cooperation between the major systemic actors is possible.

According to the neoliberal institutionalist view, the cogency of the state-centric perspective of realism has been undermined by the rapid growth in international commerce and trade. This has increased levels of interdependence, further promoting cooperation.[7] International regimes and institutions are therefore very important in helping to achieve cooperation and stability in the international system. They provide information, reduce transaction costs, make commitments more credible, and facilitate the operation of reciprocity. Institutionalized systems of cooperation in given issue areas thus promote the likelihood of cooperation and stability.[8]

"Constructivists," a group of critical theorists, share several assumptions with both realists and neo-realists. They assume that nation-states are rational actors seeking national survival, that the international system is anarchic, and that the interests of nation-states are constructed by the structure of the international system. But they also believe that the fundamental structures of international politics are "social rather than strictly material." For them, structure is determined not by the distribution of material capabilities among nation-states but rather by the product of social relationships. Social structures are made up of shared knowledge as well as of material resources and power politics. For constructivists, the "security dilemma" is a social structure based on intersubjective understandings in which nation-states do not trust each other; they therefore define their national interests in self-help terms. On the other hand, a "security community" is a social structure based on shared knowledge in which nation-states trust one another to resolve conflicts of interest without resorting to arms.[9]

Constructivists argue that, in addition to power politics, other ideas such as the rule of law and the importance of institutional cooperation influence states' behaviour. Through reciprocity nation-states learn and understand the structure of shared knowledge in the system and thus behave in a more cooperative way. Although Alexander Wendt suggests that the socially constructed structure is not easily transformed, other constructivists are more optimistic in that they suggest there is room for nation-states to pursue policies of peaceful change rather than being forced to engage in a process of struggling for power. A major difference between the realist and constructivist schools of thought, moreover, is that the latter does not separate the domestic and international political milieux. Both environments are instead considered to be part of an overall, socially constructed process.[10]

Most of the perspectives mentioned above emphasize the importance of nation-states in the international system. However, the "globalist" approach challenges this state-centric assumption. During the post–Cold War era the process of globalization has been accelerated and now a "global society" is increasingly evident. The emergence of such a society, based on systems of international economic interdependence, global communications, and an increasingly homogeneous global culture, has created broad social relationships that transcend the territorial borders of most of the active participants of international society (mainly great powers and middle powers). The process of globalization has also, however, produced new types of insecurity associated with issues concerning the environment, poverty, weapons of mass destruction, and ethnic and religious conflict (to name but a few). Globalists argue, therefore, that it is necessary to deal with the security of individuals and of groups within a global society. For them, the traditional focus on national security cannot tackle the broader security issues related to environmental hazards, inequality and poverty, mass destruction, genocide and ethnic cleansing, human rights, and minority rights.[11]

During the period of superpower confrontation, regional politics was a zero-sum type of game in which a gain to one group was a loss to the other. During that period, two superpowers directly or through regional clients suppressed or intervened in regional conflicts, including ethnocommunal conflicts. The end of the bipolar world accelerated globalization, and this process has also provided opportunities for suppressed ethnic and religious conflicts to resurface in various parts of the underdeveloped world. Religious and cultural differences, the pursuit of self-determination or autonomy, different levels of socio-economic development, political inclusion and exclusion, leadership voids, and foreign interests have all emerged to play important roles in creating collective fears of the future for different ethnic or religious groups that had no opportunities to prosper during the Cold War. Indeed these collective fears of the future have become the main cause of ethnic and religious conflicts in the underdeveloped parts of the world.[12]

During the Cold War period, realist thought prevailed. But, as we have summarized above, in the post–Cold War period the Westphalian order based on the nation-state system has been challenged. Many now argue that a substantial number of factors had made it more difficult for any one state to exercise power over its people and address issues it once considered its sole prerogative. The communications revolution, the rise of transnational corporations, increasing migration, economic integration, and the global nature of economic and environmental problems are all relevant in this context. Terrorism, drug trafficking, money laundering, and so-called "grey area" security issues are likewise emerging.[13] The increasing lack of state control, an inability to solve pressing problems, and the fact that few states' boundaries or interests coincide with the nationalities within, have all exacerbated the widespread mistrust of political leaders and institutions in many states.[14] It is further argued by globalists that when the "state" as a political unit can no longer cope with the challenges that it now faces, it will no longer be able to perform its primary function within the international system and it will therefore disappear.

To us, these assertions seem only partially correct. For example, we acknowledge that one government alone cannot control activities that thin the layer of ozone in the stratosphere or that increase the density of

carbon dioxide in the atmosphere. Resolving this type of problem therefore requires a collective effort. On the other hand, we must also argue
that the concept of the modern state is not obsolete. In the Asia-Pacific
region, for example, territorial disputes remain one of the major issues of
the day. The Senkaku or Daioyutai Islands dispute is still a source of
tension between China and Japan, a number of states are involved in a
variety of disputes in the South China Sea, the Tok-to dispute separates
Korea and Japan, and the dispute over the "Northern Territory" continues between Russia and Japan. Moreover, on the Korean peninsula
the Cold War is far from over. The die-hard repressive communist regime
in North Korea continues to pose a threat to the regional security order.

There is convincing evidence that Asian countries have increased their
military procurements over the past few decades (although the Asian
financial crisis substantially impeded this trend).[15] Some scholars would
argue that military expenditure can have a negative impact on a state's
economic performance and consequently harm its people's well-being,
but this kind of argument is supported only in the case of developed
countries and not for developing or underdeveloped countries. Many
empirical studies show that military spending can actually have a positive
impact on economic development in underdeveloped countries.[16]

We believe that these examples indicate that states are not yet obsolete. States must still be militarily prepared to protect and defend their
territory, sovereignty, and populace. Especially in North-East Asia, the
regional system still seems to be anarchic and the "self-help" mentality
prevails.

However, we do not suggest that the concept of "national security,"
with its focus on the military defence of the state, is the only important
concept in international relations and that the ideas of others, such as
constructivists or globalists, should be ignored completely. Emphasis on
other emerging security issues related to environmental hazards, poverty,
weapons of mass destruction, genocide and ethnic cleansing, and human
rights is needed as well. In particular, we must pay more attention to the
concept of human security. The concept of "human security" is discussed
in detail in the following section.

Redefining the concept of human security

In the post–Cold War period, most parts of the world are occupied with
the movements and activities of democratization and liberalization. Yet
human rights issues should also receive more attention. Although human
security has become an increasingly important issue in international politics, in most parts of the world the concept still remains underdeveloped,

hardly making it to the top of the list on any state's foreign policy agenda. Canada is the major exception. Certain industrial states (led by Japan) have also promoted human security issues in a UN context. As discussed in chapter 1, however, there is not yet much consensus within the academic and policy communities on how human security should be defined, what are the threats to human security, and how that security can be achieved (to name but a few problematic areas).

For some, human security refers to freedom from hunger, torture, imprisonment without a free and fair trial, discrimination against minorities and women, and domestic violence. It also refers to such issues as communal security, ethnic conflict (mainly prevalent in Africa and Asia), gender security, and the use of rape as a weapon of war (for example, as in the case of the former Yugoslavia in the 1990s).[17] Positively, it embraces a concept of freedom that is based on "the capacity and opportunity that allows each human being to enjoy life to the fullest without imposing constraints upon others engaged in the same pursuit." That is, "human security refers to the quality of life of the people of a society or polity. Anything which degrades their quality of life – demographic pressures, diminished access to or stock of resources, and so on – is a security threat. Conversely, anything which can upgrade their quality of life – for example, economic growth, improved access to resources, social and political empowerment, and so on – is an enhancement of human security."[18]

Human security incorporates many aspects of "comprehensive security," one of the most widely used phrases in the post–Cold War era, in terms of the inclusiveness of its security agenda. Both human security and comprehensive security deal with various non-military issues including political, economic, societal, environmental, and communal factors. In this, they move beyond the confines of the traditional notion of security that encompasses only the military dimension. However, the unit of analysis is basically different. Human security focuses on individual human beings whereas comprehensive security still regards the nation-state as the principal actor. Human security assumes that basic human needs and interests are necessary conditions for society. But it is not presumed that, without human security, national security cannot be guaranteed. Comprehensive security, on the other hand, is based on the liberal idea that non-military issues also influence national security and that institutions can make a difference by promoting security in the system. In this chapter we view "human security" as being a condition of relative safety that is free from humanitarian emergencies caused by natural or manmade disasters at the national, regional, and international levels and that also encompasses the political, military, economic, societal, communal, and environmental spheres.

Some analysts suggest that humanitarian emergencies refer to "man-made disasters such as genocide and ecological disasters such as floods and famines" and "episodes in which ethnic or revolutionary war and state repression lead to refugee flows, forced displacement of people, and massive destruction of property."[19] Others argue that humanitarian emergencies can be divided into four basic categories: (1) warfare (mainly within states); (2) disease; (3) hunger; and (4) refugee flight. In other words, humanitarian emergencies are profound social crises "in which a large number of people die and suffer from war, disease, hunger, and displacement owing to man-made and natural disasters, while some others may benefit from it."[20] The United States Mission to the United Nations defines humanitarian emergencies as crises "in which large numbers of people are dependent on humanitarian assistance ... from sources external to their own society ... and/or ... are in need of physical protection in order to have access to subsistence or external assistance."[21]

Related to the human security issue is an understanding that a humanitarian emergency in one country will not only have an impact on its own people but could spread elsewhere within the international system. So human security affects not only the human being as a unit of concern but also other units such as nation-states and systemic actors. In addressing human security issues, one can thus still think in terms of national and international security.

Although human security and national security can be mutually reinforcing concepts, they may also be in conflict with each other. Reinforcing human security in some fields may cause, intensify, or trigger other threats to national security. For example, landmines around the Demilitarized Zone on the Korean peninsula can be dangerous for individuals who live nearby. However, removal of the landmines for human security purposes might undermine South Korean national security by increasing the prospects of a North Korean *blitzkrieg*.

The recent spate of financial crises in Asian countries provides another useful example of these countervailing forces in operation (but in this case in the reverse direction). Because the South Korean government believed that the recent financial crisis threatened its national prosperity, it considered the crisis to be a threat to national security. The government therefore tried very hard to overcome the crisis by restructuring the banking system and by reforming conglomerates. But, as a result of this restructuring, the number of people unemployed in South Korea increased considerably. Consequently, the human security of those unemployed individuals was seriously threatened.

It is being argued here that the core elements of human security are concerns and interests that include issues such as human rights and that human security can supplement national and/or international security.

But we also believe that the human security paradigm cannot supplant those of national security or international security. Human security strategies, policies, and activities are needed to overcome situations of human insecurity that may have been caused by humanitarian emergencies and to prevent humanitarian crises that could lead to greater insecurity and even to conflict. But strategies, policies, and activities for human security should be carried out in such a way that they do not hamper the pursuit of national and international security. Our concept of human security is based, therefore, on a so-called "open-minded realist" or "human realist" approach. The human realist approach tries to reflect both human security and some traditional security interests.

The concept of traditional security has emphasized order and stability, whereas the existing concept of human security seems to lay greater stress on values, especially human rights, democracy, and the market economy. However, there are clear drawbacks in insisting that Western visions of democracy, market economy, and human rights be universalized.

First, no one will disagree with the argument that democracies promote human rights better than do alternative regimes. So, increasing democratization will lead simultaneously to an enforcement of human rights and a more peaceful world. But, the installation of democratic institutions in one society or polity does not automatically guarantee the human rights of minorities. After all, democracy is an instrument of majority or pluralistic rule. Free popular participation in politics, guaranteed in a democratic regime, can lead easily to the violation of human rights. For example, many people, both individually or in groups, would like to use their political power to gain an unfair advantage over their political enemies. Human rights, however, are non-majoritarian; instead, they aim to protect every human being. In democratic societies where the majority or plurality is relatively well positioned to care for its own rights and interests, one of the most important functions of human rights is to constrain that majority from exercising complete authority over other factions. Until suitable mechanisms for guaranteeing the human rights of minorities are introduced, the enjoyment of human rights will remain insecure even in democratic societies.

Enforcement of the market economy is not the end of the story for human rights activists, either. The equity issue is also a very important consideration. The market economy may be economically efficient. That is, given a limited supply of resources, market systems of allocation and distribution will produce a higher total output in terms of goods and services supplied than other economic systems. But the market system also distributes that production to those who have power within it, typically those with an income or information advantage, rather than to those specifically in need. To put it differently, although the market economy produces more overall, it is not necessarily producing more for all. In fact, the free market typically develops gross inequalities between individuals within a society in terms of income, living conditions, etc.

Today, most Asian countries are faced with a severe financial crisis, the so-called "IMF crisis." South Korea is no exception. The South Korean government, in seeking to resolve its financial crisis, has made every effort to induce foreign investment by following the suggestions and prescriptions of the United States, the International Monetary Fund, and other Western countries. It has tried very hard to open up its domestic market and to restructure its banking system and companies through big deals, mergers, and mass lay-offs in the workforce. But, to increase its national credit rating and to increase the efficiency of its economy, the South Korean government has had temporarily to abandon the equity issue. In this situation, the question that needs to be asked is who is going to be responsible for the rapidly growing number of unemployed South Koreans and for protecting their human rights? South Korea at this point in time is, therefore, a graphic example of how the operations of a market economy can have negative consequences for human rights.

Yet this evidence should not be construed to suggest that we are against the overall relative advantages of the democratic/market system as compared with the available alternatives. Quite the opposite is the case and we staunchly support that system. We are, however, suggesting that democracy and the free market system do not automatically promote improvements in the quality of life of individuals in a society. With this in mind, human security should be applied in such a way that it will be enjoyed not just by the majority of people within a democratic society but also by its minorities.

Policy suggestions

The Congress of Vienna in 1815 was perhaps the first instance in the modern era of international élites showing a distinct level of concern for human rights. The Congress not only dealt with religious freedom as well as civil and political rights, but also agreed in principle to abolish slavery. A number of anti-slavery acts and treaties followed (for example, the Berlin Conference on Africa in 1885, the Brussels Conference in 1890, the Treaty of Saint Germain in 1919, the Geneva Conference in 1926, and Great Britain's Abolition Act of 1833). The Hague peace conferences of 1899 and 1907 introduced the notion of the right of individuals to appeal to the Court of Appeal. The Peace Conference at Versailles in 1919 demonstrated its concern for the protection of minorities.[22]

At the end of World War II, international concern for human and minority rights intensified. The International Labour Organization, in particular, made important contributions to the development of human rights. It established conventions on the right to organize and bargain collectively, on the abolition of forced labour, and on ending discrimination in employment and occupation. Since its establishment, the United Nations has also played an important role in monitoring human rights violations. The 1948 Declaration of Human Rights, the Genocide Convention, and the International Criminal Court are all examples. Other regional conventions such as the European Convention on Human Rights of 1950 and the Inter-American System of Human Rights have contributed to the protection of human rights through monitoring, fact-finding, and reporting human rights violations on the national and international level. In this task they have been greatly assisted by a number of NGOs, including Amnesty International, Worldwatch, and the Minority Group.[23]

At the start of the twenty-first century, it is expected that the issue of human security will become more important in world politics. As we have seen, its emergence as a key factor in international security politics is illustrated not only by the fact that many problems we face in world politics have something to do with human security and human rights, but also by the fact that their amelioration and cure will require globally coordinated responses.

Two pressing questions present themselves: how can human security best be achieved and who should lead the effort? Certainly, efforts to enhance human security should be multidimensional in the sense that action is required at a number of levels – national, regional, and global. National governments need to assume primary responsibility for restoring the state of human security and for preventing humanitarian emergencies. However, in addressing many issues of human security, close consultation and coordination are required across national boundaries. A comprehensive and collective approach is therefore required. Institutions created to manage human security will need to perform three important functions: (1) giving early warning of humanitarian emergencies, (2) ensuring early consultation among members and interested parties, and (3) providing crisis management with regular supervision. Early warning activities will be particularly enhanced by information sharing, data gathering, and monitoring on potential human disasters. All these functions, however, can be seen as important preventative measures contributing to human security. Early consultation is needed to prevent the spread of future humanitarian crises and to secure their early resolution. Crisis management through regular monitoring and supervision of any agreements is also required.

There will also be a need to promote various channels of dialogue on future human security challenges. In this sense, "epistemic communities" – dialogues among experts on specific issues – will play a crucial role.

However, new international conventions and protocols for implementing human security can be empowered only if and when consensus emerges among the various interested parties. Achieving such consensus will, by necessity, demand a concerted effort to bridge the gap that currently exists between developed and developing (or underdeveloped) countries. A widespread conviction exists in developing and underdeveloped countries that the concept of human security is merely another tactic that developed countries are using in order to impose their values, infringe the sovereignty of less developed countries, and exploit their national interests. Claims of human rights violations in less developed countries are cited as typical examples of the "have states" pressuring their less fortunate counterparts to comply with their own policies.

As we have mentioned above, there are other related problems. Sometimes democracy and the free market system do not correlate with minority rights. As noted in chapter 1, various Asian political systems have emerged that conduct elections but that simultaneously discourage genuinely contested choices for leadership. Also, the reinforcement of human security in some countries may intensify threats to their national security. It is critical that the installation of Western norms, such as democracy and the free market system, in less well developed countries should be balanced by an appropriate recognition of the different traditional values and norms and the different national security environments that pertain to particular developing countries.

Middle powers could play a special role in developing the concept of human security and brokering its implementation at the international level. Less powerful than the UN Security Council's permanent members but more so than less developed countries, such middle powers as Australia, Canada, and Korea could take the initiative for building consensus among the world community because they threaten no one but still engender sufficient respect and command enough resources to influence the behaviour of great and small powers alike. Middle power collaboration to establish procedures and mechanisms ensuring that human security agendas are not dominated by a hegemon, or by a few great powers, could be a first, very real step to advancing that concept in ways which will transform it from an idea into a widely accepted reality.

Notes

1. For example, see Barry Buzan, Ole Waever, and Jaap de Wilde, *Security: A New Framework for Analysis* (Boulder, CO: Lynne Rienner, 1998); S. Harris and A. Mack, eds., *Asia-Pacific Security: The Economics–Politics Nexus* (Sydney: Allen & Unwin, 1997).

2. Charles Kegley and Eugene Wittkopf, *World Politics*, 4th edn (New York: St. Martin's Press, 1993).
3. Hans Morgenthau, *Politics among Nations* (New York: Alfred A. Knopf, 1973).
4. Kenneth Waltz, *Theory of International Politics* (Reading, MA: Addison-Wesley, 1979).
5. John Measheimer, "Back to the Future: Instability after the Cold War," *International Security* 15, no. 1 (Summer 1990), pp. 5–56.
6. For example, Joseph M. Grieco, "Anarchy and the Limits of Cooperation," *International Organization* 42, no. 3 (Summer 1988), pp. 485–507, and Grieco, *Cooperation among Nations: Europe, America, and Non-tariff Barriers to Trade* (Ithaca, NY: Cornell University Press, 1990).
7. Robert Keohane and Joseph Nye Jr., *Power and Interdependence* (Boston: Little Brown, 1977).
8. Robert Keohane and Lisa Martin, "The Promise of Institutionalist Theory," *International Security* 20, no. 1 (Summer 1995), pp. 39–51.
9. John Baylis and Steve Smith, *The Globalization of World Politics* (Oxford: Oxford University Press, 1997), p. 204.
10. Alexander Wendt, "Anarchy Is What States Make of It: The Social Construction of Power Politics," *International Organization* 46, no. 2 (Spring 1992), pp. 391–425; and Baylis and Smith, *The Globalization of World Politics*, pp. 204–205.
11. Baylis and Smith, *The Globalization of World Politics*, pp. 207–208.
12. See David Lake and Donald Rothchild, eds., *The International Spread of Ethnic Conflict* (Princeton, NJ: Princeton University Press, 1998); Woosang Kim, "Communal Security in Asia," presented at the conference on "Comprehensive Security: Conceptions and Realities in Asia," Green Villa, Cheju Islands, Korea, 21–22 November 1998.
13. The term "grey area" has been developed systematically by Peter Chalk. See his chapter in this volume and also his *Grey Area Phenomena in South-east Asia: Piracy, Drug Traffic and Political Terrorism*, Canberra Paper on Strategy and Defence, no. 123 (Canberra: SDSC, 1997).
14. See a Stanley Foundation report on this issue, 1993, p. 16.
15. Between 1982 and 1991, the Asia-Pacific's share of global military spending (excluding the United States and USSR) increased from 15 per cent to 25 per cent, with a faster rate of growth experienced during the late 1980s. Between 1991 and 1996, East Asian, South Asian, and Australasian countries purchased 22–29 per cent of total international arms deliveries. See Shannon Selin, *Asia-Pacific Arms Buildups Part One: Scope, Causes and Problems*, Working Paper no. 6 (Vancouver: Institute of International Relations, University of British Columbia, November 1994), pp. 2–5; and International Institute for Strategic Studies, *The Military Balance 1997/98* (London: Oxford University Press for the IISS, October 1997), p. 265.
16. For example, David Lim, "Another Look at Growth and Defence in Less Developed Countries," *Economic Development and Cultural Change* 31, no. 2 (January 1983), pp. 377–384; P. C. Frederiksen and Robert E. Looney, "Defence Expenditures and Economic Growth in Developing Countries," *Armed Forces and Society* 9, no. 4 (Summer 1983), pp. 633–645; H. Sonmez Atesoglu and J. Michael Mueller, "Defence Spending and Economic Growth," *Defence Economics* 2 (1990), pp. 19–27; James Payne and Anandi Sahu, eds., *Defence Spending and Economic Growth* (Boulder, CO: Westview Press, 1993); Uk Heo, "Modeling the Defense–Growth Relationship around the Globe," *Journal of Conflict Resolution* 42 (1998), pp. 637–657.
17. The use of "comfort women" by Japanese troops during World War II accentuates the issues of gender security.
18. Ramesh Thakur, "From National to Human Security," in Harris and Mack, *Asia-Pacific Security*, pp. 53–54.

19. Barbara Harff and Ted Gurr, "Systemic Early Warning of Humanitarian Emergencies," *Journal of Peace Research* 35, no. 5 (September 1998), pp. 551–579.
20. Raimo Vayrynen, *The Age of Humanitarian Emergencies* (Helsinki: UNU World Institute for Development Economics Research, Research for Action 1996), vol. 25, pp. 16–19.
21. US Mission to the United Nations, *Global Humanitarian Emergencies, 1996* (New York: ECOSOC section, United States Mission to the UN, 1996), p. 1, quoted from Harff and Gurr, "Systemic Early Warning," pp. 2–3.
22. Abdul Aziz Said, Charles O. Lerche, Jr., and Charles Lerche III, *Concepts of International Politics in Global Perspective* (New Jersey: Prentice Hall, 1995), pp. 262–265.
23. Said et al., p. 263, and Ian Brownlie, ed., *Basic Documents on Human Rights* (Oxford: Clarendon Press, 1992).

Part 2

"Regionalizing" human security in the Asia-Pacific

3

The concept of "human security" extended: "Asianizing" the paradigm

Withaya Sucharithanarugse

The international security environment and human society in general have been subject to rapid, widening, and deepening change since the end of the Cold War. This process has been encouraged by the trend towards globalization, and particularly by the spread of both information and information technology. It has also been facilitated by the forces of international capitalism in their rush to spread trade, investment, and financial sector liberalization to developing states. No recent example of these factors at work is more illustrative than the East Asian economic crisis. This event started off as a monetary crisis, became a financial crisis, broadened into an economic crisis, and subsequently transformed itself into a socio-political and even regional security crisis. This economic downfall caused widespread tensions between various sectors within international society, intensified economic insecurity, and raised considerable doubts about the prospects for the future.

A pervasive sense of insecurity with political, economic, social, and cultural dimensions thus spread across the Asia-Pacific region. Dealing with this phenomenon and seeking to engineer a financial recovery has become the primary focus of most governments in the region. State and private financial institutions are being drastically reorganized. This development, in turn, has precipitated large-scale job lay-offs, which, coming as they have on top of already high regional levels of unemployment (created by the general economic contraction), have created an intolerable political climate. This situation has been made even worse by an understandable collapse in consumer confidence across the region and a corresponding reduction in consumer spending. As a result, the length of time needed to make a significant economic recovery in East Asia will only be prolonged. In this environment, confusing and uncertain predictions have heightened the general feeling of insecurity amongst the peoples of the region. Furthermore, this insecurity has spread to a number of levels, passing from individuals to groups and sectors until finally assuming a state-wide and even international dimension.

The uncaring legacy

It is worth noting, however, that this expanded set of uncertainties is, in fact, building upon a legacy of pre-existing insecurities in East Asia. In the region, economic development through industrialization has been the cause of bitter and prolonged conflicts. These have largely defied resolution because state organs have never fully appreciated the need to develop effective policies for providing adequate sustenance for populations.

Natural forest reserves, for example, have been sacrificed in an unsustainable manner in order to produce agricultural products that will satisfy domestic and international markets. This has led, in turn, to ecological degradation. When coupled with severe drought and flood, this shortsightedness has created a vicious cycle of human tragedy. In addition, the pull of the market economy has promoted a pervasive culture of "racketeering" based on the cross-border smuggling of goods, drugs, labour, and prostitutes (the last two serving also to spread disease). The involuntary migration that has in fact occurred in the region is, therefore, better understood in terms of a reallocation of labour by economic forces that have entailed considerable human exploitation and suffering.

Above all else it must be recognized that no state is capable of dealing with all of these problems on its own; cooperation with other states, particularly at the regional level, is essential if these trends are to be permanently reversed. Insecurity can be seen, therefore, as being shared regionally. Although the state remains as a tangible and key unit or actor in international relations, it must be recognized that, as an effective agent for solution, it has been eclipsed by the severity of the problems that it now confronts. It is also apparent that the traditional way many Asian states have used police and/or military force as instruments for maintaining security has become increasingly ineffective. Today's "security" issues overwhelm traditional states' capacities to manage the challenges they project. These types of multidimensional problems require multilateral collaboration to generate sufficiently creative and comprehensive solutions.

Security that "cares"

Since the end of the Cold War there has, therefore, been an emphasis on "rethinking" the basic assumptions that define the boundaries of the security studies paradigm. This development has been mirrored elsewhere in the social sciences. Part of the debate that this has generated has been recorded in the "Open the Social Science" paper that was produced following a forum organized by the Gulbenkian Commission chaired by Emmanuel Wallerstein.[1] Apart from attempting to demystify the Western-biased construct of social science that has become more and more segmented, rigid, and remote from people's actual needs and concerns, this chapter goes on to suggest that the discipline should pursue an expansive and inclusive agenda. This agenda would be society based and encourage cross-disciplinary cooperation as well as a level of integration with the non-social sciences. When examining contemporary "new thinking on security," it is important to recognize that these types of factors underwrite it.

The "new thinking on security" has been pursued by scholars trying to broaden the neo-realist conception of security so that it includes a wider range of issue areas. The issues that they would prefer to see integrated into the paradigm range from economic and environmental problems to human rights and migration. From a slightly different perspective, this represents an attempt to expand the scope of security studies into three main levels of analysis. These levels would facilitate movement either down to the tier of individual or human security or up to the plane of international or global security, with regional and societal security as a possible intermediate level.

At the same time, other scholars have sought to address emerging security dilemmas while still remaining within the confines of a state-centric approach. They have done so by using diverse terms such as "common," "cooperative," "collective," and "comprehensive" security to advocate different multilateral forms of inter-state security cooperation. Neo-realists have criticized these approaches on the grounds that they are drawing security studies away from their traditional focus and methods for little reason. They suggest that these approaches lack a clear explanation or theoretical foundation and that they have failed to show any true value in terms of concrete research.[2]

The idea of "desecuritization" has also been recently developed in academia. The discussion has, however, revolved primarily around this concept's utility as a long-range political goal and not around detaching and freeing other sectors from the use of force, thus reducing and marginalizing the military sector. An advantage enjoyed by the desecuritization approach is that it reminds policy-makers, analysts, or campaigners of their responsibilities to the people-at-large when they start talking about security.

Studies incorporating consideration of the "international economy" have probably presented the strongest arguments to support a broadening of the security agenda post Cold War. These have pointed to the dangers of global liberalization causing widespread and uncontrollable system instability, especially in financial markets. They have also illuminated the darker side of trade liberalization, including the negative crossover effects that pursuing a global economy can have on environmental issues, domestic political autonomy and stability, and military self-reliance.[3]

To a degree, recent arms races in South-East Asia can also be linked to economic considerations; it has been noted that they have been largely inspired by conditions of high economic growth (see chapter 2). On that point, it is worth noting that traditional ideas about threat perceptions have had little to do with these developments. They have been driven more by causal factors such as self-confidence, self-reliance, and prestige (Myanmar may be the only exception, for its recent arms acquisitions are clearly intended to facilitate the destruction of minority resistance forces). The argument supporting this economic–security nexus is further reinforced when the dynamics of the recent financial crisis in Asia are considered.

The onset of the economic crisis has in effect curtailed the arms build-up in the region. It is worth noting that this has occurred without a great deal of misgiving and this testifies to the fact that the arms acquisition policies pursued until recently by most countries in the region were not based on real or even perceived security threats. On the contrary, it has now become apparent that the economic crisis has itself become a major security problem. In a sense it may be better to call what has occurred an outbreak of insecurity – a pervasive feeling of uncertainty amongst the general populace of the region that has been fuelled by not knowing whether economic conditions will further deteriorate, what will happen next, and when the recovery will start. In this environment, the severity of the problem has been worsened by the fact that most countries have been subjected to abrupt changes in their financial circumstances largely at the whim of international financial markets.

Governmental policy responses have further exacerbated this pervasive uncertainty. Budget cuts have drastically slowed public spending, leading to high levels of unemployment in urban areas. Cut-backs in the private sector have forced white-collar workers to seek alternative employment and, together, these pressures have led to the widespread migration of large numbers of blue-collar workers back to the countryside in several South-East Asian countries. Additional problems have flowed from the general insecurity surrounding employment prospects. There have been protests and agitation over compensation and the levels of public spending on welfare. Crime rates have increased significantly, particularly in relation to drug trafficking. Social and cultural tensions based on ethnic, religious, and even racial grounds have surfaced, and the urban destitute have resorted to looting shops and plantations.

The downfall of the Suharto regime's New Order in Indonesia on 21 May 1998 provides a stark signpost to the depth and extent of political discontent being experienced throughout South-East Asia. It has also served to highlight a secondary crisis that has arisen in the wake of the economic collapse – a lack of confidence in public leaders. In many countries the public are questioning their leaders' abilities to manage the situation either because they are incapable of doing so or because they are unwilling to do so (the suggestion being that they may be working to protect personal or commercial interests to the detriment of the general public). At the same time, several governments have shown that confidence can be restored by adopting policies of accountability and transparency. This has largely been the case in Thailand and South Korea. It is also apparent in the continuing support enjoyed by the Philippines' current president, Joseph Estrada, because he is seen to be the "people's president." The situation in Myanmar stands in stark contrast to the relative stability now being enjoyed in the Philippines. In the former country, Aung San Suu Kyi's stand-offs with the ruling State Peace and Development Council (SPDC) have introduced a new phase in a succession of crises linked directly to the worsening economic situation in the country. Collectively all of these developments reinforce the contention that economic crises must be taken very seriously lest they degenerate into other types of crisis and insecurity.

Redefining the security paradigm

From this point, our attention is naturally drawn to the issue of just where we should start the process of rethinking the whole paradigm of security. The state has traditionally been the key unit of analysis, but it is clear that the security of the "state" in developing areas is more often than not at odds with the security of the "nation." Frequently one finds that the nation is victimized for the sole cause of state maintenance. The state therefore often becomes the cause of national insecurity.

A number of specific cases in South-East Asia immediately come to mind. For example, the state of Myanmar is a compilation of nations of different ethnicity, as are the East Malaysian states of Sabah and Sarawak and Mindanao in the Philippines. In these cases, the nation not the state should be the focus of concern, but nation-building in South-East Asia has traditionally been framed in terms that encompass the development of the nation-state. This has largely been taken for granted and forced upon the people as a *fait accompli*. However, it is important to recognize that "traditional" territorial configurations in South-East Asia are orientated more towards the concept of the "nation" and not that of the "state." The "state" is primarily a Western idea that penetrated South-East Asia in order provide a legal basis for the political constructs that emerged following the disintegration of the Western empires following World War II.

To an extent, this trend has been mirrored by the security problems in Eastern Europe. This suggests that the conflict between the construct of the state and the nation is not a problem that is unique to South-East Asia. However, it would require a complete reorientation of the international system to elevate the nation to a position of ascendancy over the state. Such a process might well result in chaos. Clearly, the state-centric system, as it now exists, appears incapable of resolving such conflicts as those raging in Eastern Europe. Infusing greater sensitivity toward the idea of "nationhood" may be an interim step for addressing ongoing ethno-national disputes.

This is not to say that the idea of nation is completely free of conceptual anomalies. People of the so-called "Malay world" in South-East Asia, the Chinese diaspora, the Indians in the Maldives and Mauritius, the Muslims in southern Thailand, for example, all represent less than clear-cut ethnic or religious identities in the international community. Moreover, a number of analysts would argue that ethnicity is predominantly a social construction rather than a biological phenomenon. They contend that attention to human security problems intensified by ethnic differences would be best addressed by de-politicizing ethnicity rather than by looking at all political issues through a narrow ethnic lens.

Yet about 2,000 nationalities now inhabit the international community. Because of this tremendous ethnic diversity, we are witnessing unsuccessful accommodation between nations and states that endeavours (futilely) to integrate such socio-cultural disparities into often arbitrarily drawn state boundaries. Complicating the process even more is that the state so created is thought of as either the government, the élite, the bureaucracy, or ideology. As such the concept of "state" is bereft of people. The best we can say is that people exist for the state, not vice versa.

Our concern with the nation here is not therefore with "the nation" per se, but rather with the human beings that constitute it. Although every state aspires to become a proper "nation-state," this cannot be achieved if the people of the state cannot be protected, nurtured, and cared for. This is where human security enters in. The basic argument supporting human security rests on the realization that we all have a common duty to be concerned with all of the human beings that make up the world community, and that this sense of duty brings with it a responsibility to act or intervene on their behalf. The pursuit of "human rights" is the best-known example of this realization at work.[4]

The divisions of power politics

By focusing on people, "human security" renders meaningless the consideration of traditional territorial boundaries; even the nation and the state cannot be accorded a high priority. Human grievances are multifaceted and the chances are that, if there is one, there will be many. On closer examination such grievances may well have a political dimension that typically sees a ruling class or élite discriminating against other political groups on either racial, ethnic, historical, cultural, religious, or economic grounds (or a combination of these). This has been the case with the Chinese in Malaysia, Indonesia, and pre-1980 Thailand, and with the Vietnamese in Cambodia. It can also be seen in the relative treatment of the Javanese and non-Javanese peoples in Indonesia, the northeasterners in pre-1957 Thailand, the minorities in Myanmar, and the Singhalese and the Tamils in Sri Lanka.

Throughout history there have been examples of one ruling group weakening other groups by orchestrating political conflicts between them: typically the military against a civilian population, bureaucrats against politicians, and vice versa. There has also been a cultural dimension to discrimination: a central élite suppressing a regional élite, the high-born pitched against the *mestizo*, and the educated dominating the uneducated. Another aspect has been religious conflict: Hindus against Muslims (or the reverse), Buddhists against Christians, or Muslims against Buddhists. Finally, there has been ample evidence of economic exploitation: the case of the very rich against the poor masses, urban dwellers against the rural populace, and big business against small. Taken collectively these examples indicate that addressing human security concerns is an extremely complex matter.

On another level, the nature of and future prospects for human security rely on political systems. Politics is afforded a reasonably high priority in human affairs because the application of political power commonly defines the boundaries of human behaviour. As an extension of this, the political system of a society reflects the way that political power is being exercised. When looking at East Asia from this perspective it is worth noting that the "democratic" political systems that exist were mainly established by *force majeure* during the initial post-colonial stage of development in the region. They were not a natural outgrowth of social development but more an artificial construct. Externally, the states that embodied these political systems were crafted and tolerated fundamentally to preserve the balance of power in the international system. Internally, they drew legitimacy from claims and desires to do better than the colonial administrations or usurped regimes. Taken collectively these reasons largely explain why the principles of democracy were not embedded in the social fabric of many South-East Asian states at their birth.

The adoption of democratic systems was further stymied at the height of the Cold War by rationalizing authoritarian regimes in Asia and other developing regions as a necessary means for pursuing economic development. The fervour with which this approach was pursued succeeded in most cases in relegating the growth of democracy to the penumbra if not into the umbra. The new states of East Asia were charting unfamiliar waters when they sought to achieve their goals of development and modernity. As things turned out, authoritarian regimes led the way as East Asia launched into its revolutionary period of economic growth. In the case of Korea it was the ruling élite allied to big business that held sway, in Indonesia the coterie of Chinese entrepreneurs, in Thailand mainly the bankers and businessmen, and in Singapore and Taiwan the deftly guided hand of state regulation. However, the relentless pursuit of economic development by authoritarian regimes has also produced a legacy of economic disparity, social inequity, poor quality of life, ecological degradation, and environmental hazards. This has now created a political environment that cries for the emergence of democratization as a means of addressing these accumulated problems.

The democratization movement has been further strengthened in recent times by the increasing penetration of globalization and information technology into traditional societies. Local citizens or nationals who were pushed into the background in the past by the processes and force of development can now get assistance and support from an emerging civil service and from non-governmental organizations (both domestic and international). Human rights groups have now been joined by a host of "humanitarian" friendly societies or organizations in their pursuit of a common international agenda. Their activities, condemned by authoritarian regimes, have nevertheless succeeded in placing the issue of human suffering high on the international community's agenda.

Conceptualizing human security

Against this background, human security becomes increasingly relevant. Emma Rothschild, in her address to the Common Security Forum in Tokyo in December 1994, made it clear that the whole idea emanated from concern about the human suffering caused by the devastating catastrophe of Hiroshima. She linked common security directly to human security.[5] Others have developed this line of reasoning further, arguing that human security represents a focus on human survival, well-being, and freedom. Lincoln Chen argues, for example, that it should also be seen as the objective of all security concerns. Other forms of "security" should be seen as the means to achieve these ends, which, together, constitute human security. Applying economic, political, and environmental means to realize human security is a fairly straightforward proposition. Incorporating the means of military security does not necessarily lead to the other three ends, especially if one is conquered in battle and subjugated economically and politically in defeat. This relationship is illustrated in table 3.1.[6]

Chen has designated three key strategies for achieving human security: protection, promotion, and prevention. In situations of acute insecurity, he recommends the progressive utilization of protection measures for relief, establishing a safety-net, and supporting peace-keeping. For chronic insecurity, he believes that poverty should be the focus of concern and development the likely cure. To protect established human security regimes and to provide a warning against future challenges he suggests a preventative course of action based on information, diplomacy, and sanctions.[7]

Table 3.1 Human security

Instrumental security (means)		Security objective (ends)
Military	[Traditional security or strategy]	[?]
Economic Political Environmental	Human security	Survival Well-being Freedom

Source: Lincoln C. Chen, "Human Security: Concepts and Approaches," in Tatsuro Matsumae and Lincoln C. Chen, eds., *Common Security in Asia* (Tokyo: Tokai University Press, 1995), p. 139, with additions (in square brackets).

Asianizing the paradigm?

If the human security approach is to attain relevance in modern Asian societies it needs to be promoted and explained to the actors who frame security policy in the region. An important element in this process would be to ensure that the concept is distinct from, and not confused with, humanitarian relief activities (although these do fall within the broad scope of the human security approach). At the same time it would also need to be explained to those benefiting from the application of human security policies that it is not a single-ended charity process and that the beneficiaries need to play an active role. Unfortunately, people in developing countries are accustomed to receiving donations that are typically one-way, one-off handouts. The manner in which help is given will also be important. Experience indicates that, if people are unwilling to participate in the process because they do not believe or accept the underlying motivation, then the effort is unlikely to succeed. There is also an element of trust that needs to be taken into consideration. Politicians in South-East Asia, if not the whole of East Asia, have often been insincere and lacking in a genuine desire to help the people. It would be problematic to leave the pursuit of human security in their hands at this time.

Chen proposes that human security should address survival, well-being, and freedom of the people. To this, dignity should be added because it is a critical dimension that has always been neglected by the state and authoritarian powers. It should be acknowledged that it is not enough to recognize that all humans are born equal; rather we need to go one step further to accept that their role in society must also be equally valued. This approach reflects the traditional Eastern wisdom that rulers must seek advice from their people regardless of their social status. The cultural heritage of East Asia includes numerous stories of rulers disguising themselves and mixing with the populace so that they could listen to them and act with greater wisdom. The East Asian concept of dignity, of accepting the role of the people in society, reflects this. Besides, in traditional East Asian political thought, no matter how power is derived – be it from the mandate of heaven as is the case in Sinicized culture, through the repersonification of God as is the case with Hinduism, or through the popular election of a king as is the case with Buddhism – the power-holder is closely linked to the people.

Chen's three approaches to human security encompassing protection, promotion, and prevention deserve support. However, facilitating these processes is an issue that requires further attention. State and state organs are normally the agent and actor facilitating such processes. However, we know from experience that the state and its apparatus can produce adverse effects. Whereas in the past there was no alternative but to rely on the state for this type of support, we are now in the fortunate position of being able to access a number of "alternative" groups. These alternative groups are primarily NGOs that cover national and international areas. They possess broad networks that can be invaluable when it comes to coordinating and mounting the types of international operation that the human security approach embraces. These are groups such as the Alternative ASEAN Network, the International Network of Political Leaders Promoting Democracy in Burma, the Alternative Asia–Europe Meeting, and the Asian Network for Free Election. These international and regional groups have been very active and possess two great advantages: they have their own sources of funding and they are recognized by state authorities. These two factors suggest that it would be advisable to let them play a major role, not an auxiliary one, in promoting human security in the region. As part of any such engagement it would also be preferable to posit NGOs as bodies capable of monitoring the performance of state instrumentalities with similar tasks.

At first glance, the scope of the human security problem can appear overwhelming. Considerations of how to implement such an approach can intensify that feeling. Yet it may not be that difficult if we can first articulate the concept and then move forward steadily to reorient our perceptions towards it and to bring it to the attention of the world community. In a similar fashion, the task of actualizing human security could be achieved if it was done incrementally and according to priorities. Unlike traditional security arrangements, human security undertakings are not contingent upon the occurrence of precipitating events in order to trigger a response (as is the case with direct conflicts, confrontations, challenges, or outright invasions). To a degree, this would greatly facilitate the application of the human security approach.

On the other hand, problems would undoubtedly arise in relation to charges of interfering or intervening in the domestic affairs of states. This would be particularly prevalent in developing countries where the principle of non-interference is highly guarded. An example of this type of intercession recently occurred within the Association of South East Asian Nations when Thailand, supported by the Philippines, proposed moving from a policy of "constructive engagement" with Myanmar to one of "constructive intervention" or "flexible engagement." Indonesia came out strongly against the idea, arguing that it ran counter to ASEAN's basic principle of respecting the sovereignty of the state. Malaysia then weighed in to the argument by reportedly suggesting that Thailand would not like it if Malaysia started commenting on the treatment of Muslims in southern Thailand.[8] All in all, the exchanges on this issue and similar developments appear at times to be an almost incomprehensible defence of the state in an age characterized by growing accountability and transparency.

Another prominent example of this mode of behaviour surfaced at the ASEAN summit in Kuala Lumpur in December 1997. On that occasion, Thailand's suggestion of using the words "open society" in the final statement was blocked. In the end, the Thais had to settle for the concept of "enhanced interaction" and the brief prospect that a genuine improvement in Thai–Burmese relations would occur was lost.[9] This case brings our attention back to the observation made at the beginning of this section that articulating the case for human security may well face opposition from those who believe too strongly in the non-interventionist/non-interference philosophy. Ironically, the intervention by invitation of the International Monetary Fund in the restructuring of a number of East Asian economies has somewhat reinforced the anti-interventionists' position. The IMF's prescriptions have caused many problems for various groups of people. Therefore, we see the conflict between state and society again at play.

Conclusion

Although a number of approaches can be incorporated to advance human security, an immediate step is for East Asian governments to embrace this concept more seriously. The presence of a strong civil society will help to facilitate the adoption of policy approaches oriented to human security. Unfortunately, in most developing countries such societies are only just beginning to emerge. International organizations and international and regional NGOs have a special responsibility, therefore, to help condition developing states and their governments to accept the premises and pursue the mechanisms of the human security ethos more readily. This is the special challenge related to advancing a more egalitarian international society in an East Asian context.

In concluding it is worth reiterating the proposition presented earlier in this chapter that the approach to human security must be multidimensional in character in order to wrestle with the complexities of the real world. It is in fact this characteristic – the very complexity of the world – that commends the approach to us in the first instance. Actualizing human security, more often than not, will require regional cooperation and commitment. It will also require the concerted efforts of both public and private groups as well as individuals to be successful.

Notes

1. V. Y. Mudimbe, ed., *Open the Social Science: Report of the Gulbenkian Commission on the Restructuring of the Social Sciences* (Stanford, CA: Stanford University Press, 1996).
2. Keith Krause and Michael C. Williams, "Broadening the Agenda of Security Studies Politics and Methods," *Mershon International Studies Review* 40 (1996), pp. 229–230.
3. Barry Buzan, "Rethinking Security after the Cold War," *Cooperation and Conflict* 32, no. 1 (1997), pp. 23–25.
4. Ramesh Thakur, "From National to Human Security," in Stuart Harris and Andrew Mack, eds., *Asia-Pacific Security: The Economics–Politics Nexus* (Sydney: Allen & Unwin, 1997), p. 67.
5. Emma Rothschild, "Introduction," in Tatsuro Matsumae and Lincoln C. Chen, eds., *Common Security in Asia: New Concepts of Human Security* (Tokyo: Tokai University Press, 1995), pp. 3–5.
6. Lincoln C. Chen, "Human Security: Concepts and Approaches," in Matsumae and Chen, *Common Security in Asia*, p. 139.
7. Ibid., p. 145.
8. This process is described aptly by Jeannie Henderson, *Reassessing ASEAN*, Adelphi Paper 328 (London: Oxford University Press for the International Institute for Strategic Studies, 1999), pp. 48–55.
9. See *The Bangkok Post*, 12 December 1997, p. 3, and *The Nation* (Bangkok), 19 December 1997, p. A-3.

4

Indonesia after the fall of President Suharto: A "case study" in human security

Ikrar Nusa Bhakti

Events in Indonesia constitute a major watershed for applying the human security concept to a dynamically evolving Asia-Pacific society. Since proclaiming its independence on 17 August 1945, Indonesia's national ethos has been based on emphasizing the collective welfare of the population rather than advancing individual human rights. Too much dissent from this posture, it was feared, might precipitate a return to the days of disintegration and instability predominant in the colonial era, which could be exploited by outsiders and threaten the very existence of the new Indonesian state. Yet socio-political instability was pervasive throughout the country during the first decade of self-rule, eventually precipitating the demise of Sukarno's "Guided Democracy" in September 1965.

The Suharto government elected to overcome the state of anarchy that emerged from the army's bloody victory over the Indonesian Communist Party in 1965 and from President Sukarno's subsequent removal from office by restricting meaningful decision-making in the country to a small military élite. Civilian politicians were afforded little opportunity to influence this autocracy and democratic opposition movements were not allowed to evolve by a central government obsessed with prioritizing economic growth and maintaining political order throughout the Indonesian archipelago's 16,000 islands. Any prospect that human security (with its emphasis on *individual* happiness and quality of life) would be cultivated in these circumstances was, at best, highly remote.

Factors in contemporary political reform

The personal excesses of Suharto's family and inner circle, along with the inability of the military establishment to accept a more mature working relationship with an expanding Indonesian middle class, however, eventually worked to generate widespread and effective socio-political dissent within Indonesian society. Indonesia's current political reforms were born from aspirations that clearly reflect a human security agenda shared at least tacitly by the majority of Indonesians and that are reflected within the *Pancasila* – the Five Principles that constitute the state's founding ideology. These are: (1) Belief in One God; (2) Humanitarianism; (3) Indonesian Unity; (4) Democracy; and (5) Social Justice. Moreover, the recent intensification of their country's economic and environmental problems could not but have underscored further the importance of quality-of-life issues for millions of Indonesians.

All these factors crescendoed into what became a historical moment in Indonesian history that unfolded in May 1998 and eventually led to President Suharto's downfall. Assessing the May Revolution in some detail provides us with an instructive "test case" for ascertaining how political masses in developing societies – yearning for the most fundamental forms of human security – can transform highly autocratic political systems into ones more conducive to political reform, given the right timing and circumstances. The factors that applied to Indonesia's specific situation may not always relate to those present in other Asian societies. But they may generate some insights into how the trends that are driving the political liberalization process now in evidence throughout much of the Asia-Pacific region may be interrelated.

The Trisakti martyrs: Catalyst for reform

The death of four Trisakti University students on 12 May 1998 encouraged Indonesian university students to intensify their campaign calling for total reform. In a replay of events in 1966, when Arief Rachman Hakim (a student at the University of Indonesia) was shot to death by the military, these four students have become martyrs and heroes for the political reform movement. One day after the shooting, there were massive riots around Jakarta, Bekasi, and Tangerang in West Java. Many people believed that these riots were organized by individuals within the military establishment or by thugs operating with military backing.

The riots were amongst the worst in modern Indonesian history. Many rumours circulated concerning these riots. One was that various military personnel wanted to emulate the events that transpired during the Malari

Affair on 15 January 1974. At that time, senior military officials encouraged gangs of thugs to burn and loot shopping centres in Senen, Central Jakarta. They intended to make the people believe that those riots were undertaken by students and thus withdraw their support of student demonstration for total reform. A second rumour attributed the organization of the riots to top military officials. The Commander of the Indonesian Armed Forces, General Wiranto, for example, had good reasons to stop the student demonstrations. A strong supporter of Suharto, he had much to gain by preserving some semblance of the country's political status quo. Other rumours attributed the riots either to an intensifying power struggle among Indonesia's military élites or, conversely, to anarchists intent on demolishing symbols of development achieved under Suharto's regime. It it is quite difficult to say which of the four rumours was actually true, because the military or the police have yet to reveal publicly who the instigators really were.

The death of Trisakti University students and the mass riots failed to undermine the students' determination to topple Suharto as a prerequisite for total reform. For the second time in Indonesia's history, a student movement succeeded in forcing an Indonesian president to step down. In the end, after 32 years in power, Suharto resigned from his presidency on 21 May 1998. On the same day, B. J. Habibie was installed as President in the State Palace without convening a session of the *Majelis Permusyawaratan Rakyat* (MPR, or People's Consultative Assembly). The justification for this move was that the MPR could not convene because of security concerns stemming from the state of emergency. On that day, thousands of university students from many universities in Java, Sumatra, Kalimantan, and Sulawesi occupied the national parliament building in Jakarta.

Many factors, both internal and external, contributed to Suharto's decision to quit. The internal factors included: (1) the successful occupation of the national parliament building in Jakarta between 19 and 23 May 1998 by the students; (2) Suharto's failure to reshuffle his cabinet, even after 14 of his former aides (ministers) had sent him letters of resignation; and (3) General Wiranto's alleged statement to Suharto that the Indonesian military (*Angkatan Bersenjata Republik Indonesia* – ABRI) would no longer support him. At least two significant external factors speeded up Suharto's downfall: (1) a delay by the International Monetary Fund in providing extra funding for Indonesia (this was critical because the country desperately needed to import food and medicines but lacked foreign exchange reserves); and (2) indirect but significant US support for the student movement.

The May Revolution in Indonesia can be regarded as a genuine class revolution. In contrast to previous student movements in Indonesia, the

1998 student campaign was supported by nearly all elements within the society but was particularly spearheaded by the middle class against ensconced élites. Shopkeepers, educators, and other rank-and-file citizens supported the students by providing money, food, printing materials, T-shirts, entertainment, and short courses to strengthen the students' morale and to enhance their political capabilities.

These middle-class people can be divided into five important categories, according to their motives. These are: (1) those with a genuine desire to see political and economic reforms; (2) former student activists who had been trying to topple Suharto's regime and end his dictatorship for many years; (3) middle-class elements who became disenchanted with the Suharto family after the outbreak of the economic crisis in July 1997 (either because they lost their job or because they could not compete with the "crony capitalists" who were close to Suharto's family); (4) newcomers who jumped on the bandwagon just before Suharto's fall; and (5) former Suharto associates who wanted to "wash their hands" of their involvement with the corruption, nepotism, and collusion that had become too much a part of that regime. Appropriately, perhaps, students labelled this last group "last minute heroes."

Threats to human security

Human security issues in Indonesia have actually intensified since the fall of President Suharto. To date, Indonesia's transition from dictatorship to democracy could best be described as "going from the frying pan into the fire." Indeed, Indonesian citizens are still searching for a basis with which to formulate human security in their country. That search remains at best ambiguous and at worst frustratingly elusive.

Although there is currently freedom of expression in Indonesia, there has been no visible increase in freedom from fear, hunger, torture, etc. Indeed, outbreaks of violence, killing, and wanton destruction became daily events between the June election – to choose the People's Consultative Assembly (MPR) or Electoral College – and the MPR's October 1999 ballot to elect a new president. A list of some these traumas makes compelling reading: the extra-judicial killings by so-called "black ninja" death squads in Banyuwangi and surrounding East Java; the burning of hundreds of churches and mosques in Jakarta on 20 November 1998, Kupang (November 1998), and Ambon (19–20 January 1999); the burning of shops owned mostly by people of Chinese descent in Jakarta on 13–15 May and 20 November 1998; the slaughter of students at Semanggi near the parliament building in Jakarta on 13 November 1998; the murder and the rape of ethnic Chinese women on 13–15 May 1998; the ongoing abduction and torture of pro-democracy activists and continuing revelations of mass murders committed by the military in Aceh, North Sumatra, and East Timor. There was also pervasive and widespread looting and rioting in Jakarta, Solo (Central Java), Karawang (West Java), Lampung (South Sumatra), Kupang (East Nusa Tenggara), and Ambon (Mollucas). Last, but hardly least, there was a dramatic upsurge in street crime in Jakarta.

Obviously, the situation throughout Indonesia has become frightening in the extreme. In addition, the underlying social and political turmoil has been compounded by the depressed state of the economy. Business-people, investors, and foreign diplomats have labelled Indonesia a "dangerous place" and one to be avoided at all costs. The United States, Australia, Japan, the Netherlands, and many other foreign governments have issued travel advice warning their citizens to avoid the archipelago. In other words, Indonesia has gone from being an important actor working for the maintenance of regional security to one of South-East Asia's most explosive "flashpoints."

The leadership vacuum

As was mentioned previously, Indonesia is currently experiencing an erratic period of transition – a transition from an authoritarian regime to a democratic system. For 32 years under the Suharto dictatorship, none of Indonesia's state institutions (government, parliament, courts, etc.) was autonomous or independent. Nearly all appointments and high-level placements in government departments, military institutions, the Attorney General's Office, the Supreme Court, the People's Consultative Assembly, and state-owned enterprises had to have Suharto's blessing. Corruption, collusion, and nepotism were a day-to-day reality during the Suharto era.

It was inevitable, therefore, that the people of Indonesia and the mechanisms of the Indonesian state would be thrown into widespread chaos when Suharto was suddenly forced from office. Most government ministers, directors of state institutions, military generals, and high court judges were unaccustomed to taking the initiative themselves. More dangerous still, these people were also not accustomed to accepting responsibility for their actions. This is because they were appointed by, and trained to function simply as loyal servants to, Suharto. They were never intended to become astute and independent leaders pursuing their respective visions for the future. If they do have a collective vision for the future, it is pretty similar to the one entertained by Suharto.

To illustrate this point, on 9 November 1998 President B. J. Habibie signed decree No. 191 in order to establish the Council for Enforcement of Security and Law, but it was made public by State Secretary Akbar Tanjung only on 9 December 1998. This informal body was chaired by the President. But daily operations are overseen by the Minister of Defence (Commanding General Wiranto), who simultaneously chaired a smaller, more powerful executive committee made up of 13 people. This committee was composed of the Attorney General (Lt.-General Andi Mohammad Ghalib), the head of the State Intelligence Coordinating Board (or *Bakin*, Lt.-General Z. A. Maulani), the National Police Commander (Lt.-General Roesmanhadi), the Secretary of Development Operations (or *Sesdalopbang*, currently Lt.-General ret. Sintong Panjaitan), and nine other ministers. The aim of the new Council-at-large was, according to Minister Tanjung, to accelerate the government's reform programmes. Moreover, the Council was assigned to control and coordinate efforts to resolve crises threatening national stability.[1]

According to Akbar Tanjung, the Council did not have a place in the national command structure relative to other government agencies or ministries. "Its position will not overlap with existing bodies," he insisted.[2] On a different occasion, in Malang, East Java, the Habibie government's Coordinating Minister for Political Affairs and Security, General (retired) Feisal Tanjung, stated in December 1998 that the Council would be temporary in nature. Feisal Tanjung, who is also a member of the Council, reported: "The Council will keep monitoring security developments and will feed existing security institutions with input." It is interesting to note that, according to Feisal, the Council was formed because the existing institutions "had not been effective enough."[3]

At least on the surface, Feisal's statement appears dubious. As the minister responsible for coordinating security and political affairs, it would be reasonable to expect that he would accept responsibility for restoring law and order. But this does not appear to be the case. If this is true, then it means that his office will never work seriously to overcome the social, political, and economic crises in Indonesia. It also means that all of the existing institutions that were formed in accordance with the 1945 Constitution (for example, the presidency, the ministries, the Armed Forces, the National Police, the National Intelligence Board, the parliament, and the People's Consultative Assembly) will also have been acknowledged to have failed demonstrably both to maintain security and order and to accelerate national reform programmes.

Accordingly, the question that must be asked is why the government has rejected the students' idea to form a presidium government and a Provisional People's Consultative Assembly. Another pertinent question is why several retired generals and a number of political activists who have raised similar ideas have been accused by the Habibie regime of planning a *coup d'état* or of organizing subversive activities aimed at de-stabilizing a legal government (however, it must be added, not a legitimate government). If it is accepted that the existing institutions have been ineffective, it seems reasonable to suggest that it would better for all Indonesians if the President and the entire cabinet resigned. This would allow people who are both capable and willing to manage the country more effectively to assume power.

It is worth noting that the Council for Enforcement of Security and Law also duplicates the functions of other, already existing institutions. For example, there are at least three other government institutions that were already dealing with problems of national security, order, and stability. One is the National Resilience Institute (*Lemhanas – Lembaga Pertahanan Keamanan*) chaired by Lt.-General Agum Gumelar. Another is the Council for National Security and Defence (*Wanhankamnas – Dewan Pertahanan dan Keamanan Nasional*) personally chaired by President Habibie (although its daily operations are supervised by its Secretary General, Lt.-General Arifin Tarigan). Nor did the government seek to dissolve a third, largely duplicative institution – the Agency for the Coordination of Support for the Development of National Stability (*Bakorstanas*). This body was established during the Suharto era and was itself a replacement for the *Kopkamtib* (*Komando Operasi Pemulihan Keamanan dan Ketertiban*, or Agency for the Restoration of Security and Order). The *Bakorstanas* has been likened to an internal security agency and it is chaired by General Wiranto.

All of these agencies beg the question: why does Indonesia need so many extra institutions to maintain national stability? Is Indonesia really faced with an emergency situation so desperate that it needs yet another institution in order to resolve the many crises threatening national stability? The evident lack of satisfactory answers or explanations leads, in turn, to speculation that the Council for Enforcement of Security and Law was in fact formed to implement tougher security measures against students and anti-government activists. From that basis, another question follows: is it possible that in the foreseeable future the government will be compelled to make a statement that the country is in a state of emergency, thereby giving it the power to deal more repressively with student and political activists? The answers to such questions will largely shape the future of human security in Indonesia.

If the new government led by Abdurrahman Wahid does indeed have the political will and develops the ability to maintain security and enforce the rule of law rather than repress Indonesian citizens, another question then arises: will the daily operations of the new security council still be supervised by the Commander of the Indonesian Armed Forces? This approach would be inconsistent with recent ABRI statements claiming that the military socio-political role of the Armed Forces was being redefined and modified. It also runs counter to the demands made by the students and the general populace that the military's "dual function" (*Dwi Fungsi*) role should be abolished. In order to restore law and order, it would be more efficient for the new government simply to reinforce the three pillars of national law enforcement, namely the National Police, the Attorney General's Office, and the Supreme Court. A first step in this direction would be to appoint the National Police Commander, the Attorney General, and the Head of the Supreme Court as collective coordinators of the Council for Enforcement of Security and Law.

While militias form, socio-political questions remain

In addition to these fundamental requirements, there is also a need to understand why students still organized demonstrations demanding the abolition of *Dwi Fungsi* during the waning days of the Habibie government and why that government failed to stop corruption, collusion, and nepotism. One must also ask why there has been no adequate investigation into the wealth of Suharto, his family, and his cronies. Indeed, Indonesia's new president, Abdurrahman Wahid, reportedly has pledged to pardon Suharto if he is convicted of crimes as a result of an investigation and subsequent trial (on the grounds that his former position should afford him sufficient dignity to stay out of prison).[4] Finally, it must be ascertained why those responsible for the killing fields in Aceh, East Timor, and Irian Jaya have not yet been brought to trial. Answering these questions may tell the government much about why the general Indonesian populace is so predisposed to run amok during a time of critical political transition.

In order to overcome these crises, there is a definite need to kill the viruses and not simply to settle for reducing the fever. What the Indonesian people need is a just and civilized policy approach – a human security posture – to socio-political and economic reform, not just an approach designed to maintain the status quo and keep the current government in power. On this point, it must be recognized that Presidential Decree No. 191/1998 gave extraordinary powers to President Habibie but that it contradicted the MPR Decree No. 8/MPR/1998, which had, in fact, *abolished* previous regulations that had assigned the President such powers. This evidence indicates quite comprehensively that Habibie was following in "his professor" Suharto's footsteps by relying on the traditional security paradigm of strengthening domestic autocracy in order to maintain control over Indonesians. It is notable that he did not adopt the "human security" or "prosperity" approach that he and his spokesperson had mentioned so many times and to so many people in previous years.

In mid-December 1998 the Habibie government announced that it planned to recruit and arm a 70,000 strong civilian militia (40,000 in the first phase) to support the security forces' efforts to maintain order during the June 1999 national elections. The Coordinating Minister for Political Affairs and Security, General (ret.) Feisal Tanjung, said that the recruitment of civilians would be jointly organized by the Defence Ministry and the National Police. The government's rationalization was that the existing security forces would not be able to handle the volatile pre-election situation because there are thousands of islands in Indonesia and the ratio between the security forces and the civilian population was far from ideal. It cited an ideal ratio of 1:350 and noted that this was significantly below the existing ratio of 1:1,200.

Support for the government's plan came mostly from active and retired military generals. Both Feisal and Rudini (former Minister of Home Affairs) justified the move on the grounds that it complied with a 1982 defence and security law. Former Indonesian Vice President Try Sutrisno (also a retired army general) backed the plan by saying that the civilian militia was needed to police the "unpredictable situation." Others pointed out that the plan was in accord with Indonesia's security doctrine ("people's security and defence") and the 1945 Constitution (which states that Indonesian citizens have both a right and a responsibility to defend their country).[5]

Civilian militias are not new to Indonesia's defence system. During Indonesia's struggle for independence between 1945 and 1950, political parties established their own civilian militias (*lasykar*) to fight side by side with the regular army against the Japanese and the Dutch. During the *konfrontasi* (Indonesia's confrontation with the Malay Federation) of 1963–1966, the Indonesian Communist Party also proposed to President Sukarno that a "Fifth Force" (*Angkatan Kelima*) be established that would supplant the regular army, navy, air force, and police. In the early 1970s, the army also recruited university students as members of *Walawa* (*Wajib Latih Mahasiswa* – a military training requirement for students). The name has since been changed to *Menwa* (*Resimen Mahasiswa*, or Students' Regiment). Youth organizations such as Pemuda Pancasila, Pemuda Pancamarga, and FKPPI (The Sons and Daughters of Active and Retired Military Apparatuses) have also received paramilitary training so that they could support the government and Golkar (the ruling political party). This practice was particularly noticeable in the lead-up to past elections.

Those who opposed the government plan to raise a militia did so for four main reasons. First, they were afraid that civilian militias could be used by factions in the government or in Indonesian society that opposed moderate political elements. To support this claim they cited events that occurred during the last extraordinary meeting of the People's Consultative Assembly when the police and the military organized *Pam Swakarsa* (civilian vigilantes) to move against student demonstrations. Shortly after the "Cawang incident" (where four members of *Pam Swakarsa* were killed by the masses), the military, the police, and *Furkon* (an Islamic Forum that supports the present government on religious grounds) sought to wash their hands of the incident by claiming that they did not recruit and arm the *Pam Swakarsa*. The military and the police stated that the only *Pam Swakarsa* they recruited were from Pemuda Pancasila, Pemuda Pancamarga, FKPPI, and Banser NU (*Barisan Serba Guna Nahdlatul Ulama*). However, it was noticeable that the police did not take any action against *Pam Swakarsa* before concerns were expressed by the Minister of Education, Professor Juwono Sudarsono, together with students and political activists.

A second basis of opposition to the creation of a militia stemmed from the fear that they could be used by Golkar to intimidate supporters of opposition parties during the June 1999 election (a contingency that apparently did not materialize to any extensive degree).

A third, and genuine, fear was that the civilian militia could become a repeat of the Fifth Force, active during the PKI (Indonesian Communist Party) period. This related to a final major concern: that the role of the projected militia was too poorly defined, raising the obvious questions of what they were for and who the enemy was. It seemed all too possible that they could be employed to repress civilians who were organizing reform demonstrations.

It is easy to see that political developments in Indonesia have been moving toward a radicalization that has the potential to fragment the country and to precipitate political activities intensifying ethnic, religious, and racial upheaval. The public's favourable perception of Habibie has hardly been strengthened by his promotion of "selective" radicalization and sectarian politics. As Golkar's poor performance in the June 1999 election revealed, the government has come to be seen by Indonesia's populace as largely ineffective. This increases the degree of instability in Indonesia, endangering human security in the process.

A benchmark for the future of Indonesia as a state united by the slogan of "Unity in Diversity" was the 7 June 1999 general election. The election was relatively free and fair by Indonesian standards, with opposition parties rising to genuine prominence. This had not happened since 1955.

The 462 members of the House of Representatives (*Dewan Perwakilan Rakyat* – DPR) elected "first past the post" combined with 135 provincial

representatives (most of whom also would sit in the DPR), 38 representatives appointed by the military, and 65 "sectoral" representatives to
constitute the Electoral College or MPR.[6] Its key task, of course, was to
elect the new President and Vice President of Indonesia in October 1999.
It should also be noted that during the campaign period leading to the
June ballot, all 48 political parties that were competing were able to
conduct their campaigns without any difficulties.

No single party won a majority of the votes in the June election. Five
political factions emerged as significant: (1) the Indonesian Democratic
Party of Struggle (*Partai Demokrasi Indonesia Perjuangan* – PDI-P); (2)
the Golkar Party; (3) the United Development Party (*Partai Persatuan
Pembangunan* – PPP); (4) the National Awakening Party (*Partai Ke-
bangkitan Bangsa* – PKB); and (5) the National Mandate Party (*Partai
Amanat Nasional* – PAN). These were followed by other smaller Islamic
and nationalist parties. Even though the election was conducted in June,
the actual results were made public just before the first General Session
of the People's Representative Assembly opened on 1 October 1999. The
General Session was divided into two sessions. The first session elected a
new Speaker for the MPR, Professor Dr. Amien Rais, the chairman of
PAN. Ir. Akbar Tanjung was subsequently elected as the Speaker for the
House of Representatives. A second session convened to decide whether
the MPR would accept or reject the accountability speech of President
B. J. Habibie and to elect the new (or incumbent) President and a new
Vice President.[7]

Hopes intensified that the traumas that had been so damaging to the
human security of the Indonesian people could finally be subsiding.
However, a number of Indonesian analysts remained pessimistic about
the future of their country, even if the general election turned out more
positively than was initially expected. They felt the Indonesian people
still had to learn how to run a democracy without spiralling into social
and political chaos.[8]

The presidential election

For the second time in Indonesian history, a majority of MPR members
rejected a presidential accountability speech on 19 October 1999 (the first
time was President Sukarno's accountability speech in 1966). The MPR
had earlier voted 355 to 322 to reject the President's report on his administration of the country.[9] Habibie thus lost his chance to be re-elected
as President. There were a number of factors that caused the MPR to
reject Habibie's speech. First was the "loss" of East Timor as the result of
the 30 August referendum in which 78.8 per cent of East Timorese voted

to reject the autonomy option offered by President Habibie in favour of outright independence. Second was the worsening human security situation in East Timor, Aceh, and other areas of Indonesia. Adverse publicity about such transgressions had humiliated key sectors of the country's power structure in the eyes of the outside world.[10] Moreover, other intra-state ethno-religious cases were looming in Irian Jaya and in the Mollucas Islands. Habibie's credibility also plunged over the Bank Bali (or "Bali-gate") scandal where a substantial number of Golkar Party officials and Habibie's own supporters were involved in a major corruption scandal. Finally, General Wiranto declined Habibie's offer of the Vice Presidency on 18 October 1999, signalling that the military declined to support the incumbent as a presidential candidate.[11]

The other two presidential candidates were Abdurrahman Wahid, who was nominated by the Reform Faction and supported by the Centre Axis (Islamic political parties) in the MPR, and Megawati Soekarnoputri, who was nominated and supported by the political party that had received the most votes in the June election, the Indonesian Democratic Party of Struggle. The presidential election took place in the MPR on 20 October 1999. Wahid defeated Megawati by 373 to 313 votes, with five abstentions. The result initially sparked widespread anger among thousands of loyal Megawati supporters. They ran amok in Jakarta, Central Java, and Bali.[12] The situation, however, soon came under control when Wahid nominated Megawati to become his Vice President on the following day.[13]

Wahid is widely regarded by both politicians and independent analysts as having the will and ability to reform the country's ailing economy and to restore political legitimacy to government. Although Abdurrahman (better known by his nickname of "Gus Dur") has physical problems (he can barely see and has suffered two strokes), he is a genuine representative of the country's Muslim population. Megawati complements him as a representative of Indonesia's nationalist factions and as the leader of the winning party in the June 1999 national general election.

The election of Gus Dur as President can be seen as the best solution for the current Indonesian political environment. If Megawati had been elected as President, it might have angered both fundamentalist Islamic leaders, who were campaigning before the October election to reject a woman president, and also Suharto's remaining supporters, who were afraid that Megawati, as the daughter of the first Indonesian President (Sukarno), would exact revenge on Suharto and his former deputy, B. J. Habibie.

The election of Megawati as Vice President was also an integral part of the "best political solution." If Gus Dur and Habibie's supporters had adhered to their previous strategy of "Asal Bukan Mega" ("as long as not Megawati"), which had worked for them in the presidential election, and had chosen Akbar Tanjung (the chairman of Golkar) as Vice President, it would not only have sparked intense anger among Megawati's supporters but also have raised questions among the majority of Indonesian citizens about the legitimacy of the general election held in June. Indonesian democracy would then have been severely tested.

The newly elected President's idea of forming a national reconciliation cabinet from various members of society (political parties, ethnic groups, and religious factions) can be regarded with provisional optimism. However, Indonesia is still far from being a truly democratic country because there is still no formally designated opposition party in the national parliament. Apart from that, 5 of the 35 ministers in the new cabinet have military backgrounds, and they have control over very important positions. They are General Wiranto, Coordinating Minister for Political and Security Affairs; Lt.-General Soesilo Bambang Yudhoyono, Minister of Mines and Energy; Lt.-General Agum Gumelar, Minister of Communication; Rear-Admiral Freddy Numbery, Minister of Corrective National Apparatus; and Lt.-General (ret.) Surjadi Sudirdja, Minister of Home Affairs.[14]

Indeed, the military received the largest number of the available cabinet posts (the main political parties each have only three or four ministers). It also means that the military is laying the groundwork for a response to a domestic political crisis in the event that President Gus Dur cannot continue his five-year term. Moreover, the military can use its positions in the cabinet to manipulate Indonesian politics and to raise funds from those lucrative and powerful ministries it does control. Finally, it can resist the people's demands to end dual military functions by assuming a low-key but influential role in the country's daily political life. As an initial step in this process, it will endeavour to resist demands to try military personnel who participated in the killing, torturing, or raping of innocent Indonesian citizens in Aceh, East Timor, Irian Jaya, and other areas of the country.

Conclusion

What does this Indonesian "test case" tell us about the role of human security in contemporary Asia? Three prominent lessons seem to have emerged from the socio-political chaos and forces of political change that have dominated Indonesia since 1998. First, the Suharto government's efforts to rationalize its opposition to the development of a viable and comprehensive civil society in Indonesia failed. Its adherence to so-called "Asian values" and its insistence on imposing uncompromising functional approaches to solving deep-seated and protracted realities of poverty and alienation were found wanting when the dual challenges of financial rot and political legitimacy intensified during the mid to late 1990s. As was the case in the Philippines a decade before, "people power" became (perhaps inevitably) the dominant political force and expression of human aspirations at this critical historical juncture.

Secondly, despite the government's best efforts to control the size and context of political élite groups, Indonesian society proved quite capable of producing a viable "epistemic community" of opposition politicians, reformist technocrats, and others to guide the country through the May Revolution in such a way that the country's overall political reform was enhanced. This process was facilitated, of course, by the government's ineptitude in responding to human security concerns with very inhumane tactics. The key measuring point for success was the development of alternative socio-political power centres to the army and its allied "militias" (real or proposed) within Indonesia's broader society. To date, it appears these centres have transformed their agendas into peaceful political expression fairly effectively, as the October 1999 presidential transition illustrated. The real test will be to what extent this process is sustained during the new government's first four years in office.

Finally, human security advocates must be cautious of procedures and infrastructures introduced during various phases of political liberalization by those forces intent on preserving the status quo and their own power bases. In the Indonesian case, this was manifested by ABRI's efforts to introduce a plethora of redundant committees, institutions, and regulations to achieve the relatively simple objective of establishing a socio-political order that could be supported by the general populace. Existing institutions could be better applied to restore governmental legitimacy, bypassing the morass of bureaucratic impediments that constituted part of the original problem – a government that had lost touch with the hopes and needs of the governed.

The biggest security challenge confronting Indonesia is not how to recover its economic well-being, but how to resolve secessionist movements in Aceh, Irian Jaya, and elsewhere so as to preserve the legitimacy and cohesion of the Indonesian state. On 8 November 1999, more than 1 million people took part in a mass rally in Banda Aceh, the capital city of Aceh province, sending the loudest and clearest signal yet to Jakarta of their demand for a referendum on self-determination for that province.[15] Other provinces such as Irian Jaya and Riau are sure to follow Aceh's example unless the Indonesian central authorities move swiftly and convincingly to meet their needs and aspirations. Human security in contemporary Indonesia is certainly better than was the case in Suharto's or even Habibie's era. However, the new government cannot solve the problems of rising secessionism, inter-ethnic and religious warfare, implacable military resistance to natural justice, and economic recovery all at once over the short term. It is quite possible that democracy and human security in Indonesia may again deteriorate. It is far less likely that the Indonesian people will allow the military to dominate Indonesian politics and economy again.

Indonesia is still struggling to shape its future policies toward human security. The stakes for regional stability in it doing so successfully are unquestionably high. At the start of the twenty-first century, ordinary Indonesians have at least some reason to entertain the hope that their country will move gradually towards more democratic and prosperous times. Most of them remain acutely aware, however, of the risks accompanying the quest to infuse greater levels of democracy and compassion into their society.

Notes

1. Statement by Minister Tanjung. The full 34-strong Council for Enforcement of Security and Law comprises: 23 cabinet members; National Police Commander Lt.-Gen. Roesmanhadi; the head of the State Intelligence Coordinating Board (Bakin), Lt.-Gen. (ret.) Zaini Azhar Maulani; the Secretary of Development Operations (Sesdalopbang), Lt.-Gen. (ret.) Sintong Panjaitan; the chairman of the National Commission on Human Rights, Marzuki Darusman; and the leaders of five religious councils (Islam, Christian Protestant, Catholic, Hindu, and Buddhist) (*The Jakarta Post*, 9 December 1998).
2. *The Jakarta Post*, 9 December 1998.
3. Ibid., 11 December 1998.
4. Philip Shenon, "Indonesia's President Vows to Give Pardon to Former Leader," *New York Times*, 12 November 1999.
5. *The Jakarta Post*, 11 December 1998.
6. For a breakdown of this system, see Jose Manuel Tesovo, "No Time to Wait for Results," *Asiaweek* 25, no. 31 (6 August 1999), p. 17.
7. See, *Kompas, The Jakarta Post, Suara Pembaruan*, and other Indonesian daily newspapers between 1 October and 22 October 1999.
8. See, for example, Arief Budiman, "New Order, Old School," *Inside Indonesia* no. 58 (April–June 1999), p. 7. Budiman is a professor of Indonesian Studies at the University of Melbourne and has extensive contacts among Indonesia's élites and intellectuals. Also see T. A. Legowo, "The 1999 General Election," *The Indonesian Quarterly* 27, no. 2 (Second Quarter 1999), pp. 98–108. Legowo, Head of the Department of Social and Political Change, Centre for Strategic and International Studies, Jakarta, concluded that "if fundamental or radical changes" in Indonesia's electoral process were to be imposed by the military, counter to its pledge to remain neutral in the 1999 elections, "that will have an impact on postponing or even cancelling the elections,... [and] the democratic future of Indonesia will be seriously jeopardised" (p. 108).
9. *The Jakarta Post* and *Kompas*, 20 October 1999.
10. The Indonesian military never declared Aceh to be an area of military operations during 1989 to 1998. But the military operations to put down rebellion there during that time

were widely known by the Indonesian people. In the middle of 1998, the Armed Forces Commander, General Wiranto, declared an end to military operations there. However, the crisis situation in Aceh only intensified after Wiranto's announcement.

11. See *The Jakarta Post, Kompas*, and *Suara Pembaruan*, 19 October 1999.
12. *The Jakarta Post*, 21 October 1999.
13. *The Jakarta Post*, 22 October 1999.
14. *Editor's note*: On 15 February 2000, Wiranto was suspended from his Cabinet position pending the outcome of an Attorney General's investigation of reported human rights transgressions in East Timor in which Wiranto was implicated. Surjadi Sudirdja replaced Wiranto as Minister for Political Affairs and Security.
15. *The Jakarta Post* and *Kompas*, 9 November 1999.

5

Approaching human security as "middle powers": Australian and Canadian disarmament diplomacy after the Cold War

Carl J. Ungerer

Introduction

The purpose of this chapter is to explore some of the linkages between three sets of patterns in Australian and Canadian foreign policy over the past decade. First, it looks at how the concept of security has evolved in the official discourse of both countries. Following some earlier conceptual work in the academic literature, Australia and Canada have been among a select group of countries that have adopted and promoted a broader neoliberal framework for security dialogue. In particular, this trend has been evident in a series of publications by the former Australian foreign minister, Gareth Evans, and through the Canadian government's inquiries into its own post–Cold War peace-keeping responsibilities. Both countries have tacitly adopted Evans' "cooperative security" approach as a more inclusive and less military-focused definition of security, thereby laying much of the groundwork for the more recent focus on "human security" issues.[1]

A second theme concerns how reinvigorated notions of "middle power diplomacy" have been applied in terms of this broader security concept. Australia's commitment to cooperative middle power diplomacy has now faltered with the election of the conservative Coalition government in March 1996, but Canada, under the stewardship of Foreign Minister Lloyd Axworthy, has continued where Evans left off. Although obvious differences in the style and approach to foreign policy between Canberra and Ottawa remain, the self-identification of being a "middle power" has been a primary theme in Australian and Canadian statecraft and has informed much of their security behaviour at various times during the past decade.

Third, the chapter discusses the convergence of the first two patterns around the themes of "human security." It is argued that the main point at which notions of cooperative security and middle power diplomacy have converged with the emerging "human security" agenda has been in recent debates over arms control and disarmament. On questions of both weapons of mass destruction and conventional disarmament, Australia and Canada have attempted to blend the cooperative, coalition-building style of middle power diplomacy with the humanitarian, environmental, and development assistance themes of "human security."

Both countries under review have been active participants in Asia-Pacific cooperative security politics and, in many instances, have established indelible legacies as middle power interlocutors on human security issues in the region. Other Asian states may well view themselves as regional middle powers, but there is currently no broad consensus over which of them truly fits this category or what specifically reinforces their credentials as human security actors. Accordingly, this chapter deliberately confines its analysis to investigating how Australia and Canada, as two acknowledged Asia-Pacific middle powers, have acted as catalysts for the promotion of human security and how they have exercised creative leadership to implement it in two selected episodes. By incorporating this approach, the "middle power" typology can be demonstrated to be an important and viable dimension of the overall human security framework.

The evolving security discourse: Moving beyond comprehensive, collective, and common security

Several months before the Berlin Wall was dismantled, the Australian foreign minister, Gareth Evans, initiated a process of recasting Australia's traditional security approach to meet the changing needs of an increasingly activist middle power in the Asia-Pacific region. The 1989 ministerial statement, *Australia's Regional Security*,[2] was one of the first attempts by a Western government to widen the debate beyond a narrow definition of security based around military threats and responses.

Based in part on the emerging academic literature at the time,[3] the statement sought to project a more comprehensive security framework for Australia. The centrepiece of the statement was the assertion that security had become "multidimensional" in nature and that, as a result, states would be required to respond to a range of traditional as well as non-traditional threats to security. Among the non-military threats designated were environmental degradation, narcotics trafficking, and unregulated population flows.

The ministerial statement was the subject of considerable debate and criticism in Australia but, in retrospect, was an undoubtedly seminal contribution to the ongoing security discourse in both Australia and the Asia-Pacific region. It was, in fact, the first real attempt by an Australian government to incorporate human security issues into mainstream security dialogue. Based on the assessment regarding the multidimensional nature of post–Cold War security, the statement adopted separate concepts for Australia's security approach to South-East Asia (comprehensive engagement) and the South Pacific region (constructive commitment). Although notions of "comprehensive" and "constructive" security had been present in the academic literature for some time (and indeed were part of the existing security discourse in Asia), the ministerial statement was a conscious decision to employ these concepts in a less military-focused security policy for Australia.

The second major statement on how Australia's brand of middle power diplomacy could be applied to the changed security realities of the post–Cold War order was the publication of Evans' *Cooperating for Peace* in 1993. Following the release of the 1989 ministerial statement, Evans was keen to bring Australia's security approach under a single unifying theme that would operate as both a framework for the conduct of Australia's foreign relations and a prescription for a more secure international order. Evans dismissed the available alternatives at the time – comprehensive, common, or collective security – as either too broad or too military-focused to offer an appropriate degree of purchase over the range and complexity of emerging security issues. His preferred nomenclature – cooperative security – was defined as:

a broad approach to security which is multidimensional in scope and gradualist in temperament; emphasises reassurance rather than deterrence; is inclusive rather than exclusive; is not restrictive in membership; favours multilateralism over bilateralism; does not privilege military solutions over non-military ones; assumes that states are the principal actors in the security system, but accepts that non-state actors have an important role to play; does not require the creation of formal security institutions, but does not reject them either; and which, above all, stresses the value of creating "habits of dialogue" on a multilateral basis. For the present purposes, the immediate utility of "cooperative security" is that it does encompass, in a single, reasonably precise phrase, the whole range of possible responses to security problems through which the international community is now struggling to find its way.[4]

Naturally enough, although the "cooperative security" approach was offered as a global remedy for the problems of international security, it was one that also favoured the role of middle powers such as Australia and Canada. According to Evans, middle powers would play a crucial role within a cooperative security system through specific functions such as the development of legal regimes or providing a mediatory role in international disputes. The Cambodian peace plan orchestrated by Australia was cited as an example of the potential peace-building and peace-making activities of middle power leadership.[5]

For Canada, collective security principles have been central to its security posture over a long period.[6] Canadians emphasize that they have participated in every United Nations (UN) peace-keeping mission since 1945, as evidence of their unequivocal support for collective security approaches to international peace and security.[7] In turn, peace-keeping has provided Canada with both a clear strategic purpose and an important element of self-identification as an active, tolerant, middle power seeking negotiation rather than confrontation in international politics. These aspects of the collective security approach have been strongly supported by the Canadian people, which, in turn, has reinforced the government's peace-keeping resolve.

Despite the caution evident in more recent statements from Ottawa over Canada's commitment to participating in future conflict prevention operations in the wake of mission failures in Somalia and the former Yugoslavia, peace-keeping remains a central determinant in the organization of Canadian defence forces. But, like Evans, the current Canadian foreign minister, Lloyd Axworthy, has sought to reconstruct collective security principles for the post–Cold War environment. In a series of recent speeches and articles, Axworthy has focused Canada's collective security goals on the shift from peace-keeping to "peacebuilding" – a term that refers to preventive measures such as institution building as part of a development assistance package.[8] In what can be seen as an extension of Evans' earlier conceptual work on cooperative security, Canadian officials have taken the idea a step further – arguing that there is a link between peace-building and the humanitarian aspects of human security.

The promotion of human security in societies in conflict … poses special and complex challenges. In its focus on the political and socio-economic context of internal conflict (rather than the military aspects more typical of classic peace-keeping), peacebuilding seeks to address these challenges by working to strengthen the capacity of society to manage conflict without violence.[9]

Australian and Canadian security thinking has evolved steadily over the past decade: moving from comprehensive to cooperative security and now towards human security approaches. This has been the logical outcome of a process in which some leading middle powers have attempted to reposition themselves and their security doctrines to meet the expanding security agenda of the post–Cold War period. In short, Australia and Canada have been at the forefront of international debates concerning the range of non-traditional security approaches and have led the way on incorporating human security issues into mainstream security dialogues.

Middle power diplomacy

The second major theme in Australian and Canadian foreign policy over the past decade has been the reconstruction of "middle power" identities in international politics. To be sure, notions of "middle powers" and "middle power diplomacy" have never been far from the analysis of Australian and Canadian foreign policy. Both countries were instrumental in early efforts in the mid-1940s to raise the profile of the "middle power" category in the UN system. At the San Francisco Conference on International Organization in 1945, Canada and Australia adopted the "middle power" label as a means of distinguishing themselves from the "Big Three" (the United States, the United Kingdom, and the Soviet Union) on one side and the ubiquitous rank of smaller powers on the other. As a result, the persistent claims to middle power status by both Australia and Canada led to increasing academic attention and the establishment of middle power diplomacy as a sense of core national identity in foreign policy.[10]

Whereas Australia has traditionally viewed middle power status in terms of regional leadership, Canada favoured differentiation of international responsibilities on the basis of functionalism.[11] In Canada's view, political representation should take into account the nature of the problem being confronted and the capacity of individual states to contribute to a resolution. In this way, Canada fully expected that it would play a more significant role in the postwar order through the provision of technical and expert advice on the major questions of international peace and security.

On the basis of these criteria, Australia and Canada began directing their attention towards the application of middle power diplomacy in their own spheres of interest. Australia, under Dr. H. V. Evatt as minister for external affairs, pursued its own brand of assertive leadership through the establishment of regional institutions such as the South Pacific Commission in 1947. For Canada, the "golden years" of middle power diplomacy under Lester B. Pearson (1947–1957) were concerned mainly with playing a pivotal role between the US and European allies in the negotiations towards the Atlantic alliance. However, the brief spotlight afforded to middle powers after San Francisco was soon overshadowed by the descent into Cold War divisions between rival East and West blocs. As the Cold War progressed, the rigidity of the bipolar confrontation lessened the diplomatic room to manoeuvre for middle powers. As a result, middle power diplomacy and its academic analysis remained peripheral to the central dilemmas of superpower politics.

Following the end of the Cold War however, the middle power concept has gained a renewed currency. During the late 1980s and early 1990s as the Cold War structures began to dismantle, Australia, in particular, set about crafting a reinvigorated position on the international stage as an activist "middle power." Through a series of high-profile initiatives ranging from the protection of the Antarctic environment through to disarmament, Australia's middle power credentials gained widespread support and recognition. Moreover, the application of middle power diplomacy (i.e. coalition-building with "like-minded" countries) became a key definitional feature of both Australian and Canadian statecraft.

As a result, this heightened middle power activity began to draw increasing attention from scholars of international relations. In particular, two publications have helped to define and conceptualize the nature of contemporary middle power behaviour. Andrew Cooper, Richard Higgott and Kim Nossal's *Relocating Middle Powers* (1993) and a more recent edited volume by Cooper, *Niche Diplomacy* (1997), place the middle power concept at the centre of their analysis of Australian and Canadian foreign policy.[12] Although these authors acknowledge some of the obvious differences in approaches to particular foreign policy issues, the underlying theme of this work is the remarkable similarity of diplomatic styles and approaches among these second-tier states. As it was reconstituted in the 1990s, middle power theory emphasizes the non-structural forms of leadership based on creative and intelligent diplomacy. According to this view, the three main elements of middle power statecraft are internationalist, activist, and entrepreneurial.

Internationalist

Traditionally, middle powers have acted as key supporters of international society. One of the enduring aspects of middle power behaviour in the post–Cold War period has been their reliance on, and support for, multilateral processes. As a form of diplomatic activity however, middle power multilateralism has taken on a distinct character: the construction of "like-minded" coalitions. According to Evans and Grant, "middle powers are not powerful enough in most circumstances to impose their will, but they may be persuasive enough to have like-minded others see their point of view, and to act accordingly."[13] Middle powers are said to play a number of roles in the development of issue-based coalitions: as catalyst, facilitator, or moderator.[14] Moreover, the composition of coalitions may vary according to issues and objectives. It may be a broad-based grouping, encompassing the superpowers as well as smaller states in a defined geographic area (such as the Asia-Pacific Economic Cooperation forum), or a more narrowly focused consortium dealing with specific concerns (such as the Australia Group, which deals with chemical and biological weapons). The focus on issue-based coalitions in the definition of middle powers builds on the associated concept of "niche diplomacy": the view that middle powers will direct their attention towards issues when they can demonstrate a high degree of resources and qualifications.[15]

Activist

A second dimension of middle power diplomacy is the distinction between active and latent diplomatic capabilities. In part, middle powers are identified by their position across the spectrum of diplomatic activity from accommodative or reactionary policies at the one end to combative or heroic initiatives at the other.[16] Although a number of states in the international system would claim membership of this assertive middle power category – particularly some of the newly industrializing countries in East Asia – the contemporary definition of middle powers privileges those states that have the diplomatic resources to pursue initiatives at the global level. Such initiatives can take the form of brokering solutions to international crises, creating institutions to advance niche issues, or providing technical, expert advice in the context of a multilateral negotiation. In this way, being a middle power is as much about the utilization of existing resources in creative and intelligent ways as it is about having the requisite "clout" to do so.

It would be misleading to suggest, however, that only middle powers are capable of initiating creative policy options at the international level. What distinguishes middle powers from smaller states is their ability to highlight policy agendas and bring them to the attention of the international community as a whole. Alternatively, middle power initiatives may be seen as having greater credibility than the policies of larger states because they are unlikely to be the sole beneficiaries of any negotiated outcome.[17]

Entrepreneurial

Above all, the essential quality of contemporary middle power diplomacy is the exercise of entrepreneurial leadership. Cooper, Higgott, and Nossal and the analysis of Evans and Grant have both suggested that, with the decline of hegemonic leadership in the international system following the end of the Cold War, the middle power label has become associated most closely with non-structural forms of political leadership.[18] It is what the Canadian foreign minister, Lloyd Axworthy, has described as "soft power."[19] Much of the applied theory on middle power leadership has been drawn from the earlier work of Oran Young.[20] Young was concerned with how non-structural forms of leadership were used in the creation and maintenance of international regimes. In addition to the traditional form of structural or hegemonic leadership, Young suggested that there were at least two additional categories – entrepreneurial and intellectual leadership – at play in international negotiations. According to him, an entrepreneurial leader "relies on negotiating skill to frame issues in ways that foster integrative bargaining and to put together deals that would otherwise elude participants."[21] In contrast, the intellectual leader "produces intellectual capital or generative systems of thought that shape the perspectives of those who participate in institutional bargaining."[22]

In what can be seen as a direct application of Young's leadership categories to Australia's middle power diplomacy, Evans and Grant have argued that:

[T]here has to be in most cases a degree of intellectual imagination and creativity applied to the issue – an ability to see a way through impasses and to lead, if not by the force of authority, then at least by the force of ideas.... [W]hat middle powers may lack in economic, political or military clout, they can often make up with quick and thoughtful diplomatic footwork.[23]

The preceding discussion has traced how two conceptual patterns in Australian and Canadian diplomacy have evolved over the past decade. In both cases, the broadening of the security agenda and the revival of the middle power concept have followed the development of some new language and intellectual trends in the literature on international relations. But the promotion of these concepts has also been driven by the changed circumstances of international politics; or what John Gerard Ruggie has termed "hegemonic defection."[24] In particular, two important aspects of the leadership question are worth noting here.

First, the prior hegemonic position of the United States was predicated around notions of power based on military/security capabilities. The common assumption of the emerging international order is that the nature of power and security has changed and that a diplomatic capacity to deal with the new multipolar system rests as much on qualitative attributes as it does on quantitative capabilities. Secondly, the issue of what now constitutes leadership in the international system must take into account the changes to the policy agenda of international relations. Increasingly, as writers on human security have shown, states are counting social and economic issues (in addition to traditional military concerns) among the primary threats to national sovereignty. In the diplomatic space created by this diffusion of interests and capabilities in the international system, middle powers are much better placed to prompt creative policy responses. In this context, the work by Cooper, Higgott, and Nossal usefully moves the debate on middle power behaviour beyond a preoccupation with material capabilities – whether it be size, level of GDP, or geography – towards an appreciation of how middle powers are able to influence international political relations through a different style of leadership.

Human security and the new disarmament agenda

So far, this chapter has explored two dominant themes in Australian and Canadian diplomacy over the past decade: cooperative security and middle power diplomacy. But the practical application of cooperative middle power security diplomacy has been more difficult for both Australia or Canada than policy-makers in those two states might first have expected. The need, as always, to blend principle with pragmatism in the conduct of official relations has tainted the application of initiatives across the expanded "human security" agenda, or what Evans had lumped together under the rubric of "good international citizenship" issues.[25] The mere fact that Evans had elevated "good international citizenship" issues (i.e. development cooperation, human rights, and the environment) to the forefront of Australia's core national interests was not sufficient to allay predictable criticisms that realism and idealism do not make perfect partners in the harsh world of international politics.[26]

As Australia discovered in the first half of the 1990s, and Canada realized in the second half, the most convenient point at which the twin goals of cooperative security and middle power diplomacy converge with the expanded "human security" agenda has been in the debates over arms control and disarmament. There were several reasons for this. First, disarmament issues conformed to the regime-building aspects of cooperative, peace-building diplomacy. They related to the construction and maintenance of international legal norms to deal with one of the primary legacies of the Cold War – namely, the proliferation of weapons of mass destruction. Moreover, structural changes brought about by the end of the Cold War led to heightened expectations for multilateral security agreements on disarmament. In this context, the United Nations' main disarmament forum – the Geneva-based Conference on Disarmament (CD) – assumed a much greater importance. Arguably, no two states were more aware of this trend and its potential opportunities than Australia and Canada. Both had invested considerable political capital in the CD and in multilateralism more generally for a number of decades.

Secondly, disarmament was the one area where middle powers felt they could provide a degree of political leadership in negotiations. Australia and Canada had been schooled in the history of nuclear deterrence and carried with them years of expert technical knowledge on arms control matters. This, combined with what Evans and Grant called "quick and thoughtful diplomatic footwork," was the perfect ingredient for progressing the disarmament agenda once the bipolar system had broken down. The absence of structural leadership was an additional reason for middle powers wanting to advance initiatives. Nowhere had the limited nature of US leadership been found more wanting, for example, than in the nuclear non-proliferation debates of the previous few years. The non-aligned movement (with India among the most vocal) had consistently argued that further horizontal proliferation of nuclear weapons was inevitable while the nuclear weapons states remained unprepared to uphold their side of the disarmament bargain under the 1968 Nuclear Non-proliferation Treaty (NPT). The explicit declaration of nuclear arms proliferation in South Asia in May 1998 was perhaps the clearest evidence yet of what Hedley Bull warned during the Cold War years would be the "revolt against the West" if the great powers ignored their global responsibilities.[27]

Finally, and perhaps most importantly, the disarmament agenda became the easiest and most palatable avenue to pursue cooperative, middle power objectives. As the focus on the other main elements of the human security agenda (human rights, the environment, and development assistance) became increasingly bogged down in criticisms over economic opportunism and political interference, disarmament was the one area of the new internationalist agenda that permitted middle powers such as Australia and Canada to play an assertive leadership role without being challenged by domestic and international audiences at every turn. In fact, active and constructive internationalism on disarmament issues became a direct source of political legitimacy for Australia and Canada in relation to important aspects of civil society – both at home and abroad. Although not the source of any particular electoral goldmine domestically, there were sufficient political incentives for both states to advance their disarmament credentials outside either moral imperatives or national interest calculations. Both Australia and Canada found that, unlike human rights, the environment and development assistance, disarmament diplomacy was regarded by a wide cross-section of community groups as a valuable application of foreign policy resources.

The convergence of cooperative middle power diplomacy and human security issues is evident in a range of disarmament initiatives undertaken by Australia and Canada over the past decade. The following section looks at two specific examples. The first was Australia's efforts to conclude a Chemical Weapons Convention (CWC) in the early 1990s, and the second was the Canadian government's more recent sponsorship of a treaty to ban anti-personnel landmines.

Australia and the Chemical Weapons Convention

One of the first targets of Australia's reinvented middle power diplomacy after the Cold War was the negotiations towards a ban on chemical weapons. The international community had long recognized the abhorrent qualities of chemical weapons. From the widespread use of mustard gas in World War I through to the more recent chemical attacks on Kurdish separatists in Iraq, governments and their citizens were well aware of the horrific and debilitating nature of these weapons. Despite nearly 20 years of negotiations in the Conference on Disarmament, however, the bipolar security structures of the Cold War had limited any real progress towards a comprehensive ban on chemical weapons.

By 1991, the principal stumbling block to finalizing a chemical weapons ban was the lack of an agreement on key aspects of the draft convention, which had left 20 per cent of the final document in "square brackets" (i.e. disputed or alternative language). The Australian government nevertheless sought to capitalize on the improved climate in international arms control negotiations by submitting a compromise draft treaty to the CD in March 1992.[28] Australia's "Model CWC" was the first attempt by any state to present a treaty text free from alternative language and footnotes. The initiative proved decisive. Less than 12 months after the presentation of the Australian text, the Chemical Weapons Convention was signed by 129 states in Paris. It was an obvious example of how creative and intelligent middle power diplomacy could be used to secure international security objectives.

Aside from the welcome diplomatic kudos, Australia's reasons for pursuing the CWC had much to do with human security principles. The use of chemical weapons throughout the Cold War was invariably directed against civilian populations. The Stockholm International Peace

Research Institute had recorded numerous allegations of chemical weapons attacks throughout the 1980s, including the following countries or groups: South Africa in Angola 1982 and 1988; the CIA in Cuba 1978–1982; and the Soviet Union against the mujahedin.[29] However, the most blatant and persistent use of chemical weapons against civilians was the Iraqi attacks against Kurds during the years 1984–1988. More recently, a 1995 sarin gas attack in a Tokyo subway by members of the "Supreme Truth" religious sect highlighted the continuing dangers of chemical weapons to the security and well-being of individuals in society. As the actions of the Japanese sect revealed, chemical weapons remain relatively easy to make and use by terrorist groups – particularly in small doses intended for civilian populations.

There were additional reasons for Australia's chemical weapons initiative. The building of an effective international legal regime against the production and use of chemical weapons meant that Australian defence forces would no longer have to prepare for a chemical attack. Moreover, a strong chemical weapons regime supported and overlapped with other key aspects of the new internationalist agenda. In particular, Australia had expressed concerns over the environmental and human rights aspects of chemical weapons use – making representations to Iraq following the attacks against the Kurds and other representations to the United States over the potential environmental damage caused by the destruction of chemical weapons at Johnston Atoll in the South Pacific.[30] Taken together, these aspects of Australia's chemical weapons initiative demonstrated the application of a broader notion of security and a clear demonstration of "good international citizenship" or human security goals.

The Ottawa Process: The Canadian Landmines Treaty

The most visible blend of middle power advocacy on disarmament issues and human security principles has been the recent Canadian efforts to construct an international treaty on anti-personnel landmines. The "Ottawa Process" derived its name from the series of diplomatic conferences organized by the Canadian government during 1996 and 1997. These sought to "fast-track" an international agreement banning landmines from the inventory of the world's military arsenals. The end product of these deliberations was the signing of a Convention on the Prohibition of the Use, Stockpiling, Production and Transfer of Anti-personnel Mines and Their Destruction in Ottawa by 122 states in early December 1997.

Three important aspects of the Ottawa Process are worth noting in terms of the link between middle powers and human security. First, the Canadian government overtly represented the Ottawa Process as a central plank in its efforts to promote human security issues as part of a broader foreign policy agenda. In a paper written shortly before the Convention was signed, Canadian Foreign Minister Lloyd Axworthy argued that Canada had a leading role to play in support of human security issues in the developing world. In addition to Canada's contribution to peace-building, humanitarian assistance, and economic development, Axworthy nominated the Ottawa Process as an example of what a middle power could do to influence international peace and stability after the Cold War. In his paper, Axworthy made a clear distinction between traditional arms control measures (such as the NPT and the Comprehensive Test Ban Treaty) and the more people-centred approach of the landmines treaty.[31]

Secondly, the rationale behind Canada's landmines initiative was based on two key arguments: (1) that landmines were an indiscriminate killer of civilians (particularly women and children); and (2) that they were an invisible barrier to economic development. In this way, the Canadians shifted the disarmament debates from a general argument about the building of international peace and security to the specific social and economic concerns of human security. The arguments put forward by Canada as to why a treaty banning landmines was necessary related directly to the humanitarian values of human security: the disruption of food supplies; the contamination of soil and water; and the economic loss of productive workers.[32]

The third important link between the landmines treaty and human security was the style of diplomacy adopted by Canada. The Ottawa Process was different from previous disarmament initiatives in that the Canadian government took its lead from a community of non-governmental organizations (NGOs). For several years after the signing of the 1980 UN Convention of Certain Conventional Weapons (CCW), the International Committee of the Red Cross and other NGO groups working in countries such as Angola and Cambodia began a global campaign to ban landmines. The regulatory provisions under Protocol II of the CCW (which deals with mines) were considered ineffective and insufficient to bring about a complete elimination of landmines. These concerns were put to Canada and a small group of other countries during the 1996 session of the CD by a group calling itself the International Campaign to Ban Landmines – a coalition of over 350 NGOs. Canada decided at that meeting to remove the landmines issue from the bureaucratic and sometimes cumbersome committee system of the CD and to run a parallel treaty-making process using its own resources. Reflecting the disillusionment with traditional multilateralism, the main slogans associated with the landmines campaign were "no exemptions, no exceptions" and "an agreement open to all but hostage to none."

Beneath the jingoism lay a deeper shift in the patterns of Canada's middle power diplomacy. For the first time, international civil society norms were incorporated directly into the foreign policy programme of an industrialized Western state. Moreover, the Canadian government explicitly sought to construct a response to the landmines issue that gave primacy and legitimacy to non-state actors in the diplomatic negotiations. This was a far cry from the status of NGO groups only a few year earlier at the 1995 NPT Review and Extension conference at which one diplomat commented that NGOs had been "banished to the rafters" of the General Assembly hall in New York. In short, the Ottawa Process revealed some of the changing patterns and linkages of international politics between individuals and global security issues acknowledged by the recent academic work on human security.

The Asian dimension

How then does Australian and Canadian middle power diplomacy relate to the problem of human security as it is manifested in Asia's emerging security order? It is evident that, at least in the area of disarmament, the policies and initiatives of Australia and Canada have met the criteria for effective middle power leadership. In both cases assessed here, they overcame initial regional scepticism and reached closure on their stipulated policy objectives, with the majority of regional states fully supporting their campaigns.

In the case of the CWC, China initially entertained serious reservations over what it viewed as excessively intrusive verification procedures. But Australia took care to consult with Chinese representatives at every stage of the negotiation process to ensure a successful outcome. Australia had organized a number of conferences and seminars for East Asian and South Pacific countries to explain the relevance of the treaty to those that may not initially have felt chemical weapons were a direct security concern to themselves. At the end of the process, most countries in the region were committed to early signature and ratification of the CWC and, as one American official highly familiar to the process observed, "the Australian Government deserves much of the credit for this."[33]

Engaging Asian states in the Ottawa Process was managed by Canada along similar lines. Various Asia-Pacific countries participated in the preliminary conferences organized after the UN Conference on Disarmament failed to agree to an anti-personnel landmine treaty in April–May 1996. This was the case notwithstanding the fact that many Asia-Pacific countries – including Australia, China, India, Indonesia, Pakistan, and Russia – remained convinced that the CD was the most appropriate venue for negotiating a landmines treaty. Some Asian states, such as

China, Singapore, and South Korea, had become substantial producers and distributors of landmines. Still others had mined areas of limited military significance in order to harass or control elements of their own populations.[34]

Despite these barriers, the Canadians were determined to sustain the momentum of the Ottawa Process as a means of bypassing the increasingly cumbersome negotiating environment of the CD. The process also served as an example to other Asia-Pacific powers of how to advance one's diplomatic agenda beyond normal multilateral channels if the objective is so compelling as to warrant it. The Foreign Affairs and International Trade Department, for example, focused strongly upon various inter-Asian dialogues concerning landmines as contributions to its own cause. These included a July 1997 report prepared by a Regional Seminar for Asian Military and Strategic Studies Experts convened in Manila and sponsored by the International Committee of the Red Cross, which argued that landmines are seldom used in accordance with traditional military purposes and that the "appalling humanitarian consequences in the end of anti-personnel mines have far outweighed their military utility."[35] Recommendations of a special ASEAN Regional Forum (ARF) demining seminar held in Australia the following month were also incorporated by the Canadians into their own "fast-track" landmines agenda.[36] As the above episodes demonstrate, most Asia-Pacific states accepted the arguments put forward by Australia and Canada that chemical weapons and landmines were a direct threat to the security of individuals, thus reinforcing the link between effective middle power diplomacy and the pursuit of human security objectives in the region.

Conclusion

Contemporary middle power behaviour offers a potentially useful entry point into the practical study of human security issues. Arguably, no states have been more receptive to, or accommodative of, human security principles than Australia and Canada. In fact, these two leading middle powers have been at the forefront of international debates that recognize the changing nature of security and the means by which to provide a more secure environment for individual citizens, both at home and abroad.

Rather than attempting to address separately each of the environmental, humanitarian, and social issues related to the concept of human security, however, it has become convenient for middle powers to frame their response to particular disarmament issues in terms of a broader definition of security. Disarmament initiatives such as the treaties on chemical weapons and landmines became highly appropriate vehicles through which Australia and Canada could progress the combined aspects of human security and, in Australia's case, promote its credentials as a "good international citizen." Moreover, the disarmament agenda has allowed middle powers to avoid much of the inevitable criticism directed toward isolated initiatives related to the new internationalist agenda such as human rights or the environment.

This chapter began by examining Australian and Canadian discourses on security, their respective practice of middle power diplomacy, and the recent convergence of those first two patterns around human security issues. It was argued that, in the area of disarmament in particular, Australian and Canadian diplomacy has blended the cooperative, peace-building focus of contemporary middle power statecraft with the combined humanitarian, environmental, and social concerns of human security. This is not to suggest that all such Australian and Canadian disarmament initiatives have followed this path or, indeed, that there have not been significant differences in the approaches of each country to the specific examples raised. What is significant is that, through their respective promotion of middle power security diplomacy, Australia and Canada have been actively engaged in a process whereby the traditional dividing lines between national security and human security have been increasingly blurred.

Notes

1. The concept of "human security" is an attempt to broaden the definition of security and security studies away from a narrow focus on military capabilities and the use of force by states. According to Ramesh Thakur, "human security refers to the quality of life of the people of a society or polity. Anything which degrades their quality of life – demographic pressures, diminished access to or stock of resources, and so on – is a security threat." As such, the concept encompasses a broad range of concerns including human rights, the environment, and social issues. See Ramesh Thakur, "From National Security to Human Security," in Stuart Harris and Andrew Mack, eds., *Asia-Pacific Security: The Economics-Politics Nexus* (Sydney: Allen & Unwin for the Australian National University, 1997), pp. 52–80. Evans' approach to "cooperative security" is outlined in Gareth Evans, *Cooperating for Peace: The Global Agenda for the 1990s and Beyond* (Sydney: Allen & Unwin, 1993) and Gareth Evans and Bruce Grant, *Australia's Foreign Relations in the World of the 1990s*, 2nd edn (Melbourne: University of Melbourne Press, 1995), p. 102.
2. *Australia's Regional Security*, Ministerial Statement by Senator Gareth Evans, Minister for Foreign Affairs, 6 December 1989. For a rigorous analysis of Evans' policy approach, consult Greg Fry, ed., *Australia's Regional Security* (Sydney: Allen & Unwin, 1991).
3. Evans' work appears to have been influenced in particular by two important sources of academic writing on the changing nature of security: first, the series of publications from the Copenhagen School, including in particular the work of Barry Buzan; and, second,

the application of some of that earlier European literature to the Asia-Pacific context by academics at the Australian National University. Reflecting the first approach is Buzan's *People, States and Fear: The National Security Problem in International Relations* (London: Wheatsheaf Books, 1983). Illustrative of the second (Asia-Pacific) strand is Andrew Mack and Paul Keal, eds., *Security and Arms Control in the North Pacific* (Sydney: Allen & Unwin, 1988).

4. Evans, *Cooperating for Peace*, p. 16.

5. Ibid., pp. 25–97.

6. Background is provided by James G. Eayrs, *In Defence of Canada: Peacemaking and Deterrence* (Toronto: Toronto University Press, 1972), and by Geoffrey Hayes, "Canada as a Middle Power: The Case of Peacekeeping" in Andrew Cooper, ed., *Niche Diplomacy: Middle Powers after the Cold War* (New York: St Martin's Press, 1997), pp. 73–89.

7. See the current Canadian foreign minister's recent assertions to this end in Lloyd Axworthy, "Canada and Human Security: The Need for Leadership," *International Journal* 52, no. 2 (Spring 1997), pp. 183–196.

8. These views are consolidated in ibid.

9. Department of Foreign Affairs and International Trade (DFAIT), Canada, "Peacebuilding and International Security" at http://www.dfait_maeci.gc.ca/ONU2000UN/fa-07txt-g.html, 1998.

10. Kim Nossal, *The Politics of Canadian Foreign Policy* (Scarborough, Ontario: Prentice Hall, 1997), pp. 53–60.

11. Michael Tucker, *Canadian Foreign Policy: Contemporary Issues and Themes* (Toronto: McGraw-Hill Ryerson, 1980), pp. 6–7.

12. Andrew Cooper, Richard Higgott, and Kim Nossal, *Relocating Middle Powers: Australia and Canada in a Changing World Order* (Vancouver: University of British Columbia Press, 1993), and Cooper, *Niche Diplomacy*.

13. Evans and Grant, *Australia's Foreign Relations*, p. 345.

14. Cooper, Higgott, and Nossal, *Relocating Middle Powers*, pp. 24–25.

15. Cooper, *Niche Diplomacy*, pp. 1–24.

16. Ibid.

17. See John Ravenhill, "Cycles of Middle Power Activism: Constraint and Choice in Australian and Canadian Foreign Policies," *Australian Journal of International Affairs* 52, no. 3 (November 1998), pp. 309–327.

18. Cooper, Higgott, and Nossal, *Relocating Middle Powers*, p. 12, and Evans and Grant, *Australia's Foreign Relations*, p. 348.

19. Axworthy, "Canada and Human Security."

20. Oran Young, "Political Leadership and Regime Formation: On the Development of Institutions in International Society," *International Organization* 45, no. 3 (Summer 1991), pp. 281–308.

21. Ibid., p. 293.

22. Ibid., p. 298.

23. Evans and Grant, *Australia's Foreign Relations*, p. 374.

24. John Gerard Ruggie, "Multilateralism: The Anatomy of an Institution", *International Organization* 46, no. 3 (Summer 1992), p. 593.

25. The notion of "good international citizenship" is embodied as a core theme in many of the essays found in Stephanie Lawson, ed., *The New Agenda for Global Security: Cooperating for Peace and Beyond* (Sydney: Allen & Unwin for the Australian National University, 1995). Also see Evans and Grant, *Australia's Foreign Policy*, pp. 300–341.

26. See Richard Leaver and Dave Cox, eds., *Middling, Meddling, Muddling: Issues in Australian Foreign Policy* (Sydney: Allen & Unwin, 1997).

27. Hedley Bull, "The Revolt against the West," in Hedley Bull and Adam Watson, eds., *The Expansion of International Society* (Oxford: Clarendon Press, 1984), pp. 217–228.
28. Martine Letts, Robert Mathews, Tim McCormack, and Chris Moraitis, "The Conclusion of the Chemical Weapons Convention: An Australian Perspective," *Arms Control* 14, no. 3 (December 1993), pp. 311–332.
29. See the 1984–1990 editions of the Stockholm International Peace Research Institute, *World Armaments and Disarmament* (Oxford: Oxford University Press).
30. Evans and Grant, *Australia's Foreign Relations*, pp. 159, 166.
31. Axworthy, "Canada and Human Security", pp. 183–184.
32. John English, "The Ottawa Process. Paths Followed, Paths Abroad," *Australian Journal of International Affairs* 52, no. 22 (July 1998), pp. 121–132.
33. James F. Leonard, "Rolling Back Chemical Proliferation," *Arms Control Today* 22, no. 8 (October 1992), p. 15.
34. See Kevin P. Clements, "Limiting the Production and Spread of Landmines," *Pacific Research* 7, no. 1 (February 1994), pp. 3–4.
35. "Anti-Personnel Mines: What Future for Asia?" Press Release, Canadian Department of Foreign Affairs and International Trade, 24 July 1997, at http://www.mines.gc.ca/english/documents/declaration.html.
36. "Summary Report of the ARF Demining Seminar," at http://www.aseansec.org/politics/arf4xg.html.

Part 3

Applying human security to key issue areas

6

Asian values and human security cooperation in Asia

Hyun-Seok Yu

Throughout the 1980s, Western scholars tried to explain the somewhat puzzling but nonetheless remarkable economic success occurring in East Asia. Many scholars concluded that, among other factors, Asia's intellectual and social tradition – what we now call "Asian values" – was the hidden ingredient explaining Asian economic success. Asian values include attachment to the family as an institution, deference to societal interest, thrift, respect for authority, valuing consensus over confrontation, and emphasizing the importance of education. Collectively these had laid the foundation for many Asian states achieving rapid material progress by enabling social stability, unity, and economic efficiency. Because the "Asian economic miracle" was mainly led by the four so-called "dragons" (South Korea, Taiwan, Hong Kong, and Singapore), Asian values generally referred to Confucian ideas, and the main focus of debate was on the relationship between these values and the rapid economic growth being realized in the region.

As several of these countries (including South Korea and Taiwan) have also moved toward political liberalization, the Asian values issue has gradually shifted toward examining several political dimensions. The leaders of some Asian states, along with various scholars in the region, overtly proud of their remarkable economic performance and impressive record of political developments, began to argue that an Asian model based on Asian values could be an alternative to capitalism and liberal democracy as applied in other regions. Some even went so far as to assert that the Asian model is superior to liberal democracy. They argued, first, that the West's headlong pursuit of individualism has brought about the breakdown of the family, intensified drug problems, and increased violence and social decay. Secondly, individual freedom and liberal democracy are not necessarily "universal" values and, in many cases, they would not be suitable for Asia. Therefore, expecting Asia to accept the extra-regional conceptions of democracy and human rights at face value is unreasonable.

Currently, the debate over Asian values is moving into a third stage, as most Asian countries are facing severe economic difficulties. Now some scholars are taking the offensive, arguing that previously lauded Asian social and cultural mores have also caused the economic crash in Asia. The gloomy economic realities of Asia are now being interpreted as evidence of Asian values gone wrong. The attachment to family has suddenly become "nepotism." The importance of personal relationships rather than formal legality becomes cronyism. Consensus has become "wheel-greasing" and corrupt politics. Conservatism and respect for authority have become "rigidity" and an inability to innovate. Whether it is about democracy, human rights, or economic growth, the controversy surrounding Asian values remains unresolved and it continues to act as a source of tension, not only between Asia and the West, but also within Asia.

This chapter deals with the issue of Asian values in the context of Asia's potential for human security cooperation. As noted in both chapters 1 and 2, human security emphasizes the welfare of individuals and the quality of life of the people of a society or polity. It also refers to freedom from hunger, attack, torture, and imprisonment without a free and fair trial, and to guarantees against discrimination on spurious grounds. In a positive sense, human security means the freedom to exercise the capacity and opportunity that allow each human being to enjoy life to the fullest without imposing constraints upon others engaged in the same pursuit. Human rights violations therefore threaten human security. Ramesh Thakur has observed that human security issues are closely connected to peace. He notes that the "democratic peace thesis" suggests that democracies rarely go to war against one another and that democracies also promote human rights better than alternative regimes. Consequently, increasing democratization will lead simultaneously to an enhancement of human rights and a more peaceful world.[1]

For the sake of regional stability, there are two major tasks. The first is that there should be an effective measure to control human rights violations both domestically and internationally. This is because the abuse and violation of human rights can lead to violent conflicts spreading across borders: the group whose rights are being abused can resort to arms in retaliation; the conflict can entangle neighbouring countries; the scale of the human rights abuses can lead to international involvement and intervention. The important point here is that human rights issues are no longer domestic matters but are now a matter of legitimate international concern. Secondly (and this is related to the first point), in order to have international institutions that promote cooperation in elevating human rights (and therefore enhance human security), there needs to be a shared understanding of just what "human rights" are. In this sense, it is very important to formulate a concept of democracy and human rights that can be universally accepted by the countries in the region.

It is argued here that the current "Asian values" debate is misplaced; it is going in the wrong direction and will have only a negative impact on building up a commonly shared conception of human rights in the Asian region. For this reason we need initially to go beyond the current discussion of "Asian values," which is based on a false dichotomy between East and West. More attention must be directed toward the immediate task of formulating a universally acceptable concept of human rights. A proper vision of human rights should incorporate traditional cultures such as Confucianism and this attempt should not be viewed as the rejection of prevalent human rights thinking; instead, it should be perceived as an effort to improve it.

The Asian values debate: Development and limitations

The so-called "Asian values debate" intensified with the signing of the Bangkok Declaration on Human Rights in April 1993 by 40 East and South-East Asian states, including China, Malaysia, Indonesia, Singapore, and Korea.[2] In the words of a government spokesman for Singapore (whose leaders have been particularly outspoken participants in the debate), the Declaration "stakes out a distinctive Asian point of view" on human rights.[3] The governments of countries that signed the Declaration argue that Asian states, because of their "unique" values and special historical circumstances, are justified in adopting an understanding of human rights and democracy that is fundamentally different from that prevailing in the West. According to these states, Western diplomacy focusing on human rights is simply part of an effort to assert political and economic hegemony over Asia. The Bangkok Declaration, along with views presented during its signing, sparked a heated debate.

That debate raged not only between Asia and the West but also among Asians. It was fuelled even more by a now-famous interview given by Lee Kuan Yew, the former prime minister of Singapore and one of the most outspoken Asian leaders campaigning against Western hegemony. In his interview with *Foreign Affairs* (March/April 1994), he implied that Western-style democracy is not applicable to East Asia, asserting that, in the East, "the ruler or the government does not try to provide for a person what the family best provides." This self-reliant and family-oriented culture was identified as the primary reason for East Asia's economic success. In Lee's view, the moral breakdown of Western societies can be attributed to too much liberal democracy and too many individual rights. Consequently, the Western political system is not suited to family-oriented East Asia.[4]

I will argue that this embodiment of "Asian values" has several problems. First, as other commentators have already suggested, there is no such thing as "Asian values."[5] Asians, broadly defined, make up more than 60 per cent of the world's population and it is absurd to argue that there is one set of values that represents such a huge demographic composition. Even in East Asia, referring to a single set of values involves the forced blending of many of the world's intellectual traditions – Confucianism, Buddhism, and Islam, to name but three. The term "Asian values" in the current "Asian values debate" is often used to denote Confucian values.

The second major problem with the "Asian values debate" is that it has been fuelled and shaped by the opinion of prominent figures such as Lee Kuan Yew and Dr. Mahathir and then given further life by responses to those views from both the West and Asia. These selective views are wrongly referred to as being representative of definitive "Asian views." The fact is that, although these perspectives contain some interesting points and arguments, they do not represent the consensus of all Asian people. In other words, the term "Asian values" often misleads non-Asians. Asia's intellectuals and politicians have not even come close to unanimity about the notion of Asian values propagated by the concept's leading promoters.

In fact there has been much criticism toward "Asian values" inside Asia. Kim Dae Jung, the President of South Korea, argues that Lee Kuan Yew has projected misleading arguments in order to reject Western-style democracy and to provide an excuse for his total intolerance of dissent. Contrary to Lee's claim, Asia has democratic philosophies that are as profound as those to be found in the West. Kim mentions the ideas of Meng-tzu, a Chinese philosopher who preached that the people come first, the country comes second, and the king comes third. In addition, the ancient Chinese philosophy of *Minben Zhengchi*, or "people-based politics," teaches that "the will of people is the will of the heaven" and that one should "respect the people as heaven" itself.[6]

The most critical problem with the current "Asian values debate" is that it wrongly leads people to believe that Asians do not honour human rights or that various Asian philosophies such as Confucianism are totally incompatible with the Western conception of human rights. How such misunderstandings occur was well illustrated in a speech made by Zbigniew Brzezinski, the former National Security Advisor to President Jimmy Carter. He argued that the "Asian values" doctrine ("which rejects the notion of inalienable human rights") is one of the main challenges to democracy and human rights.[7] Wei Jingsheng, a well-known dissident expelled from China, and Nobel Peace Prize winner and East Timorese dissident Jose Ramos Horta both consequently criticized this type of "misconception" about "Asian values." They asserted there is nothing intrinsically anti-democratic about genuine Asian philosophies and that such Western constructs as those postulated by Brzezinski were intellectually contemptuous of all Asians. Their criticism implies that in the "Asian values debate" Westerners have got the wrong idea about "Asian values" and that this is because some authoritarian leaders in Asia have used the concept as a justification for their non-democratic rule.[8] In fact, Brzezinski was correct in his assertion about the Asian values *doctrine* (which has a clearly ideological dimension). But this is not the same thing as saying that "genuine Asian philosophies" are anti-democratic.

It is contended here that the Asian values debate should not be about whether or not Asian values can be presented as an alternative to Western democratization. As Joseph Chan has proposed, "'Asian values' need not be understood as a set of values entirely distinct from and in opposition to Western values, but simply as those values that many people in Asia would endorse and that would guide them in their search for a political morality."[9] According to the Confucian tradition, the social distance between the state and the individual is much closer than that embraced by Western liberalism. Therefore, the core of the "Asian values debate" (especially pertaining to human rights) should be about the proper relationship between the state and individual in light of promoting human rights.

The human rights conception in Asia and the West

In order to promote human rights regionally there should be a commonly acceptable understanding of human rights by countries in the region. In other words, since Asia is the most diverse region in terms of culture, religion, ethnicity, and language, it is necessary to have a consensus on the norms and institutions of human rights among countries in the region. The tension between Asia and the West and even within Asia regarding human rights is the result of differing interpretations of that concept. In all candour, it is extremely difficult to present a set of views on human rights that would truly represent all of the Asian states. Each country has a different set of views on human rights. Some Asian countries accept the idea of universal human rights, while others stress the legitimacy of tolerating different understandings and human rights practices as a reflection of different historical traditions and cultural backgrounds. Secondly, Asian countries' views on human rights also vary according to the type and intensity of a given issue. Asian policy-makers, for example, might share an understanding of human rights with Western states as a matter of general principle but, when the implications of a specific position are weighed in depth, serious disagreements can arise over how critical human security considerations really are to the issue at hand.

Imposing trade sanctions as part of a "linkage policy" to compel different human rights behaviour has been a recurrent case-in-point over the past few years. Despite the inherent difficulty of identifying "Asian" human rights postures, it is correct to say that differences regarding human rights really have emerged between Asia and the West. The most striking difference is that Asian culture views individuals as an element of society and emphasizes their responsibilities and duties within it. Western liberal democracy is based on the concept of the individual, who has inborn and inalienable rights. A government that restricts any of these rights can be justified only on the basis of consent. On the other hand, human rights in the Asian (more correctly Confucian) tradition are understood as relating to other individuals' rights as well as to society as a whole. The anecdote that Lee Kuan Yew mentioned in his interview at least clarifies this aspect. In Singapore, any customs or police officer who sees someone behaving suspiciously can require that person to have a urine test. In America, it would be a violation of the suspected individual's rights, but in the view of many Asian states it would be acceptable for the sake of the welfare of that individual as well as of the society.

The "East–West difference" in approaching the problem of human rights does not necessarily mean that the two cultures' images are always incompatible. Much of the controversy arises over secondary principles of human rights. Joseph Chan argues that Asian states and the West do not differ in their positions on basic principles. What causes difficulties, he asserts, is what he terms "mid-level principles," which can help determine the scope and limits of rights and duties. Indeed, there is a possibility that Asia and the West could formulate a commonly acceptable conception of human rights. Chan suggests that "Asian political moralities would probably diverge significantly from the strand of liberalism, which is arguably a very influential vision of political morality in the United States. Most Asian political moralities would probably endorse the principles of perfectionism, moralism, and paternalism. While endorsing basic human rights, they would allow these midlevel principles to affect the scope of those rights."[10] He goes on to say: "What is involved in the development of human rights norms in Asia is Asians' search for a coherent political morality. This is an important task for each Asian society – a task that should not be understood in terms of a contest between Asians and Westerners."[11]

There is ample evidence that Asia has a rich tradition of democracy-oriented philosophies that accommodate the importance of human rights. As I noted above, Chinese philosopher Meng-tzu's dictum that people have the right to rise up and overthrow their government in the name of heaven shows the importance of human rights. A native philosopher of Korea, Tonghak, went even further, advocating that "man is heaven" and that one must serve people as one does heaven. South Korean President Kim Dae Jung claims on this basis that there are no ideas more fundamental to democracy than the teachings of Confucianism, Buddhism, and Tonghak.[12] Besides these human rights-oriented philosophies, there are many democratic traditions and institutions in Asia including freedom of speech and the board of censor system. Some might argue that these traditions and ideas are meaningless given the region's poor contemporary human rights record and the low level of political democratization of many Asian states. But Chan argues that the violations of human rights by Asian states should be separated from the values that Asians really cherish. His argument deserves attention because Western societies, despite their long tradition of democracy and concept of universal human rights, are guilty of many human rights violations of their own – including discrimination against minorities and dual standards on policies regarding human rights violations (e.g. Australia's Cold War policy toward East Timor, which leaned toward Indonesia).

It is true, however, that there has been no *universal* conception of human rights in Asia. Confucianism, as represented by the thought of Confucius and Meng-tzu, does not incorporate the idea of human rights. Rather, it puts great emphasis on duties arising from social roles in human relations; on the virtues of respect for the elderly and filial piety; and on mutual trust and care between family members.[13] In the sense that Confucian ideas tend to limit the role of rights in human relationships to a minimum fallback mechanism to protect the vulnerable party against exploitation and harm, they could be viewed as contradicting the Western conception of human rights. However, it is more accurate to view Confucian ideas of human rights as based on different ideas of how relationships should develop between individuals and between an individual and the community or the state. Confucian ideas on the relationship between the state and the individual and the Western conception of human rights could actually complement each other if duty and reward are viewed as common variables in both approaches.

Therefore, once Western states accept that there is room for improvement in their own conception of human rights (which means Westerners acknowledging that there are values other than Western liberalism that could enrich human rights conceptions), traditional cultures such as Confucianism have much to contribute to the modern discourse on human security and to the development of human rights norms. We often witness the rights of the socially vulnerable (the poor, the elderly, ethnic minorities, women, etc.) being violated, even in societies that have a long tradition of human rights protection. This tendency has intensified as the process of globalization has accelerated and the neoliberal ideology that champions market principles and non-interventionism gains worldwide acceptance.[14] In this situation, the role of the state in protecting the rights of the socially weak is important. Although it is the state that most frequently threatens human security (through war, repression, systemic discrimination, and so on), it is equally true that it is only the state that can protect the socially weak from the tyranny of the market and enhance human rights principles.

The important point here is that the norms and institutions of human rights and liberal democracy are not permanent visions but are continually evolving. Recently, many Westerners have felt that serious problems have arisen in their own countries as a result of an overemphasis on liberal values and individual rights. Bilahari Kausikan claims that the most trenchant criticisms of extreme individualism, of liberal democracy, and of key elements of Western-style systems have been voiced by Westerners themselves.[15] This realization once more underscores the possibility that the two sets of socio-cultural values (Asian and Western) could complement each other and contribute to developing a new conception of human security that can be shared by both Asia and the West. As the precondition for this, traditional cultures of Asia such as Confucianism must be transformed in light of the spirit of human rights. As Chan argues, vibrant and transformed Confucianism could supply rich ethical norms and virtues that would take their place alongside Western concepts of human rights to guide people's behaviour, effectively tempering an otherwise overly rigid rights-based culture often found in Western societies.[16]

Conclusion: Regional cooperation to elevate human rights

The best word to characterize the Asian region is "diversity." In addition to ethnic, religious, and cultural diversity, there are different views of the notion of human rights among countries in the region. In order to promote human security in Asia, a coordinated regional strategy for human rights is critical. As a precondition for this coordinated effort, there must be a shared regional view on what should constitute human rights.

The major difficulty in achieving this objective is cultural diversity among the countries in the region. Many Asia-Pacific countries – including Australia and New Zealand – are not comfortable with Dr. Mahathir's position or Lee Kuan Yew's stance within the "Asian values" debate. Moreover, the most fundamental policy of the Association of South East Asian Nations (ASEAN) since its foundation in 1967 has been "non-interference" in a country's affairs. Moreover, ASEAN's new recruits, e.g. Viet Nam and Myanmar, do not want intervention in their domestic matters by external forces.

How can we, in this situation, develop a concept of human rights that can be accepted by all countries of the region, and pursue joint measures to promote human security there? A good starting point would be to promote the collective realization among Asian peoples that the current "Asian values" debate is mainly shaped by controversy over the views of several outspoken Asian leaders. This controversy digresses from the real issue. Basically, the key question is not about which set of values is superior to others. The current "Asian values" debate is based on a false dichotomy between Asian and Western values concerning human rights, and has a negative impact on building up a commonly shared conception of human rights.

The real issue, then, is the social distance between the individual and the state. Some Asian states are still prone to exploit the closeness between the state and the individual in their culture, rationalizing it as a basis for maintaining their non-democratic rule. This trend should not be allowed to shape the core of the "Asian values" debate. In fact that kind of non-democratic system is not acceptable in the Confucian values system. A proper distance that guarantees individual human rights to the maximum extent must be cultivated in *all* Asia-Pacific societies at the dawn of a new century.

Notes

1. Ramesh Thakur, "From National to Human Security" in Stuart Harris and Andrew Mack, eds., *Asia-Pacific Security: The Economics–Politics Nexus* (Sydney: Allen & Unwin, 1997), pp. 72–73.
2. Within the East Asian region, Japan did not sign the Declaration under pressure from the United States.
3. "Asian Values Revisited," *The Economist* 368, no. 8078 (25 July 1998), p. 25.

4. Fareed Zakaria, "Culture Is Destiny: A Conversation with Lee Kuan Yew," *Foreign Affairs* 73, no. 2 (March/April 1994), pp. 109–126.
5. I am not persuaded by an attempt to explain social phenomena with cultural factors. This so-called "cultural approach" is able to present plausible explanations only of something that has already happened. In other words, when it comes to predictive power, the cultural approach is hardly impressive. I do not deny the importance of culture. But the concept of "Asian values," which first won wide acceptance in academia as a factor explaining the East Asian economic miracle, has proven, with hindsight, to be nothing more than an explanation scholars came up with to explain something they could not explain otherwise.
6. Kim Dae Jung, "Is Culture Destiny? The Myth of Asia's Anti-Democratic Values," *Foreign Affairs* 73, no. 6 (November/December 1994), pp. 189–194.
7. Zbigniew Brzezinski, "The New Challenges of Human Rights," *Journal of Democracy* 8, no. 2 (April 1997), p. 4.
8. Wei's views were offered at the Forum 2000 conference hosted by former Czech Republic president, Václav Havel, and recounted in *Inside China Today*, 23 June 1999. This source can be found on the Internet at http//www.insidechina.com/special/weijing/weijingbio.php3. Horta's views were expounded in an address on "Human Rights and Morality vs Pragmatism and Real Politik," Human Rights Oration, 13 December 1998, Alfred Dreyfus Anti-Defamation Unit at B'nai B'rith, Sydney. The address is reprinted on the Internet at http//www.pactok.net.au/docs-et/jrhsp131298.html.
9. Joseph Chan, "An Alternative View," *Journal of Democracy* 8, no. 2 (1997), p. 42.
10. Ibid., p. 40.
11. Ibid., p. 41.
12. Kim Dae Jung, "Is Culture Destiny," p. 194.
13. Chan, "An Alternative View," p. 44.
14. Jeremy Brecher and Tim Costello, *Global Village or Global Pillage* (Boston: South End Press, 1994).
15. Bilahari Kausikan, "Governance That Works," *Journal of Democracy* 8, no. 2 (April 1997), pp. 24–34.
16. Chan, "An Alternative View," p. 45.

7

Human rights and culture: Implications for human security

Wilfrido V. Villacorta

At no time in Asia have human rights been more relevant than during the recent Asian financial crisis. Too often in this part of the world has it been claimed that democracy must conform to so-called "Asian cultural values." Oriental tradition is said to give premium to social harmony, the supremacy of the community's good over individual interest, preservation of customs and revered institutions, and respect for seniority and authority. These values are what were supposedly responsible for the much-vaunted "East Asian miracle." The implication is that human rights and freedoms are more obstacles than stimuli to economic growth. However, the political and economic crises faced by some Asian countries today are mainly attributed to the lack of transparency in governance. In political systems where power is concentrated at the centre and where freedoms are curtailed, corruption and cronyism are more likely to occur. This is true, regardless of what a particular society's "cultural" foundations may be.

The trend towards democratization facilitates and accelerates acceptance of human security as an alternative to the traditional notion of security, which is state centred. It helps the cause of human security that the big powers no longer concern themselves as much with ideological conflict. The post–Cold War international order justifies giving more importance to civil society and the non-military dimensions of security. Security discourse now tends to include a populace's economic and social well-being as well as its general health and safety. The past few ministerial meetings of the ASEAN Regional Forum, for example, have not limited themselves to traditional issues of security but have addressed such human security concerns as transnational crimes and international terrorism.[1]

Asian values: Fact or fiction?

Samuel Huntington is often cited by those who perceive inherent difficulties in transplanting the Western democratic model to non-Western countries. He observes that "the traditionally prevailing values in East Asia have differed fundamentally from those in the West and, by Western standards, they are not favorable to democratic development. Confucian culture and its variants emphasize the supremacy of the group over the individual, authority over liberty, and responsibilities over rights."[2]

In post-colonial Asia, it became fashionable among leaders of emerging independent states in the region to underscore the "Asian way" of governance and to differentiate it from those Western political systems from which they had recently been liberated. Asian élites spoke of the "middle way" between democratic ideals that project uncompromising socio-political equality and the sweeping but suspect promises of the Soviet communist bloc (and its Chinese and South-East Asian derivatives) that unfettered class equality could be reasonably envisioned and achieved. The new Asian sovereignties of India, Pakistan, Indonesia, Malaysia, Myanmar, the non-communist Indochinese states (South Viet Nam, Laos, and Cambodia), and the Philippines, as well as the older but now more autonomous polities of South Korea and Thailand, called themselves democratic, but claimed to be "enriched" by the traditional values of paternal authority and communitarian spirit. Burmese leader U Nu adopted Buddhist socialism; Jawaharlal Nehru spoke of "democratic collectivism" as the basis of Indian socialism; Mohammed Ayub Khan introduced "basic democracy" for Pakistan's Islamic state; Abdul Rahman of Malaysia proclaimed the *Rukun Negara* national philosophy; Indonesia's Sukarno established a "guided democracy." When Ferdinand Marcos declared martial law in the Philippines in the early 1970s, he resuscitated the *barangay*, a pre-colonial concept that he used to name the political units in his "constitutional authoritarianism." The message of all these "Asian" models was that there should not be a blind application of the Western paradigms of governance and development; they must be adapted to local conditions.[3]

At present, the leading proponent of the need to Asianize political systems in the region is the former Singaporean prime minister, Lee Kuan Yew. Although he sees many positive features in American society, he finds "parts of it totally unacceptable: guns, drugs, violent crime, vagrancy, unbecoming behavior in public – in sum the breakdown of civil society." He avers that Asians prefer a well-ordered society that allows them to enjoy what freedoms they have to the maximum extent. In contrast, the West allows "the expansion of the right of the individual to behave or misbehave as he pleases" at the expense of orderly society.[4]

Lee deplores the fact that the idea of the inviolability of the individual has been turned into dogma.[5] Even some Westerners share this regret. Zbigniew Brzezinski, for example, argues that civic freedom has been divorced from the notion of civic responsibility in the West and the context of patriotic citizenship, which involve the willingness to serve and to sacrifice. Freedom has been transformed into "a self-validating absolute" arising from the emphasis on "the maximization of individual satisfactions and the minimization of moral restraints."[6] Recent events such as school shootings in Colorado and Oregon carried out by children infatuated with cult worship and the wild gyrations of stock markets orchestrated by international hedge funds are illustrative and tend to support this line of argument, structured as it is along cultural lines.

What makes Lee Kuan Yew's cultural explanation more interesting, however, is his idea of the role of genetics. The following quotation is illustrative:

Genetics and history interact. The Native American Indian is genetically of the same stock as the Mongoloids of East Asia – the Chinese, the Koreans and the Japanese. But one group got cut off after the Bering Straits melted away. Without that land bridge they were totally isolated in America for thousands of years. The other, in East Asia, met successive invading forces from Central Asia and interacted with waves of people moving back and forth. The two groups may share certain characteristics, for instance if you measure the shape of their skulls and so on, but if you start testing them you find that they are different, most particularly in their neurological development, and their cultural values.[7]

This outlook represents one very distinct interpretation of how the evolution of cultures shapes security perceptions. Asian decision-makers viewed their environment from a distinct cultural and institutional context – an argument that Lee unconsciously shares with the so-called "constructivist" school of international relations. Perceptions (i.e. "knowledge") accumulated and practices refined over time gave Asians distinct and shared experiences that have transcended individual Asian polities or states. These intersubjective understandings constitute a shared "Asian" identity that can be managed and transformed only by "knowledgeable and capable" Asian decision-makers.[8]

The problem with this perspective of Asian "uniqueness" is that it fails to explain the forces of change or to predict what discourse will drive "knowledge" or shape a particular order at a specific time in history. In modern times, for example, Asian cultures have proven to be just as susceptible to desiring and accruing material capabilities and gains as have their Western counterparts. Asian Triads appear to have more in common with brutal, zero-sum Western criminal counterparts than with traditional Confucianist values of reverence toward immediate family and central authority. These types of apparent incongruities have led analysts such as Fareed Zakaria to raise the following questions:

If culture is destiny, what explains a culture's failure in one era and success in another? If Confucianism explains the economic boom in East Asia today, does it not also explain that region's stagnation for four centuries. In fact, when East Asia seemed immutably poor, many scholars – most famously Max Weber – made precisely that case, arguing that Confucian-based cultures discouraged all the attributes necessary for success in capitalism. Today scholars explain how Confucianism emphasizes the essential traits for economic dynamism. Were Latin American countries to succeed in the next few decades, we shall surely read encomiums to Latin culture.[9]

There are, of course, Western scholars who concur with the view that culture in general, and an "Asian way" more specifically, is a key factor in explaining how political systems and geographic regions evolve historically. S. M. Lipset, for example, has asserted that culture explains in large measure the success or failure of democracy.[10] So too has Lucien Pye, who insisted that in many Asian societies "making decisions means taking risks, while security lies in having no choices to make." Power resides in the person of officials and the attitudes that motivate them (what constructivists would view as "agents") and not in the actual offices or institutions that they occupy (i.e. "structures"). Because power is thus personalized, "legitimacy is associated with private behavior and personal morality becomes a public issue."[11] Pye's classic studies of Asian authority structures, as well as those conducted by Amir Santoso, who identifies the Javanese tradition of according respect to elders and superiors as underscoring the evolution of Indonesian "democratization," would appear to provide ample evidence of this theory's validity.[12]

But such conclusions are hardly uncontested. To say that culture influences political predispositions does not necessarily lead to the conclusion that democracy is antithetic to the Asian political legacy. The reverse could be true. There were, for example, early traces of democratic thought as early as the Theravada Buddhist scriptures.[13] In the *Digha Nikkaya* and the *Mahjimma Nikkaya*, the Buddha spoke of the equality of all men and women. In his discourse with the *Vijjians*, he emphasized the importance of consultation and free choice of leaders. His teachings on the *Dharma Raja* (the virtuous ruler) referred to the need for a moral ruler who is obliged to serve the people. An abusive ruler must be resisted and replaced. We can also find the tradition of democracy in the Philippines, where the first anti-colonial revolution in Asia took place in 1896. This revolution against Spain was inspired by liberal democratic principles and led to the establishment of the first Asian republic and democratic constitution.

Culture and human rights

The degree and forms of political participation may differ from one culture to another, but such differences are transcended by human rights, which are acknowledged by the United Nations and by international law to be universal. Human rights, in fact, are congruent with the preservation and respect of indigenous cultures.

It is, therefore, a contradiction in terms to claim that cultural imperatives necessitate the temporary suspension of human rights. The experiences of the Philippines under Marcos and Indonesia under Suharto have demonstrated the dire consequences of such rationalization. These aberrations have taken their toll not only on cultural growth but also on economic development and political stability, which are the supposed justification for authoritarianism.

As the Cold War has disappeared into history, the *raison d'être* of authoritarian regimes has come under increased challenge. Ethnonationalists in Eastern Europe, South-East Asia, and elsewhere are increasingly imposing their aspirations for sovereign and cultural autonomy against reactionary élites and autocratic societies unaccustomed to having their traditional political control over such groups questioned so openly. More fundamentally, opposition elements in many authoritarian political systems are evolving into credible, even dynamic, political forces in their own right. They have embraced democratization as the panacea for overcoming political exclusion or marginalization. They are supported in their quests to win greater power by liberal democratic societies whose leaders are convinced that if the emerging nationalities are governed by democratics like themselves they will be less prone to fight wars and more able to provide the basic necessities of life.

But critics continue to find fault with newly democratized or redemocratized political systems as they struggle to provide basic services and to reconcile nationalism with freedom in newly liberated societies. Nationalists with authoritarian leanings often magnify the failings of former socialist governments, such as occurred in the Soviet Union, to evoke nostalgia for the *ancien régime* when there was more concern for order than for rights and freedom. In evaluating the record of "new democracies," however, it must be remembered that their economic problems were brought about not by the restoration of human rights and democratic institutions but by the corruption of those in charge of distributing basic resources and generating opportunities for all citizens to enjoy greater levels of prosperity. As a matter of fact, it is respect for human rights and the democratic environment that enable the citizenries of troubled, underdeveloped societies to debate problems freely and derive more appropriate strategies for confronting them. The gradual evolution of municipal governments in Chinese villages independent of the Chinese Communist parties and the more spontaneous rise of a real political opposition to Slobodan Milosevic's rule in Serbia following the Kosovo conflict are cases in point. Culture became less important than providing basic supplies and services – i.e. human security – at grass-roots levels, and the central authorities were deemed incapable or unwilling to fulfil this basic requirement.

Unravelling the "East Asian miracle"

Before the onset of the financial crisis, prominence was assigned to the "East Asian miracle." The newly industrializing economies (NIEs) of the region – South Korea, Taiwan, Hong Kong, and Singapore, and, more recently, Malaysia, Thailand, and Indonesia – were upheld as the models that should be emulated by the developing world. The economic growth of the region's "original" NIEs, the "dragons" of South Korea, Taiwan, Hong Kong, and Singapore, was allegedly facilitated by their common authoritarian, Confucian tradition. In the case of the new "tigers" – Malaysia, Thailand, and Indonesia – economic momentum was supposed to have been aided by authoritarian rule. These Asian "dragons" and "tigers," of course, did not follow a single approach to economic development. South Korea and Taiwan had varying degrees of protectionism and government intervention in the earlier years of their economic development, whereas Hong Kong and Singapore, now counted among the "tigers," adopted laissez-faire measures. What the political élites of these societies did have in common, however, was a single-minded determination to combine an emulation of Western-style market capitalism with a distinctly "Asian" brand of political centrism, thus setting themselves apart from the risks of political accountability incurred by élites in Western cultures.

If this constituted the "model approach" for pursuing an East Asian miracle, such a path was short-lived. Paul Krugman was one of the first to question the authenticity of the "East Asian miracle."[14] But it took a genuine, region-wide financial crisis to prove that fast-tracked economic growth would be difficult to sustain in conditions bereft of social equity and human rights and with limited popular participation.

To date, it appears as if the worst implications of Krugman's analysis of economic vulnerability in the region have been sidestepped. The recent dynamism of liberal democratic growth in the region, along with the growth of financial transparency and accountability demanded as a remedy for escaping the region's financial crisis, is clearly undercutting the stereotype of Asia as a haven of authoritarianism. The maturation of democracy in Japan, India, and the Philippines and the democratization of Taiwan and South Korea attest to the universal workability of democratic institutions. The recent compliance of Thai and South Korean banking and commercial sectors with stringent International Monetary Fund guidelines for opening up their operations for all to see reinforces trends of political liberalization in the region. We find increasingly in these countries the same (or at least very similar) commitments to civil rights and freedoms found in the West. What makes this development so impressive is that, in most of these countries, democracy has had to blend with age-old cultural institutions and practices and has had to endure resistance from anti-democratic factors such as initial one-party rule and well-ensconced military or police establishments.[15]

Does economic growth necessarily lead to human security?

Despite the apparently continued viability of most Asian economies, problems remain. The *Human Development Report* for 1996 of the United Nations Development Programme (UNDP) provided a balance sheet of human development in the Asia-Pacific region that graphically portrays both the recent triumphs and the still outstanding challenges in this context.[16]

Health

By 1993, life expectancy region-wide was more than 85 per cent of that in the industrial countries. On the other hand, more than 2 million people are infected with HIV. In the rural areas of South-East Asia and the Pacific, only 55 per cent have access to safe water, and only 41 per cent have access to basic sanitation.

Education

Between 1990 and 1991, the tertiary enrolment ratio in South-East Asia and the Pacific rose from 4 per cent to 16 per cent. In East Asia, more than 100 million boys and girls do not attend school at the secondary level.

Income and poverty

In the period 1960–1993, per capita income in East Asia grew more than 5 per cent a year – the highest rate in the world. But in 1990, nearly 170 million people in East Asia were still living below the poverty line.

Women

Women constitute 19 per cent of parliamentary representatives in East Asia – 1.6 times the proportion in the industrial countries. Female tertiary enrolment doubled between 1970 and 1990 in South-East Asia and the Pacific. However, in East Asia – excluding China – 1 million women are illiterate. Maternal mortality is 442 per 100,000 live births in South-East Asia and the Pacific, compared with only 95 in East Asia.

Children

In East Asia between 1960 and 1993, infant mortality declined from 146 per 1,000 live births to 42. Nearly 95 per cent of one-year-olds in South-East Asia and the Pacific are immunized. On the other hand, more than a third of children under 5 in South-East Asia and the Pacific are malnourished. Nearly 1 million children in East Asia die before the age of 5.

Population and urbanization

Between 1930 and 1992, the fertility rate declined more in East Asia, South-East Asia, and the Pacific than in the industrial countries. But the population in East Asia (excluding China) was projected to be 79 per cent urbanized by the year 2000 (up from 36 per cent in 1960), increasing the pressure on infrastructure and basic services.

What are the implications of these trends? Deepak Nayyar offers the timely reminder that economic development in a democracy requires that "people are at the center of economic development not only as its beneficiaries but also as the main actors." He further asserts that "people can impart a sense of purpose to society only when they are enthused by a sense of achievement based on an improvement in their living conditions and a widening of opportunities in their daily existence."[17] The statistics provided in the above categories reveal both the promises and the perils entailed in the human security ethos to which Nayyar is referring: the dangers of failing to satisfy even the most basic human expectations and the immense benefits of satisfying them well.

Democracy, liberalization, and the financial crisis

This brings us to the relationship between democracy and the financial crisis, and to how that linkage might relate to the broader question of culture as a factor in any "Asian miracle."

The history of the financial crisis, which emanated from speculative attacks on Asian financial systems from mid-1997 onward, requires a separate analysis that is far beyond the scope of this chapter. In the context of human security and culture, however, the crisis has provided us with several key lessons. Two, in particular, stand out. First, it has certainly underscored the direct connection between irresponsible financial management and human security. At the same time (and somewhat in contrast), it has generated increased scepticism in affected countries about the benefits of fast-paced economic liberalization. Both of these "lessons" will be assessed in some detail here.

That non-disclosure and widespread corruption proved to be a fact of Asian financial life should hardly be surprising, given that political democratization is only a recent phenomenon in many Asian cultures and other socio-economic sectors are under less pressure to reform at the same pace as central political institutions. In a non-democratic business environment where human rights and freedoms are hardly a priority consideration, such factors as an employee's welfare or a small investor's security are scarcely protected. Moreover, the press is often muzzled in scrutinizing the privileged echelons of a developing state's financial infrastructure. Consequently, transparency and accountability do not exist in corporate governance or in state regulatory mechanisms ostensibly designed to exercise corporate oversight. This absence makes conditions ripe for financial corruption and especially vulnerable to the vagaries of international market fluctuations.

The human security ramifications of corporate failure throughout East Asia during 1997–1998 were starkly evident. Thai entrepreneurs who were stalwarts in such diverse industries as telecommunications and construction were suddenly unemployed or, at best, took their places on the street corner hawking fruit and trinkets. Powerful South Korean industrial unions became impotent overnight and thousands of their constituents were thrown out of work, precipitating massive social unrest just at the time when that country's most liberal government in modern history, led by President Kim Dae Jung, was assuming office. Malaysian Prime Minister Mahathir accused Western stock manipulators of deliberately undercutting his country's – and the entire region's – economic development. Perhaps the most conspicuous casualty from a human security perspective was the de facto death of institutional approaches to market liberalization that, in turn, could have spilled over to facilitate greater political liberalization. Western institutional approaches to free trade and multilateral security as represented by the Asia-Pacific Economic Cooperation forum and by the ASEAN Regional Forum (ARF) were exposed as fragile and all too abstract agents of regional progress for "the common Asian citizen" at a time when personal savings were decimated by currency devaluation and central governments were demanding that their subjects literally turn over family jewellery and artefacts so that their precious metals could be melted down to bolster depleted state treasuries. The "misery index" (to recall the infamous phrase employed by a recent American president) was on graphic display throughout Asia during 1997–1998.

A welcome offshoot of the crisis, however, was the realization that democracy is the best political system for responding to an economic downturn. Authoritarianism may induce fast-tracked economic growth in many cases, but we have learned from postwar Asian history that it is only a matter of time before the social costs are exposed and the economic and political consequences of corruption and cronyism – the handmaidens of authoritarian rule – catch up and take their toll.

In particular, we have seen that the currency turmoil has brought political turbulence to two of the most afflicted countries in the region: Indonesia and Malaysia. It did not lead to permanent political instability in three other stricken countries: South Korea, Thailand, and the Philippines, although the last two have had their share of labour strikes. What is noteworthy is that these three countries have a common element: a democratic political system that permits freedom of expression and press freedom.

The rise of new democracies in South-East Asia is inevitable. The signs are clear in Indonesia, Malaysia, and Singapore. The political contagion will spread to Viet Nam, Myanmar, Laos, and Cambodia. We can anticipate the confluence of liberalized markets and the ascent of democracy in the South-East Asian subregion. One positive outcome of the financial crisis is that it has unwittingly served as a stimulus to democratization in South-East Asia. As John Kenneth Galbraith stressed, "[f]reedom of expression and public participation in government are widely heralded as social virtues; it is too little noticed that beyond a certain point in economic development they become socially necessary and politically inescapable."[18]

At the same time, the Asian financial crisis has generated widespread scepticism in afflicted countries about the wisdom of fast-paced liberalization. Owing to advances in communications technology, huge amounts of money can move in an extremely short period of time and, if targeted maliciously, can wreak havoc in financial markets. The integration of financial markets has destabilized individual markets because of the sudden and huge capital movements that occur. It is intriguing that US$1,000 billion is traded in global currency markets every day, whereas only US$10 billion is needed for world exports on a daily basis.[19]

There are inherent dangers in a situation where US$1,000 billion floats around world financial markets whose only purpose is to secure higher rates of return. That amount is greater than the foreign exchange reserves of the 12 largest national economies and, if misapplied, can destabilize entire regions. Central banks used to be able to regulate exchange rates. But now that the amount of money being traded in the hands of speculators is so large, central banks simply do not have the reserve resources to protect their financial systems. This means that states have lost a significant amount of their political power, which includes the capacity to remain in control of how they fare in the international economy.

As globalization intensifies, economies and financial markets have to adjust to a worldwide framework that emphasizes the free market. Conformity to this framework is necessary in order to make countries competitive. However, despite efforts towards structural reform in the international marketplace, there will always be losers as well as winners in this arena. This will have implications for the type of groupings that will emerge among countries at varying levels of economic performance and for their behaviour on such key issues as free trade, currency valuation, and foreign investment.

An uncontrolled increase in the number of losers in the global competition of international political economics would lead to widespread alienation among developing economies in Asia and elsewhere from a global financial system that appears to have little relevance or affinity to their specific interests. This development, in turn, would generate forms of international conduct inimical to global peace and prosperity: incessant trade conflicts, backtracking on liberalization commitments, and reversion to protectionism, militarization, terrorist activities, and wars waged by governments desperate for international causes that would deflect popular dissatisfaction.

Interestingly, the acknowledged czar of financial markets, George Soros, thinks that there has been too much "market fundamentalism." In his book, *The Crisis of Global Capitalism*, he contends that financial markets which are inherently unstable cannot be self-correcting and that social needs cannot be met by giving market forces free rein:

Capital is more mobile than the other factors of production and financial capital is even more mobile than direct investment. Financial capital moves wherever it is best rewarded; as it is the harbinger of prosperity, individual countries compete to attract it.[20]

According to Soros, market fundamentalism "has rendered the global capitalist system unsound and unsustainable." He concludes that "capitalism, with its exclusive reliance on market forces, poses a different kind of danger to open society" and that "market fundamentalism is today a greater threat to open society than any totalitarian ideology."[21]

Human security and human emancipation

The above analysis relates to the need for developing countries and for the individuals inhabiting them to feel they are in control of events and trends to the extent that they can have at least some impact on the basic forces that may shape and change them. In most instances, this means no more than gaining sufficient control of those processes directly related to securing the most fundamental components of life. In the 1994 UNDP *Human Development Report*, the fundamental components of human security were identified: food, health, economic welfare, environment, personal well-being, community and political participation. Global, regional, and national security are now more directed at the security of people and the security of the planet.[22] As intimated above, financial security – particularly the right of small entrepreneurs, depositors, and shareholders to be guaranteed the protection of the value of their wealth – has also recently become a major concern. Perhaps most importantly, human security is inherently tied to human freedom and human rights.

The link between security and "human emancipation" is succinctly explained by Professor Ken Booth:

"Security" means the absence of threats. Emancipation is the freeing of people (as individuals and groups) from those physical and human constraints which stop them from carrying out what they freely choose to do ... Security and emancipation are two sides of the same coin. Emancipation, *not power or order*, produces true security. Emancipation theoretically is security.[23]

Human emancipation is thus at the core of human security and human rights. These inviolable rights encompass guarantees of the conditions necessary to benefit rational beings.[24] Such freedom, of course, can on occasion precipitate certain insecurities in its own right. Ideally, emancipation leads to human beings coming to terms with their cultures and societies and to a better understanding of the forces of social change. In doing so they are able to integrate emancipation with social responsibility more effectively than if freedom is measured totally in terms of satisfaction or frustration with one's own destiny in life. In no small measure, this too constitutes a key aspect of human security.[25]

Mass political participation, according to the United Nations Development Programme, is a process of enlarging people's choices. It involves the ability of an electorate to influence and control decision-making processes and the relationships that collectively constitute state or other decision-making units. Meaningful political participation, moreover, empowers the people with the freedom to choose and change governance at every level, including institutions such as the family, the workplace, the market, and the school system, which, in themselves, establish particular patterns of authority and power structures.

The challenges and pressures of globalization provide greater justification for both political and economic democratization. The financial crisis showed the necessity of modernizing the state and the political élite. Early on, King Sihanouk of Cambodia realized that charismatic leadership is no longer the order of the day. He wrote that "it is no longer enough these days to merely move the masses or inspire unity; today's leaders need to be more like chairmen [sic] of boards of multinationals, expert in trade, finance, foreign investments and it doesn't hurt to know how to work a computer."[26]

Moreover, Arthur Schlesinger, Jr., observes that integration and disintegration feed on each other: "Globalization is in the saddle and rides mankind, but at the same time drives people to seek refuge from its powerful forces beyond their control and comprehension. They retreat into familiar, intelligible, protective units. They crave the politics of identity. The faster the world integrates, the more people will huddle in their religious or ethnic or tribal enclaves."[27]

Conclusion

Emphasis on human security is a positive development in security studies. It is a reflection of the global trend in which the pressure to cultivate and sustain democracy is intensifying. Part and parcel of this is an acknowledgement that the people's security is more important than that of the state. In this sense, the cultural aspects of security clearly become more important, although debate over how they do so has yet to be resolved. It may be that culture drives perceptions and understandings about what must be "secured" at different levels of analysis (the individual, the state, or an international system) or it may be that it acts more as a constant referent or foundation against which periods of great historical change can be measured by Asians and by other peoples. The latter function is hardly unique to Asian security needs but is clearly a human security need.

Accordingly the growing prominence and appeal of human security may be that it is not culturally based at all but is anchored to the realization that human rights are not antithetic to any one indigenous or "unique" culture. People's rights and aspirations are not a disruptive factor in state security but are rather a stabilizing element that can be applied to facilitate sustained development in emerging states and societies. As human rights and human security become more significant in the discourse among states, it is to be hoped that they increasingly underwrite Asian and international economic stability and enhance democratization. Asian cultures will be strengthened to the extent that these quests are successful.

Notes

1. For summaries, see the Australian Department of Foreign Affairs (DFAT) "ARF" Web site at http://www.dfat.gov.au/arf_meet.html.
2. Samuel Huntington, "American Democracy in Relation to Asia," in Robert Bartley et al., eds., *Democracy and Capitalism: Asian and American Perspectives* (Singapore: Institute of Southeast Asian Studies, 1993), p. 38.
3. Wilfrido Villacorta, "Democracy in Asia," *Proceedings of the Workshop on Democracy* (Vatican: Pontifical Academy of Social Science, 1997), pp. 88–89.
4. Fareed Zakaria, "Culture Is Destiny: A Conversation with Lee Kuan Yew," *Foreign Affairs* 73, No. 2 (March/April 1994), p. 111.
5. Ibid., p. 112.
6. Zbigniew Brzezinski, *Out of Control: Global Turmoil on the Eve of the 21st Century* (New York: Charles Scribner's Sons, 1993), p. 69.
7. Fareed, "Culture Is Destiny," p. 117.
8. Ronald L. Jepperson, Alexander Wendt, and Peter J. Katzenstein, "Norms, Identity and Culture in National Security," in Peter J. Katzenstein, ed., *The Culture of National Security: Norms and Identity in World Politics* (New York: Columbia University Press, 1996), pp. 33–75. A specific application of this to the Asian situation is briefly assessed by Muthiah Alagappa, *Asian Security Practice: Material and Ideational Influences* (Stanford, CA: Stanford University Press, 1998), especially pp. 18, 60.
9. Fareed, "Culture Is Destiny," p. 125.
10. S. M. Lipset, "The Centrality of Political Culture," in Larry Diamond and Marc Plattner, eds., *The Global Resurgence of Democracy* (Baltimore, MD: Johns Hopkins University Press, 1992), pp. 135–137.
11. Lucien W. Pye, *Asian Power and Politics: The Cultural Dimensions of Authority* (Cambridge, MA: Belknap Press, 1985), pp. 22–23.
12. According to Javanese culture, open criticism is a source of conflict: "If there is a need to criticize, the best way would be to discuss it privately with one's superiors." See Amir Santoso, "Democratization: The Case of Indonesia's New Order," in Anek Laothamatas, ed., *Democratization in Southeast and East Asia* (Singapore: Institute of Southeast Asian Studies, 1997), p. 37.
13. Villacorta, "Democracy in Asia," p. 89.
14. See Paul Krugman, "The Myth of Asia's Miracle," *Foreign Affairs* 73, no. 6 (November/December 1994), pp. 62–78.
15. Villacorta, "Democracy in Asia," p. 89.

16. United Nations Development Programme, *Human Development Report* (New York: Oxford University Press, 1966), p. 39.
17. Deepak Nayyar, "Democracy, Markets and People in the Context of Globalization," *Public Policy* 2, no. 1 (January–March 1998), p. 81.
18. John Kenneth Galbraith, *The Culture of Contentment* (Boston and New York: Houghton Mifflin, 1992), p. 8.
19. Elmar Altvater and Birgit Mahnkopf, "The World Market Unbound," *Review of International Political Economy* 5, no. 3 (Autumn 1997), p. 460.
20. George Soros, *The Crisis of Global Capitalism: Open Society Endangered* (London: Little, Brown, 1998), p. xix.
21. Ibid., pp. xx–xxii.
22. Ingvar Carlsson, Shridath Ramphal et al., *Our Global Neighbourhood: The Report of the Commission on Global Governance* (Oxford: Oxford University Press, 1998), p. 336.
23. Ken Booth, "Security and Emancipation," *Review of International Studies* 17, no. 4 (October 1991), p. 317.
24. Edmund Espina et al., *Comprehensive Course on Human Rights* (Quezon City: Task Force Detainees of the Philippines, 1991), p. 38.
25. Erich Fromm, *Fear of Freedom* (London: Routledge & Kegan Paul, 1960), p. 9.
26. Norodom Sihanouk with Bernard Krishar, *Charisma and Leadership* (Tokyo: Yohan Publications, 1990), p. xxii.
27. Arthur Schlesinger, "Has Democracy a Future?" *Foreign Affairs* 76, no. 5 (September/October 1997), p. 10.

8

"Grey area phenomena" and human security

Peter A. Chalk

This chapter aims to broaden the terms of reference through which international and regional security are understood in the contemporary era, particularly with regard to the prominence of so-called "soft," non-traditional security threats or "grey area phenomena" (GAP). It analyses certain features of the current global system that are exacerbating the occurrence and growth of these influences, many of which are found with particular clarity in South-East Asia. The chapter concludes that, in order to deal with GAP, it is imperative that this subregion's states commit themselves to more forceful and innovative action at both the national and international levels.

The changing nature of security in the post–Cold War era

With the collapse of the Soviet bloc in Eastern Europe in the late 1980s and early 1990s it appeared that the international system might be on the threshold of an era of unprecedented peace and stability. Politicians, diplomats, and academics alike began to forecast the imminent establishment of a new world order, increasingly managed by democratic political institutions. These, it was believed, would develop within the context of an integrated international economic system based on the principles of the free market.[1] As this new world order emerged, it was assumed that serious threats to international stability would decline commensurately.

However, the initial euphoria that was evoked by the end of the Cold War has since been replaced by a growing sense of unease that threats at the lower end of the conflict spectrum may soon assume greater prominence. Such concern has been stimulated largely by the remarkable fluidity that now characterizes international politics, in which it is no longer apparent exactly who can do what to whom and with what means. Moreover, it appears that, in this new world "order," violence and the readiness to risk and inflict death are increasingly being used by the "weak" not so much as a means of expressing identity but as a way of creating it.[2] As Richard Latter observes, such dynamics are likely to reduce inter-state conflict only at the expense of an increase in pandemic threats that fall below the level of conventional war.[3]

Stated more directly, the geopolitical landscape that now faces the global polity lacks the relative stability of the linear Cold War division between East and West. There is no large and obvious equivalent to the Soviet Union against which to balance the United States, the world's sole remaining superpower. Indeed, few of today's dangers have the character of direct military aggression emanating from a clearly defined sovereign source. Security, conflict, and general threat definition have become more diffuse and opaque, lacking the simple dichotomies of the Cold War era. The challenges that will face the global community in the new millennium are likely to evolve as "threats without enemies," with their source internal, rather than external, to the political order that the concept of "national interest" has traditionally represented.[4] In commenting on this new strategic environment, former Central Intelligence Agency Director James Woolsey has remarked: "We have slain a large dragon, but now we find ourselves living in a jungle with a bewildering number of poisonous snakes. And in many ways, the dragon was easier to keep track of."[5]

Making sense of these changes will require a holistic, non-linear approach to security that goes beyond the relatively parsimonious assumptions of *realpolitik* that informed international politics for so many years. Traditional spatial notions of security, of national stability defined purely in terms of territorial sovereignty (reflected on a larger scale by the containment doctrines of the Cold War), simply do not work in today's more complex geo-strategic environment.[6] Tomorrow's world will be a GAP world, a setting in which standard, military-based conceptions of power and security will have, at most, only limited relevance.

Such considerations are of particular importance to the South-East Asian region for two main reasons. First, many of the GAP challenges that confront policy-makers today thrive in areas that lack strong state structures, in terms of both national cohesiveness and established systems of civil and legal justice. Ethno-religious separatism and extremism, for instance, are likely to be especially common in states where there are extensive cultural differences between élite and non-élite primal identities and where there is no effective overarching "glue" to subsume such variations to a greater sense of national identity. Equally, organized illicit activities such as narcotics smuggling and human trafficking require the existence of malleable criminal and social justice structures if they are to flourish and avoid the strictures that would otherwise be imposed on ingrained systems of personal clientelism.[7]

South-East Asia, in many ways, is ripe for both intensified ethnic conflict and accelerated flows of illegal trafficking. The region contains a number of ethno-religious minorities that are experiencing erosions of their traditional authority structures owing to the process of modernization that has been enacted by the majority to consolidate its dominance over the state.[8] The resulting sense of insecurity and alienation has already provided the basis for increasingly serious forms of atavistic conflict based on such forces as militant Islam. Aggravating the situation has been the willingness of corrupt elements of certain South-East Asian security, political, and judicial establishments to participate directly in GAP activities as a way of supplementing low personal incomes and boosting inadequate agency budgets. Thai, Burmese, and Cambodian complicity in heroin trafficking and Indonesian involvement in piracy would be two such examples. Official connivance of this type has, obviously, done little to enhance the efforts of those who seek a tighter and more effective national response strategy.

Second, many South-East Asian nations exhibit resistance towards intrusive and interventionist monitoring or law enforcement mechanisms. The norm of non-interference in internal affairs, which essentially dates back to the 1976 Treaty of Amity and Cooperation, remains extremely strong in the mindset of the Association of South East Asian Nations (ASEAN) and continues to form the crux of the group's collective sense of security and self-identity. The rejection of a 1998 Thai proposal to formalize a doctrine of "flexible engagement," which would have allowed member states to discuss one another's domestic affairs more frankly and even institute more intrusive policies, is indicative of this continued preference for what is now, somewhat disparagingly, referred to as the "ASEAN way."[9] Such loosely configured security norms may well be conducive to the generation of cordial regional relations – at least at the rhetorical level – allowing, as they do, tough issues to be side-stepped or simply ignored. However, they are hardly appropriate for the type of intrusive regional and international action that is needed to combat contemporary soft security challenges, the sources for most of which tend to be internal rather than external. In this context, ASEAN itself could be seen as integral to the GAP problem as it is emerging in South-East Asia.

The notion of grey area phenomena

Grey area phenomena (GAP) can be loosely defined as threats to the stability of sovereign states by non-state actors and non-governmental processes and organizations.[10] Although many GAP problems come to involve violence, not all do. Those that manifest themselves in an aggressive manner are typically associated with the activities of non-state actors such as international crime syndicates, drug trafficking organizations, and terrorist groups. Non-violent GAP forces are more generally related to the threat posed by non-governmental processes and influences such as uncontrolled or illegal immigration, famine, and the transnational spread of diseases such as HIV and cholera. Whenever GAP influences are associated with violence and aggression, however, such conflict is generally organized, and employed for either political or economic purposes, and characteristically falls short of major conventional warfare.[11]

All GAP issues, whether violent or not, represent a direct threat to the underlying stability, cohesion, and fabric of the modern sovereign state. However, unlike the challenge posed by traditional security concerns such as overt external aggression, the GAP threat is of a somewhat more transparent and insidious nature. This is because it typically stems from a context that exists outside formal state structures and can only occasionally be directly linked to, or identified with, another polity, power faction, or global ethno-religious bloc. As Holden-Rhodes and Lupsha observe, this characteristically gives rise to an "ooze factor" situation whereby the effects of GAP are often ignored or, when recognized, factored into a viable political policy action equation only once they have reached a major destabilizing stage within the state(s) concerned.[12] Moreover, because GAP are not directed or controlled by states, traditional defences that governments have erected to protect themselves and their citizens are generally impotent against them.[13]

GAP threats also blur the previously clear dividing lines between the domestic and international spheres of security. Issues such as terrorism, drug trafficking, and environmental degradation may emanate from within states; however, their effects are generally not contained, typically having an impact that is truly transnational in nature. Further compounding the situation is that, in many cases, the impact of one GAP influence will have consequences for another. Hence we see political extremists moving into organized international criminal activity for revenue purposes; global warming encouraging the spread of disease; and environmental degradation stimulating mass unregulated population flows.

Grey area phenomena are not new. Problems such as famine, disease, drugs trafficking, terrorism, and organized crime have all existed for many years. What is new, however, is that the realities of the current global context are working to facilitate the occurrence and growth of these threats, especially those of the non-state (as opposed to the non-governmental process) variety. Four in particular stand out.

The "dollarization" of the globe

The economic success of capitalism and its accompanying system of materialism have led to the so-called "dollarization" of the globe. Today, in both the developed and particularly the developing world, to possess dollars is to possess power and influence; it is the mark of success. Not only has this served to provide powerful motivating rationales for enhancing financial wealth – often by whatever means possible – it has also allowed non-state actors to acquire treasuries and, hence, power of sufficient magnitude that their influence now matches or even surpasses that of many sovereign states.[14]

The dollarization of the international system is essentially a consequence of the permeation of Western commercial values throughout the globe via electronic communications and widespread travel. Through television, the movies, and enhanced transnational mobility, relatively unsophisticated and discontented audiences around the world have been increasingly exposed to the quasi-political distortion of materialism that is inherent within the Western/capitalist socio-economic value system. Personal meaning and satisfaction have, as a result, come to be defined in terms of driving a "flashy" car, wearing designer clothes, owning expensive jewellery, living in exotic surroundings – in short, having access to and enjoying the very best that Western consumerism and commercialism can offer.[15]

The quickest and easiest way to such riches, and the satisfaction they appear to engender, is through crime. This is especially true in regions where relative deprivation[16] is perceived to be especially great and legitimate economic opportunities are lacking (something that applies to most of the non-Western developing world). In these instances the possession of wealth and power has become far more important than considerations of the means used to acquire them.[17] The result has been the emergence of so-called "black dollar" groups – organizations seeking material wealth on the back of sustained criminal activities, which can cover anything from arms and narcotics trafficking, to gem smuggling, piracy, and even the illicit trade in human body parts.

The resurgence of atavistic forms of identity

Since the end of the Cold War, there has been a major resurgence of religious fundamentalism (Islamic and others) and other atavistic forms of identity such as ethnicity. This particular feature of the present international system is helping to sustain, and in certain instances create, highly destabilizing sub-national communal conflicts, many of which have involved armed factions that are prepared to utilize terrorist strategies as either a primary or a secondary mode of struggle. Such effects have been felt on a truly global scale. States throughout Western and Central Europe, Africa, Central Asia, South Asia, and East Asia have literally been torn apart as a result of political terror instigated by armed groups justifying their actions on the basis of a self-proclaimed right to national or religious self-determination.[18]

Although ethno-religious communal conflict is hardly new (many internal insurgencies during the Cold War had specific ethnic or religious overtones), there are at least two interrelated factors working to amplify primal conflict in the present international system. First, there has been the perceived failure of regimes that have defined themselves on the basis of unifying secular belief systems such as communism, pan-Africanism, and pan-Arabism. Unable to adapt to rates of change that today come in minutes, days, and months, not years or decades, and failing to satisfy the increasingly diverse demands of rapidly expanding populations, governments throughout the developing world (and, in certain instances, the developed world) appear to have failed. The resulting discontinuity, disequilibria, and apparent chaos have stimulated demands for alternative models of development, while, at the same time, people have sought new frameworks of personal meaning to replace the obsolete universalist doctrines of the Cold War era. The combined effect has been a resurgence of atavistic ideology, with groups increasingly turning to primordial identities based on religion and ethnicity (or an amalgamation of the two) as a way of ameliorating both their frustration and their discontent.[19]

Secondly, the disintegration of the imposed order of the Cold War has allowed ethno-religious forces to take on greater freedom and autonomy in their own right. No longer concerned by global ideological imperatives, neither Washington nor Moscow has an interest (and, at least in Russia's case, the capability) in containing regional hostilities – conflicts that, in many cases, were deliberately engineered as part of their respective national security policies (see below). The lifting of the superpower "lid" in this fashion has lent an unprecedented "fluidity" to world politics, unleashing a whole variety of ethnic, religious, and territorial tensions that had, hitherto, been effectively capped or at least controlled.[20]

This particular effect of the post–Cold War era has been felt most acutely in multi-ethnic states that have had no previous experience of ethnic accommodation. In such instances, nationalism has typically drawn upon ethnicity[21] as a relational concept, creating boundaries between "insiders" and "outsiders" that have been further entrenched and radicalized by the calls of politicians, nationalists, and demagogues to cleanse and purify their particular "ethnies" from all contaminating and alien influences.[22]

The proliferation of weaponry

We are currently living in an age in which organized violence has become a tool that is increasingly available to sub-state actors and groups. The basic division between the government, army, and people – the bedrock of the trinitarian concept of conventional warfare – has collapsed as a result of the production and diffusion of armament technology. This de-structuring, rooted in the mass production and proliferation of basic and advanced combat weapons, has made it increasingly difficult for the state to monopolize violence and has given a variety of organizations options that were formerly reserved to the government and its armed forces.[23] A systematic review of ongoing ethnic strife, for instance, shows that the total value of the military hardware used annually by sub-state armed groups has been as high as US$3.5 billion in recent years, nearly a quarter of the value of the orthodox trade in major weapons in 1992.[24]

During the Cold War, the United States and the USSR both made ex-tensive use of "war by proxy" as a way of indirectly pursuing their global objectives.[25] In large part, this was due to the constraints that were placed on conventional warfare as a result of the development and pro-liferation of atomic weapons of mass destruction. The nuclear factor represented a qualitative change in both the destructiveness and the pre-dictable consequences of war. As Steve Weber observes, for the first time in the history of the modern states system, a great power's use of total force against its nuclear-armed adversary would absolutely ensure a re-distribution of capabilities that would be unfavourable to both. Not only could a full-blown nuclear exchange not be won; it would also inevitably lead to the destruction of both superpowers and their immediate partici-pation in the system.[26]

This realization, enshrined in the strategic dogma of Mutually Assured Destruction, forced both the United States and the USSR (and their re-spective allies) to abandon the use of all-out war as a viable, or rational, tool of statecraft. At the same time, given that any direct confrontation could easily escalate across the nuclear threshold, conventional wars fought immediately between the superpowers were similarly ruled out. This obliged both the United States and the USSR to find new ways of settling their differences. The result was the introduction of "war by proxy" whereby both sides (as defined by the North Atlantic Treaty Organisation and the Warsaw Pact) attempted to pursue their territorial, economic, and political goals through surrogate actors.[27]

In a number of instances, the adoption of proxy armies involved the transfer of extensive armouries to regions of intense East–West rivalry. Following the Soviet invasion of Afghanistan in 1979, for instance, the United States embarked on a huge covert operation to train, arm, and finance rebel Muslims to resist the occupying Soviet army. It is believed that Washington spent in excess of US$3 billion in military aid, reaching a peak of US$600 million a year just before the USSR withdrew in 1989. One study estimates that, by 1987, some 65,000 tons of weapons were being transferred each year to the Afghan rebels via Pakistan.[28]

Playing out the Cold War in this manner has ensured that there is now not only a global supply of arms useful to GAP actors, but also the knowledge of how to foment, organize, and sustain insurgency. Such technological and intellectual diffusion has provided GAP practitioners with the means to match and, in certain instances, surpass the capabilities of nation-states. As Steven Metz observes, the full effects of this particular legacy of the Cold War have still to be realized and will, in all likelihood, be felt for many years to come.[29]

Globalization

The international system is now more globally interdependent than at any other time in history. Whether measured on the basis of information flows, foreign investment, financial transactions, the total volume of world trade, government-to-government contact, or people-to-people links, the figures all show major increases, especially over the past 20 years.[30] While it is not necessary to spell out these developments in terms of specific statistics – the trends are both clear and well known – the consequences for GAP do require some elucidation.[31]

Perhaps of most importance to GAP is the shrinking of the globe as a result of technological developments that have made virtually every corner of the planet quickly accessible. Today one can physically move from one part of the world to another in the same time (if not more rapidly) that it used to take to journey from one city or county to another, with such international travel being largely open to all.[32] If the word "physically" is removed from the above sentence, the world is reduced to mere seconds and even microseconds. Real-time events happening on one side of the globe can be observed from distant jungle locations simply by accessing Cable Network News or the British Broadcasting Corporation via a generator. Money moves even faster, with an estimated US$1 trillion being electronically transferred around the globe each day (compared with an annual trade of US$155 billion between the United States and Japan).[33]

This transnationalization of world politics has worked to the advantage of GAP actors. In particular, it has allowed groups to shift capital, to communicate, and to move on a genuinely global scale – exploiting favourable tactical and logistical environments that may exist many miles from their home base. In today's global world, GAP players have the potential to operate with the same speed, precision, and international dimension as decision-makers in advanced nation-states.[34] Indeed, given the fact that borders and jurisdictional frontiers continue to be viewed as sacrosanct by most polities in the present international system, it could be argued that GAP actors are actually able to function more effectively than governments. As Cherif Bassiouni observes:

These phenomena which transcend national boundaries are not hampered by political and diplomatic considerations, nor do they suffer from the impediments created by bureaucratic divisions among the national organs of law enforcement and prosecution. The international response to phenomena which know no national boundaries [has thus been] piecemeal, divided, and more frequently than not, devoid of any effective efforts at international cooperation.[35]

Grey area phenomena in South-East Asia

The above influences of dollarization, arms proliferation, globalization, and heightened forms of atavistic/primordial identity are combining to exacerbate and sharpen the threat posed by GAP in the post–Cold War international system. In many ways, these factors are emerging with particular clarity and focus in South-East Asia, creating a regional-specific pattern that is likely considerably to heighten the scope and potential for GAP in the coming years.[36]

The emphasis on economic prosperity and power conceived in terms of wealth is as strong in South-East Asia as anywhere on the globe. Indeed it could be argued that the desire for material progress has emerged as one of the major defining characteristics of the region and one that largely underpins the normative perceptions of many in the region. In a number of respects this material drive has served the region well, powering the "tiger" economies of Singapore, Malaysia, Indonesia, Thailand, and Hong Kong to the point that they are now amongst the most dynamic anywhere in the world.[37]

On a more negative note, however, the need and ever constant desire for wealth and opulence have provided a fertile ground for the growth of more insidious GAP influences. The emphasis on achieving high rates of economic growth as quickly as possible has had an extremely negative impact on the environmental viability of the region. Indeed, according to a 1996 poll conducted by the Asian Development Bank, atmospheric and freshwater pollution as a result of unsustainable industrialization were already being ranked as by far the most important environmental issues facing policy-makers in the region.[38] Rivers in East Asia are currently ranked as amongst the most polluted anywhere in the world, with those in Manila, Bangkok, and Jakarta thought to carry three to four times the world levels of raw sewage, household garbage, construction debris, and market waste.[39]

The craving for instant material gratification (itself amplified by the severe economic disparities generated by the region's rush to wealth) has additionally encouraged a number of groups to engage in various illicit activities as a way of quickly fulfilling their material aspirations. The result has been the gradual evolution of a parallel underground economy throughout South-East Asia, which is currently being powered by a range of illicit activities including drug trafficking, loan sharking, protection rackets, money laundering, piracy, and prostitution rings. The effective regulation of these "ventures" has been undermined by the crisis of governance in a number of South-East Asian states, where the involvement of corrupt elements of certain judicial, political, and security structures has allowed crimes to proliferate or at least go unchecked.

Drug-induced corruption, for instance, has been a recurring problem in Thailand, facilitating the regional and international diffusion of narcotics from the Golden Triangle. A case in point was the 1992 decision by the United States government to refuse a visa application from Narong Wongwan, leader of the prominent Justice and Unity Party, after it became apparent that he was linked to a major drug-trafficking operation based in Myanmar. More recently, in 1996, a former member of parliament (MP) from the Chart Thai Party, Thanong Siripreechapong, was extradited to the United States to face legal proceedings in connection with his participation in a major Thai–US drug-smuggling ring that had been active between 1977 and 1987. A variety of other former and current officials, including Mongkohl Chongsuthanamanee, MP, and Vatana Asavaname, a former deputy interior minister, have been similarly "fingered" by the US government for their involvement in the Golden Triangle drug trade.[40]

Equally, one of the reasons piracy is believed to have emerged with such "clarity" in Indonesian territorial waters stems from the protection that a number of organized maritime gangs have almost certainly received from the country's armed forces. Indeed, members of the international shipping community have repeatedly claimed that pirates operating around the Riau archipelago and more generally throughout the Java Sea specifically benefit from close association with Indonesian military and customs units – allowing gangs quickly to seize cargo ships and disperse their payloads. The desire to supplement low incomes through the protection of extra-legal business "opportunities" almost certainly plays a role in such connivance.[41] As Jon Vagg noted in 1995:

[E]conomic development [has] ... meant that prices rose and incomes fell from 1989/90 on. This could have provided an incentive for piracy for civilian and basic-grade military personnel alike, and the rise of piracy that took place from early 1990 on. In addition, in as much as the armed forces hold a substantial degree of [power], it is possible that they condoned, assisted and "taxed" non-military pirates just as they would many other illegal enterprises.[42]

The "black dollar" organizations that sustain this organized criminal activity have been quick to recognize and exploit certain natural features of South-East Asia that are conducive to their illicit designs. The more important of these are:

- relatively porous land and maritime borders, which are conducive to smuggling;
- large and essentially un-monitorable archipelagic coastlines, which facilitate illicit maritime activities such as piracy;
- extensive hinterlands made virtually unpenetrable by dense jungle, deep valleys, and steep mountain ranges, which have helped to create fortified "no-go" grey areas beyond the formal control of the government;
- at least with respect to the Golden Triangle, near-perfect climatic and topographical conditions for the growth and cultivation of the heroin poppy, which is vital for heroin production.

The scope of organized criminal activity in South-East Asia – sometimes referred to as the "cancer" of the region's legitimate capitalism – should not be underestimated. For example, well over half of all acts of piracy that take place around the world occur in South-East Asia; Indo-China represents one of the most prolific areas of the globe with respect to the sex trade and heroin trafficking; and money laundering afflicts financial institutions from Hong Kong to Cambodia. Moreover, in 1995, delegates at an annual Interpol meeting in Beijing were informed that the world's largest and most sophisticated organized crime rings originate from South-East Asia, run, for the most part by the Hong Kong Triad network.[43]

South-East Asia has also been affected by the global resurgence of atavistic, primordial forms of identity. New strains of ethnic violence have boiled over in Indonesia; Islamic extremism is emerging as a powerful force in Malaysia, Indonesia, Thailand, and the Philippines. Ethno-religious tension has surfaced in Myanmar. And armed separatist movements continue to pose serious problems for a variety of states across the region, including rebel groups in Aceh, Irian Jaya, and East Timor (all in

Indonesia), Pattani (southern Thailand), and Mindanao (southern Philippines). These influences are not only encouraging a heightened level of general civil disobedience, but also serving to sustain the activities of established ethno-separatist groups as well as generate a new breed of highly militant religious organizations.[44]

The emergence of primordial identity in South-East Asia is hardly surprising given its heterogeneity: the region is home to all the world's major belief systems and at least 32 separate ethno-linguistic groups.[45] Many of these groups have been arbitrarily "lumped" together in states that were originally created purely on the basis of Western imperial designs – the sanctity of whose borders has since been vigorously upheld by successive post-colonial South-East Asian governments. The result has been the creation of a number of post-colonial state structures throughout South-East Asia that are "weak" in the sense that they contain significant sectors of population who do not identify strongly either with their ruling groups or with territorial boundaries (for example, Indonesia, the Philippines, and Myanmar).[46]

Whereas the momentum of modernization has managed to deflect internal ethnic and religious tensions in a number of places such as Singapore, Malaysia, central Indonesia (at least until mid-1997), and central–northern Thailand, in others it has served merely to exacerbate regional alienation by undermining traditional authority and socio-economic structures. This is especially true in outlying, remote areas that have suffered from administrative and economic neglect as a result of the introduction of development programmes whose prime purpose has been to further the interests and preferences of the dominant community. For these regions – which include southern Thailand, the southern Philippines, and the outer wings of the Indonesian archipelago – the unifying ethos of secular modernization has not only acted as a major stimulant for the basis of a new sense of communal identity (ethnic, religious, or both). It has also worked to reinforce the separatist "credentials" and legitimacy of established local rebel groupings. The tendency of South-East Asian élites periodically to crack down on outbursts of communal identity with draconian internal counter-measures has further heightened this sense of regional alienation.[47]

In at least three areas – Aceh (located on the northern tip of Sumatra in Indonesia), Pattani (southern Thailand), and Mindanao (southern Philippines) – the resurgence of regional primordial identity has been additionally exacerbated by the political influence of Islam. Feeding off the contemporary force of fundamentalist extremism, communal empathies in these three regions have not only been heightened, but also been increasingly militarized – spawning violent and, at times, highly destructive campaigns of terror and internal unrest. Perhaps the most vivid example of this is in Mindanao, where ongoing Moro separatist activity is increasingly being channelled through extremist Islamic organizations such as the Moro Islamic Liberation Front and the Abu Sayyaf Group.[48]

Compounding the threat posed by these "commercial" and "spiritual" GAP influences are the two instrumental variables of weapons proliferation and globalization – both of which, again, find particular expression in the South-East Asian subregion. There is no shortage of combat weapons (both basic and more advanced) in South-East Asia, thanks, largely, to the considerable stocks left over from the Cold War conflicts in Cambodia and Afghanistan. Added to these are the supplies that are being smuggled out of the former USSR and Eastern Europe by crime syndicates utilizing Russian, Chinese, Afghan, and Pakistani munition "pipelines."[49]

The extent of these various weapons sources should not be underestimated. In Cambodia, for example, the United Nations Transitional Authority seized more than 300,000 arms and in excess of 80 million rounds of ammunition between 1991 and 1993. This is believed to be only a fraction of the total amount of weaponry disseminated to the country during the 1980s (largely by China, the United States, and Thailand) to facilitate local resistance against the Vietnamese-backed (and Soviet-supported) Cambodian government.[50] Afghanistan provides an even more telling case in point. Indeed, it is believed that by 1989 enough weapons had been transferred to the country (by either the United States or the USSR) that every able-bodied male could be armed in one way or another. Of perhaps greatest concern is the fact that, of the 900 American Stinger missiles supplied to the Afghan militia during the civil war, the fate of as many as 560 is still not known.[51]

The type of weaponry currently being diffused throughout South-East Asia is truly extensive. It includes, *inter alia*, M16 and AK47 assault rifles; light-weight grenade launchers; squirt-less flame throwers; surface-to-air missiles; portable anti-tank weapons; light and heavy machine guns; rocket-propelled grenades; and landmines and other demolition material.[52] The lethality of these various munitions is phenomenal and needs to be emphasized to illustrate the type of firepower to which GAP actors in South-East Asia now have access.

Finally, South-East Asia has also emerged as a major transportation, communications, and financial hub, with an intense network that connects the region not only locally but also internationally with the major centres of Europe, the wider Asia-Pacific, the South Pacific, and North America. More than one-third of the world's merchant fleet currently use sea lanes of communication that pass through South-East Asia, making the subregion one of the busiest and most important maritime trading corridors in the world.[53] Rapid economic growth has contributed to the regional development of prominent global banking systems, free-wheeling stock exchanges, and money markets that are now fully integrated with established financial centres such as London, Tokyo, and New York. Finally, major domestic and international airports at Manila, Singapore, Bangkok, Hong Kong, Kuala Lumpur, and Jakarta have ensured that, in terms of global and regional access, South-East Asia is as open and easily traversed as any area in the world.

All of this has helped with the regional and international diffusion of GAP influences, allowing threats such as terrorism, organized crime, piracy, and disease both to emanate from and to migrate to South-East Asia. We have, as a result, witnessed Middle Eastern terrorists planning and carrying out operations in the Philippines and Thailand; Burmese drug cartels "bouncing" narco-dollars between European, American, and Asian financial institutions markets, leaving a virtually untraceable money trail in the process; the growth of a vibrant South-East Asian underground economy run by a variety of Russian, Japanese, and Chinese organized crime gangs; pirates attacking British, Dutch, Greek, and Cypriot registered merchant vessels anywhere from Indonesia to Hainan; and HIV being carried from the tourist sex markets of Bangkok, Chiang Mai, and Manila to countries as far away as the United States, Australia, and Germany.

The future

States, at least in the realist world, have tended to categorize security according to internal and external spheres, shying away from cooperation lest future enemies be strengthened.[54] Such an approach, however, is completely at odds with the "realities" of security in the contemporary world. If the challenges of today are to be effectively dealt with, governments must commit themselves to innovative reform and action at both the national and international levels.

Nationally, states must be prepared to initiate far-reaching interagency operations and countermeasures that cross military, health, nongovernmental, and civilian law enforcement jurisdictions. Internationally, more attention needs to be devoted to establishing regulatory inter-state forums that are able to coordinate and integrate multilateral responses in a fully comprehensive manner. Contemporary GAP issues blur and distort the traditional distinctions between internal/external and military/non-military dimensions of security. It is therefore imperative that, in responding to these challenges, states are able to mobilize strategies and tools that are similarly complex and multidimensional in nature.

In South-East Asia, both national and international preparedness against GAP remains inadequate. Inter-agency cooperation has been confounded by the severe bureaucratic competition that afflicts many of the region's security and public management establishments. Exacerbating the situation has been the direct involvement of corrupt governmental officials and elements of the military in GAP activities, which has, in certain cases, heightened tolerance of personal clientelism at the expense of law and social justice. The inevitable consequence of these operational disequilibria has been the manifestation of policy decisions that are erratic, discontinuous, and generally characterized by a pervasive quality of inertia.[55]

In terms of international cooperation, effectiveness has been undermined by the implementation of ad hoc, piecemeal responses that have lacked any real degree of proactive, long-term planning. This relatively hesitant acceptance of a more integrated and formalized approach to security planning stems from the familiarity that South-East Asian states feel towards bilateral cooperation and the process of gradually strengthening modalities of coordination through minimalist inter-governmental coordination as and when necessary.[56]

Dealing with these shortcomings will require political determination and the active input of all states in the region. The crucial question, thus, revolves around whether South-East Asian security and political leaderships are prepared to adapt to the demands and challenges of their post–Cold War regional security environment. It is still too early for a definitive answer to be given to this central question. It is clear, however, that in the absence of a firm commitment to develop more effective means to deal with GAP influences history is likely to record the end of the Cold War as an episode that ushered in a Pacific century that turned out to be far from peaceful.

Notes

1. A detailed survey of these proposed changes was provided by the *World Economic Outlook* (Washington DC: IMF, 1991); see especially pp. 26–27.
2. See, for instance, "Terrorism and the Warfare of the Weak," *The Guardian*, 27 October 1993.
3. Richard Latter, *Terrorism in the 1990s*, Wilton Park Papers no. 44 (London: HMSO, 1991), p. 2.
4. See David Abshire, "US Foreign Policy in the Post–Cold War Era: The Need for an Agile Strategy," *Washington Quarterly* 19, no. 2 (Spring 1996), pp. 42–44: Simon Dalby, "Security, Intelligence, the National Interest and the Global Environment," *Intelligence and National Security* 10, no. 4 (October 1995), p. 186; and Gwyn Prins, "Politics and the Environment," *International Affairs* 66, no. 4 (October 1990), pp. 711–730.
5. Quoted in John Ciccarelli, "Preface: Instruments of Darkness: Crime and Australian National Security," in John Ciccarelli, ed., *Transnational Crime: A New Security Threat?* (Canberra: ADSC, 1996), p. xi.

6. Dalby, "Security, Intelligence, the National Interest and the Global Environment," p. 186.
7. See, for instance, Steven Metz, "Insurgency after the Cold War," *Small Wars and Insurgencies* 5, no. 1 (Spring 1994), pp. 73–74.
8. Amitav Acharya, "A New Regional Order in South-east Asia: ASEAN in the Post–Cold War Era," *Adelphi Paper* 279 (1993), p. 20.
9. See, for instance, "ASEAN Way Prevails in Tea Party's Polite Talk," *The Australian*, 30 July 1998, p. 6.
10. This conceptualization is based on a paradigm first developed by Jim Holden-Rhodes and Peter Lupsha in 1992. See Jim Holden-Rhodes and Peter Lupsha, "Gray Area Phenomena: New Threats and Policy Dilemmas," *Criminal Justice International* 9, no. 1 (January/February 1993), pp. 11–17, and "Horsemen of the Apocalypse: Gray Area Phenomena and the New World Disorder," *Low Intensity Conflict and Law Enforcement* 2, no. 2 (Autumn 1993), pp. 212–226.
11. Peter Chalk, *Grey Area Phenomena in Southeast Asia: Piracy, Drug Trafficking and Political Terrorism* (Canberra: Strategic and Defence Studies Centre, Australian National University, 1997), p. 5.
12. Holden-Rhodes and Lupsha, "Gray Area Phenomena," p. 12.
13. Richard Matthew and George Shambaugh, "Sex, Drugs, and Heavy Metal: Transnational Threats and National Vulnerabilities," *Security Dialogue* 29, no. 2 (June 1998), p. 165.
14. Ibid., 15; Holden-Rhodes and Lupsha, "Horsemen of the Apocalypse," pp. 219–220.
15. Metz, "Insurgency after the Cold War," pp. 71–72. See also Andrew Scott, *The Dynamics of Interdependence* (Chapel Hill: University of North Carolina Press, 1982); and Ronald Dore, "Unity and Diversity in Contemporary World Culture," in Hedley Bull and Adam Watson, eds., *The Expansion of International Society* (Oxford: Clarendon Press, 1984), pp. 407–424.
16. It was Ted Gurr who first developed the idea that relative deprivation could serve as a powerful motivating influence for aggression. For further details see Ted Gurr, *Why Men Rebel* (Princeton, NJ: Princeton University Press, 1970).
17. Metz, "Insurgency after the Cold War," p. 70.
18. Chalk, *Grey Area Phenomena in Southeast Asia*, p. 7.
19. Metz, "Insurgency after the Cold War," pp. 66–71; Holden-Rhodes and Lupsha, "Horsemen of the Apocalypse," pp. 217–218.
20. Peter Chalk, *West European Terrorism and Counter-Terrorism: The Evolving Dynamic* (London: Macmillan, 1996), p. 65; Metz, "Insurgency after the Cold War," p. 70.
21. Whereas civic conceptions of the nation regard it as a community of shared culture, common laws, and territorial citizenship, ethno-nationalism conceives the nation as a vernacular community of genealogical descent. See Anthony Smith, "The Ethnic Sources of Nationalism," *Survival* 35, no. 1 (Spring 1993), p. 55.
22. See, for instance, David Welsh, "Domestic Politics and Ethnic Conflict," *Survival* 35, no. 1 (Spring 1993), pp. 63–80; Smith, "The Ethnic Sources of Nationalism," pp. 48–62; Ted Gurr, "Peoples against States: Ethnopolitical Conflict and the Changing World System," *International Studies Quarterly* 38, no. 3 (September 1994), pp. 347–377; Ted Gurr, "Communal Conflict and Global Security," *Current History* 94, no. 592 (May 1995), pp. 212–217; Donald Horowitz, "Ethnic and Nationalist Conflict," in M. Klare and D. Thomas, eds., *World Security. Challenges for a New Century* (New York: St. Martin's Press, 1994), pp. 175–187; and Donald Horowitz, *Ethnic Groups in Conflict* (Berkeley, CA: University of California Press, 1985).
23. Chalk, *West European Terrorism and Counter-Terrorism*, p. 1. See also Martin van Creveld, *The Transformation of War* (New York: Free Press, 1991), pp. 192–193; and Holden-Rhodes and Lupsha, "Gray Area Phenomena," p. 12.

24. Aaron Karp, "The Arms Trade Revolution: The Major Impact of Small Arms," in Brad Roberts, ed., *Weapons Proliferation in the 1990s* (Cambridge, MA: MIT Press, 1995), pp. 64–65. See also Aaron Karp, *Arming Ethnic Conflict* (Lanham, MD: United Nations University Press, 1996).

25. War by proxy is defined by the US Army as "the use of military capabilities up to, but not including, sustained combat between regular [national] forces." See TRADOC pamphlet, *US Operational Concept for Low Intensity Conflict* (Department of the Army, Ft. Monroe, Virginia, No. 524–44), p. 2.

26. See Steve Weber, "Realism, Detente and Nuclear Weapons," *International Organization* 44, no. 1 (Summer 1990), pp. 55–82.

27. Chalk, *West European Terrorism and Counter-Terrorism*, pp. 39–41.

28. "The Covert Arms Trade," *The Economist*, 12 February 1974, pp. 19–21.

29. Metz, "Insurgency after the Cold War," p. 67. See also Holden-Rhodes and Lupsha, "Horsemen of the Apocalypse," p. 218.

30. Kal Holsti, *International Politics* (Englewood Cliffs, NJ: Prentice-Hall, 1995), p. 71.

31. Mark Zacher has done some detailed and useful work on the growth in international interdependence in recent years. For a particularly good source of statistical information, see "The Decaying Pillars of the Westphalian Temple: Implications for International Order and Governance," in James Rosenau and Ernst-Otto Czempeil, eds., *Governance without Government* (Cambridge: Cambridge University Press, 1992), pp. 58–101.

32. Holden-Rhodes and Lupsha, "Gray Area Phenomena," p. 13.

33. Official US trade statistics compared with figures from market surveys conducted by the Federal Reserve Bank of New York, the Bank of Japan, and the Bank of England. Cited in International Monetary Fund, "International Capital Markets: Part I. Exchange Rate Movements and International Capital Flows," *World Economic and Financial Surveys* (April 1993), p. 4. See also Holden-Rhodes and Lupsha, "Horsemen of the Apocalypse," p. 217; Allen Meyerson, "Currency Markets Resisting Powers of Central Banks," *New York Times*, 25 September 1992; and "A Survey of International Financial Markets," *The Economist*, 21 July 1990, pp. 50–78.

34. Holden-Rhodes and Lupsha, "Horsemen of the Apocalypse," p. 217; Matthew and Shambaugh, "Sex, Drugs, and Heavy Metal," pp. 163–166.

35. Cherif Bassiouni, "Effective National and International Action against Organised Crime and Terrorist Criminal Activities," *Emory International Law Review* 4 , no. 1 (Spring 1990), p. 36.

36. See Acharya, "A New Regional Order in South-east Asia," pp. 17–30; and N. Ganesan, "Rethinking ASEAN as a Security Community in Southeast Asia," *Asian Affairs* 21, no. 4 (Winter 1995), pp. 217–221.

37. See, for instance, Clark Neher, *Southeast Asia in the New International Era* (Boulder, CO: Westview Press, 1994), pp. 16–18.

38. Asian Development Bank, *Ranking of Environmental Issues by Asian Policy Makers* (Harvard: Harvard Institute for International Development, 1996). The perceived importance of water pollution and freshwater depletion was indexed at 16 on a scale of 0–20. This compares with 9 for air pollution and deforestation; 8 for solid waste; 7 for soil erosion; 6 for biodiversity loss; and 3 for wildlife loss, fish depletion, desertification, and climate change.

39. "Cleaning up in Asia," *The Australian*, 19 May 1997; "Factors That Contribute to River Pollution," *New Straits Times*, 13 October 1997.

40. Chalk, *Grey Area Phenomena in Southeast Asia*, p. 49.

41. See Peter Chalk, "Contemporary Maritime Piracy in Southeast Asia," *Studies in Conflict and Terrorism* 21, no. 1 (January–March 1998), p. 94.

42. Jon Vagg, "Rough Seas? Contemporary Piracy in South-East Asia," *British Journal of Criminology* 35, no. 1 (Winter 1995), pp. 76–77.

43. See, for instance, Chalk, "Contemporary Maritime Piracy in Southeast Asia," p. 89; Bertil Lintner, "The Drug Trade in Southeast Asia," *Jane's Intelligence Review Special Report No 5* (April 1995); Carl Grundy-Warr, Rita King, and Gary Risser, "Cross-Border Migration, Trafficking and the Sex Industry: Thailand and Its Neighbours," *Boundary and Security Bulletin* 4, no. 1 (September 1996), pp. 86–97; and "March of the Triad Army," *The Australian*, 26 June 1997.

44. See, for instance, Peter Chalk, "Political Terrorism in South-East Asia," *Terrorism and Political Violence* 10, no. 2 (Summer 1998), pp. 118–134.

45. Acharya, "A New Regional Order in South-east Asia," p. 19.

46. Ibid., pp. 19–20. For an excellent general account of the consequences of the "weak" post-colonial state structures for internal stability, see Kal Holsti, *War, the State and the State of War* (Cambridge: Cambridge University Press, 1996).

47. Ibid., p. 20. See also Michael Leifer, *Dilemmas of Statehood in Southeast Asia* (Singapore: Asia Pacific Press, 1972), p. 37; and David Brown, "From Peripheral Communities to Ethnic Nations: Separatism in Southeast Asia," *Pacific Affairs* 61, no. 1 (Spring 1988), pp. 51–77.

48. See, for instance, Peter Chalk, "The Davao Consensus: A Panacea for the Muslim Insurgency in Mindanao?" *Terrorism and Political Violence* 9, no. 2 (1997), pp. 79–98; and Peter Chalk, "The Muslim Insurgency in the Southern Philippines," report prepared for the Australia/Israel Jewish Affairs Committee, Melbourne, 1999.

49. For two good accounts of weapons trafficking out of the former USSR and Eastern Europe, see Matti Joutsen, "Organised Crime in Eastern Europe," *Criminal Justice International* 9, no. 2 (March/April 1993), pp. 11–17; and Joseph Serio, "Organised Crime in the Former Soviet Union: Only the Name Is New," *Criminal Justice International* 9, no. 4 (July/August 1993), pp. 11–17.

50. See Mats Berdal, "Disarmament and Demobilisation after Civil Wars," *Adelphi Paper* 303 (1996), pp. 18–20; and Tara Kartha, "The Proliferation and Smuggling of Light Weapons within the Region," paper presented before the Council for Security Cooperation in the Asia Pacific (CSCAP) Working Group on Transnational Crime, Manila, May 1998, pp. 6–7.

51. Prashant Dikshit, "Proliferation of Small Arms and Minor Weapons," *Strategic Analysis* 17, no. 2 (May 1994), pp. 195–196; Prashant Dikshit, "Technology: Fillip to Terrorism and Light Arms Proliferation," *Strategic Analysis* 18, no. 5 (August 1995), p. 629; and Chris Smith, "The International Trade in Small Arms," *Jane's Intelligence Review* 7, no. 9 (1995), pp. 427–428. According to Dikshit, Stinger surface-to-air missiles are capable of attaining speeds up to 2,600 km/hour, making them lethal to all aircraft up to an altitude of 3.5 km. During the Afghan conflict, 340 Stingers were fired at Soviet aircraft, achieving a kill rate of 79 per cent.

52. See, for instance, Lintner, "The Drug Trade in Southeast Asia," p. 5; and Dikshit, "Technology," p. 630.

53. John Noer, "Southeast Asian Chokepoints," *Strategic Forum* 98 (December 1996), p. 1.

54. Matthew and Shambaugh, "Sex, Drugs, and Heavy Metal," p. 165.

55. Chalk, *Grey Area Phenomena in Southeast Asia*, p. 85.

56. Ibid., pp. 89–90.

9

Refugees and forced migration as a security problem

William Maley

With the outbreak of the war in the Balkans in 1999, the world was transfixed by the spectacle of Kosovar refugees fleeing in their hundreds of thousands from an onslaught unleashed against them by paramilitaries under the control of Yugoslav President Slobodan Milosevic. Apart from the awesome humanitarian challenge that this posed to agencies committed to relieving the sufferings of the refugees, these obviously unexpected population movements created major concerns for the neighbouring states of Albania and Macedonia – suddenly burdened by inflows with which they were poorly equipped to cope – as well as for the democratically run Montenegrin republic of the Yugoslav Federation, which also received its share of traumatized Kosovars. The crisis of displacement of course highlighted yet again the perils of going to war without appropriate planning for contingencies which the use of force could easily generate. But, in a wider sense, it also pointed to the ways in which refugee flows and forced migration can impinge dramatically upon the security of states and territorial units, as well as reflect the breakdown of "security" in any meaningful sense for the wretched victims themselves. Specifically, it showed that refugee movements are linked to broader political, social, and military developments; that refugees can move fast, and in vast numbers; and that refugee movements may be difficult to manage, since each refugee is a unique individual with distinct wants, interests, and hopes.

The aim of this chapter is to explore these themes in more detail. It is divided into four sections. In the first, I discuss the ways in which refugees can be defined, paying particular attention to the problems of those who may fall outside narrow or legalistic definitions. In the second, I examine various reasons why the positions and circumstances of refugees should be of concern to both citizens and governments. In the third, I examine in turn the evolution of mechanisms for what is (somewhat unfortunately) termed "burden-sharing" in respect of refugees; the ongoing problem of responding appropriately to particular types of refugee flow; some of the forms of collective response that are available, and some of their strengths and weaknesses. In the final section, I take up the specific question of what steps might be taken to prevent the emergence of refugee problems, and argue that, rather than seeking to eliminate the problem of refugees by excluding them physically from our shores, we need to confront the repressive dispositions of refugee-creating states by promoting processes of liberal and democratic transformation.

What is a "refugee"?

The definition of "refugee" is important because of the growing understanding that there are certain individuals who are denied the protection that the state should provide to its citizens, and who are therefore in need of a different form of protection. Those who are denied proper protection but remain *in situ* can draw for protection on the broad corpus of rules known as human rights law. For those who have been displaced, however, a different and additional set of rules and principles may come into play, namely those that we associate with international refugee law.

The starting point in understanding the core meaning of refugee is the definition offered in Article 1A(2) of the 1951 Convention Relating to the Status of Refugees. This provides that the term "refugee" shall apply to any person who, "owing to well-founded fear of being persecuted for reasons of race, religion, nationality, membership of a particular social group or political opinion, is outside the country of his nationality and is unable or, owing to such fear, is unwilling to avail himself of the protection of that country; or who, not having a nationality and being outside the country of his former habitual residence ... is unable or, owing to such fear, is unwilling to return to it." Further provisions address the position of those who possess dual nationality, the circumstances in which individuals cease to be refugees, and the (limited) circumstances in which the Convention will not apply to those who might otherwise appear to be covered. Although the matter is not beyond debate, the better view is that the definition is *constitutive* – that is, a person becomes a refugee when the criteria it sets out are met in fact; being a refugee under international law is not dependent upon some State Party to the Convention determining that a claimant to refugee status is indeed a refugee.

There are, however, a number of limitations in this definition that it is important to highlight.[1] First, it applies only to those who have at some point crossed an international frontier, although they need not have been *driven* across a frontier; the phenomenon of the refugee *sur place*, who after departing without difficulty from his or her country of nationality is then unable to return because of changed circumstances at home, is well known. Secondly, it covers only those with a well-founded fear of being *persecuted*. The Convention itself does not define persecution, but some states have adopted the view that persecution arises only when individuals are in some sense *singled out*; on this view, if a state is repressive but in a way that deprives all persons of freedom in equal measure, "persecution" is not present.[2] Others have taken the view that only the state can persecute, with the implication that those fleeing the predations of armed militias in disrupted states have no basis for claiming refugee status. Thirdly, it is concerned only with persecution *on certain grounds*; persecution on grounds other than those enumerated in the Convention offers no basis for protection.

As a result of these three limitations, there are important groups whom the everyday usage of the word "refugee" would capture who are nevertheless not embraced by this technical legal definition, and who as a consequence do not enjoy the legal protections of the 1951 Convention. First, the Convention definition does not embrace internally displaced persons, even though in the modern world they are both numerically significant and often in circumstances of extreme desperation.[3] Take as an example those Kosovars displaced by persecution at the hands of Milosevic's militias. Those who have entered Albania or Macedonia are legally in a quite different situation from those who have fled to Montenegro, for the latter remain on the territory of Yugoslavia, although in a unit of the Yugoslav Federation that has in effect repudiated the extreme nationalism of Belgrade and sought to offer the displaced Kosovars some protection. Secondly, the Convention definition does not embrace those who are victims simply of economic penury, natural disaster, or environmental degradation – although loose talk about "economic refugees," a term that owes its origins to the Nazis' description of those who fled 1930s' Germany as *Wirtschaftsemigranten*,[4] should not disguise the fact that one can both desire a better life economically and at the same time be the victim of persecution on one of the grounds set out in the 1951 Convention.

It is because of these lacunae that serious efforts have been made by scholars (if not by policy-makers, for whom the 1951 Convention definition of refugee represents a kind of lowest common denominator) to put forward definitions of refugee that more closely mirror the scope of ordinary language. Zolberg, Suhrke, and Aguayo define refugees as "persons whose presence abroad is attributable to a well-founded fear of violence, as might be established by impartial experts with adequate information."[5] Andrew Shacknove has suggested that a refugee is a person deprived of basic rights, with no recourse to his or her home government, and with access to international assistance.[6] Neither of these definitions is unproblematical, given the degree of conceptual stretching that on occasion has been associated with the notion of "violence" and the scope for debate over the precise substance of "basic rights,"[7] but at least they carry us beyond some of the constrictions that arise if one limits one's concern solely to those persons whom the 1951 Convention definition would capture.

Rationales for concern

Why should we worry about refugees? For citizens of consolidated liberal democracies, the risk that *they* will be forced to flee their homes as a result of violence or human rights violations is negligible. Refugees seem to inhabit another world altogether, one with which it is difficult for the more fortunate citizens in developed countries to identify. However, in my view there are powerful reasons – legal, moral, and political – why we should take note of the plight of refugees.

From a purely legal point of view, many states have accepted responsibilities towards refugees by signing and ratifying the 1951 Convention. The key obligation that the Convention imposes, in Article 33.1, is that of *non-refoulement*, namely that no contracting state "shall expel or return ('refouler') a refugee in any manner whatsoever to the frontiers of territories where his life or freedom would be threatened on account of his race, religion, nationality, membership of a particular social group or political opinion." A state that fails to meet its obligations under the Convention runs the risk of blemishing its reputation as a good international citizen, and of inviting other states to ignore treaties that *they* find burdensome, something that might not be at all in the first state's interest.

Beyond this legal consideration is a range of moral reasons why the plight of refugees should be of concern. To explore these in detail would take us far beyond the scope of this chapter, but a number of general points stand out, which will carry different weights in the eyes of different observers. First, responsibilities to refugees can be grounded in a responsibility to *protect the vulnerable* when the model of "assigned responsibility" embodied in a system of states with special duties to their citizens has broken down – as is the case when people are forced to flee their homeland or are denied security within its borders.[8] It is vulnerability that is at the core of the refugee experience, and whereas being a refugee is fortunately beyond the worst nightmares of most residents of free countries, being vulnerable is not.[9] Secondly, responsibilities to refugees can be defended on the basis of the "humanitarian principle," that there is "a duty incumbent upon each and every individual to assist those in great distress or suffering when the costs of doing so are low."[10] According to such arguments, we sacrifice our own humanity when we tolerate practices that affront the very notion of humanity. Thirdly, from the very nature of a free polity, one can build a *prima facie* case for duties towards those who flee from a society in which freedom is denied: a "free" country that seeks to return such persons compromises the integrity of its commitment to freedom as a basic good. Fourthly, and somewhat more specifically, one may be driven by special duties of a communitarian character to assist refugees who share a common heritage and history, which explains the relative hospitality with which groups as diverse as Afghan Muslims and Kosovar Albanians have been received even when entering a neighbouring state in large numbers. It is also worth noting that it is not simply individuals who bear duties towards refugees; as Stanley Hoffmann has argued, "it remains the duty of each country to open its own borders as widely as possible, without looking for excuses or waiting for others to act."[11]

That said, states are much less likely to be swayed by ethical arguments of this sort, which focus on *human* security, than by arguments of interest. And it is undeniable that considerations of interest have led to a wide range of measures in recent years by which states have sought to exclude potential asylum seekers from their territory, notably in Europe through the operation of the Schengen Agreement and the Dublin Convention. In some cases, the implementation of such measures has been justified by reference to the need to preserve an effective system of asylum for those with a well-founded fear of persecution. In others, however, the rhetoric that surrounds the removal of undocumented entrants is cast very much in terms of the security "threat" posed by increased "trafficking" in human beings and uncontrolled migration. In a country such as Australia, this seems bizarre when one contemplates the oceanic protection enjoyed by an island continent, and the minute numbers of the undocumented arrivals in Australia when compared with the hundreds of thousands of persons accommodated in a matter of weeks by states such as Albania or Macedonia.

However, there are more legitimate worries of a political and strategic kind that may rightly preoccupy liberal governments. First, refugee movements may be extremely costly to countries of first asylum. It is often overlooked that the countries to which the largest refugee movements occur are typically far from prosperous, and can provide bearable living conditions only with the greatest difficulty, or at the expense of programmes to assist their own citizens. Secondly, refugee flows may be politically destabilizing to host countries, and contribute to the disintegration of either fragile domestic political structures or patterns of social consensus. This is especially the case if they cause a delicate ethnic balance to shift in a divided society and, should this occur, regional stability may be sorely tested. In this case, refugee movements can pose a genuine, as opposed to a spurious, security problem.[12]

The response to the political and strategic problems that refugees may pose should not, however, be to cast forced migrants into an abyss or to block their movement to countries in which they will be safe. It should rather be to explore measures to prevent catastrophic refugee flows in the first place by eliminating the conditions that drive people to flight, and to ensure that the responsibility for those who have no option but flight is appropriately shared and efficiently managed through multilateral structures. It is to these issues that I now turn, addressing first the history of multilateral action, then some of the contemporary challenges it faces, and finally the types of long-term pre-emptive steps that deserve attention.

A collective response: Precedents and problems

Refugee movements of the dimensions witnessed in the twentieth century have cried out for multilateral responses rather than discrete actions by individual states. Refugee movements can have extensive ramifications for the well-being of entire regions, by exhausting the resources of those bodies initially charged with managing a refugee flow, which are then obliged to call on others for assistance if a humanitarian catastrophe is to be avoided. This happened in 1921, when the President of the International Committee of the Red Cross, Gustav Ador, appealed for action through the League of Nations to address the overwhelming burden of Russian refugees.[13] Since then, a range of international institutions have played roles in managing refugee crises, discharging functions as diverse as offering protection, providing sustenance, and facilitating resettlement or repatriation.

The League of Nations responded to Ador's request by appointing the renowned explorer Dr. Fridtjof Nansen as High Commissioner for Russian Refugees. He held office from 1921 until his death in 1930, and his great creation was the institution of the "Nansen Passport," an identity document for displaced Russians (subsequently extended to a number of other groups) which greatly eased the difficulties faced by individual refugees in travelling and seeking employment. In 1931, the League of Nations established the Nansen International Office for Refugees, which was required to terminate its operations by the end of 1938 and charged with undertaking humanitarian relief operations. Legal and political protection of refugees, on the other hand, was transferred to the League Secretariat, which found the task acutely embarrassing once refugees began to flee from Nazi Germany, at that time a powerful League member. The result was the establishment of the High Commission for Refugees Coming from Germany, which was not directly funded by the League. The High Commissioner, James G. McDonald, served from October 1933 to December 1935, and his resignation letter powerfully denounced the policies of the German government.[14] However, although the League somewhat expanded the authority of his successor as High Commissioner for Refugees from Germany, it appointed to the position a League official, Sir Neill Malcolm, who made it clear that he had no intention of challenging Berlin's policies. With the expiry of the Nansen Office approaching, the League Assembly decided on 30 September 1938 – at a meeting ironically overshadowed by the notorious Munich agreement on the same day, which ratified the dismemberment of Czechoslovakia – to replace the Nansen Office and the office of High Commissioner for Refugees from Germany with a new office of High Commissioner for Refugees under the Protection of the League of Nations. This position was filled from 1 January 1939 by Sir Herbert Emerson.

More important than these changes, however, was a parallel development arising from the July 1938 Evian Conference, which had been called at the initiative of President Franklin Roosevelt to address the problems of German (and, since the *Anschluss* of February 1938, Austrian) refugees. This was the creation of a permanent Intergovernmental Committee on Refugees (IGCR), directed first by George Rublee and then from February 1939 by Sir Herbert Emerson jointly with his League responsibilities. The IGCR, in contrast to the League, enjoyed the support of the United States, and was notable for being directed to the devising of long-range programmes of assistance, and from 1943 for combining protection, support, and resettlement functions. The outbreak of World War II naturally limited quite severely the ability of the IGCR to realize its objectives, but as a model for future frameworks for assistance it was of considerable significance.

In November 1943, the United Nations Relief and Rehabilitation Administration (UNRRA) was established to provide relief services to augment the military activities of the Allies following the anticipated invasion of Europe. However, its approach to its task was not well received by the United States (its main source of funds), which saw it as overly accommodating to Soviet political objectives.[15] The result was the establishment of the International Refugee Organization (IRO). The Preparatory Commission of the IRO assumed the functions of both UNRRA and the IGCR from 1 July 1947. The IRO itself formally came into existence on 20 August 1948 and lasted until it went into liquidation on 1 March 1952.[16] The IRO was much the most elaborate agency thitherto devised to address refugee problems, and developed elaborate programmes dealing with protection, sustenance, and resettlement. It resettled 1,038,750 refugees between July 1947 and December 1951, with the principal countries of resettlement being the United States (31.7 per cent), Australia (17.5 per cent), Israel (12.7 per cent), and Canada (11.9 per cent).[17]

Yet if UNRRA suffered from US hostility, then so equally did the IRO from Soviet hostility. The USSR (and other states of the Soviet bloc) declined to join. Furthermore, its costs came to be seen as burdensome by the United States, which supplied the not inconsiderable sum of US$237,116,355 to the organization, or 59.5 per cent of the total contributions received during the body's operational life.[18] With US aid priorities shifting to the European Recovery Programme, and Palestinian refugees supported by a distinct body (the United Nations Relief and Works Agency for Palestine Refugees in the Near East), a smaller agency to deal with *protection* of refugees seemed the most important priority. The result was the establishment by the UN General Assembly of the Office of the United Nations High Commissioner for Refugees, with a three-year mandate from 1 January 1951. With the cessation of the IRO's *resettlement* operations, these tasks were taken on board from 1 February 1952 by the Provisional Intergovernmental Committee for the Movement of Migrants from Europe. It is an indicator of the intractability of refugee problems that both these bodies remain key actors in the management of protection and resettlement, the former universally known as UNHCR, and the latter now a fully fledged independent agency, the International Organization for Migration, both based in Geneva.

Since 1950, there have been eight High Commissioners: Gerrit van Heuven Goedhart (1950–1956); Auguste Lindt (1956–1960); Felix Schnyder (1960–1965); Sadruddin Aga Khan (1965–1977); Poul Hartling (1978–1985); Jean-Pierre Hocké (1986–1989); Thorvald Stoltenberg (1990); and Sadako Ogata (since 1991). Their names are worth recording, for UNHCR is peculiarly an agency whose energy and morale are shaped from the top, and some High Commissioners have been notably more successful than others.[19] Although protection of refugees is an integral part of UNHCR's mandate, it should never be overlooked that "protection of refugees is ultimately a matter of host-country policy."[20] UNHCR's vulnerability arises from the fact that its operations are funded by voluntary as opposed to assessed contributions, and it may take a courageous High Commissioner to press the cause of protection if important donors have no interest in seeing the protection mandate effectively discharged in a particular case. Curiously enough, the best guarantor of UNHCR's ability to discharge its protection function may well be its increasing use to provide emergency assistance not only to refugees, but to war victims *in situ*; UNHCR has been widely praised for its performance in the former Yugoslavia, not least because its officers in the field proved in general to be far more sensitive to the moral dilemmas faced by the international community than did some other UN officials. As one critical observer put it, "the UNHCR staffers told the truth unswervingly."[21] Since UNHCR, like all the international organizations created to address refugee crises, is to a considerable extent a creature of the domestic and international politics of the states that created it and fund it, this was no small achievement.

This, then, is the architecture for the multilateral management of refugee crises. However, it is far from the case that the existence of such structures guarantees seamless efficiency once a refugee crisis emerges. Refugee crises are neither predictable nor smooth, and it is virtually impossible for agencies such as UNHCR to "preposition" scarce resources in anticipation of particular crises, since to do so would involve isolating those resources from refugee communities in other parts of the world whose needs might be immediate and pressing. The "protective mandate" of UNHCR now embraces far more people than simply those who are refugees within the 1951 Convention definition, and this confronts UNHCR with the need to balance different responsibilities at many different stages of its activities. In the short term, a great deal of UNHCR's work involves the provision of emergency assistance to those who have been displaced and for whom no durable solution is apparent. This can itself be a source of political difficulty, not only because of the resource commitments involved, but also because sprawling refugee camps can themselves be political resources,[22] especially if they are used as a safe haven for guerrillas and others who remain involved in the politics of the countries from which they have fled. Attacks in the course of "hot pursuit" against such guerrillas can put at risk both aid workers and the noncombatants whom they are seeking to protect. Beyond this, moral complexities arise from the very notion of haven for those whose activities may have triggered disaster in the first place, for example the Rwandan *génocidaires* who then buried themselves amongst refugees when the regime that nurtured their murderous activities was overthrown.[23]

In general, three types of durable solution to refugee crises have been contemplated: voluntary repatriation; settlement in the country of first asylum; and resettlement in a third country. In many cases voluntary repatriation is exactly what refugees themselves want. It is striking, for example, that the collapse of the communist regime in Afghanistan in April 1992 triggered the largest and fastest spontaneous repatriation of refugees in UNHCR's history: once the political circumstances that had prompted their flight changed, they stood ready to return. For others, however, repatriation is not a possibility; for example, large numbers of Palestinians displaced in 1948 were unable ever to return to their homes, and died in exile.[24]

If those for whom repatriation is impossible cannot integrate elsewhere – either in the country of first asylum or in some country of resettlement – their presence is likely to complicate greatly the relations between their host and the country from which they have fled. Other states with an interest in the stability of such regions may need to consider creative means of easing the burden on countries of first asylum. In some cases, this will involve financial assistance. This is certainly the case in East Timor, where the UNHCR targeted US$29 million in Major Special Programmes and Emergencies funding for 1999 – the largest amount for an Asia-Pacific locale and the fourth-largest allocation in its total budget after the Balkans, Africa's Great Lakes region, and the Commonwealth of Independent States. The expense was merited, however, as nearly 108,000 East Timorese refugees were repatriated between early October and late November 1999 by the UNHCR alone.[25]

In other cases, it may be necessary to devise processes for offering resettlement to those most in need. However, past such experiments have enjoyed only mixed success, even in a purely domestic context. One need only recall the Thai Army's effort during the early 1990s to resettle 1.2 million domestic farmers living on degraded forest land in Thailand's north-east so that loggers could convert the evacuated areas into corporate pulp plantations.[26] Refugee populations located across various borders in Indo-China and Thailand, moreover, place enormous burdens upon state resources and disrupt local ethnic and political equilibrium. Again, the Thai Army's recent efforts to repatriate Kurin refugees to Myanmar by force, where they would face inevitable persecution, readily come to mind. Indeed, a major challenge facing the UNHCR and other relief agencies is complicity in the strategies of parties to conflicts that have (purposely) created refugee populations.[27]

A recent and important example of a more successful resettlement programme was the so-called "Comprehensive Plan of Action" for dealing with the outflow of asylum seekers from Viet Nam to neighbouring states.[28] The initial response to large-scale Vietnamese outflows was not encouraging from a humanitarian point of view. In 1978–79, Malaysia "put its 'push-off' policy into full effect, rejecting more than 50,000 Vietnamese who attempted to land, and threatening to send away 70,000 more who were already in camps."[29] In June 1989, with a further outsurge under way, states meeting in Geneva agreed to a set of arrangements under which Vietnamese asylum seekers would receive temporary protection in countries in which they first arrived, with a commitment from traditional "resettlement" states, notably the United States, Canada, Australia, and France, to resettle those found to be refugees under the 1951 Convention. Although some questions about the quality of procedures were raised,[30] approximately 80,000 refugees were resettled under the Comprehensive Plan.

An alternative approach is to detach refugee *protection* from the idea of refugee *resettlement*. This approach, associated in particular with the writings of James Hathaway, has generated lively debate. Its proponents have rightly noted both that the 1951 Convention confers a right not of resettlement but of non-refoulement, and that, as the "refugee" programmes of developed countries may select for resettlement those whose resettlement prospects are greatest rather than those who are most in need of protection, the international refugee regime runs the risk of failing to provide protection to those who need it most. Temporary, if nonetheless finitely structured, protection is likely to be more attractive to states, and therefore capable of reinvigorating a wider protective regime.[31]

To critics of this approach, these proposals have two weaknesses. The first – perhaps a weakness not so much of the proposals themselves as of the climate in which they are being offered – is that governments may welcome the proposal to shift from permanent to temporary protection, but without offering temporary protection of the carefully designed type that Hathaway and his associates are proposing. Australia in 1998 saw a proposal for merely temporary protection figure prominently in the policy of the extremist One Nation party of Pauline Hanson,[32] and a similar policy had been used, albeit briefly, in the early 1990s.[33] The second, even more worrying, weakness is that a regime of merely temporary protection inevitably leaves refugees in a state of limbo, psychologically if not materially. The fear that can blight a refugee's life for years can be dispelled only by a more permanent resolution of the crisis of displacement to which the experience of flight gives rise.

Democratization as a solution

I would like to conclude by offering some observations on the *politics* of refugee movements. Whereas Western politicians are inclined to paint pictures of a world in which the citizens of developed countries are besieged by "economic refugees" squeezing "genuine refugees" out with their bogus claims, what is more striking is the *reluctance* of most people to quit their homes on merely economic grounds. Migration, forced or otherwise, is a complex phenomenon[34] but, given the socio-cultural bonds that link people to particular communities, the decision to exchange a high level of social certainty for a deeply uncertain future is not one to be taken lightly. This is why many countries with deeply impoverished segments in their populations are not necessarily major sources of "forced migration"; India comes immediately to mind.

It is therefore in the realm of politics that enduring solutions to refugee crises are to be found, and the expansion of the scope of liberal democracy is in my view the most promising political solution. Democratization is of course a complex process, not without its risks in transitional periods,[35] and hardly capable in short order of generating a democratic political culture, a consensually unified national élite, effective political institutions, or a high level of political institutionalization.[36] Nonetheless, liberal democracies seem broadly to be marked by three characteristics that make them more congenial for their residents and therefore less likely to put them to flight. First, whereas war between democratic and non-democratic states is relatively common, democracies in general do not go to war with each other.[37] Although NATO's armed crusade does not look to be a particularly effective way of democratizing Serbian politics, in the long run the replacement of the Milosevic regime with a democratic one is essential if the problem of population displacement in the Balkans is to be overcome. Secondly, democracies meet the basic needs of ordinary people better than do autocracies. There has not been a famine of note in any democracy for over half a century. Electoral politics in open societies militate against indifference to extreme suffering within a population. Thirdly, it is increasingly appreciated that democracies offer economic advantages that autocracies cannot. Although central planning was discredited by the Soviet experience, claims that an "authoritarian advantage" in the economic sphere outweighed the case for democracy continued to echo in different circles. Since the Asian financial crisis, those echoes have grown increasingly faint.[38] There are good reasons to believe that, in the long run, liberal democracy will expand its writ simply because of the comparative advantage it offers both élites and masses in the economic sphere.

The past 20 years have witnessed a very substantial increase in the scale and scope of forced migration, and as one observes with horror the misery of the victims it is all too easy to give in to despair. For that reason, it is all the more important to end on a note of hope. From the slaughter of the Western Front to the gas chambers of Auschwitz, from the carnage of Viet Nam and Afghanistan to the killing fields of Cambodia and Rwanda, the twentieth century was a dark one, and it ended under the shadow of Kosovo. Fortunately, we have it within our power to make the twenty-first century a brighter one, and many people of goodwill are committed to building a better future in which broader ethical concerns for human security are not subordinated to more traditional conceptions of national security. It is difficult to believe that their efforts will not win at least some rewards.

Notes

1. See Guy S. Goodwin-Gill, *The Refugee in International Law* (Oxford: Oxford University Press, 1996).
2. On this interpretation and its defects, see James Crawford and Patricia Hyndman, "Three Heresies in the Application of the Refugee Convention," *International Journal of Refugee Law* 1, no. 2 (April 1989), pp. 155–179.
3. See Janie Hampton, ed., *Internally Displaced People: A Global Survey* (London: Earthscan Publications, 1998).
4. Gil Loescher, *Beyond Charity: International Cooperation and the Global Refugee Crisis* (New York: Oxford University Press, 1993), p. 17.
5. Aristide R. Zolberg, Astri Suhrke, and Sergio Aguayo, *Escape from Violence: Conflict and the Refugee Crisis in the Developing World* (New York: Oxford University Press, 1989), p. 33.
6. Andrew Shacknove, "Who Is a Refugee?" *Ethics* 95, no. 2 (January 1985), pp. 274–284 at p. 282.
7. See William Maley, "Peace, Needs and Utopia," *Political Studies* 33, no. 4 (December 1985), pp. 578–591.
8. See Robert E. Goodin, "What Is So Special about Our Fellow Countrymen?" *Ethics* 98, no. 4 (July 1988), pp. 663–686.
9. On the need to protect the vulnerable, see Robert E. Goodin, *Protecting the Vulnerable* (Chicago: University of Chicago Press, 1985); Philip Pettit, *Republicanism: A Theory of Freedom and Government* (Oxford: Oxford University Press, 1997), p. 5.
10. Mathew J. Gibney, "Liberal Democratic States and Responsibilities to Refugees," *American Political Science Review* 93, no. 1 (March 1999), pp. 169–181 at p. 178.
11. Stanley Hoffmann, *Duties beyond Borders: On the Limits and Possibilities of Ethical International Politics* (Syracuse: Syracuse University Press, 1981), pp. 224–225.
12. See Myron Weiner, "Security, Stability and International Migration," *International Security* 17, no. 3 (Winter 1992–93), pp. 91–126.
13. Claudena M. Skran, *Refugees in Inter-war Europe: The Emergence of a Regime* (Oxford: Oxford University Press, 1995), pp. 84–85.
14. Ibid., pp. 234–236.
15. See Loescher, *Beyond Charity*, p. 49.
16. For a detailed history, see Louise W. Holborn, *The International Refugee Organization. A Specialized Agency of the United Nations: Its History and Work 1946–1952* (London: Oxford University Press, 1956).
17. Ibid., p. 433.
18. Ibid., p. 122.
19. For more detailed discussions of UNHCR's performance, see Loescher, *Beyond Charity*, pp. 129–151; Shelly Pitterman, "International Responses to Refugee Situations: The

United Nations High Commissioner for Refugees," in Elizabeth G. Ferris, ed., *Refugees and World Politics* (New York: Praeger, 1985), pp. 43–81; Alex Cunliffe, "The Refugee Crises: A Study of the United Nations High Commission for Refugees," *Political Studies* 43, no. 2 (June 1995), pp. 278–290; S. Alex Cunliffe and Michael Pugh, "The Politicization of UNHCR in Former Yugoslavia," *Journal of Refugee Studies* 10, no. 2 (June 1997), pp. 134–153; Thomas G. Weiss and Amir Pasic, "Reinventing UNHCR: Enterprising Humanitarians in the Former Yugoslavia, 1991–1995," *Global Governance* 3, no. 1 (January–April 1997), pp. 41–57.

20. Pitterman, "International Responses to Refugee Situations," p. 58.

21. David Rieff, *Slaughterhouse: Bosnia and the Failure of the West* (New York: Touchstone, 1996), p. 206.

22. On the politicization of refugees and the problems that this can create, see William Shawcross, *The Quality of Mercy: Cambodia, Holocaust and Modern Conscience* (New York: Simon & Schuster, 1984); Howard Adelman, "Why Refugee Warriors Are Threats," *Journal of Conflict Studies* 28, no. 1 (Spring 1998), pp. 49–69; Fiona Terry, "The Paradoxes of Humanitarian Aid," *Agenda* 5, no. 2 (1998), pp. 135–146.

23. On the Rwandan genocide, see Philip Gourevitch, *We Wish to Inform You That Tomorrow We Will Be Killed with Our Families: Stories from Rwanda* (New York: Farrar Straus & Giroux, 1998); *Leave None to Tell the Story: Genocide in Rwanda* (New York: Human Rights Watch, March 1999).

24. On the events of this period, see Benny Morris, *The Birth of the Palestinian Refugee Problem, 1947–1949* (Cambridge: Cambridge University Press, 1987).

25. See the UNHCR's "Timor emergency update" web site at http://www.unhcr.ch/news/ .media/timor/latest.htm.

26. Paul Handley, "The Land Wars," *Far Eastern Economic Review* 154, no. 44 (31 October 1991), pp. 15–16.

27. For a typical case study, see Chupinit Kesmanee, "Moving Hilltribe People to the Lowlands: The Resettlement Experience in Thailand," in Hari Mohan Mathur, ed., with the collaboration of Michael M. Cerna, *Development, Displacement and Resettlement: Focus on Asian Experiences* (New Delhi: Vikas Publishing House, 1995), pp. 244–254.

28. For a detailed discussion of the Comprehensive Plan of Action, see W. Courtland Robinson, *Terms of Refuge: The Indochinese Exodus and the International Response* (London: Zed Books, 1998).

29. Dennis McNamara, "The Origins and Effects of 'Humane Deterrence' Policies in Southeast Asia," in Gil Loescher and Laila Monahan, eds., *Refugees and International Relations* (New York: Oxford University Press, 1989), pp. 123–133 at p. 125.

30. See Arthur C. Helton, "Refugee Determination under the Comprehensive Plan of Action: Overview and Assessment," *International Journal of Refugee Law* 5, no. 4 (1993), pp. 544–558.

31. For a detailed elaboration of these views, see James C. Hathaway, ed., *Reconceiving International Refugee Law* (The Hague: Martinus Nijhoff, 1997).

32. See Chandran Kukathas and William Maley, *The Last Refuge: Hard and Soft Hansonism in Contemporary Australian Politics* (Sydney: Centre for Independent Studies, Issue Analysis no. 4, 16 September 1998).

33. See *Australia's Refugee Resettlement Programs: An Outline* (Canberra: Department of Immigration, Local Government and Ethnic Affairs, 1991).

34. See Mike Parnwell, *Population Movements and the Third World* (London: Routledge, 1993), pp. 11–28.

35. See Adam Przeworski et al., *Sustainable Democracy* (Cambridge: Cambridge University Press, 1995), p. 110.

36. See William Maley, "Peace-keeping and Peacemaking," in Ramesh Thakur and Carlyle A. Thayer, eds., *A Crisis of Expectations: UN Peacekeeping in the 1990s* (Boulder, CO: Westview Press, 1995), pp. 237–250 at pp. 247–249.
37. On the "liberal peace" thesis, see Michael Doyle, *Ways of War and Peace* (New York: W. W. Norton, 1997), pp. 284–300.
38. See Stephen D. Wrage, "Examining the 'Authoritarian Advantage' in Southeast Asian Development in the Wake of Asian Economic Failures," *Studies in Conflict and Terrorism* 22, no. 1 (January–March 1999), pp. 21–31.

10

Environmental security

Lorraine Elliott

Introduction

Every so often a new phrase enters the lexicon of international relations. "Environmental security" is one such phrase. As a normative concept, it illuminates debates about what security means in a post–Cold War world – security for whom and from what – and about the kinds of strategies and policies that will ensure that security. To paraphrase Norman Myers, what will "buy more security – real, enduring and all-round security."[1] This chapter considers environmental security in the context of debates about the relationship between traditional security and human security. It begins by examining environmental degradation as a component of human security. It then explores how, if at all, environmental concerns might integrate traditional security approaches and strategies with those more applicable to the human security agenda. The final section examines some of these themes in the context of environmental degradation in Pacific Asia.

Human security

In its 1994 *Human Development Report*, the United Nations Development Programme (UNDP) elaborated a clear and sophisticated understanding of human security and its component parts. Human security, the

UNDP argued, is universal, interdependent, and people centred, best achieved through early prevention rather than later intervention. Rather than a concern with weapons or with territory, "it is a concern with human life and dignity."[2] Human security is, however, more than security reduced to the level of the individual or an emphasis on "the individual's welfare."[3] It is conceptually and practically interwoven with global security. As Canadian Foreign Minister Lloyd Axworthy observes, human security "acknowledges that sustained economic development, human rights and fundamental freedoms, the rule of law, good governance, sustainable development and social equity *are as important to global peace* as arms control and disarmament."[4]

The relationship between human security and traditional security is therefore embedded in complexity. It provides an opportunity to recognize different kinds of threats, not to states but to peoples and communities, and to reassess the probability of insecurities. The Commission on Global Governance observed, for example, that "threats to the earth's life support systems, extreme economic deprivation, the proliferation of conventional small arms, the terrorising of civilian populations by domestic factions and gross violations of human rights ... challenge the security of people far more than the threat of external aggression."[5] These are, as Ken Booth suggests, "problems of profound significcnce"[6] and ones that place "emancipation at the centre of new security thinking."[7] The UNDP also anticipated human security as an antidote to more traditional security emphases, which Walt summarizes as "the threat, use and control of military force"[8] and the "likelihood and character of war."[9] Its 1994 Report argued that "for too long the concept of security has been shaped by the potential for conflict between states ... equated with ... threats to a country's borders."[10] Human security, the UNDP suggested, invoked a "profound transition in thinking."[11] How, then, does environmental security fit within this transition?

Environmental security: Securing the environment

Protection of the environment is crucial to human security. It is a decisive factor in economic vitality. A secure environment is fundamental to individual and community health and well-being and, in some cases, to survival (the ultimate security challenge). It is, if nothing else, "the essential support system on which all other human enterprises depend."[12] As Gareth Porter explains, "increasing stresses on the earth's life support systems and renewable natural resources have profound implications for human health and welfare that are at least as serious as traditional military threats."[13] The UNDP also made it quite clear that equitable access to resources and environmental services was a central component of human security. Protection of the environment – environmental security – is important also because it is a fundamental ethical principle that the environment should be protected and sustained, not abused and degraded. Yet, as Gwyn Prins reminds us, environmental security is a goal. What we have, he argues, is environmental insecurity.[14]

The nexus between human security and protection of the environment has been acknowledged as a fundamental international principle. Principle 1 of the Rio Declaration – the statement of principles adopted at the 1992 United Nations Conference on Environment and Development (UNCED, or the Rio Summit) – states that "human beings are at the centre of concerns for sustainable development. They are entitled to a healthy and productive life in harmony with nature." The irony is, of course, that human activity is the cause of environmental insecurity. In other words, the human security dilemma is that the causes of human insecurities are located in the practices of human economy and society as well as the structures that inform and constitute those practices.

It is clear that human activity is changing the environment – and not for the better – in a way unlike that of any other era.[15] Extensive and excessive resource use, energy-inefficient lifestyles, industrialization, and the pursuit of economic growth are inextricably linked to environmental degradation, within and across state borders. The agenda of contemporary environmental concerns and their social, economic, and ecological impacts is a long one. It includes atmospheric pollution, ozone depletion, and climate change; deforestation, desertification, and land degradation; loss of biodiversity, species, and habitat; air and water pollution; the impacts of urbanization and industrialization, including the increased production of toxic and hazardous waste; depletion of non-renewable and renewable resources, including water and arable land. Air pollution, water pollution, marine pollution, depletion of fish stocks, and loss of arable land all contribute to health insecurities, food insecurities, and economic insecurities – in other words, to human insecurities. Poor environmental practice exacerbates disasters of nature such as floods and landslides. These, in turn, increase human insecurity.

There is also a fundamental inequity in the environmental and human insecurity problem. The industrialized world accounts for about one-quarter of the world's population. Yet it consumes about three-quarters of the world's energy and resources, and produces a similar proportion of the world's waste and pollution.[16] The social and economic consequences of environmental degradation and resource depletion will, on the other hand, more quickly exacerbate the already-existing misery and despair in the poorer parts of the world. The most immediate and disproportionate impact of environmental degradation will be felt by those who are already marginalized in society and who have contributed less to environmental decline – the poor, women, and indigenous peoples for example. Up to 1 billion people could be displaced or made further insecure as a result of inundation of coastal regions through climate-change-induced sea-level rises, through changes in agricultural zones and loss of croplands, or because low-lying island countries simply cease to exist. The loss of forests (along with the practices that contribute to deforestation) threatens loss of habitat and subsistence to millions of forest dwellers and indigenous peoples as well as increasing the vulnerability of poor peasants to land-clearance schemes and development programmes. Up to 1.2 billion of the world's people are threatened by the impacts of desertification.[17]

Thousands of committed people have worked hard to keep environmental issues on the international agenda since the 1992 Rio Summit. Negotiation and debate on environmental issues have continued apace. Within the UN system and outside it, any number of committees, working groups, expert panels, subsidiary bodies, and commissions, convened by governments, intergovernmental agencies, scientific bodies, and non-governmental organizations, have continued to focus on expanding our understanding of environmental problems and on the search for solutions. Much has also been made in those years of the imperative for a global partnership (as Agenda 21 has it) in support of our common future (as the World Commission on Environment and Development described it). As the President of the Republic of the Maldives reminded the industrialized countries in a speech in 1995, "environmental security is a common good that we share together or forfeit forever."[18]

Yet despite the many thousands of words on paper – in conventions, protocols, declarations, communiqués, statements of principle, management programmes and action plans – and despite some local successes, environmental degradation continues to worsen. The United Nations Environment Programme's (UNEP) first *Global Environmental Outlook*, prepared for the 1997 General Assembly Special Session to Review the Implementation of Agenda 21 (the programme for action adopted at UNCED), states unequivocally that "from a global perspective the environment has continued to degrade during the past decade ... progress towards a sustainable future is just too slow."[19] The political will is lacking; the funds are not forthcoming; economic goals take precedence over environmental ones. There has been much activity but not enough action and the prognosis for environmental security, and the human security to which it makes a fundamental contribution, is not good.

Overcoming the global environmental crisis in the interests of the environment and human security requires new and invigorated forms of governance informed by the imperatives for cooperation and involving not only states and governments but a strengthened civil society. It requires new norms and values, ones that emphasize interdependence, precaution and prevention, intra- and inter-generational equity, and the pursuit of local and global environmental justice. These are the values that the UNDP suggests are crucial to human security. But it is not clear that they have found much place in the pursuit of traditional security. Indeed, in many cases, it is precisely these values that have been undermined by such an agenda.

This brings us to the second theme of this analysis – the relevance of environmental security to the project of reconciling human and traditional security (if, indeed, such reconciliation is possible) and whether or not the intellectual and policy tools of the traditional security agenda are amenable to securing the environment.

Environment and security: Accommodation or subversion?

The environmental nexus between traditional and human security (or insecurity) has been acknowledged in international law. Principle 24 of the 1992 Rio Declaration states that warfare is inherently destructive of the environment; Principle 25 observes that "peace, development and environmental protection are interdependent and indivisible"; and Principle 26 requires that states should solve their environmental disputes peacefully. Environmental concerns have been accommodated within traditional security circles, although not always welcomed by its most conservative proponents. But this has been done in a way that, despite some interesting conceptual and operational advances, does little to address the real problems of environmental insecurity or human security. It is not clear that "environmental security," in the way it has been captured by the traditional agenda, meets the common security test outlined by proponents of human security. For this reason, a human security approach to environmental degradation (and environmental security) may serve more as a challenge to the normative assumptions and the policy prescriptions of the traditional security agenda.

In traditional security circles, environmental security brings environmental degradation within the more traditional framework of security geopolitics. It stands as shorthand for the likelihood for "major environmental changes to generate and intensify conflict between and within states."[20] This version of the environmental security project seeks to understand better the dynamics of this relationship and to identify the kinds of environmental degradation that might disrupt national, regional, or even international security, and how they might do so.

Much attention is paid to conflict or tension over scarce (or potentially scarce) resources, particularly water and arable land and the environmental services they support. Freshwater is a fragile and finite resource: it constitutes only about 2.5 per cent of the world's water resources and even less than that is available for human use.[21] Global demand for freshwater is increasing as the world's per capita water supply continues to decline, from 17,000 m^3 in 1950 to 7,000 in 1997.[22] By the end of the 1980s, 80 countries with over 40 per cent of the world's population were facing water scarcities, along with the environmental and human insecurities that result. Water, and especially clean water, is fundamental to life: without it people die. The inter-state dimensions of water insecurity are highlighted by the extent of shared (that is, transboundary) water resources. Over 150 major river systems are shared by two countries and a further 50 are shared by between three and twelve countries. Per capita arable land is also on the decline. Contributing factors include population pressures, land degradation and desertification, the impact of urbanization, and the technological and biophysical limits of irrigation. The decline in available land for agriculture is unevenly distributed, with developing countries, particularly in Asia and Africa, suffering a disproportionate loss.[23] While the possibility of intra- and inter-state tensions and conflict over land resources features in the environmental conflict literature, immediate human insecurities are central to these concerns. These include loss of food productivity, increased malnutrition and related health problems, and involuntary movement of peoples.

The web of causality between environmental degradation and conflict is further complicated by what the World Commission on Environment and Development called "differences in environmental endowment"[24] – inequities in the distribution and use of resources, in the causes of environmental degradation, and in vulnerabilities to environmental change. "All too often," Myers argues, "the result is civil turmoil and outright violence, either within a country or with neighbouring countries."[25] Environmental scarcity is further linked to "population movement, economic decline and the weakening of states," and expected to exacerbate the potential for violence, disrupt "legitimised and authoritative social relations,"[26] and have "serious repercussions for the security interests of both the developed and the developing worlds."[27] As the UN Secretary-General's *Agenda for Peace* suggested, ecological damage becomes a new risk for stability.[28]

This particular environmental security narrative has been incorporated into more traditional security doctrine at national, regional, and international levels in which environmental degradation is labelled a "non-military threat." In this "renaissance" version of security, "new issues and challenges are being subsumed under old ... approaches."[29] The US government's National Security Strategy recognizes that the "stress from environmental challenges is ... contributing to political conflict."[30] NATO's Strategic Concept refers to the "environmental dimensions of security and stability."[31] Environmental threats to security have also made their way onto the Security Council agenda. The 1992 Security Council Heads of State meeting identified "non-military sources of instability in [*inter alia*] ... the ecological fields" as "threats to peace and security."[32] In the face of such potential threats, and despite an emphasis on their non-military nature, the option of a "direct military response" to "poor environmental behaviour"[33] is not excluded from strategic considerations. States, Lothar Brock argues, could "use military force in order to protect themselves from [the] social consequences of global environmental decay."[34] Indeed, the possibility that "environmental problems in one country affecting the interests of another could easily come within the purview of the Security Council"[35] – a kind of "environmental collective security" – is taken as a serious possibility. However, the security referent (that is, security for whom) remains the state or the international system of states. Environmental degradation is a problem for the traditional security agenda only if it is a likely contributor to conflict, might threaten state or international security, or might require military intervention of some kind.

There is little attention to human security in this version of the environmental security project. The threats are to states (and if also to persons, only incidentally). The traditional agenda is expanded to include non-military threats but the normative assumptions about traditional security remain. The cause of conflict is operationally irrelevant. Environmental degradation is thus "securitized" and environmental security is "militarized." Environmental (in)security becomes synonymous with environmental threats to the state. Strategic and defence bureaucracies continue to define the threat to "national" security and appropriate responses to those threats.

Exploring environmental security as a human security concept has a number of implications for the traditional security agenda. Rather than "reconciling" the two, it suggests that there is a tension between them which cannot be bridged. The military model of environmental security masks the extent to which the pursuit of traditional security contributes to other forms of insecurities, including, in this case, environmental ones. It also fails to reveal the theoretical limitations of traditional security for identifying and responding to other forms of insecurity. It is, Dalby argues, "practically dysfunctional as the discursive framework for any political arrangement" for addressing "pressing global problems."[36]

The practices of war and preparation for war, which still constitute a central component of the traditional security agenda, continue to have a direct and indirect impact on the environment. "Arms competition and armed conflict," the Brundtland Commission argued, "create major obstacles to sustainable development."[37] The "wanton disruption of the environment by armed conflict"[38] and the unintended (or at least overlooked) environmental consequences of war damage terrestrial and marine ecosystems and contribute to air and other forms of pollution. The use of defoliants for area denial during the Viet Nam war, for example, destroyed 14 per cent of Viet Nam's forests and severely damaged economically and ecologically important mangrove swamp ecosystems[39] as well, of course, as directly affecting the non-combatant population. Deliberate and "unintended" environmental damage during the 1990–91 Gulf conflict included atmospheric and marine pollution, environment-related health trauma in local populations, and damage to local ecosystems as a result of bombing, use of military vehicles, and excessive waste management and water consumption demands.[40] Indeed, pursuit of the traditional security agenda during the Cold War has left us with a legacy of environmental insecurity: nuclear and toxic waste; landmines; the "unintended" environmental consequences of war and war-preparation; increased environmental pressures as refugees flee conflict; sacrifice areas used for testing; lost opportunity costs; excessive and disproportionate resource use and pollution. Further, when it comes to conflict, environmental protection norms are almost always sacrificed in the interests of the conduct of war. In practice, environmental degradation in wartime has been subject to little or no accountability and is poorly covered in international law. The provisions of the 1977 Environmental Modification Convention are "ambiguous and limited"[41] and the injunctions in Protocol 1 to the Geneva Conventions, which requires combatants "to limit environmental destruction," are "vague and permissive."[42]

Defence establishments in a number of countries have begun to address the environmental consequences of this resource profligacy and environmental disregard. Environmental security has therefore become operationalized as "environmentally responsible defence," acknowledging the impact of defence-related activities on the environment and demonstrating an apparent willingness to "green the military" through balancing readiness and stewardship doctrines. Military establishments are encouraged to implement environmental management strategies; to conserve resources; to protect heritage and habitat; to develop more environmentally benign weapons acquisition and disposal strategies. Any such operational attention to stewardship matters is to be welcomed from an environmental point of view, although the motivation is often driven more by the economic consequences of declining defence budgets, or by occupational health and safety requirements, than by environmental values.

Debates about the defence dimensions of the environmental agenda are now turning to the issue of "proactive" or "protective" environmental defence,[43] which would seem to engage more specifically with preventive security (recalling the UNDP's emphasis on early prevention) in the context of broader foreign policy goals. In the United States, the Department of Defense's environmental security programme has supplemented its original focus on environmental management and stewardship with an emphasis on defence environmental cooperation as a contribution to democratization and better governance. Defence forces in many countries are already well experienced in disaster response and relief activities. Defence support may also contribute to the development of civilian capabilities in areas such as anti-poaching and interdiction of smuggling activities, both of which are important to support species protection and the conservation and management of maritime and terrestrial ecosystems. The use of military assets and resources – such as personnel, data, technical and scientific capacities, environmental clean-up expertise, disaster response capabilities – for environmental monitoring and early-warning purposes is also being advanced,[44] although almost always with the caveat that national security interests should not be compromised.

The emphasis on environmentally responsible defence and preventive environmental defence is advanced in terms of a "paradigm shift ... a different way of viewing ... present boundaries and roles" in which the "threat-based [military] is under assault by the notion of a capabilities-based one."[45] Or as Sherri Goodman, US Under-Secretary of Defense for Environmental Security, suggests, thinking about environmental concerns within the military "challenges us to embrace change, to let go of old paradigms and preconceived notions about how to do business."[46] Although militaries world-wide are being tasked for non-combat missions and are venturing into the theatre of operations other than war, there would still seem to be little to justify claims about subversion of military purpose or a paradigm shift that might be more hospitable to human security concerns. Within the military, the view is still dominant that attention to environmental concerns beyond limited operational stewardship takes the military too far from its traditional role, that any such involvement runs the risk of dulling the sword, undermining "core business," and compromising the readiness doctrine. The military, it is argued, can "ill-afford peacetime activities that detract from wartime readiness."[47] Descriptions such as that offered of the US Navy's new attack submarine, destined for fleet service in 2004, which draws attention simultaneously to its environmentally benign weapons system and to "its future capabilities as a killing machine,"[48] still demonstrate an intuitive militarism that is fundamentally at odds with the ethical foundations of environmental protection and human security.

The normative assumptions that inform a "militarized" environmental security remain caught in realist assumptions about states, geopolitics, and threat which do little to advance the cause of environmental protec-

tion or human security. The geopolitical metaphors of traditional security
– borders and boundaries and, ultimately, power acquired through dominance and deterrence – cannot account for the ecological or human imperatives of addressing environmental degradation. They marginalize a
fundamental aspect of environmental change from the environmental security debates. Ecosystems do not coincide with the political space that is
the state, and the concepts of sovereignty and territorial integrity that are
fundamental to geopolitical security are "difficult (if not impossible) to
maintain within an ecological frame of reference."[49] The traditional idea
of an enemy "other," and the strategies that this engenders, are increasingly inappropriate for defining contemporary insecurities and for determining policy responses when faced with threats without enemies.
Certainly the environment is not the enemy. Rather the "threat" lies in
the everyday activities of humans, corporations, and states, humans primarily in pursuit of quality of life, and corporations and states in pursuit
of profit or economic security. The answer to the question who or what is
being made secure, and from whom (or what), is not "us" (or "states")
and "the environment," but is, or at least should be, "the environment"
and "us." Traditional military responses are inappropriate here; as Renner argues, they "cannot reverse resource depletion or restore lost ecological balance"[50] and, as the Brundtland Commission noted, there are
"no military solutions to environmental insecurity."[51] The practices of
"traditional security" are also potentially poorly adapted to meeting human security challenges. Meeting the imperatives of environmental protection requires cooperation rather than conflict. It requires openness and
transparency rather than secrecy in the claimed interests of national security. As strategic analysts James Winnefeld and Mary Morris suggest,
addressing environmental degradation challenges the "customarily closed
domain of national security and strategy planning."[52]

From a human security perspective, a focus on environmental threat
and conflict places too much emphasis on traditional security (modified or
not) and not enough on the environment or on people. A traditional
security model of environmental security also provides little scope for
understanding how "poverty, injustice, environmental degradation and
conflict interact in complex and potent ways."[53] Where poverty is factored into the analysis it is often in such a way that the structural conditions that force the poor into unsustainable practices (which are never
as environmentally destructive as those of the world's far less numerous
richest peoples and countries) are ignored or discounted as "security"
concerns.

Understanding environmental security in security terms rather than
environmental ones also diverts attention from the more immediate and
real insecurity problems of environmental degradation and narrows pol-

icy options by focusing on symptoms rather than causes. In elaborating his concept of preventive defence, former US Defense Secretary Perry argued that security "depends equally as much on *preventing* the conditions that lead to conflict and on helping to create the conditions for peace."[54] Yet, as Jessica Mathews points out, the "underlying cause of turmoil is often ignored. Instead governments address the ... instability that results."[55] Although instability is also a contributor to human insecurity, the responses are (or at least should be) to address the *causes* of instability as a means of overcoming human and environmental insecurity. Preventing or overcoming environmental degradation will make a greater contribution to human security and, indeed, to national and international security than will mobilizing the narratives and practices of traditional security in response to that degradation.

The intellectual challenge of environmental security is one thing. The implementation challenge is quite another. Despite debates about the importance of meeting non-military threats to security, the kinds of funds required to address environmental insecurities are simply not forthcoming. Expenditure for international agencies such as UNEP in the decade 1982 to 1992 totalled only US$450 million, the equivalent of less than five hours of global military spending for the same period of time.[56] The funds available to institutions such as the Global Environment Facility total, for the latest three-year replenishment, something in the vicinity of US$2 billion (for the incremental costs to developing countries of addressing the global component of climate change, ozone depletion, biodiversity loss, and ocean pollution).

A small UN expert study group on Military Resources to the Environment identified "preservation of the environment [as] one new channel for the vast energies released by the end of the Cold War."[57] The UNDP made it clear that "capturing the peace dividend"[58] was a central requirement for the move to human security. A considerable environmental peace dividend could be achieved with even small cuts. The UNDP has suggested that a 3 per cent reduction in military expenditure would have resulted in a peace dividend of about US$1.5 trillion by the year 2000.[59] Yet a report from the Worldwatch Institute notes that, although global military spending has declined since the end of the Cold War, about three-quarters of the increase in peace spending has been directed towards addressing the legacy of Cold War militarism – de-mining, weapons dismantling, repatriation of refugees who fled war and violence. What is more, since the end of the Cold War, the balance between war and peace spending has continued to lean heavily in the direction of the former: US$140 spent globally on military goods and services for each US$1 spent on peace.[60] The Gulf Allies were able to find $US60–70 billion for their efforts against Iraq at the beginning of the 1990s,[61] but cannot find anywhere near that amount to support environmental security in its ecological or human security sense.

Environmental security viewed through a traditional security lens remains a conventional view of security, even if it identifies a nonconventional set of threats. As noted above, resistance to preventive environmental defence remains among those responsible for the "enforcement" of the traditional security agenda. There is also a strong resistance to the "welfarizing" of security as a concept. Mohammed Ayoob argues, for example, that moving beyond the traditional military-oriented definition of security "runs the risk of making the term so elastic as to detract seriously from its utility as an analytical tool."[62] Gleick suggests that what is required is not a "redefinition of international or national security" but a "better understanding of the nature of certain threats."[63] Others are sceptical of this apparently new-found strategic interest in environmental concerns, arguing, as Ronnie Lipschutz and John Holdren have done, that it represents little more than "strategic analysts ... busy combing the planet for new threats to be countered."[64] Scholars such as Daniel Deudney and Lothar Brock caution against adopting the term "security" to focus attention on environmental degradation. In their view, it sends us off in the wrong direction, locking environmental concerns into an inappropriate, state-centric framework and invoking the "emotive power of nationalism."[65] Letting military and security planners get involved in debates about environmental degradation and human security is seen to be rather akin to leaving the fox in charge of the chickens.

Pacific Asia

Environmental scarcity is a feature of Pacific Asia. This means not just the availability of traditional resources such as fish, timber, oil, and gas but also the availability and quality of environmental services including clean air, unpolluted water, arable land, and ecosystem and habitat diversity. The patterns that link economic activity, environmental inequity, and social and political tensions to human and traditional insecurities are reproduced here. Human health and welfare are closely linked to environmental scarcity. Subsistence lifestyles in the region remain heavily dependent on the "exploitation of land, forests and water resources"[66] and still constitute the basic means of survival for over half the region's population, making them vulnerable to environmental degradation and scarcity. However, countries in the region are also increasingly high-consumption countries with growing urban populations and unsustainable demands for energy. This transition from a rural-based economy – what

Vervoorn calls the "industrialisation of Asia within the world economy"[67] – contributes disproportionately more to environmental decline in the region, further exacerbating environmental inequities between rich and poor.

Most of the region's environmental problems have been identified in one forum or another as likely causes of instability, conflict, or violence, although there is little compelling evidence, as Dupont observes, that environmental scarcity has been a "primary cause of any major subnational or inter-state conflict."[68] However, the potential for tension over resource issues, pollution, waste management, and environmental degradation is growing. Environmental decline within states exacerbates other kinds of political and social instabilities, especially in the context of poverty, internal colonization, and inequitable access to resources and environmental services. Competing groups include "tribal communities, peasants, fisher[people], miners, loggers and corporations."[69] Environmental management strategies can often contribute further to inequities if they "ignore concerns about human equity, health of ecosystems, other species and the welfare of future generations."[70] This is particularly so if access to resources is disproportionately privatized in corporate hands, when market-based pricing structures are implemented for scarce resources such as water, or when resource management infrastructure, such as dams, has severe ecological and social consequences. Environmental problems in the region are also taking on an increasingly transboundary dimension, with potential consequences for security relationships between states.

Several environmental scarcity issues in Pacific Asia stand out as particularly challenging in human and traditional security terms. Deforestation represents perhaps "the most visible evidence of the rate of environmental change" in the region.[71] On average, 1.2 per cent of forest land is lost every year, at least part of it as a result of illegal activities, often in frontier forest areas. At least 15 per cent of national land area in the region is affectd by soil degradation and over one-third of the region's arable land is vulnerable to desertification.[72] The social consequences of deforestation and land degradation include shortfalls in food production and exacerbation of poverty, as well as conflict over land tenure and access to forest lands and, in some cases, unplanned movement of peoples within countries and across borders.

Almost half the countries in the region face water stress of some kind as a result of continued overuse of water for agriculture and domestic and industrial uses, compounded by severe pollution of available water resources. The impact on local communities can be severe, and drought and economic hardship can increase competition for water resources within states. Where water is a shared and transboundary resource there is potential for tension and even conflict over disrupted water flows or up-stream activities affecting downstream water quality, especially if political relationships have been corroded by other factors. Much attention here has focused on the Mekong, which is shared by six countries, on the Tumen and Yalu rivers between China and North Korea, and on the water agreements between Malaysia and Singapore.

The maritime environment adds a further dimension to the human and traditional insecurities associated with resource and environmental issues. The potential for inter-state conflict is high where competition for access to both living and non-living resources coincides with overlapping sovereignty claims or intrusion into exclusive economic zones, or involves transboundary sources of pollution and degradation.[73] Over-fishing of most of the region's fisheries has disrupted an economic resource and diminished a major source of protein for the region's people, thus exacerbating human insecurity. Confrontation between states over illegal fishing activities and over access to increasingly scarce fish stocks is already a problem in the region.

Rising energy demands, slowed only temporarily by the economic crisis, are complicit in increased problems of air pollution and resource scarcity. Coupled with a likely decline in regional energy self-sufficiency, concerns over the maintenance of secure energy supplies have increased the potential for confrontation over resources such as oil and other hydro-carbons and over energy infrastructure such as pipelines and dams. Nuclear capability further complicates the environmental and traditional security dimensions of energy scarcities, raising concerns over the environmental and human impacts of nuclear accidents, some of which could have potential transboundary consequences, and tensions between countries over the transportation and storage of nuclear wastes.[74] Energy use is also a major factor in regional air pollution. Almost all the region's major cities exceed the World Health Organization's guidelines on particulates and sulphur dioxide, and the human insecurity costs can be high. Transboundary atmospheric pollution, particularly particulate-laden smoke and industrial acid rain, has also emerged as a real cause of friction between regional neighbours. The so-called haze incidents in South-East Asia, arising from land-clearing fires primarily in Kalimantan and Sumatra, affected human and ecosystem health, agriculture, tourism, and transportation not only in Indonesia but also in Malaysia, Brunei, Singapore, and Thailand.

Environmental decline and resource scarcity therefore clearly complicate the security challenges facing the region in a post–Cold War world. Environmental integrity is compromised, human security is undermined, and the potential for environment-related instabilities within states and confrontation between them is not to be discounted. These so-called non-traditional security threats have now been inscribed on the agenda of official security institutions in the region, such as the ASEAN Regional Forum, as well as within the Track II process mobilized under the Council for Security Cooperation in the Asia Pacific and the ASEAN Institutes of Strategic International Studies network. The focus remains on the likelihood of environment-related conflict and violence between states or in situations where internal instability is deemed a threat to regional security.[75] In the face of such possibilities, a regional environmental security policy must ensure that the security problems of environmental scarcity are more firmly integrated into regional security architecture in order to avoid conflict, enhance cooperation, and build confidence. An environmental security policy should also devise an early warning system and spell out what will be done where scarcity-related tensions are evident and likely to worsen.[76]

However, the kinds of resolution mechanisms that arise from this modified traditional security approach can go only so far in dealing with the likely insecurity consequences of environmental scarcity in the region. On their own, they are inadequate to the task of preventing environmental conflict within or between states. More attention is required to amelioration of the likely causes of conflict through prudent environmental policies and overcoming environment-related human insecurities. Most governments in the region have established environment ministries and related agencies, instituted environmental protection programmes, and adopted various legislative initiatives to improve environmental quality. Environmental cooperation and programmes for joint action are institutionally well developed under ASEAN, although the impact of such programmes on the state of the environment in South-East Asia has been limited. The institutional framework for cooperative dialogue on the environment in North-East Asia is less well developed but not entirely absent. For the most part, however, environmental policy debates in the region are not couched in terms of their importance for regional security, despite the obvious connections. Environmental degradation continues and, with it, the likely insecurity consequences for peoples and, potentially, for states.

A regional environmental security policy therefore needs to ensure that strategies for regional environmental cooperation are strengthened and implemented for both environmental and security reasons. This requires political will, substantial resources (including greater attention from the international community), better flow of information, the adoption and transfer of environmentally sound technologies, legal structures to implement regional agreements, commonly accepted environmental standards, and immediate response capacity for environmental emergencies.[77] Finally, policies on resource and environmental management must take account of the human security dimensions of environmental scarcity. A regional environmental security policy must recognize and respond to the social and economic drivers of environmental decline, facilitate an equitable sharing of rights to and responsibilities for habitat and resources, and ensure that local communities are included in environmental decision-making and implementation.

Conclusion

If "environmental security" as a concept and as a policy is to have some impact on how we think about and pursue security, it may be best achieved not through abandoning the concept but through continuing to emphasize and pursue a human security framework. Such an approach should at least move those engaged in traditional security and defence thinking from identifying "non-military threats" to focusing on "operations other than war" as the fundamental intellectual and operational purpose of "traditional" security planners and agents. In the final analysis, however, human security requires more than a rethinking of threats. It requires a rethinking of what security means, who it is for, and how it is to be achieved. Environmental security, Richard Falk argues, "requires a willingness to make ... fundamental changes."[78] Those changes have not yet been made, in either the security agenda or the environmental agenda. As then UN Secretary-General Boutros Boutros-Ghali reminded, indeed cautioned, his audience at the end of the Rio Summit in 1992, "one day we will have to do better."[79]

Notes

1. Norman Myers, *Ultimate Security: The Environmental Basis of Political Stability* (Washington DC: Island Press, 1996), p. 218.
2. See United Nations Development Programme (UNDP), *Human Development Report 1994* (New York: Oxford University Press, 1994), p. 22.
3. Ramesh Thakur, "From National to Human Security," in Stuart Harris and Andrew Mack, eds., *Asia-Pacific Security: The Economics–Politics Nexus* (Sydney: Allen & Unwin in association with the Department of International Relations and the Northeast Asia Program, Research School of Pacific and Asian Studies, Australian National University, 1997), p. 53.
4. Lloyd Axworthy, "Canada and Human Security: The Need for Leadership," *International Journal* 52, no. 2 (Spring 1997), p. 184; emphasis added.
5. Commission on Global Governance, *Our Global Neighbourhood* (Oxford: Oxford University Press, 1995), p. 79.
6. Ken Booth, "Security and Emancipation," *Review of International Studies* 17, no. 4 (October 1991), p. 318.

7. Ibid., p. 321.
8. Stephen M. Walt, "The Renaissance of Security Studies," *International Studies Quarterly* 35, no. 2 (June 1991), p. 213.
9. Ibid., p. 212.
10. UNDP, *Human Development Report 1994*, p. 3.
11. Ibid., p. 22.
12. Barry Buzan, "New Patterns of Global Security in the Twenty-First Century," *International Affairs* 67, no. 3 (1991), p. 433.
13. Gareth Porter, "Environmental Security as a National Security Issue," *Current History* 94, no. 592 (May 1995), p. 218.
14. Gwyn Prins, "Putting Environmental Security in Context," in Gwyn Prins, ed., *Threats without Enemies* (London: Earthscan, 1993), p. xiv.
15. For more, see Lorraine Elliott, *Global Politics of the Environment* (London: Macmillan, 1998).
16. UNDP, *Human Development Report 1992* (New York: Oxford University Press, 1992), p. 35; and Aaron Sachs, "Upholding Human Rights and Environmental Justice," in Lester R. Brown et al., eds., *State of the World 1996* (New York: W.W. Norton, 1996), p. 144.
17. William C. Burns, "The International Convention to Combat Desertification: Drawing a Line in the Sand?" *Michigan Journal of International Law* 16, no. 3 (Spring 1995), p. 834.
18. H. E. Maumoon Abdul Gayoom, *A Warning from the Small Island States: Our Fate Will Be Your Fate*, Address by the President of the Republic of the Maldives to the Second Municipal Leaders' Summit on Climate Change, Berlin, 27 March 1995, p. 10.
19. United Nations Environment Programme, *Global Environmental Outlook-1: Executive Summary*, 1997, at http://www.unep.org/unep/eia/geo1/exsum/ex3.htm.
20. Marvin S. Soroos, "Global Change, Environmental Security and the Prisoner's Dilemma," *Journal of Peace Research* 31, no. 3 (August 1994), p. 318.
21. Eric Rodenburg and Dirk Bryant, "Water: Conditions and Trends," in World Resources Institute, *World Resources 1994–95* (New York: Oxford University Press, 1994), pp. 181–182.
22. UNDP, *Human Development Report 1998* [Overview], at http://www.undp.org/undp/hdro/97.htm.
23. Richard H. Moss, "Resource Scarcity and Environmental Security," *SIPRI Yearbook 1993* (Oxford: Oxford University Press, 1993), p. 32; Alan Dupont, *The Environment and Security in Pacific Asia*, Adelphi Paper 319 (London: Oxford University Press and International Institute for Strategic Studies, 1998), pp. 44–45.
24. World Commission on Environment and Development (WCED), *Our Common Future* (Oxford: Oxford University Press, 1987), p. 292.
25. Norman Myers, "Environment and Security," *Foreign Policy*, no. 74 (Spring 1989), p. 24.
26. Thomas F. Homer-Dixon, "On the Threshhold: Environmental Changes as Causes of Acute Conflict," *International Security* 16, no. 2 (Fall 1991), p. 91.
27. Thomas F. Homer-Dixon, "Environmental Scarcities and Violent Conflict: Evidence from Cases," *International Security* 19, no. 2 (Summer 1994), p. 36.
28. Boutros Boutros-Ghali, *An Agenda for Peace*, Report of the Secretary General pursuant to the Statement adopted by the Summit Meeting of the Security Council on 31 January 1992, 47th Session, Security Council S/24111; General Assembly A/47/277, 17 June 1992, p. 5.
29. Michael C. Williams and Keith Krause, "Preface: Toward Critical Security Studies," in Keith Krause and Michael C. Williams, eds., *Critical Security Studies* (Minneapolis: University of Minnesota Press, 1997), p. xix.

30. Kent Hughes Butts, "Why the Military Is Good for the Environment," in Jyrki Käkönen, ed., *Green Security or Militarised Environment* (Aldershot: Dartmouth Publishing, 1994), p. 86.
31. NATO, "Security Architecture," in *NATO Handbook* (Brussels: NATO, 1998), at http://www.nato.int/docu/handbook/hb10200e.htm.
32. Betsy Baker, "Legal Protection for the Environment in Time of Armed Conflict," *Virginia Journal of International Law* 33, no. 2 (1993), p. 356.
33. Julian Oswald, "Defence and Environmental Security," in Prins, *Threats without Enemies*, p. 129.
34. Lothar Brock, "Peace through Parks: The Environment on the Peace Research Agenda," *Journal of Peace Research* 28, no. 4 (November 1991), p. 410.
35. Crispin Tickell, "The Inevitability of Environmental Security," in Prins, *Threats without Enemies*, p. 23.
36. Simon Dalby, "Contesting an Essential Concept: Reading the Dilemmas in Contemporary Security Discourse," in Krause and Williams, *Critical Security Studies*, p. 21.
37. WCED, *Our Common Future*, p. 294.
38. Arthur Westing, "The Environmental Component of Comprehensive Security," *Bulletin of Peace Proposals* 20, no. 2 (1989), p. 131.
39. Jeremy Leggett, "The Environmental Impact of War: A Scientific Analysis and Greenpeace's Reaction," in Glen Plant, ed., *Environmental Protection and the Law of War* (London: Belhaven Press, 1992), p. 69.
40. Ibid.; Jozef Goldblat, "Legal Protection of the Environment against the Effects of Military Activity," *Bulletin of Peace Proposals* 22, no. 4 (1993), pp. 399–406; and Odelia Funke, "National Security and the Environment," in Norman J. Vig and Michael E. Kraft, eds., *Environmental Policy in the 1990s*, 2nd edn (Washington DC: CQ Press, 1994).
41. Johan Jørgen Holst, "Security and the Environment: A Preliminary Exploration," *Bulletin of Peace Proposals* 20, no. 2 (June 1989), p. 124.
42. Merrit P. Drucker, "The Military Commander's Responsibility for the Environment," *Environmental Ethics* 11, no. 2 (Summer 1989), p. 145.
43. Ian Finlayson, "Environmental Security and the Australian Defence Force," in Alan Dupont, ed., *The Environment and Security: What Are the Linkages?*, Canberra Papers on Strategy and Defence no. 125 (Canberra: Strategic and Defence Studies Centre, Australian National University, 1998), pp. 65–75.
44. See Gordon MacDonald, "Environmental Security," IGCC Policy Brief, February 1995, no. 1; Butts, "Why the Military Is Good for the Environment"; and Peter Crabb, Julie Kesby, and Laurie Olive, eds., *Environmentally Responsible Defence* (Canberra: Australian Defence Studies Centre, 1996).
45. Lt.-Col. Richard J. Rinaldo, "The Army as Part of a Peace Dividend," *Military Review* 73, no. 2 (February 1993), p. 46.
46. Sherri W. Goodman, "Supporting Defence Reform through Technology Innovation," Third Annual SERDP Symposium, 3 December 1997, at http://www.ceq.cso.uiuc.edu/denix/Public/ES-Programs/Speeches/speech-38.html.
47. Rinaldo, "The Army as Part of a Peace Dividend," p. 52.
48. Sandra I. Meadows, "Navy Casts Multimission Sub for Pollution-Free Dominance," *National Defense* 81, no. 526 (March 1997), p. 28.
49. Peace Research Institute, Oslo (PRIO), *Environmental Security: A Report Contributing to the Concept of Comprehensive International Security* (Oslo: PRIO/UNEP, 1989), p. 18.
50. Michael Renner, *National Security: The Economic and Environmental Dimensions*, Worldwatch Paper 89 (Washington DC: Worldwatch Institute, 1989), p. 38.
51. WCED, *Our Common Future*, p. 301.

52. James A. Winnefeld and Mary E. Morris, *Where Environmental Concerns and Securities Strategies Meet: Green Conflict in Asia and the Middle East* (Santa Monica, CA: RAND, 1994), p. iii.
53. WCED, *Our Common Future*, p. 291.
54. Cited by Sherri W. Goodman, "The Environment and National Security," Address to the National Defense University, 8 August 1996, at http://www.loyola.edu/dept/politics/hula/goodman.html.
55. Jessica Tuchman Mathews, "Redefining Security," *Foreign Affairs* 68, no. 2 (Spring 1989), p. 166.
56. Mosafa K. Tolba, Osama A. El-Kholy et al., *The World Environment: 1972–1992: Two Decades of Challenge* (London: Chapman & Hall, 1992), p. 592.
57. Maj. Britt Theorin, "Military Resources to the Environment," *Bulletin of Peace Proposals* 23, no. 2 (1992), p. 120.
58. UNDP, *Human Development Report 1994*, p. 8.
59. UNDP, *Human Development Report 1992*, p. 9.
60. Worldwatch Institute, "Peace Expenditures Rise But Still Not Sufficient," Press Release, 1994, at gopher://gopher.igc.apc.org:70/00/orgs/worldwatch/worldwatch.news/3, p. 1.
61. Johan Holmberg, "Whither UNCED?" *IIED Perspectives*, no. 8 (Spring 1992), p. 8.
62. Mohammed Ayoob, "The Security Problematic of the Third World," *World Politics* 43, no. 2 (1991), p. 259.
63. Peter H. Gleick, "Environment and Security: The Clear Connections," *Bulletin of Atomic Scientists* 47, no. 2 (April 1991), p. 17.
64. Ronnie Lipschutz and John P. Holdren, "Crossing Borders: Resource Flows, the Global Environment and International Security," *Bulletin of Peace Proposals* 21, no. 2 (1990), p. 126.
65. Daniel Deudney, "The Case against Linking Environmental Degradation and National Security," *Millennium* 19, no. 1 (Winter 1990), p. 461; and Brock, "Peace through Parks."
66. Alvaro Soto, "The Global Environment: A Southern Perspective," *International Journal* 47 (Autumn 1992), p. 694.
67. Aat Vervoorn, *Re-orient: Change in Asian Societies* (Oxford: Oxford University Press, 1998), p. 157.
68. Dupont, *The Environment and Security in Pacific Asia*, p. 75.
69. Lim Teck Ghee and Mark J. Valencia, "Introduction," in Lim Teck Ghee and Mark J. Valencia, eds., *Conflict over Natural Resources in South-east Asia and the Pacific* (Singapore: Oxford University Press, 1990), p. 3.
70. Sandra Postel, *Dividing the Waters: Food Security, Ecosystem Health and the New Politics of Scarcity*, Worldwatch Paper no. 132 (Washington DC: Worldwatch Institute, 1996), p. 7.
71. Vervoorn, *Re-orient*, p. 166.
72. Sandagdorj Erdenebileg, "Environment and Security: Definitions and Concepts," in Kent Butts, ed., *Conference Report: Environmental Change and Regional Security* (Carlisle Barracks, PA: Center for Strategic Leadership, US Army War College, 1997), p. III-6.
73. Up to 70 per cent of coastal and maritime pollution is from land-based sources and often transgresses sovereign maritime boundaries.
74. The region's most recent nuclear accident, at Tokai in Japan late in September 1999, raised concerns again about the potential for a Chernobyl-like accident, affecting the environment and human health across the region. Taiwan's agreement with North Korea for the storage of Taiwan's nuclear waste generated some degree of political tension between Taiwan and both South Korea and China.

75. Little attention is paid in official forums to the direct and indirect consequences of military activity and traditional security budgets for the environment or the complicity of militaries, in some countries, in environmental degradation or policies on resource use.
76. Richard Matthew, "The Environment and Security: Definitions and Concepts (Presentation II)," in Butts, *Conference Report*, p. III-18.
77. These ideas are developed further in Lorraine Elliott, *Environment, Development and Security in Asia Pacific: Issues and Responses*, Plenary paper delivered to the 13th Asia Pacific Roundtable, Kuala Lumpur, 30 May to 2 June 1999.
78. Richard Falk, *On Humane Governance: Toward a New Global Politics* (Cambridge: Polity Press, 1995), p. 169.
79. Cited in Tony Brenton, *The Greening of Machiavelli: The Evolution of International Environmental Politics* (London: Royal Institute of International Affairs and Earthscan, 1994), p. 231.

11

Maritime security in the Asia-Pacific

Jin-Hyun Paik and Anthony Bergin

Overview

The Asia-Pacific region is a community of maritime nations. There are few Asian-Pacific states that do not have significant maritime frontiers and strong maritime interests. The commercial and strategic significance of the sea in the Asia-Pacific region requires little elaboration. The sea is a major source of food for the region, and the sea lanes are the lifelines of the Asian-Pacific economies, which are heavily dependent on unimpeded access to raw materials, markets, and investment opportunities. The region also encompasses a number of strategic straits, some of which lie across the vital oil supply routes from the Persian Gulf. All these resources, of course, relate directly to the welfare of those inhabiting the Asia-Pacific region and thus to their "human security" imperatives.

This strong maritime orientation dictates the security, political, as well as economic outlooks of all states in the region. Any analysis of the geopolitics in the Asia-Pacific must account for this maritime character (which for a long time has been taken for granted). As the economies of the region have prospered and extra-regional influences have declined, so governments have turned their attention more closely to the security of their own maritime interests. As a result, maritime issues are at the forefront of current regional security concerns. Of the 30 or so conflict points in the region, more than a third involve disputes over islands, continental shelf claims, exclusive economic zone (EEZ) boundaries, and other offshore issues. Many emerging regional security concerns – such as piracy, pollution from oil spills, safety of the sea lines of communication, illegal fishing and exploitation of other offshore resources, and other important elements of economic activities – are essentially maritime.

These concerns, in fact, are reflected in the significant maritime dimension of the current arms acquisition programmes in the region, for example, the maritime surveillance and intelligence collection systems, fighter aircraft with maritime attack capabilities, modern surface combatants, submarines, anti-ship missiles, naval electronic warfare systems, and so on. Unfortunately, some of these new capabilities are more offensive and inflammatory, and, in conflict situations, potentially prone to the possibilities of inadvertent escalation. For this reason, maritime concerns are well represented in current proposals for regional confidence-and-security-building measures, of which about a third are intended to address maritime matters directly, while others have a significant maritime dimension. It is therefore important that regional mechanisms be instituted to deal with these maritime issues – both to address the cause of tension and to manage and reduce such tension. By doing so, the region's maritime politics will be addressing human security more directly and more effectively.

Another urgent task to improve the maritime security environment in the Asia-Pacific region is to build a solid maritime regime based upon the common understanding of rules governing the use and protection of the ocean. In this regard, the law of the sea is particularly important. In fact, the Asia-Pacific region is characterized by a number of features that give prominence to certain law of the sea issues. For example, the Asia-Pacific region includes two of the largest archipelagic states in the world. It also includes a number of major straits that have increased in strategic and maritime significance since the end of World War II. There are, moreover, a number of maritime boundary disputes as well as sovereignty disputes over both islands and maritime areas. The United Nations Convention on the Law of the Sea (hereinafter, the LOS Convention), which came into force on 16 November 1994, deserves particular attention. The LOS Convention obviously does not resolve all the outstanding maritime issues. But it could be an important basis for maintaining peace and stability in the Asia-Pacific ocean by clarifying and refining rules applicable to ocean affairs and providing a mechanism for peacefully settling disputes in the event of conflicts.

When examining maritime issues in the Asia-Pacific region from the viewpoint of the international law of the sea, it must be stated that "the individual" is not seen as the ultimate and intended beneficiary. The dominant emphasis in the law of the sea is on sovereign entitlement and state authority. What, then, is the linkage to human security? A perspec-

tive of international law that views the individual as the ultimate beneficiary is chiefly of relevance in the field of human rights and related areas
of fundamental human welfare. Nevertheless, issues related to ocean
management, particularly in the areas of the environmental health of
the oceans and resolving sea-use conflicts, can be brought down below the
level of the nation-state, to communities and ultimately to the level of the
individual. With such a perspective in mind, this chapter first examines
maritime issues that could pose a threat to security in the Asia-Pacific.
We then explore the appropriate measures to be taken to enhance regional maritime security. Particular attention will be paid to the relevance
and role of legal rules in improving the maritime security environment.

Major maritime issues in the Asia-Pacific

Outstanding maritime issues in the region can conveniently be divided
into five categories: (1) disputes about the sovereignty of offshore islands;
(2) issues of maritime boundaries; (3) the protection of seaborne trade;
(4) resource conflicts; and (5) the maintenance of law and order at sea.

Island disputes

It has been pointed out that disputes over territory have been the most
important single cause of war between states in the past two or three
centuries. As one scholar observed some time ago, there is some kind of
sanctity about state territories.[1] It is often argued that the psychological
importance of territory is quite out of proportion to its intrinsic value,
economic or strategic.[2] Thus territorial disputes inevitably involve serious
threats to international peace and security. The danger of confrontation
is all the more serious when important natural resources are at stake.

The main offshore territorial dispute in the Asia-Pacific is over the
Spratly Islands in the South China Sea. Within the South China Sea, the
Paracel Islands and Macclesfield Bank have also been sources of dispute,
but the Spratly Islands are contested by six different claimants. They are
the most strategically important, lying in the key sea lines of communication (SLOCs) between the Strait of Malacca and North-East Asia's
great industrial powers.[3] The question of who owns the 400-plus rocks,
reefs, and islands within the South China Sea was largely ignored until
1970s. At that time, however, the area became a possible target for exploration by multinational oil companies. Motivated by the desire to
extend control over sea-based resources, neighbouring states in the area
have increasingly come into verbal conflict and even sporadic military
confrontation over who exercises sovereignty over the Spratlys. During

the 1980s and 1990s, most states found themselves in a race to bolster their claims to sovereignty by gaining occupation of those islands that can support a physical presence. Currently, Viet Nam occupies over 20 islets or rocks, China occupies 8, Taiwan 1, the Philippines 8, and Malaysia 3 to 6.

The race for occupation of the Spratlys has increased the likelihood of conflict, resulting in at least two major cases of military intimidation in recent years, one of which led to military conflict (China and Viet Nam in 1988 and China and the Philippines in early 1995). This particular territorial dispute thus remains one of the most dangerous flashpoints in the region. Although all the claimants have endorsed the use of peaceful means to overcome their differences, it is worrying that all claimants, except Brunei, have stationed troops in the contested area. With time, most of the claimants will be in a good position to project military power into the South China Sea. Progress in the informal South China Sea workshops hosted by Indonesia has been slow because of the different approaches, priorities, and agendas of China and the South China Sea states, but some cooperation has been achieved in non-contentious areas such as the conduct of marine scientific research, the preservation of the ecosystem, and pollution control.[4]

There are three major island disputes in the seas of North-East Asia: namely the dispute over the Senkaku Islands (or Daioyutai) between Japan and China; the dispute over the Tok-to (or Takeshima) between Korea and Japan; and the dispute over the Northern Territories (or Southern Kuril Islands) between Russia and Japan. Like the Spratlys, the three island disputes in North-East Asia, unless carefully managed, could also erupt into major regional conflict. The island disputes in North-East Asia have also recently come to the fore owing to the regional states' moves to extend their maritime jurisdictions by establishing 200-mile exclusive economic zones.[5] One of the consequences arising from such extended maritime jurisdiction is the overlapping of competing jurisdictions and, thus, the necessity of delimitation. In North-East Asia, where the distance between the coastal states does not exceed 400 miles, the question of boundary delimitation inevitably arises. Moreover, the extension of maritime jurisdiction also exacerbates the decade-long island disputes in the region, because the boundaries cannot be delimited unless the sovereignty disputes over the islands are resolved one way or another.

The intensity of these territorial disputes cannot be explained in terms of the economic or strategic value of the islands in dispute. Rather, in each case the dispute has become a volatile element of domestic politics. Certainly, historical animosities between Japan and other claimant states are a complicating factor in the Senkaku and Tok-to disputes. The risk of a military takeover of any of the disputed islands, however, seems unlikely. The political and human costs would be huge, while the economic and security benefits would be relatively small. But there is a risk that agitators on either side may precipitate a crisis by undertaking provocative acts, which would raise nationalist passions and make conflict resolution difficult.

Maritime boundaries

In the North-East Asian region, there are currently three maritime boundary agreements in force.[6] The geographic circumstances of the area require the conclusion of a few more bilateral and trilateral agreements to complete maritime boundaries. Yet two factors make the boundary delimitation in this area particularly thorny. First, there exist some very difficult territorial disputes in the region. Unless these territorial disputes are resolved, which is highly unlikely, it may not be possible to delimit the boundaries. Secondly, as the continental shelf dispute in the early 1970s showed, coastal states appear to be in serious disagreement about which laws should apply to boundary delimitation in the region. Moreover, the region's complicated geography and the uncertain nature of the seabed make delimitation an extremely difficult issue.

In the South-East Asian sub-region, on the other hand, there are currently over 20 maritime boundary agreements in force.[7] However, given the greater number of coastal states and the complicated geographical nature of the region, there still remain a number of important boundaries to be delimited. In fact, the geographical circumstances relating to the delimitation of maritime boundaries in South-East Asia are far more complicated than those found in North-East Asia. This area has a series of highly complicated territorial disputes as well, involving the ownership of uninhabited islands and coral outcroppings (most of them in the South China Sea).

The attitude of regional states towards boundary delimitation has been summarized by Sam Bateman as follows: "few countries appear to have assigned any great priority to the delimitation of maritime boundaries and some (e.g.: the Philippines, Russia and North Korea) have no agreed boundaries at all. Indonesia is the one country which has pursued its maritime boundary negotiations assiduously with agreement, wholly or in part, to seven of the seventeen boundaries required."[8] Furthermore, overlapping national maritime jurisdictions will continue to pose significant problems for marine environmental management and marine resource development in the Asia-Pacific.

SLOC security

The Asia-Pacific region as a whole enjoyed the highest rate of economic growth in the world in the 1980s and 1990s. If the region's economic strength continues to grow (and signs are good that its current financial crisis is dissipating), so too will its share in world trade. The medium of this expanded trade is shipping, which carries over 98 per cent of all goods traded. Thus the increased importance of Asia-Pacific trade means a remarkable growth in sea-borne trade traversing the Pacific Ocean. Against this backdrop, the security of merchant shipping in the region is a subject that certainly deserves continued attention.

In 1995, shipments in the Asia-Pacific region surpassed 1.5 billion tonnes, comprising over one-third of the world's maritime trade volume. Generally, crude oil is the biggest single cargo in terms of volume through the sea lanes of South-East Asia, while industrial products are the dominating cargo in terms of value. The SLOCs of South-East Asia handle 54 per cent of the total two-way trade of South-East Asian countries, 42 per cent of Japan's trade, and 46 per cent of Australia's trade.[9] Major shipping routes in the Asia-Pacific region are constricted at key straits such as Malacca, Sunda, Lombok, and Makassar straits. The South China Sea provides shipping routes connecting North-East Asia and the Middle East.

With the demise of Cold War confrontation, it is generally acknowledged that the prospects of a global conflict extending into East Asia and the consequent threat to the security of sea lanes are rather remote. However, this does not necessarily mean that threats to the security of the sea lanes cease to exist. In fact, although the end of the Cold War has certainly resulted in the decline of activities by the traditional naval powers in the region (the United States and Russia), it has also led to the rather paradoxical situation where more navies of regional powers have begun to assert themselves in regional waters, apparently to fill the power vacuum.[10]

China's naval capability, for instance, has expanded over the years from a coastal defence role to an ability to project power further offshore. This capability has assumed greater significance in the South China Sea, where territorial disputes remain unresolved. It is clear that Japan has the potential capability in technology and financial resources to go beyond its legitimate task of protecting its waters within 1,000 nautical miles from its mainland. Indeed, a long-range sea lane defence strategy is in prospect, indicated by the Japan Defence Agency's recent acceleration of defence procurement requests to cover Japan's "surrounding areas" more credibly.[11] Although these proposals have thus far been tempered by other Japanese government agencies, China's rising military power and on-going Japanese apprehensions about the United States' long-term intentions to balance China in the East and South China Sea could yet lead to a more independent and powerful Japanese maritime power.

Other countries in the region, including Taiwan, South Korea, and most ASEAN countries, are also planning to acquire more powerful naval forces and to develop their maritime capabilities. Such naval arms build-ups stem from growing concerns about the region's strategic environment and differing national interests, that is, the urge to protect and expand a sphere of influence and the fear of losing it. The states concerned thus pay heed to the geo-strategic dimension of their rivalries. The result is that, despite the reduction in the US and Russian maritime presence, the maritime security environment in the Asia-Pacific is becoming more complicated. There will be more navies of consequence, and an increased risk of incidents between maritime forces. This could result in a potentially unstable regional maritime environment. Of particular concern is disruption of SLOCs by conflicts involving actions by China to enforce its claims to sovereignty over Taiwan or the Spratly Islands, or to oil fields disputed with Viet Nam.

The other issue related to SLOC security is a navigational regime. Three specific categories of navigational controls – innocent passage, transit passage, and archipelagic sea lanes passage – are designed in the Law of the Sea Convention to balance the rights of user or maritime states with the interests of coastal states. Some coastal nations interpret the navigation regimes differently from the maritime powers. The former are generally interested in imposing controls in waters under their jurisdiction for purposes of national security and environmental protection. The latter tend to interpret the rules to permit a maximum degree of navigational freedom. The most important unresolved issues in the Convention, which could affect the security of the SLOCs in the Asia-Pacific region, are discussed below.

First, it is beyond dispute that a foreign vessel enjoys the right of innocent passage through the territorial sea of the coastal state. However, it has long been controversial whether or not the right of innocent passage applies to all ships, including warships or ships carrying nuclear or other inherently dangerous or noxious substances. In particular, the right of innocent passage for warships has been a much debated issue in the international community, and many coastal states have been reluctant to permit passage without prior authorization or at least notification. Further, general state practice remains conflicting. The history of foreign invasion and traditionally sensitive security concerns in East Asia has caused many coastal states in the region to have strong reservations on the right of foreign warships to innocent passage through their coastal waters.[12] Despite the adoption of the LOS Convention, this issue remains unresolved, and has become a potential source of conflict.

Secondly, under the Convention, straits used for international navigation are subject to the new regime of transit passage. Transit passage is defined as the exercise of freedom of navigation and overflight solely for the purpose of continuous and expeditious transit in normal modes of operation. It is generally understood that submarines are free to transit international straits submerged, since that is their normal mode of operation. As far as passage in the international straits is concerned, controversy appears to lie not in its military aspect but rather in its commercial aspect. For example, a question frequently concerns the rights of a strait state to interfere with transit passage because of suspected pollution incidents, and the scope of corresponding enforcement measures that can be taken by a strait state.[13] The strait states' regulatory response to accidents and pollution that heavy use of the straits has caused could be a serious source of conflict in the region, where there are some 20 important international straits.

Thirdly, under the LOS Convention, an archipelagic state may designate sea lanes and air routes suitable for the continuous and expeditious passage of foreign ships and aircraft through or above its archipelagic waters. Such archipelagic sea lanes must include all normal passage routes and all normal navigational channels. There are two important archipelagic states in the region, Indonesia and the Philippines. The Convention assigns responsibility to these states for designating sea lanes in coordination with the competent international organization, the International Maritime Organization (IMO). However, much uncertainty remains over the balance between maritime states and archipelagic states. Specifically, the respective roles and power of the IMO and of archipelagic states in designating sea lanes are subject to various interpretations. Given that the designation of archipelagic sea lanes is a potentially potent device for regulating navigation, it is not difficult to envisage a source of conflict unless common interpretation of an archipelagic regime is agreed.

The other challenges to the free passage of ships through SLOCs in the post–Cold War Asia-Pacific encompass obstruction due to maritime accidents or disasters, damage by piracy, unilateral declarations restricting the use of specific waters, and intentional obstruction of shipping by, for example, mining of a critical SLOC.[14] Although SLOC protection lends itself to cooperative regimes, some balance is needed between the concerns of maritime nations to keep the sea lanes open and as unregulated as possible and those nations whose coastlines abut the strategically important sea lanes and whose main concerns are associated with marine safety and traffic management issues.

Resource conflicts

Competition for scarce marine resources is another source of conflict in the region. It has been mentioned that territorial and boundary issues are becoming more acute, mostly because of the resources involved. In particular, fish that used to be found in abundance in the region have become very scarce owing mainly to over-fishing. Many national fishing grounds such as the Yellow/East China Sea and the Gulf of Siam have long been depleted of fish. This situation has made fisheries one of the most contentious maritime issues in the region. Currently, the fishing regime in North-East Asia that has been in force for the past four decades is going through a fundamental transformation because regional countries have either established or are about to establish 200-mile EEZs. New bilateral fishery agreements based on the regime of the EEZ have replaced,[15] or are expected to replace in the near future, the old treaties that had regulated fishery relations among the regional countries.

The transition to the era of the EEZ may be inevitable, but the path to a new regime is strewn with many thorny issues.[16] In South-East Asia, illegal fishing in foreign EEZs has become a cause of tension among regional states. There have been many incidents where the Thai navy, for example, has used force to prevent Thai fisherpeople from being arrested in neighbouring states' waters. It remains to be seen what will happen when the Thai navy acquires more power-projection capabilities. The Malaysian navy has been prompted to examine its rules of engagement in light of these developments. It may be necessary to introduce new incidents-at-sea agreements to prevent the escalation of low-level conflicts into greater ones over the near future. Such agreements are designed to prohibit or contain the consequences of inherently dangerous or inadvertent military activities by articulating codes of conduct for military forces and mandating crisis consultation and communication.[17]

Law and order at sea

Piracy has also become an issue of international importance and concern. The threat posed by piracy in South-East Asian waters has exhibited a marked rise since the end of the Cold War. Attacks rose from 3 in 1989 to 60 in 1990, before reaching an all-time high of 102 in 1991. Between 1992 and 1997, 511 separate attacks were recorded, representing an annual incident rate of 85. Indeed, South-East Asia is by far the most piracy-prone region of the world. The lethality of piracy attacks also appears to be on the increase. During the first half of the 1990s, with 557 ships boarded, 442 crew were taken hostage, 29 were assaulted, 45 were injured, and 55 were murdered. Piracy thus constitutes a direct threat to the lives and welfare of the citizens of a variety of flag states. Particular concern has been expressed about the navigational hazards to ships, often carrying dangerous cargoes, and the potential danger to navigation and the marine environment these ships may pose if left unattended while steaming at full speed and under attack by pirates in confined waters.

The fight against the international narcotics trade now has substantial international maritime dimensions, as has the problem of the passage of illegal migrant peoples. The major importation of drugs is usually made by sea through secretion in the structure of shipping containers, in containerized goods, and in vessel compartments; concealment in trawler cargo, coastal traders, and yachts; transfers at sea from mother ships to trawlers; crews bringing commodities ashore; and throwing narcotics overboard for local trawler or yacht recovery. Insurance frauds involving both ships and cargoes are another continuing source of major concern in the growing field of international crime. It has been estimated that maritime fraud costs the international community more than £13 billion annually. There is particular concern in the Asia-Pacific regarding cargo deviations, that is, vessels not arriving at their nominated destination but unloading the cargo elsewhere, where it is sold and the vessel scuttled or re-registered, and phantom ships, namely vessels with false identities. The safe carriage of dangerous cargoes such as nuclear materials and liquefied natural gas is also an emotive and controversial environmental issue of particular importance to the Asia-Pacific scene. Concerns are raised in relation to the lack of notification to coastal states of the routes the shipments take, to legal issues relating to the shipment of nuclear materials through sensitive ocean areas, and to the liability of the states involved in the shipments should there be an accident.[18] In the case of nuclear materials, the declarations of nuclear-free zones may also raise difficult issues because of inconsistency with commitments made under the LOS Convention.

Measures to enhance maritime security in the Asia-Pacific

In the post–Cold War Asia-Pacific, the urgent task of all regional states and maritime powers with interests in the region should be to support a stable and secure maritime regime as well as to implement maritime confidence-building measures. Such a maritime regime is a fundamental prerequisite not only for enhancing security at sea but also for further maritime cooperation among regional states. Perhaps the first priority is to agree upon the common reference point for the use and protection of the ocean. In this regard, it should be noted that the global ocean regime, as sets of authoritative norms for the jurisdictions and uses of the ocean, received its most complete expression in the LOS Convention. This framework is a good basis for building a more stable maritime regime in the region.[19] Obviously, ratifying and adhering to the LOS Convention will not solve all the problems confronting the region. Nevertheless, it will surely play a long-term stabilizing role by curing and preventing the growth of state practice at variance with the universal norms so established.

Along with such regime-building efforts, various maritime confidence-and-security-building measures should be explored. As the maritime security environment gradually changes, the idea of regional agreements on the prevention of incidents at sea particularly deserves more attention. The need for such agreements has become real, owing mainly to the increased naval presence of many states in confined regional waters. Moreover, such agreements would subsequently facilitate development towards something more important in the future.

It has been suggested that the importance of maritime information and databases to the sustainable development of marine and coastal areas could even lead to a new discipline of marine informatics. This would involve studying how to supply decision-makers with the high-quality integrated information they require to make decisions on complex issues of sustainable development.[20] Although at the individual level citizens have a right to know, to understand, and to access information about their marine environment, the biggest problem about information sharing in the Asia-Pacific is that, with such a complicated situation regarding maritime jurisdiction and unresolved maritime boundaries, states may be less willing to cooperate in case they are perceived to be compromising their sovereignty.

With respect to the territorial/boundary and resources issues, the prospects for resolving territorial disputes are slim. Given the enormous difficulties related to resolving ongoing sovereignty disputes, it is better to divorce the question of sovereignty from the more technical boundary negotiations. Furthermore, in light of the complexities of the geographical and other situations in the region, a more functionally oriented approach is preferable to a jurisdiction-oriented approach such as boundary delimitation. Regional states should be encouraged to resolve pressing issues of environmental protection and resource development without incorporating underlying sovereignty and boundary issues. For instance, the states may address fishery problems, which motivated them to establish the 200-mile zone, from a regional perspective by promoting a coordinated policy of conservation and effective enforcement procedures. They may also work out cooperative arrangements for the development of seabed mineral resources. Since such arrangements could be established without prejudice to underlying territorial and maritime boundary issues, they might constitute optimal solutions that would defer more politically charged issues to the indefinite future. Given the rather sensitive political relations between various regional states, this approach may be more constructive.

To maintain law and order at sea, multilateral maritime surveillance regimes might be considered for dealing with particular problems such as piracy and oil spills in international waterways. In 1992, for example, Malaysia, Singapore, and Indonesia agreed to cooperative efforts to combat the increasing threat of piracy in the Strait of Malacca. The three countries are now discussing the establishment of a common surveillance system over the Strait, to provide shared radar coverage of all traffic through the waterway. Obviously, there is little enthusiasm in the region at this stage for proceeding with a full-blown regional maritime surveillance regime. Short of a structured maritime surveillance regime, arrangements for the exchange of maritime information and data would be very important as potential maritime confidence-and-security-building measures in their own right and a prerequisite for other forms of maritime security cooperation including maritime surveillance.

Conclusion

It has been previously emphasized that the LOS Convention could be a solid basis for building a stable regional maritime regime and thus enhancing maritime security in the Asia-Pacific. However, despite the seemingly strong support for the LOS Convention in the region, there are considerable doubts concerning the precise rules for governing the use of the ocean since many LOS provisions lack clarity and are subject to varying interpretation. In this sense, a stable maritime regime for the Asia-Pacific requires agreement on how to apply the terms of the Convention. In fact, the necessity of developing a uniform, coherent maritime regime through commonly acceptable interpretations is more acute in this part of the world than in any other region, mainly because outlooks and behaviour pertaining to important aspects of ocean use diverge substantially among the coastal states in the region. In this respect, the following three points should be emphasized.

First, it is important to enhance openness and transparency as regards maritime regimes and the practice of regional states. In fact, the LOS Convention requires coastal states to give due publicity to the charts or lists of geographical coordinates related to their baseline or jurisdictions and to deposit a copy of each such chart or list with the Secretary-General of the United Nations.[21] Considering that a number of unfortunate incidents have occurred in recent times that can be traced to uncertainty on such matters, this would seem essential for building a stable regional ocean regime.

Secondly, the LOS Convention offers a pacific settlement system that would substantially contribute to the development of uniform practice and interpretation of the Convention. It also provides the basis for further development of law by providing general principles and a framework for issues such as marine environment and marine scientific research. Regional states should make the most of such mechanisms and frameworks to settle future disputes and to promote greater cooperation.

Thirdly, regional states should intensify their efforts to develop a more harmonious and solid maritime regime. In particular, regional states could reach greater consensus about controversial rules of the law of the sea that are inconsistent with the national policies of certain states. For instance, the United States and the Soviet Union signed a joint statement in 1989 on the innocent passage of warships in each other's territorial seas. Attached to the joint statement, the two governments issued a Uniform Interpretation of the Rules of International Law Governing Innocent Passage, which sets forth in more detail the common interpretation of the Convention governing innocent passage in territorial seas.[22] Similar measures could be taken by regional states with respect to various controversial issues. In addition, regional maritime councils or other coordinating bodies could be established for the purpose of coordination and strengthening cooperation among regional states.

All of these measures relate to the broader task of interrelating maritime resources and issues more effectively to the needs of individuals inhabiting the Asia-Pacific maritime region. Out of necessity, maritime security politics remains the current domain of state-centric bargaining and coordination. As greater expertise is required to negotiate and resolve increasingly complex LOC-related issues, however, the need to cultivate epistemic communities of experts to identify possible solutions to future maritime conflicts and for grass-roots support to enact these solutions will intensify. As a result, ways of conducting the business of maritime diplomacy in the Asia-Pacific are bound to undergo substantial and far-reaching change.

Notes

1. A. O. Cukwurah, *The Settlement of Boundary Disputes in International Law* (Manchester: Manchester University Press, 1967), p. 10.
2. Evan Luard, *The International Regulation of Frontier Disputes* (London: Thames & Hudson, 1970), p. 7.
3. For a detailed study of the Spratly dispute, see for example Mark Valencia and Jon Van Dyke, "Comprehensive Solutions to the South China Sea Disputes: Some Options," in Sam Bateman and Stephen Bates, eds., *The Seas Unite: Maritime Cooperation in the Asia Pacific Region* (Canberra: Strategic and Defence Studies Centre for the Australian National University, 1996), pp. 223–262.

4. See Ian Townsend-Gault, "Preventive Diplomacy and Pro-Activity in the South China Sea," *Contemporary Southeast Asia* 20, no. 2 (August 1998), pp. 171–190.
5. For more on recent developments, see Jin-Hyun Paik, "Territorial Disputes at Sea: Situation, Possibilities, and Prognosis – With Particular Reference to Northeast Asian Seas," in Mohamed Jawhar Hassan and Ahmade Raffie, *Bringing Peace to the Pacific* (Kuala Lumpur: ISIS Malaysia, 1997), pp. 319–334.
6. The first boundary in the region was delimited between South Korea and Japan in the continental shelf area through the Korea Strait north of Tsushima Island in 1974. In 1986 and 1990, respectively, North Korea and the Soviet Union (now Russia) agreed on their territorial sea boundary and continental shelf and EEZ boundaries in the northern East Sea (or Sea of Japan).
7. For details of maritime boundary agreements in force in the East Asian region, see Jonathan I. Charney and Lewis M. Alexander, eds., *International Maritime Boundaries*, vols. 1 and 2 (Dordrecht and Boston: Martinus Nijhoff, 1993).
8. Sam Bateman, "Economic Growth, Marine Resources and Naval Arms in East Asia – A Deadly Triangle?" *Marine Policy* 22, no. 4–5 (1998), p. 303.
9. United States Pacific Command, *Asia-Pacific Economic Update*, Summer 1996.
10. For regional naval developments, see Dick Sherwood, ed., *Maritime Power in the China Seas: Capabilities and Rationale* (Canberra: Australian Defence Studies Centre, 1994).
11. Japan's new National Defence Programme Outline adopted in November 1995 emphasized the importance of that country building a capability of acting more efficiently to defend Japan's "surrounding areas" in future contingencies. This principle was further reinforced in 1997 when the Diet approved a revised set of U.S.–Japan Defense Guidelines, which committed the Japanese to support US military operations in future "regional contingencies" more comprehensively.
12. The following states in the East Asian region require either authorization or notification for the innocent passage of foreign warships: Bangladesh, Myanmar, China, India, Indonesia, Republic of Korea, Democratic People's Republic of Korea, and Pakistan.
13. For details, see B. A. Hamzah and Mohd. Nizam Basiron, *The Straits of Malacca: Some Funding Proposals* (Kuala Lumpur: ISIS Malaysia, 1997).
14. For details, see Henry Kenny, *An Analysis of Possible Threats to Shipping in Key Southeast Asian Sea Lanes* (Alexandra, VA: Center for Naval Analysis, 1996).
15. For example, the new Korea–Japan fishery agreement, which entered into force in January 1999, has replaced the bilateral agreement of 1965. The new treaty has been strongly opposed by fisherpeople in both countries.
16. For a discussion of the dangers related to the transition to the EEZ in North-East Asia, see Jin-Hyun Paik, "Exploitation of Natural Resources: Potential for Conflicts in Northeast Asia," in Sam Bateman and Stephen Bates, eds., *Calming the Waters: Initiatives for Asia Pacific Maritime Cooperation* (Canberra: Strategic and Defence Studies Centre for the Australian National University, 1996), pp. 171–184.
17. See Stanley Weeks, "Incidents at Sea Agreements and Maritime Confidence-Building Measures," in Bateman and Bates, *The Seas Unite*, pp. 79–94.
18. For an analysis of the difficult questions raised by the transport of radioactive wastes from Europe to Japan through the Asia-Pacific region, see Grant Hewison, "Return Shipments of Radioactive Wastes from Europe to Japan," unpublished paper presented at the meeting of the Working Group on Maritime Cooperation of the Council for Security Cooperation in the Asia Pacific, Tokyo, Japan, November 1997.
19. Strong support for, and commitment to, the LOS Convention is evident in the Asia-Pacific region. The following regional states are now parties to the LOS Convention:

Australia, China, Indonesia, India, Japan, Malaysia, Mongolia, Myanmar, New Zealand, the Marshall Islands, the Philippines, Belau, Russia, Nauru, South Korea, Singapore, Western Samoa, the Solomon Islands, Sri Lanka, and Viet Nam.

20. Roger Bradbury, "Marine Informatics: A New Discipline Emerges," *Maritime Studies*, no. 80 (January/February 1995), pp. 15–22.
21. Articles 16, 75, and 84 of the LOS Convention.
22. For the text of the statement with the attached Uniform Interpretation of Rules of International Law Governing Innocent Passage, see *International Legal Materials* 28 (1989), pp. 1444–1447.

12

Human and economic security: Is there a nexus?

Leong Liew

Introduction

Since the end of the Cold War, there has been a shift in emphasis in security issues away from "national security" to "human security." According to Ramesh Thakur, "national security" focuses on "military defense of the state" whereas "human security" emphasizes "the individual's welfare."[1] The emphasis given to the defence of the state during the Cold War does not mean that the welfare of an individual was considered unimportant. On the contrary, individual welfare was considered important but it was conditional upon the existence of a secure state. During the Cold War, national leaders perceived that the security of their nations was under threat and therefore placed the security of the state ahead of an individual's welfare. Today, with the end of the Cold War, armed conflicts are mainly inter-ethnic rather than inter-state.[2] The traditional threat to states from other states is declining, but new forms of threats – terrorism, organized crime, political instability, and poverty – are rising. Moreover, closer international integration of financial, commodity, and even labour markets has shifted governments' focus away from national security to economic security as the important determinant of individual security. People in the West today worry less about war than about unemployment, and economic rather than national security is now the major concern of public policy.[3] What then is the nexus between human and economic security? Is there a nexus? In this chapter, I explore some of the literature in the fields of economics and political science to derive some suggestive answers to these two questions.

Some definitions

Initially, one has to be clear about the concepts "human security" and "economic security." Are they two separate variables or is economic security simply a subset of human security? Some authors from a variety of disciplines regard economic security simply as a subset of human security.[4] If this is the case, there is no causal relationship between the two concepts and an examination of any "nexus" would be mundane. In this chapter, I treat human security and economic security as two distinct and separate variables. Human security is defined here as conditions that enable humans to be free from physical risk and physical danger, to live in a sustainable environment, and to have economic welfare. This approximates the definition used by de Sherbinin but, unlike de Sherbinin, I do not consider economic security to be necessarily synonymous with economic welfare.[5]

Economic security can be considered at two levels: micro and macro. At the micro level, it embodies two aspects. One is institutional security of the market, which requires the existence of institutions that enable the successful functioning of a market economy. Security of property rights and security of contracts are generally accepted by most economists as the most important of these institutions. The other aspect is economic security of the individual, which is security of employment and income. The former aspect relates to security of private assets, including human and intellectual capital, and sanctity of contracts; the latter relates to the security of the stream of income from those assets. The security of the stream of income of an individual is not just about how secure his or her employment is. It is also about how high or low a society's guaranteed minimum income is relative to average income. It is in effect the security of access to a certain level of consumption to which people are accustomed. At the macro level, economic security concerns a state's economic security. It concerns the effectiveness of the state, through its trade policies and foreign relations, in protecting and enhancing the collective economic security of its citizens.

The consumption set that can be afforded by an individual indicates his or her level of economic welfare. The absolute income level of an individual is a good measurement of this consumption set. It includes all sources of income, private as well as government financial and non-financial transfers.[6] Since economic welfare is related to consumption, it includes "health security," which is to have access to good and affordable medical care. A high level of economic security does not necessarily accompany a high level of economic welfare; it is possible to have one without the other, and they may sometimes be inversely related. The middle classes in the United States, Western Europe, and Australia are today, for example, materially very well off, but they suffer from high insecurity of employment and income. The middle classes in the newly industrialized countries of East Asia share the same experience as their Western counterparts. The middle classes in East Asia have reaped significant material benefits from the globalization of their national economies, but the Asian financial crisis has shown that this has come with a price of increased vulnerability of their economies and a lower level of economic security. Workers in the former Soviet Union and in Maoist China were not well off economically; they had very low standards of living compared with those enjoyed in the West, but they enjoyed a high degree of employment and income security. Although the minimum guaranteed income in Western Europe and Australia is higher than in Maoist China, the gap between the minimum guaranteed income and average income was much lower in Maoist China, which had one of the most equal income distributions in the world.

Aside from economic welfare, human security includes freedom from both physical risk and physical danger and living in a sustainable healthy environment. To be free from risk and physical danger is to have personal security. To have personal security is to be free from any form of arbitrary punishment, imprisonment, and violent crime.[7] These freedoms do not include the freedom from economic risk or from negative market outcomes for the individual, which have more to do with economic security.

Individual economic security and human security

A case has been made that economic security and human security are separate variables, but what is the form of the relationship between them? Are they positively or inversely related? Is the relationship unidirectional – economic security determines human security or vice versa – or are they mutually dependent? These questions are explored in turn in this and in subsequent sections.

One can infer four major arguments from the literature concerning the relationship between individual economic security and human security.[8] The first can be labelled the "neo-Darwinian view" and it finds support in some of the neo-classical economic studies that have examined the relationship between tax and labour supply, and between social security and saving. It suggests an inverse relationship between individual economic security and human security. According to this view, economic insecurity provides the incentive for the individual to perform paid work[9] and to save. An absence of economic insecurity (as a consequence, for example, of the existence of a generous welfare system) lowers the incentive for individuals to work. Moreover, the disincentive to work affected by a generous welfare system is reinforced by the high level of personal taxation that has to be levied on those who work to sustain the provision of such a generous system. The neo-Darwinian view suggests that in the long run a generous welfare system would cause a loss of the work ethic, which ultimately will adversely affect individual economic welfare.

On the question of private saving, Martin Feldstein has found that each dollar of social security wealth in the United States reduces private saving by between two and three cents and the overall impact of the social security programme is to reduce private saving by 60 per cent.[10] The implication of Feldstein's research finding for human security is that the existence of a social security system reduces private saving and thereby adversely affects investment. This reduces economic growth and therefore has a long-term negative impact on human security. The belief in an inverse relationship between economic security and the individual incentive to work and save was very strong in the 1980s, and it drove many of the economic and social policies of conservative political leaders such as Prime Minister Thatcher in the United Kingdom and President Reagan in the United States.

A high level of economic security for the individual does not necessarily have to be financed through high levels of personal taxation. Governments of a small number of resource-rich countries with low populations such as Kuwait and Brunei are able to provide high levels of individual economic security without the need to resort to high rates of taxation. The people of these countries, however, would eventually suffer from the "winner's curse."[11] The good fortune of their citizens, according to this argument, makes them soft and unprepared for the rigour of competition, which they must face when their natural resources are exhausted. These countries are moreover easy targets of aggression from their larger and more powerful neighbours and have to rely continuously on Western powers for security.[12]

Although an inverse relationship between economic security and human security finds support from aspects of neo-classical economics, some critics of neo-classical economics also lend their indirect support to this view. The well-known economic historian Joseph Schumpeter viewed innovation as the driving force behind the dynamism of capitalism. Unlike neo-classical economics, his theory does not focus on price competition as a driving force of capitalist development. Instead, it is "competition from the new commodity, the new technology, the new source of supply, the new type of organization ... competition which commands a decisive cost or quality advantage and which strikes not at the margins of the profits and the outputs of the existing firms but at their foundations and their very lives."[13] He coined the term "creative destruction," which embodies the idea that an old economic structure has to be destroyed before a new one that is better suited to a changed business environment can be created. Economic security for the individual has the connotation of stability, of absence of change, and this violates the principle of creative destruction. Schumpeter would argue that complete economic security for the individual is unattainable, and that any attempt to achieve it would ultimately fail because the forces of capitalist competition would destroy those who seek to preserve the old ways of doing things. In the Schumpeterian world, economic insecurity is the catalyst for change and development. Sunset industries must be allowed to fail lest they become a burden to sunrise industries, and outdated institutions must be replaced with modern institutions to accommodate and to facilitate change.

The classical social democrat or radical position on the relationship between individual economic security and human security is diametrically opposite to the neo-Darwinian view. It holds that there is a positive relationship between individual economic security and human security. Supporting arguments for this position can be found in some of the literature on population growth. Early research on fertility was heavily influenced by Gary Becker, who formulated a model where both low incomes and low opportunity cost of time as a result of a lack of market opportunities for the poor encourage the procreation and raising of children. When households enjoy high incomes and experience high opportunity cost of time, they will opt for quality rather than quantity of children.[14]

Instead of the opportunity cost of time, M. T. Cain focuses on economic insecurity as an important variable explaining fertility. According to Cain, economic insecurity and low incomes are responsible for the high population growth in many developing countries. In developing countries, small markets and restrictive labour mobility limit job opportunities and sources of saving. In the absence of a social welfare net, children are the only guaranteed source of old-age pension for many people.[15] As population increases, labour supply increases as well and this puts pressure on wages. Families that rely primarily on selling their labour for income therefore have the incentive to maximize the number of their children to maximize household income. The consequence of many families maximizing the number of their children is to increase the labour supply and so depress wages even further. Another consequence is that fewer public resources per capita are available for government subsidies to the poor for education and health. Education and health are important factors influencing long-term labour productivity, and smaller subsidies to the poor for these two services have an adverse impact on their long-term economic welfare.[16]

Thus the argument for a positive relationship between individual economic security and human security is strong for developing countries, but what about for industrialized countries? Could a case be made that the relationship between individual economic security and human security is positive in these types of state? The answer is "yes," but a different argument has to be used. In industrialized countries, there is access to public pensions and overpopulation is not a problem.[17] The factor that can explain a positive relationship between individual economic security and human security in industrialized countries is economic risk. Returns to investment are positively correlated with levels of risk, but many individuals are risk averse. In fact, the less wealthy a person is, the more risk averse the person is likely to be. The economic welfare of a society depends on having a large number of entrepreneurs who are prepared to take risks to invest in projects for individual profit and in the process create wealth and jobs for the rest of the population. Risk-taking is less likely among the less wealthy when the safety-net available to support those who fail is perceived to be non-existent or inadequate. Failure in a business venture for the less wealthy could mean a fall from a spartan but nevertheless comfortable level of living to poverty. For the wealthy, it could mean a dramatic fall in standards of living, to a level well below the norm.

The source of the conflict between economic conservatives and classical social democrats over the relationship between individual economic security and human security is their opposing views of human nature. Economic conservatives tend to hold the view that human beings are natural free-riders, always trying to get something for nothing. The classical social democrat has a more altruistic view of human nature, believing that human beings are not natural free-riders who are forced to work because of economic insecurity. In this view, people work not just because of economic insecurity but also because it gives them purpose and connects them to society. The reluctance of less wealthy people to invest in a business to be self-employed instead of remaining unemployed or working in a not entirely satisfactory job is related to risk aversion, not laziness. Unemployment is caused not by people who are unwilling to work but by the unavailability of jobs at at least the subsistence wage.[18] In the classical social democrat view, economic security is likely to enhance economic welfare and hence human security by providing social insurance for risk-taking. Whereas conservatives tend to emphasize the problem of "moral hazard"[19] in the economy, classical social democrats tend to emphasize the cooperation between individuals.

What is the available evidence that supports or counters these perspectives? As one would expect, evidence exists to back both arguments. Andrew Schotter reported a series of experiments that suggested repeated transactions between individuals increase free-rider behaviour because individuals take time to learn that free-rider behaviour can improve their economic payoffs.[20] On the other hand, Roland McKean argued that repeated social interactions provide "opportunities for application of social pressure," which contribute to the successful enforcement of informal rules and ethical conduct. Continuous social interactions increase the importance of individual reputation and collective sanctions become effective deterrents against free-rider behaviour. However, reputation is important to the individual and collective sanctions work only in the presence of small numbers of people. With large numbers, the effectiveness of deterrence is compromised by informational and enforcement problems and moral hazard is more likely.[21]

Most Western industrialized governments tend to adopt a middle neoliberal position between the conservatives and the classical social democrats. In this middle position, the form of the relationship between individual economic security and human security is seen to be an inverted U. At low levels of individual economic security, increases in economic security improve economic welfare and hence human security. There is a threshold, however, beyond which further increases in economic security reduce economic welfare and human security. The neoliberal view recognizes the importance of a basic safety-net to provide a modicum of individual economic security, but it also recognizes that too much economic security for the individual can reduce the incentive to work and to save. This type of theorizing provides the intellectual justification for welfare targeting of the poorest while allowing the market to dictate outcomes for those of the population who are better off. This is the ideology of Tony Blair's "New Labour" in Great Britain and of the Hawke–Keating Labor governments of the 1980s and the first half of the 1990s in Australia. It is also the ideology behind the policies transforming command economies to market economies.[22]

The dominant Japanese management view on the relationship between individual economic security and human security differs from the middle neoliberal position.[23] It is still a middle position like that of Western industrialized states, but the form of the relationship is not an inverted U. From the Japanese management perspective, the specific form of the relationship depends on whether one is looking at inter-group or intra-group interaction. Intra-group cooperation is a form of social insurance and it provides economic security through risk-sharing among members of a group, which encourages individual risk-taking. Inter-group competition, however, is fostered to provide the incentive to achieve higher economic welfare. Intra-group cooperation and inter-group competition together form the foundation for long-term economic growth and guarantee human security. Japanese industrial organization is the best example of this belief in action. *Keiretsu* business groups enable risk-sharing in innovation between the manufacturing J-firm and its suppliers. Suppliers compete to remain within the *keiretsu* for the benefits of assured markets, and this competition between suppliers and cooperation between the suppliers and the manufacturer make the manufacturer internationally competitive.[24] Within the J-firm, cooperation is emphasized with a view to improving the competitiveness of the firm.[25] In other words, internal cooperation is designed to facilitate external competitiveness. Intra group, the relationship between economic security and human security is seen to be positive, whereas inter group, this relationship is seen to be negative.

This Japanese management approach to individual economic and human security emphasizes the importance of institutions and finds support from the institutional school of economics. The school sees that continuous interaction of institutions and organizations in the face of competition drives institutional change. Institutions are "rules of the game in a society"; they are "humanly devised constraints that shape human interaction,"[26] and organizations are "groups of individuals bound by some common purpose to achieve objectives."[27] "Competition forces organizations to continually invest in skills and knowledge to survive." Key competency acquired by individuals and organizations will determine their "perceptions about opportunities and hence choices that will incrementally alter institutions."[28]

There is a subtle yet important difference between the view on competition expressed here and the view implicit in Schumpeter's "creative destruction." Schumpeter emphasized discrete historical jumps; North emphasizes incremental and evolutionary changes. According to North, change is path dependent. Incremental and evolutionary changes are consistent with maintenance of individual economic security. Discrete historical jumps are not; they imply dramatic changes and upheavals. The Japanese view of capitalist development is closer to North's view than to Schumpeter's perspective. Internal stability and the promise of economic security for the individual encourage risk-taking by a group, which improves its external competitiveness and, theoretically, advances long-term economic welfare and human security.

State economic security and human security

The four major arguments concerning the nexus between economic security and human security discussed above focus on the issue at the micro level. In this section, the problem is discussed at the macro or state level. At the state level, the issue centres on the effectiveness of the state, through its trade policies and foreign relations, in protecting and enhancing the economic security of its citizens as a group. Economic security involves securing current sources of raw materials and finding new ones, as well as protecting current and new markets for domestic producers. On one side of the argument, it can be seen how economic security enhances human security. Guaranteed access to raw materials and continued access to existing markets and expansion of foreign markets are obviously good for the economic welfare of a country. On the other side, however, efforts to achieve economic security could be a source of conflict. Japan's attempt to enhance its economic security in the 1930s was an important factor driving that country into World War II. Recently, efforts by China and some of its neighbours to secure potential rich sources of energy in the South China Sea are behind the territorial disputes among these players.

Policies implemented by states to protect domestic markets may enhance the economic security of domestic producers. States have used strategic trade policies successfully to develop new industries, penetrate world markets, and enhance a nation's economic welfare. All these policies have the potential to enhance the economic security and economic welfare of a nation but, when advocates of "free trade" dominate world politics, they also have the potential to generate conflicts with the nation's trading partners in today's world. Although bilateral trade disputes on their own are unlikely to lead to serious retaliatory conflicts that could harm human security, they can inflame other disputes severely enough to cause a major conflict.[29] The ongoing trade dispute between the United States and China and the disputes between these two nations over Taiwan, human rights, and weapons exports, for example, are sources of tension that could conceivably lead to a serious conflict between them.[30]

Market institutional security and human security

Liberal theory predicts a positive correlation between market institutional security and human security.[31] Market institutional security in the form of economic rights, particularly property rights and rights to secure contracts, is regarded in liberal theory as an important prerequisite for economic development and the promotion of human security. Although the case for a positive relationship between market institutional security and human security is strong, there are also strong alternative arguments that suggest this relationship is complex and cannot easily be represented in simple linear terms.

Baumol and Olsen, among others, emphasized the importance of private property rights for human security. Baumol made the distinction between productive and unproductive entrepreneurship. In his view, productive entrepreneurship creates wealth; unproductive entrepreneurship merely redistributes wealth. Property rights are one of the "rules of the game" that determine whether a society encourages productive or unproductive entrepreneurship. When private property rights are impeded or are inadequately protected, entrepreneurs concentrate their efforts on protecting their existing wealth and redistributing other people's wealth, and neglect production. Baumol illustrated his argument with examples from feudal China. He explained that official positions were highly coveted in feudal China because weak legal protection of property rights allowed imperial officials to depredate the general population. Wealth gained through productive entrepreneurship could easily be lost to the predatory actions of officials. The consequence of this, according to Baumol, was low levels of productive investment and economic development.

Olsen contrasted the behaviour of roving predators with that of stationary bandits to illustrate the importance of secure private property rights for economic growth and hence human security. He painted a picture of life in a locality where anarchy reigns. In our anarchical society, uncoordinated theft by roving bandits destroys the incentive to produce, making the local population and bandits worse off as a result. The incentive to produce is improved, according to Olsen, if the bandit chief makes a commitment to the locality by establishing himself or herself as a warlord. Uncoordinated theft is replaced by organized theft. A secure warlord will have the incentive to provide security and other public goods that will stimulate economic activity. An insecure warlord with temporary tenure will have no incentive to provide public goods that complement other inputs in production. Instead, productive assets will either be confiscated or be left to run down.

In China, township and village enterprises (TVEs) appear to provide a counter-example to the importance of private property rights. The property rights of Chinese TVEs are vague and insecure but competition for investment funds among community governments appears to be effective in keeping a check on their predatory actions towards the TVEs.[32] The presence of ample investment alternatives for capital in other localities substitutes for a lack of formal property rights protection in providing market institutional security.

Most of the traditional literature on property rights focuses attention on the state or the "ruler" or "warlord" as the only potential threat to property rights. But other actors are potential threats as well. Once attention is drawn away from those threats in the traditional literature, property rights violation could be interpreted in a different light. As Przeworski and Limongi have observed, organized workers have threatened the property of capitalists, and landless peasants have threatened the property of landlords.[33] Hence, property rights violation need not always be negative, since historically the poor have had to violate property rights in local common-pool resources to survive. The local commons as a source of food and fodder during bad years serve as insurance for the poor. Enforcement of property rights over the commons induces the conservation of scarce resources and internalizes externalities, and is good for the environment, but it can be detrimental to the well-being of the poor.[34]

A similar argument could be used to justify redistributing land from rich landlords to landless peasants. A lack of market institutional security may be a reason for personal security because violence by the poor is forestalled. The key is whether property rights violation is a one-shot confiscation or whether it is continuous. When land reform is carried out as a one-shot move and strong commitments given by the state that there will be no further redistribution of land are believed, then there should be no economic disincentive to production. Land reform in Taiwan in the 1950s is one example of a successful land reform backed by the force of the state. It was a one-shot move that made a positive contribution to Taiwan's postwar economic miracle. The People's Republic of China had a programme of land reform too, but constant changes in property rights and inappropriate agricultural policies undermined agricultural production and threatened human security.[35]

Organized workers may threaten the property rights of capitalists, but it can be argued that this leads to more equal incomes and a more harmonious society. More importantly, it is debatable whether organized labour will necessarily undermine human security by disadvantaging owners of capital and lowering their incentive to invest. Proactive organized labour may be able to impose a numerator management strategy, rather than the denominator strategy favoured by owners of capital, which some research has shown to strengthen rather than weaken the long-run competitiveness of the firm.[36] A numerator management strategy focuses on research and development to create new products and markets. This is opposite to a denominator strategy, which focuses on cost-cutting.

Saint-Paul and Verdier add another interesting twist to the argument on income redistribution by suggesting that wealth redistribution does not need to have a negative impact on economic development, and by inference human security, if the income is redistributed as public education. Public education, according to these analysts, is an investment in human capital, which plays an indispensable role in promoting economic growth.[37] Moreover, the amount of positive externalities generated by education is large. Consumers of education do not internalize all its benefits. Funds redistributed away from the wealthy to fund public education benefit the wealthy from the positive externalities generated by a better-educated population. All things equal, owners of capital will derive a higher return from their investment with a better-educated workforce.

The protection of property rights and the enforcement of contracts in places such as Italy and post-communist Russia are often provided by organized crime. Provision of these services by organized crime tends to flourish in places where state authority is weakest.[38] The provision of these services is incidental to other predatory actions of organized crime, and they do not ultimately contribute to economic welfare but in fact undermine personal security and have an adverse impact on human security. So, although protection of economic rights may be important for the development of human security, the experience of Russia shows that the mechanism through which this protection is obtained is equally important.

Democracy, economic security, and human security

A substantial amount of the literature that deals with the relationship between democracy and economic welfare, especially that written by scholars trained in economics, focuses on the impact of democracy on the protection of property rights. Olsen saw democracy as an effective tool of good governance for guaranteeing the protection of economic rights.[39] Dornbusch and Edwards took the opposite position and argued that democracy may create the incentive to appropriate capital.[40] On the other hand, Saint-Paul and Verdier pointed out that, even if democracy leads to redistribution of wealth, it is not detrimental to growth if the redistribution is delivered as public education, as we just considered.[41] Thus, democracy may not be bad for human security even if it may be bad for economic security. In fact, democracy may not necessarily be bad for economic security. Dornbusch and Edwards focused on the impact of democracy on owners of capital, but democracy may enhance the economic security of owners of labour, who form the majority of society. Industrial democracy could increase the economic security enjoyed by workers by making it more difficult for owners of capital to dismiss them. Another argument for a positive link between democracy and economic security has been put forward by A. K. Sen, the Nobel laureate in economics, who has argued that adversarial politics and a free press play an important role in famine prevention.[42]

The argument that an autocratic government is conducive to economic growth was popularized by Huntington, who argued that democracy leads to popular demands for high consumption.[43] This has an adverse impact on profits and investment and therefore undermines growth and economic welfare.[44] Hong Kong, Singapore, South Korea, and Taiwan have often been cited as examples of authoritarian rule being successful in enhancing economic welfare. However, there are many other examples, such as North Korea and Zimbabwe, of authoritarian rule being the antithesis of economic growth and economic welfare. The available evidence is still inconclusive as to whether democratic or authoritarian regimes are best for economic welfare.[45]

Even if the evidence for an inverse relationship between democracy and economic welfare is strong, economic welfare is only one aspect of human security; personal security is another aspect. Personal security includes freedom from any form of arbitrary punishment and imprisonment, which is best guaranteed by a democratic system. Moreover, according to Congleton, democracies are more concerned with the wellbeing of the environment than are authoritarian regimes. This, reasoned Congleton, is because an autocrat receives a greater share of national income than the median voter in a democracy. As a result, his or her opportunity cost of forgone income from environmental controls is higher.[46]

Democracy has been treated as the independent variable, and economic security and economic growth as the dependent variables, in our discussion so far on the relationship between these three variables. It is perfectly legitimate to specify democracy and economic security as dependent variables and make economic growth the independent variable. Economic growth provides greater economic security and a higher level of economic welfare, but it is not clear that rising economic incomes will turn an authoritarian political system into a democratic one. Przeworski and Limongi, in a statistical study of 135 countries between 1950 and 1990, found that the birth of democracy is not an inevitable consequence of economic development, but a high level of economic development improves the chances that a democracy will survive once it is in existence. They found that democracies with per capita incomes above US$6,005 (at constant 1985 prices and purchasing power parity values) are likely to exist forever.[47]

Conclusion

There is obviously a nexus between human and economic security. A wide range of literature, mainly from the disciplines of economics and political science, was used to establish the existence of such a nexus. But the relationship between human and economic security is complex and my analysis of the literature is unable to come up with a clearly defined causal relationship. There are two main reasons for this. First, the arguments in the literature differ according to differences in ideology or theoretical approaches. The Thatcherite and the social democratic views on the relationship between economic and human security are at opposite ends of the spectrum. The former envisages an inverse relationship, the latter a positive relationship. The neoliberal and Japanese management views sit somewhere in between, but the form of the relationship that they envisage differs. The form of the neoliberal relationship varies according to the level of economic security. In the Japanese management case, the relationship depends on the subject of analysis, whether it is inter group or intra group.

The second reason for different interpretations of the relationship between economic and human security is that some factors impact on both human security and economic security in the same direction but other factors affect one of them in one direction and the other in another direction. The impact of democracy on human and economic security, for example, is multi-directional. Democracy may lead to violations of the property rights of owners of land and/or capital but this may enhance the economic security of poor peasants and workers. Democracy may discourage investment and can have a negative effect on economic welfare and thus human security. In other instances, however, it may ensure personal protection and enhance the environment, and promote human security.

Notes

1. Ramesh Thakur, "From National to Human Security," in Stuart Harris and Andrew Mack, eds., *Asia-Pacific Security: The Economics–Politics Nexus* (Sydney: Allen & Unwin, 1998), p. 53.
2. See Samuel P. Huntington, *The Clash of Civilizations and the Remaking of World Order* (New York: Simon & Schuster, 1996) pp. 35–36.
3. A survey undertaken in the United States found that "43 percent of the population knows a friend or family member who has lost his or her job." Another survey found that a significant majority of workers suffer from some anxiety about losing their jobs. See Frank Calamito, "Reflections on the Downsizing Debate," *HR Focus* 73, no. 7 (July 1996), pp. 9–12.
4. Alex de Sherbinin, "Human Security and Fertility: The Case of Haiti," *Journal of Environment & Development* 5, no. 1 (March 1996), pp. 28–39; Ian Gough, "Economic Institutions and the Satisfaction of Human Needs," *Journal of Economic Issues* 28, no. 1 (March 1994), pp. 25–49; and Jessica T. Matthews, "Power Shift," *Foreign Affairs* 76, no. 1 (January/February 1997), pp. 50–66.
5. de Sherbinin, "Human Security and Fertility," p. 37.
6. In economics, economic welfare is normally measured only by real income or consumption.

7. Economic security, health security, and personal security are the three kinds of security identified by President Clinton that American voters are most afraid of losing. See Mickey Kaus, "Maximum Security," *The New Republic* 209, no. 24 (13 December 1993), pp. 17–19. I have included freedom from arbitrary imprisonment as an aspect of personal security. This aspect is not of concern to most Americans and was not covered in the *New Republic* article.

8. The word "infer" is used here because the literature does not explicitly discuss the relationship between individual economic security and human security.

9. "Work" is defined as more than just having a job; it is viewed as being in a job where the necessary amount of effort is applied to achieve an acceptable output.

10. Martin Feldstein, "Social Security and Saving: New Time Series Evidence," *National Tax Journal* 49, no. 2 (June 1996), pp. 151–171; and Martin Feldstein, "Social Security, Induced Retirement and Aggregate Capital Accumulation," *Journal of Political Economy* 82, no. 5 (September/October 1974), pp. 905–926.

11. The concept of the "winner's curse" originates from bargaining theory. It denotes a situation where the winner of an auction has offered a bid that exceeds the worth of the item on offer. See John McMillan, *Games, Strategies and Managers* (New York: Oxford University Press, 1992), pp. 137–141, for an elaboration.

12. The Iraqi invasion of Kuwait in 1992 and the continuing dependence of Kuwait on Western military force are constant reminders of the "winner's curse."

13. Joseph Schumpeter, *Capitalism, Socialism and Democracy* (New York: Harper, 1942), p. 84.

14. Gary Becker, "An Economic Analysis of Fertility," in National Bureau of Economic Research, ed., *Demographic and Economic Change in Developed Countries* (Princeton, NJ: Princeton University Press, 1960), pp. 209–240.

15. M. T. Cain, "Fertility as an Adjustment to Risk," *Population and Development Review* 9, no. 2 (June 1983), pp. 688–702.

16. G. Psacharopoulos, "Returns to Education: An Updated International Update and Implications," *Journal of Human Resources* 20, no. 4 (Fall 1985), pp. 583–604; and John Strauss and Duncan Thomas, "Human Resources: Empirical Modelling of Household and Family Decisions," in Jere Behrman and T. N. Srinivasan, eds., *Handbook of Development Economics: Volume 3A* (Amsterdam: North-Holland, 1995), pp. 1883–2023.

17. The generosity of public pensions varies across countries. Although public pensions do not eliminate economic insecurity altogether, they provide sufficient incentive to produce a low population growth.

18. The subsistence wage differs according to how rich a country is.

19. "Moral hazard" is defined as self-interested misbehaviour due to inadequate information or information being too costly to acquire, which places limits on the types of contract that can be written and enforced. See Paul Milgrom and John Roberts, *Economics, Organization and Management* (Englewood Cliffs, NJ: Prentice-Hall, 1992), p. 129. It is important to note that there are many non-conservative and left-leaning economists who believe there is a moral hazard problem. The difference is they are more likely than conservatives to believe that appropriate incentive schemes can be found to elicit cooperative behaviour.

20. Andrew Schotter, *Free Market Economics* (Oxford: Blackwell, 1990), pp. 100–101.

21. Roland N. McKean, "Economics of Trust, Altruism, and Corporate Responsibility," in Edmund S. Phelps, ed., *Altruism, Morality, and Economic Theory* (New York: Russell Sage Foundation, 1975), pp. 29–44.

22. It must be noted that economic reform has yet to bring the expected material benefits to many of the former command economies. Many of their citizens have experienced a

reduction in their levels of human and economic security. Among the former command economies of Central and Eastern Europe, only Poland's economy in 1997 was larger than it was in 1989. See figure 3 in Joseph E. Stiglitz's "Whither Reform: Ten Years of the Transition," paper presented at the annual World Bank Conference on Development Economics, Washington, DC (28–30 April 1999). China is a lone star performer among former command economies. China's economy has more than quadrupled in size since its communist leaders started instituting market reforms in 1978.

23. This is derived from examining studies on the so-called Japanese style of management or industrial organization. Two representative studies are Masahiko Aoki, "Toward an Economic Model of the Japanese Firm," *Journal of Economic Literature* 28, no. 1 (March 1990), pp. 1–27, and Airoyuki Odagiri, *Growth through Competition. Competition through Growth* (Oxford: Clarendon Press, 1992). But perhaps the best-known study on this topic in the West is Chalmers Johnson, *MITI and the Japanese Miracle* (Stanford, CA: Stanford University Press, 1982). The economic crisis in Japan has not changed the core management style of the J-firm. The crisis is more the result of a banking crisis caused by inappropriate sequencing of financial liberalization than of a deficient corporate management system. See, for example, Takeo Hoshi and Kashyap Anil, "The Japanese Banking Crisis: Where Did It Come from and How Will It End?" *NBER Macroeconomics Annual 1999*.

24. Odagiri, *Growth through Competition*, pp. 136–165.

25. Aoki, "Toward an Economic Model," p. 10.

26. Customs and social norms as well as laws and official regulations are rules.

27. Douglass C. North, *Institutions, Institutional Change and Economic Performance* (Cambridge: Cambridge University Press, 1990), pp. 3–5.

28. Douglass C. North, "The New Institutional Economics and Third World Development," in John Harriss, Janet Hunter, and Colin M. Lewis, eds., *The New Institutional Economics and Third World Development* (London: Routledge, 1995), p. 23.

29. They can certainly be serious enough to sour relations between two nations. Japan–USA trade disputes have led to various books published in each country that are critical of the other or view the other as a long-term threat. The best-known book by Japanese authors that has been translated to English is Shiataro Ishihara and Akio Marita, *Japan That Can Say "No"* (Tokyo: Kobunsha, 1989). One book published in the United States has the ominous title, *The Coming War with Japan* (New York: St Martin's, 1991). The tension between the United States and China led to the publication of a book in China with a title that was inspired by the book by Ishihara and Morita: Song Qiang, Zhang Cang Cang, Qiao Bian, et al., *China Can Say "No"* [Zhongguo Keyi Shuo Bu] (Hong Kong: Mingbao Chubanshe, 1996).

30. Andrew J. Nathan and Robert S. Ross, *The Great Wall and the Empty Fortress: China's Search for Security* (New York: W. W. Norton, 1997), pp. 73–78.

31. William Baumol, "Entrepreneurship: Productive, Unproductive, and Destructive," *Journal of Political Economy* 98, no. 5 (October 1990), pp. 893–921; North, *Institutions, Institutional Change and Economic Performance*; Marcus Olsen, "Dictatorship, Democracy and Development," *American Political Science Review* 87, no. 3 (September 1993), pp. 567–576; and Gerald W. Scully and Daniel J. Slottje, "Ranking Economic Liberty across Countries," *Public Choice* 69, no. 2 (1991), pp. 121–152.

32. Gabriella Montinola, Yingyi Qian, and Barry Weingast, "Federalism, Chinese Style: The Political Basis for Economic Success in China," *World Politics* 48, no. 1 (October 1995), pp. 50–81.

33. Adam Przeworski and Fernando Limongi, "Political Regimes and Economic Growth," *Journal of Economic Perspectives* 7, no. 3 (Summer 1993), pp. 51–69.

34. Pranab Bardhan, "Research on Poverty and Development Twenty Years after Redis-

tribution with Growth," *World Bank Research Observer* (Annual Conference Supplement 1995), pp. 59–70.

35. Chih-ming Ka and Mark Selden, "Original Accumulation, Equity and Late Industrialization: The Cases of China and Capitalist Taiwan," *World Development* 14, no. 10/11 (October/November 1986), pp. 1293–1310.

36. Leong Liew, "Management and Organization in Chinese Industry: From Mao to Deng," *Review of Radical Political Economics* 30, no. 2 (Spring 1998), pp. 46–86.

37. Gilles Saint-Paul and Thierry Verdier, "Education, Democracy and Growth," *Journal of Development Economics* 42, no. 2 (December 1993), pp. 399–407.

38. Arthur A Goldsmith, "Economic Rights and Government in Developing Countries: Cross-national Evidence on Growth and Development," *Studies in Comparative International Development* 32, no. 2 (Summer 1997), pp. 29–44.

39. Olsen, "Dictatorship, Democracy and Development," *passim*.

40. Rudiger Dornbusch and S. Edwards, *The Macroeconomics of Populism in Latin America* (Chicago: Chicago University Press, 1991). This is more likely to occur, however, if the median voter is relatively poor. See T. Persson and G. Tabellini, "Politico-Economic Equilibrium Growth: Theory and Evidence," mimeo, cited in Saint-Paul and Verdier, "Education, Democracy and Growth," p. 399.

41. Saint-Paul and Verdier, ibid.

42. Sen's work on famines was one of his many achievements that won him the Nobel Prize in 1998. An excellent survey of his work on famines can be found in Jean Dreze and Amartya Sen, *Hunger and Public Action* (Oxford: Clarendon, 1989).

43. Samuel P. Huntington, *Political Order in Changing Societies* (New Haven, CT: Yale University Press, 1968).

44. It is interesting to note that Huntington's work had a great impact in China when the supposedly liberal Zhao Ziyang was Party General-Secretary. Many of his key advisers advocated an ideology of neo-authoritarianism (*xinquanweizhuyi*) based on fast-paced market reforms, but with an authoritarian political system to ensure stability.

45. Przeworski and Limongi, "Political Regimes and Economic Growth."

46. Roger D. Congleton, "Political Institutions and Pollution Control," *Review of Economics and Statistics* 74, no. 1 (February 1992), pp. 412–421.

47. Adam Przeworski and Fernando Limongi, "Modernization: Theories and Facts," *World Politics* 49, no. 2 (January 1997), pp. 155–183.

13

Seeking human security from nuclear weapons: Recent non-traditional initiatives

Marianne Hanson

The issue of nuclear weapons has become a very real concern in the Asia-Pacific region. Attention was dramatically focused on the region when India and Pakistan conducted nuclear tests in May 1998, but, even prior to these events, disturbing developments in North Korea, as well as the seemingly permanent retention of nuclear weapons by key players in the region (China, the United States, and Russia), meant that the Asia-Pacific has become one of the most intensely nuclearized regions of the world.

These weapons have usually been viewed as a traditional, rather than a human, security issue and it may seem incongruous that a chapter on nuclear weapons should appear in this volume. They have, after all, been overwhelmingly associated with the traditional "realist" reference points of preparation for military conflict and the pursuit of self-help in an anarchical international environment.

Yet, although these weapons remain firmly associated with traditional security thinking, it is possible to make the argument that the possession, use, or threat of use of nuclear weapons should also be viewed within a human security framework. If human security includes safety and protection from "sudden and harmful disruptions in the patterns of daily life,"[1] if its issues are those that "strike directly home to the individual,"[2] and if addressing these threats requires "action and cooperation at different levels – global, regional and local,"[3] then there is a case to be made for examining the issue of nuclear weapons from a broader perspective than has been done in the past. There are a number of factors –

including humanitarian, developmental, and environmental – attendant on the possession and use of nuclear weapons that are intrinsically related to acknowledged human security concerns. Also relevant is the fact that some notable and recent attempts – emanating from the Asia-Pacific region – to regulate the possession and prevent the use of these weapons have been conducted on a non-traditional basis, implying a shift away from state-based negotiations and reflecting a greater incorporation of non-state actors into these processes. This again is consonant with policies increasingly associated with the search for human security.

Human security and nuclear weapons: Rationales for linkage

This chapter will argue that there are at least five reasons why the possession, use, or threat of use of nuclear weapons warrant a human security analysis. From the outset it should be said that there is nothing particularly new or startling about the first four points raised here; any serious consideration of the effects of the use of nuclear weapons would uncover these issues fairly quickly. In past decades, particular issues noted here – especially the potential cost to civilian human life – have been individually highlighted as part of a critique of nuclear strategy conducted by various peace groups. This chapter aims to restate these essential points collectively, and moreover to do so as part of a broader analysis which argues that together nuclear weapons constitute a serious threat to overall human security. This threat is especially prevalent in the Asia-Pacific region today.

Humanitarian factors

The first and most important of these points revolves essentially around humanitarian factors: nuclear weapons are targeted at civilian populations and rely overwhelmingly for their impact on the threat of a massive loss of life in the state of a targeted adversary. In effect, civilian populations are held hostage to a military system that uses weapons of a destructive nature vastly different from any previously devised. It is widely recognized and accepted that nuclear warfare remains incomparably destructive relative to any other method of warfare and that there is no protection against its horrible effects. Certainly, during the Cold War, there were attempts to move away from a counter-city targeting strategy (which focused on urban civilian populations) towards a counter-force strategy (which focused on military hardware and personnel), but these remained largely unconvincing as workable strategies. Restricting damage to specific areas and delineating between civilian and military targets were simply not possible with weaponry that was diffuse, rather than discrete, in its impact. In any case, the very basis of nuclear deterrence, the foundation of security policy for nuclear weapons states, remained implicitly tied to the threat of widespread destruction of civilian areas and high loss of life (even if this was not overtly stated to be the case). The presence of strategic – as differentiated from theatre – nuclear missiles in the arsenals of the superpowers highlights this point. Indeed, what is notable about the doctrine of nuclear deterrence is the scant attention paid to the humanitarian implications of such a policy.

These fundamental humanitarian implications need reasserting here. At its heart, the use, and by implication the threat, of nuclear attack violates international humanitarian law, which seeks to regulate the conduct of warfare. The two core principles of humanitarian law governing the actual conduct of armed conflict (*ius in bello*) specify, first, that parties to a conflict must distinguish between combatants and non-combatants, and, secondly, that it is prohibited to cause superfluous injury or unnecessary suffering. Both of these principles would be violated in the extreme by resorting to nuclear warfare. (Indeed, injuries would continue in subsequent generations also, as the deformities and illnesses of postwar Hiroshima and Nagasaki children demonstrated, thereby raising additional legal questions of inter-generational justice.) It seems surprising therefore that nuclear doctrines were developed without an adequate assessment of the humanitarian consequences of their use and indeed that the doctrine of nuclear deterrence continues to rely on the threat of massive civilian deaths.[4] Discussions in late 1998 and early 1999 by some members of NATO on the Alliance's nuclear strategy have raised questions about the desirability of a "no first use" policy[5] and have demonstrated some awareness of these humanitarian implications. Adding to the debate, Canada's foreign minister stated that "any discussion of using Alliance nuclear capabilities – *even in retaliation* – raises very difficult questions of means, proportionality and effectiveness that cause us significant concerns."[6] That is, even in the event of nuclear attack, and cognizant of the principles of humanitarian law, there are serious moral impediments to responding in kind by killing large numbers of civilians for the actions of their leaders.

Certainly there developed, since 1945, a strong taboo against the use of nuclear weapons and this taboo appeared to underwrite the actual practice of refraining from using nuclear weapons.[7] But there is quite clearly a disjuncture between official security policies that rely on nuclear deterrence and the widespread sentiment that the actual use of such weapons would be too awful to consider.[8] The danger, of course, is that a nuclear doctrine based on the unexamined mantra of deterrence and heedless of the laws of war can too easily translate, especially in moments of crisis, into practice, overriding any examination of moral implications that might until then have held such a policy in check.

There have been attempts to impose a legal framework on the nuclear question. Most recently, and reflective of civil society concerns, was the advisory opinion of the International Court of Justice (ICJ) which stated that the use or threat of use of nuclear weapons would generally be contrary to international law.[9] The indiscriminate destructiveness of a nuclear or thermonuclear device pits nuclear weapons against the human rights principles outlined in the Charter of the United Nations and the two human rights Covenants.[10] In sum, any use of nuclear weapons, targeted as these weapons are at civilian populations and carrying the destructive potential that they do, would be catastrophic and would violate fundamental human rights and humanitarian law. This factor remains at the core of objections to the use or threat of use of nuclear weapons from a human security perspective.

Citizen–state relations

The second factor in an analysis of nuclear weapons as a human security concern is the issue of citizen–state relations and the risks and fears imposed on a population whose leadership embarks on the acquisition of nuclear weapons. At stake here is, first, the issue of consent in relationships between the citizen and the state, and, secondly, the state's ability to provide protection to its citizens. These are explicitly related to the point noted above, namely that civilian populations are in effect held hostage in nuclear calculations. It can be argued that, even in democracies where processes of government are transparent, individuals may have relatively little say in determining the security policies of their governments or how these policies will be operationalized. However, any decision to embark on a process of nuclearization automatically brings with it nuclear risks to all citizens, not just to those who might have been instrumental in determining security policies or who constitute the military forces of that nation. This factor of state actions and consequences for civilians becomes even more acute in undemocratic societies, where the processes of decision-making may be even more closed to citizen input. Whatever the case, the burden of threat is not confined to military targets or even to political and decision-making élites, but rather casts a shadow over all citizens indiscriminately.

At a wider level, the question of the survival of the state and its ability to fulfil its protective function for its citizens in the event of a nuclear attack comes into play. If we take it as given that the primary function of the state is to provide security for its citizens and that this security is vital if the state is to fulfil its secondary function – namely promoting the general welfare of its citizens – then it becomes apparent that the possibility of nuclear attack, which may render the state helpless, severely tests the protective link between state and citizen. John Herz was one of the earliest writers to point out that the advent of nuclear weapons called the territorial function of the state into question and rendered the primary unit of the international system vulnerable to overwhelming devastation, ushering in what he called a new "condition of permeability."[11] In this case, survival would depend not on one's own actions or on those of the state, or on any set of defensive arrangements prepared by the state, but rather on the sanity and rational behaviour of one's opponents.[12] As a result of this, individuals might no longer perceive that the state can provide the level of protection it was able to do prior to the advent of nuclear weaponry. This in turn means that security becomes a much broader concern, linking at once the security of an individual human being with the activation of effective negotiations, rules, and norms at a regional and global, rather than simply at a state-based, level.

Nuclear weapons and the environment

A third factor in any analysis of nuclear weapons from a human security perspective concerns the enormous environmental implications attendant on their use. (It should be noted that even the non-aggressive practice of nuclear testing has drawn widespread condemnation on environmental grounds.) Not only would an attack result in widespread casualties, it would also render uninhabitable vast tracts of territory and increase levels of radiation over an even wider region. Uniquely among weapons devised by humans, nuclear weapons have the potential to damage in an instant and possibly for decades – depending on the scale of the attack – areas once host to a variety of plant and animal life forms.[13]

Apart from the immediate damage caused, there would remain significant obstacles to the restoration of normal life in such an area. When one recalls the difficulties faced by states in Europe attempting to restore their agricultural, industrial, and social infrastructures after World War II, it becomes apparent that such an attempt after nuclear warfare would be profoundly more difficult. The problem would be felt more acutely by underdeveloped states, but it is by no means clear that even advanced developed economies could sustain attendant levels of damage and restore adequate social, agricultural, industrial, and economic environments. The widespread destruction of cultural assets would also occur. Thus it can be argued that the use of nuclear weapons would have severe impacts on human environments, on prospects for development, and on economic well-being, all of which would collectively diminish the quality of life for those able to survive such an event.

Nuclear weapons and terrorism

Fourthly, there is the very real spectre of terrorist use of nuclear weapons, a fear that has grown markedly since the ending of the Cold War. The acquisition of nuclear material by terrorist or other subnational groups has become a key international security concern, evidenced by recent efforts to establish control over fissile material and effect the safe transfer of nuclear weapons from certain regions to established and authorized control.[14] Again, this problem raises questions about the effectiveness of state activities in regulating nuclear weapons and the vulnerability of the individual to sudden and destructive attacks, in this case from unexpected or even unknown quarters.

Moreover, the concept of nuclear deterrence clearly fails in such cases; assuming that a terrorist organization resorts to nuclear attack, it is highly unlikely that a nuclear weapons state, assuming it can locate the whereabouts of the antagonists, will launch a nuclear missile in retaliation. Even if it is accepted that it is nuclear deterrence that has kept the nuclear peace in the past 50 years (itself a questionable assumption), there is no likelihood that a nuclear response – which would kill many more than the initial perpetrators – would be considered. Very little, therefore, may stand in the way of averting such an attack. And if nuclear material remains available in a strategic culture that maintains the status quo, that is, the retention of tens of thousands of warheads by the nuclear weapons states, then the very existence of these arsenals poses a potential terrorist threat to human security.

It must be acknowledged, of course, that conventional weapons also present many of the hazards and difficulties noted in the above points. States have not always respected international humanitarian law; it could, for instance, be argued that the civilian casualties incurred during the firebombings in Tokyo and Dresden were commensurate with the indiscriminate destruction seen at Hiroshima and Nagasaki. All reflected a clear determination to target civilian populations. Similarly, security calculations involving conventional weapons can also present many of the difficulties noted in relation to the second factor, whereby citizens may feel powerless against the will of élites to engage in specific security strategies that threaten to jeopardize the individual's life. In an environmental context, there are numerous examples of prolonged conventional warfare rendering areas inhospitable and destroying vital infrastructure, while terrorist attacks have to date involved the use of conventional (and, in a few cases, chemical) weapons. The point here is not that these developments are restricted to nuclear warfare, but rather that, because of the qualitatively different nature of this warfare, they become much more amplified and represent a far greater threat to the well-being of citizens than does the rise of such developments as a result of conventional warfare. Moreover, popular views upholding human rights and international humanitarian law, good governance, respect for the environment, and the need for stable development have increased in recent decades. International humanitarian law has progressed greatly since 1945 and it is unlikely that such targeting of civilians and loss of life would be acceptable to the international community today, particularly if it was to be inflicted by nuclear weaponry. In sum, although these concerns are not attached solely to nuclear arsenals, they become magnified by their association with this class of weaponry.

Nuclear insecurity

This leads to the fifth factor identified here as a human security issue: increasingly, it would appear that people and states are seeking security not *with* nuclear weapons, but rather *from* nuclear weapons.[15] Indeed, where once it was felt that nuclear weapons can *give* security (still, of course, the philosophy behind deterrence theory), there is a growing sense that measures must be taken to protect citizens and states *from* nuclear weapons.

The domestic public support for the tests conducted by India and Pakistan in May 1998 demonstrates that the former view is by no means obsolete. Yet that popular support reflected an obsessively nationalist sentiment and showed little consideration of the damaging security consequences that may have flowed from the tests. It is likely, for instance, that the security of both these countries has been diminished, rather than enhanced, by the decision to adopt overtly aggressive nuclear stances. Reflecting the preponderant rejection of nuclear capabilities is the fact that the overwhelming majority of states have signed and abide by the Nuclear Non-Proliferation Treaty (NPT), and there is growing public revulsion at the testing or proliferation of nuclear weapons. This latter element was most evident when China and France resumed testing after observing a self-imposed moratorium in the early 1990s and also manifested itself in the widespread public and official state condemnation of the Indian and Pakistani tests at the international level.

The activities of groups such as Abolition 2000 and Pugwash have become intense with the ending of the Cold War. Notable public declarations, such as the December 1996 *Statement on Nuclear Weapons by International Generals and Admirals* and the February 1998 *Statement by*

International Civilian Leaders as part of the *State of the World Forum*,[16] demonstrate that individuals are seeking a greater input into security planning. This process would thus no longer remain the exclusive pursuit of states and their leaders. Equally interesting were moves by certain states to sponsor discussion and reports by non-state actors to address nuclear arms control issues. It is two of these initiatives that will now be examined.

Non-traditional approaches to furthering arms control: Two regional initiatives

Importantly, the growing sentiment that sees nuclear weapons as a threat to security has favoured the rise of innovative and non-traditional initiatives which seek to regulate the possession of these weapons and to put pressure on the nuclear weapons states to disarm. The ending of the Cold War reinforced a view that seeking security from nuclear weapons might now be conducted through the involvement of actors not normally associated with military planning and defence. Moreover, the time was opportune for the incorporation of individuals and non-governmental organizations (NGOs) into the traditionally state-governed processes of arms control. In many ways, this represented the development of "new thinking" about security; these changing policy-making approaches to nuclear weapons and security add to the argument that this issue can be viewed within a human security perspective. Traditional negotiating forums, bilateral and multilateral, remain in place, but it is now accepted that these might be usefully supplemented by non-state processes.

The Canberra Commission on the Elimination of Nuclear Weapons

The Canberra Commission on the Elimination of Nuclear Weapons was convened in 1995 by the then Australian prime minister, Paul Keating, to make the case, if it could be made, for the complete elimination of nuclear weapons. The evolution of a nuclear elimination debate at the international level provided the context for this. The Henry L. Stimson Center and the Federation of American Scientists, for example, together with other institutions in the United States were beginning to challenge the conventional wisdom in American foreign policy that simply reaffirmed the doctrine of nuclear deterrence and that claimed that nuclear weapons elimination was impractical and in any case undesirable, even in the post–Cold War environment. The work of these groups put together and amplified the strategic and political arguments against the continued possession of nuclear weapons and was a reflection of evident widespread public opinion against this class of weapon. Such developments helped to shape Keating's view that a bold state-sponsored initiative on the nuclear question was now needed and that Australia was well placed to convene this.[17]

The Commission brought together a group of 17 independent specialists on the strategic, political, military, and legal aspects of nuclear weapons. Included were academics, former prime ministers, ambassadors, and civilian and military leaders. Two of the most important Commissioners had been closely involved with the US military: General Lee Butler was former Commander in Chief of the US Strategic Air Command, and Robert McNamara a former US Secretary for Defense. What was notable about this period and the makeup of the Commission was that the argument for elimination was being made not by fringe or radical organizations urging unilateral disarmament, but rather by respected and acknowledged specialists on the military and political issues attendant on the possession or use of nuclear weapons. Following a series of meetings over a 10-month period, the Commissioners' *Report*, delivered in August 1996, concluded that assertions of nuclear weapons' utility were no longer viable and that an important window of opportunity existed for their elimination.[18]

The *Report*'s fundamental message was that maintaining nuclear arsenals serves no useful purpose and that, unless significant moves were made towards elimination, the international community could expect to see the further and unwanted spread of these weapons to other states as well as the risk of accidental or terrorist use. It noted that in today's world, where security threats all too often come in the form of ethnic conflicts, state disintegration, humanitarian disasters, environmental degradation, or economic crisis, nuclear weapons seem at best irrelevant and at worst – because of their destructive capacities and the danger of accidental, terrorist, or "irrational" use – a threat to the very continuance of life.[19] The *Report* argued that nuclear weapons were useless in the battlefield. They were likely to kill as many "friendly" as "enemy" forces. They were not useful as deterrents against conventional attack or attack by biological or chemical weapons (neither were they useful in responding to such attacks). The only utility that *might* remain for these weapons is that they are perceived as necessary for deterring a nuclear attack by another state. The *Report* noted, however, that this sole utility implies the continued existence of nuclear weapons and that any such utility would disappear if nuclear weapons were eliminated.[20]

The *Report* recommended phased steps to elimination, which involved taking nuclear forces off alert, removing warheads from delivery vehicles, ending the deployment of all non-strategic weapons, ending nuclear testing, increasing reductions in US and Russian arsenals, and embarking on a no-first-use policy. It also outlined a number of reinforcing steps needed, including action to prevent horizontal proliferation, the further development of effective monitoring and verification regimes, and the agreement of a ban on the production of fissile material for explosive purposes.[21]

The change of government in Australia before the Commission could complete its programme meant that the *Report* was not publicized and promoted to the same extent that its original sponsors would have wished. Nevertheless, the *Report* has been incorporated into several other governmental and non-governmental studies on nuclear arms control and has generated a significant amount of attention to the question of elimination.[22]

Initiating the Canberra Commission – an approach that applied state patronage to a group of independent analysts in the interests of furthering arms control – represented a singularly different kind of disarmament activity for Australia. It was highly innovative and creative; no other national government had unilaterally backed and funded any similar initiative. It also demonstrated the active leadership element of what the Labor government of the day had termed "good international citizenship."[23] The sponsors of the Commission devised a previously untried method of exerting diplomatic influence and sought to pursue a course of action at the international level that would challenge the nuclear status quo and, it was hoped, provide new directions for international security discussions. While not in any way diminishing the achievements of traditional forums such as the Conference on Disarmament, the decision to establish a group of persons who could prepare a *Report* that would then be submitted to the United Nations as well as to the Conference on Disarmament, effectively side-stepped many of the time-consuming and bureaucratic difficulties usually encountered in traditional, state-based multilateral negotiations. In sum, the Canberra Commission initiative, together with its product, the *Report*, demonstrated that addressing vital nuclear security issues could be enhanced by utilizing non-traditional methods and non-traditional actors.

The Tokyo Forum on Nuclear Non-Proliferation and Disarmament

A second attempt emanating from the Asia-Pacific region to address the nuclear weapons issue which combined state patronage with non-state actors was the Tokyo Forum on Nuclear Non-Proliferation and Disarmament. (The Tokyo Forum process is ongoing at the time of this writing.) This initiative was a direct response to the South Asian tests of May

1998 and the attendant prospect of further unravelling of the nuclear non-proliferation regime. The Forum (originally titled the "Conference on Urgent Actions for Nuclear Non-Proliferation and Disarmament") was jointly sponsored by the Hiroshima Peace Institute, the Japan Institute of International Affairs, and the Japanese government. (Japan's foreign ministry acts as the secretariat for the Forum.) The initiative was announced by Japan's then foreign minister (and subsequently prime minister), Keizo Obuchi, on 4 June 1998, merely days after the tests conducted by India and Pakistan. Stressing the non-governmental nature of this initiative, Obuchi noted that the Forum's activities would differ from "discussions among governments" and that it would be representative of a broader group of voices from "all possible realms on this subject."[24] The Forum was scheduled to hold a total of four meetings between August 1998 and July 1999. The process has involved 21 participants from 17 different countries, including former diplomats, disarmament specialists, and academics acting in their independent capacities and not necessarily representing the views of their own home governments. The membership includes four Canberra Commissioners; indeed, the entire initiative owes a debt to the Canberra Commission in terms of its form and content. (Unlike the Canberra Commission, however, and in an attempt to focus greater attention on non-proliferation issues, the Tokyo Forum includes representatives from India and Pakistan.)

The Forum's wider aim has been to discuss nuclear disarmament issues on a global scale, although its chief concern remains the threats following from the South Asian tests and their impact on regional and global security. Substantial debate has focussed on whether the Forum's report should specify a time-bound framework for nuclear elimination and what status should be accorded to India and Pakistan in light of their tests. It was said that this report would constitute the "last large-scale proposal for nuclear disarmament in the twentieth century."[25] According to NGO sources, it will specifically address current problems in nuclear proliferation and disarmament, the issue of nuclear weapons at regional levels such as the Middle East, North-East and South Asia, nuclear disarmament, primarily related to the United States and Russia, fissile material, verification arrangements, and the improvement of the non-proliferation regime.[26]

The Forum – itself a non-state gathering – has also attracted substantial interest from the wider NGO community in Japan and elsewhere concerned with nuclear issues. Forum member Nobuo Matsunaga, vice-president of the Japan Institute of International Affairs, noted at the third meeting that one of the characteristic trends of international relations after the Cold War was the "increasing roles and importance of NGOs and international organisations" in such processes.[27] This has been amply demonstrated by the parallel NGO conferences that have been held at each of the Forum's meetings, and in the process by which citizens' recommendations have been presented for consideration at the Forum's meetings.[28]

The Forum's report will not be presented to the Japanese government until after the fourth meeting in July 1999 and without reviewing its contents it is not possible to comment here on what its actual impact might be on arms control processes at the regional and international levels.[29] Yet the importance of the exercise is that, like the Canberra Commission, the Tokyo Forum seeks to shift the arms control debate in positive directions by the use of unorthodox methods. The Japanese government – despite its sensitivities to the US security relationship restricting its extent of involvement in the Forum – still perceived some value in sponsoring it. That it did so confirms the trend of assigning epistemic communities and NGOs greater significance – a pattern established initially by the Canberra Commission.

It must be noted that there remains a great gulf between, on the one hand, those recommendations discussed and proposed by the Canberra Commission and the Tokyo Forum and, on the other, the inaction of the nuclear weapons states themselves. The latter have shown themselves unwilling to move towards substantially lower levels of nuclear armaments, despite the changed global circumstances of the post–Cold War era. Both the United States and Russia had, of course, reduced their arsenals since the mid-1980s, primarily through the START I Treaty. Additionally, the indefinite extension of the NPT in 1995 and the completion of the Comprehensive Test Ban Treaty in 1996 contributed to the sense that much had been achieved in arms control in the half-dozen or so years after the Cold War ended. Yet the United States and Russia continue to possess tens of thousands of nuclear weapons, have made very little progress beyond START I, and show firm resistance to calls made in the United Nations General Assembly or in the Conference on Disarmament for further reductions. France, the United Kingdom, and China, for their part, have also resisted calls for elimination. All these factors have led non-nuclear weapons states to conclude that the nuclear powers have not fulfilled their obligation, outlined in the NPT, to disarm.[30]

Realistically (and despite the best efforts of those involved in the Canberra Commission and the Tokyo Forum), the climate for arms control looked unpromising as the 1990s drew to a close. Those involved in these initiatives certainly recognize the obstacles in the path of disarmament and acknowledge that elimination, if it occurs, will be a long and difficult process, but note that it is one for which it is nonetheless worth striving. The essential point here is that ultimately it will be the actions of states rather than of non-state groupings that will determine the course of elimination; despite this, there is a growing sense that innovative methods and coalition-building between states and other actors can assist the assessment of security threats and the formulation of ideas to reduce them. Learning from these instances of civil–diplomatic interaction may be helpful in devising strategies for arms control regimes that support and reinforce the notion of an inclusive international society.

The Asian dimension

The recent nuclear tests conducted by India and Pakistan, North Korea's test of a long-range nuclear-capable ballistic missile (in August 1998), and the recent initiative by the United States and Japan to move toward developing a theatre missile defence system to neutralize Chinese and North Korean nuclear capabilities all signal that the Asia-Pacific is a region largely devoid of nuclear arms control and disarmament initiatives. Some analysts have observed that the arms control environment in Asia has suffered compared to that in Europe because Asia was unable to establish a Cold War legacy of negotiating from distinct geopolitical blocs commensurate to NATO and the Warsaw Pact.[31] In fact, a number of such initiatives have unfolded in the Asia-Pacific over the past quarter-century. This subsection will review briefly the more noteworthy ones that underscore the determination of many Asia-Pacific parties to pursue and strengthen prospects for regional cooperation in reducing nuclear arsenals.

Perhaps the oldest continuing nuclear disarmament measure in the region is the South Pacific Nuclear Free Zone (SPNFZ) Treaty signed by the members of the South Pacific Forum at Rarotonga in August 1985. All five established declaratory nuclear weapons powers (the United States, Russia, China, the United Kingdom, and France) now honour this nuclear-weapon-free zone or NWFZ (with the United Kingdom, France, and the United States signing its protocols in March 1996, after the French completed their last series of underground nuclear tests in the Muraroa Atoll). The negotiation of SPNFZ, or "spinfizz" as it is commonly known, was part of a larger "human security drama" involving New Zealand and the United States. New Zealand's Labour government had challenged Washington's postwar extended nuclear deterrence posture by declaring New Zealand an NWFZ soon after coming to power in July 1984. By doing so, New Zealand alienated its larger ally to the extent that it was extricated from the ANZUS alliance with the United States and Australia. But it also called attention to a number of moral arguments against nuclear weapons postulated by its prime minister, David Lange, and to the effectiveness of various grass-roots organizations in that country in persuading approximately 70 per cent of its population that a nuclear deterrence strategy was, at best, irrelevant and, at worst, immoral relative to New Zealand's own defence requirements. Such groups as Peace Movement Aotearoa, the Women's International League for Peace and Freedom, and Scientists Against Nuclear Arms were all active in pressing successfully for the passage of the Nuclear Free Zone Bill introduced by Lange in 1985.[32]

The NWFZ legacy was taken up by the Association of South East Asian Nations (ASEAN) in December 1995 when its member states signed the Bangkok Treaty, establishing a Southeast Asian Nuclear Free Zone (SEANFZ).[33] Modelled largely on the SPNFZ precedent, SEANFZ went further than its predecessor in defining an NWFZ purview by including the exclusive economic zones and the continental shelves of signatory states. Like the SPNFZ, however, it gave each signatory the right of discretion in allowing US naval units or those of other nuclear powers to visit their ports without explicit verification of those units' nuclear content (a practice known as the "right of innocent passage"). The impetus for SEANFZ, however, was largely state centric in origin rather than generated by independent anti-nuclear movements. A human security element was present, however, insofar as the ASEAN states wished to isolate resource disputes in the East China Sea and their own underdeveloped offshore resource areas from future regional conflicts that might otherwise have impeded their own national development. Airzal Effendi, the Indonesian chairman of a working group set up to draft the treaty, expressed this rationale by noting that "[p]revention is better than cure. We are very much afraid of technology services which are developed day by day and they might want to make smaller armaments but big explosive power."[34] In other words, the ASEAN signatories did not want to be pulled into a regional nuclear arms race that would include the development of tactical nuclear weapons designed for use in contested territorial waters. China has since signalled it would ratify the SEANFZ; the other nuclear powers have yet to do so.

A human security element has also shaped the politics of nuclear arms control in North-East Asia, primarily in regard to the Korean peninsula. Recent US diplomatic action has dissuaded North Korea – labelled in many quarters as a nuclear weapons "rogue state" – from fully developing its nuclear weapons capacity. The October 1994 Agreed Framework is a classic example of a state indicating its intention to relinquish the elements of prime military power in return for access to food and fuel resources it could otherwise not provide to its own people. More recently, South Korean Prime Minister Kim Jong-pil admitted that South Korea had attempted to develop nuclear weapons but had relinquished the project when former South Korean President Park Chung-Hee was as-

sassinated in October 1979 and when prospects intensified for the establishment of a Korean peninsula nuclear free zone in the late 1980s and
early 1990s.[35] Indeed, a far-reaching Joint Declaration on a Non-Nuclear
Korean Peninsula was signed during one of the brief intervals of inter-
Korean détente at the end of December 1991. Both sides promised to
pursue the peaceful use of nuclear energy, to ban nuclear weapons, and
to agree not to build nuclear enrichment facilities. The Joint Declaration
also called for a joint commission to negotiate the implementation of joint
inspections. The treaty soon succumbed to renewed suspicions by the
South and the United States that the North was embarking on the covert
development of nuclear weapons. But it also reflected a deep-seated desire by Koreans on both sides of the Demilitarized Zone to avoid a war
involving weapons of mass destruction against their own people. President Kim Dae Jung justified his "Sunshine Policy" towards North Korea
by reiterating this sentiment. Expressing his government's determination
to "end the Cold War legacy of animosity and confrontation," Kim announced a North Korean policy "based on firm security [but leading] to
genuine reconciliation."[36] How flexible Kim is willing to be in response
to North Korea's demands that US forces withdraw from the South as a
precondition for a Korean peace treaty, however, remains uncertain. A
unilateral South Korean decision to modify or drop its reliance on the US
extended deterrent – including its nuclear component – may be the ultimate test that South Korea will need to pass before Korean unification
can actually occur. Also related to this are moves to establish a Northeast
Asian Nuclear Weapons Free Zone, moves that have nevertheless been
resisted to date by the nuclear weapons states in the region.[37]

Conclusion

The threat posed by nuclear weapons should no longer be viewed as
something separate from human security concerns. This analysis has
argued that, while nuclear weapons continue to be perceived as a traditional security issue, there are a number of factors accompanying this
class of weaponry that warrant a closer association with the emerging
paradigm labelled "human security." That dominant doctrines of nuclear
strategy have largely ignored the potential cost to human security only
reinforces the need for such a reassessment. Moreover, it is clear that, in
recognition of the current impasse in arms control processes and the need
to reiterate fundamental humanitarian norms to enhance global security,
new, more inclusive processes that combine the support of states with
non-traditional methods became important in the 1990s, even if their
actual impact on policy-making remains relatively low. These new points

of intersection between governmental and non-governmental processes will, in all likelihood, grow in significance in coming years and seek to apply increasing pressure on nuclear weapons state actors, who remain, for the moment at least, the key decision-makers of security policy.

Notes

1. Department of Foreign Affairs and International Trade, Canada, "Notes for an Address by the Honourable Lloyd Axworthy, Minister of Foreign Affairs, to a Meeting of the Mid-America Committee 'Global Action, Continental Community: Human Security in Canadian Foreign Policy'," Chicago, Illinois, 9 September 1998.
2. United Nations, *Human Development Report 1994*, as cited in the Report of the Commission on Global Governance, *Our Global Neighbourhood* (Oxford: Oxford University Press, 1995).
3. Ibid.
4. E. J. Hogendoorn, who researches in the Arms Division of Human Rights Watch, and commenting chiefly on conventional weapons, notes that new weapons systems continue to be developed without any such assessment of their humanitarian implications. See "The Human Rights Agenda: The Further Development of Arms Control Regimes," *Disarmament Diplomacy*, no. 34 (February 1999), p. 6.
5. NATO's 1991 Strategic Concept had failed to endorse a "no first use" policy; ahead of the unveiling of a new Strategic Concept in April 1999, questions were raised in December 1998 by Germany's foreign minister about whether the organization should now adopt such a policy. This suggestion was, however, soon dismissed, with the US Secretary of State claiming a "reaffirmation of our current NATO nuclear strategy." Press Conference by Secretary of State Madeleine Albright, Brussels, 8 December 1998.
6. Address by the Honourable Lloyd Axworthy, Minister of Foreign Affairs, to NATO's North Atlantic Council Meeting, 8 December 1998 (emphasis added).
7. On the evolution of these normative constraints, see Richard Price and Nina Tannenwald, "Norms and Deterrence: The Nuclear and Chemical Weapons Taboos," in Peter Katzenstein, ed., *The Culture of National Security: Norms and Identity in World Politics* (New York: Columbia University Press, 1996), pp. 114–152.
8. Andrew Butfoy, in outlining the paradox of a security policy dominated by a concept of deterrence that involves the theoretical use of what are essentially unusable weapons, refers to a "parallel, abstract world divorced from day-to-day diplomacy." See Butfoy, "The Future of Nuclear Strategy," in Craig A. Snyder, ed., *Contemporary Security and Strategy* (London: Macmillan, 1999), p. 166.
9. International Court of Justice, *Communique*, 8 July 1996. This was the result of a citizens' initiative, the World Court Project, in which more than 1 million people petitioned the ICJ to consider the legality of nuclear weapons. The Court's advisory opinion has been interpreted by some observers as allowing a loophole for the use of nuclear weapons: as part of its ruling, the Court had noted that it was unable to determine whether, in extreme circumstances of self-defence, in which the survival of the state was under threat, the use of nuclear weapons is legal or not. Clearly this reflected indecision over the matter rather than legal permission for the use of nuclear weapons in self-defence. In any case, even self-defence is widely seen as not justifying genocide, and overwhelmingly the ICJ's decision has been interpreted as indicating that the threat or use of nuclear weapons would be generally contrary to international law.

10. For an examination of the Court's ruling, see Andrew Mack, "Delegitimising Nuclear Weapons: The World Court Decision," *Pacific Research* 9, no. 3 (1996), pp. 3–5.
11. John Herz, *The Nation-State and the Crisis of World Politics* (New York: McKay, 1973), p. 121.
12. On this point, see also Richard J. Harknett, "Territoriality in the Nuclear Era," in Eleonore Kofman and Gillian Youngs, eds., *Globalization: Theory and Practice* (London: Pinter, 1996), pp. 138–149.
13. Certainly the destructive potential of nuclear weapons has increased dramatically since the bombings of 1945, making it clear that damage – human and environmental – will be greater than at these attacks.
14. The Cooperative Threat Reduction scheme, between the United States and the successor states of the USSR, is a notable example that seeks to monitor nuclear materials in the wake of the break-up of the Soviet Union.
15. This conceptual shift ties in with Ramesh Thakur's observations that "human security, with its emphasis on the individual's welfare" demonstrates a "freedom *from*: from want, hunger, attack, torture ... and so on." Ramesh Thakur, "From National to Human Security," in Stuart Harris and Andrew Mack, eds., *Asia-Pacific Security: The Economics–Politics Nexus* (Sydney: Allen & Unwin, 1997), p. 53.
16. The full text of both these statements can be viewed at http://www.worldforum.org/initiatives.
17. Keating seemed to be aware of the substance if not the details of these existing debates in the United States. He noted that "many ideas for a nuclear weapons-free world are on the table, but there has never before been a government-sponsored exercise to develop a comprehensive and practical approach to the problem." Statement by Prime Minister Keating to the Inaugural Meeting of the Canberra Commission on the Elimination of Nuclear Weapons, Canberra, 19 January 1996.
18. *Report of the Canberra Commission on the Elimination of Nuclear Weapons* (Canberra: Commonwealth of Australia, 1996).
19. Ibid., p. 29.
20. Ibid., p. 24.
21. Ibid., pp. 49–65.
22. The *Report*'s recommendations were incorporated, for instance, into the Stimson Center Steering Committee Report of March 1997 and the report of the Committee on International Security and Arms Control of the National Academy of Sciences of June 1997 (both of which acknowledged the work of the Canberra Commission as instrumental in laying the groundwork for the elimination debate) as well as the 1997 Final Report of the Carnegie Commission on Preventing Deadly Conflict. For an analysis of the *Report*'s impact, see Marianne Hanson and Carl Ungerer, "The Canberra Commission: Paths Followed, Paths Ahead," *Australian Journal of International Affairs* 53, no. 1 (April 1999), pp. 5–17.
23. The concept of good international citizenship had been raised by Australia's foreign minister, Gareth Evans, as early as 1988, but was most clearly articulated in his co-authored book, *Australia's Foreign Relations in the World of the 1990s* (Melbourne: Melbourne University Press, 1991), pp. 40–41.
24. Quoted in Ministry of Foreign Affairs, Japan, "Press Conference by the Press Secretary," 5 June 1998, at http://www.mofa.go.jp/announce/press/1998/6/605.html.
25. A point noted by Michael Krepon, President of the Stimson Center and Chairperson of the Drafting Committee for the Forum's report.
26. Yukari Shigenobu and Akira Kawasaki, "Tokyo Forum Sets up Drafting Committee," *Peace Depot News Letter*, no. 4, 1 May 1999.
27. Quoted in ibid.

28. Additionally, citizen groups, including victims of the Hiroshima and Nagasaki bombings, have held meetings with foreign ministry representatives, the first time that Japanese Ministry of Foreign Affairs officials have appeared on an NGO nuclear elimination panel in Japan. See Hiro Umebayashi, "The New Agenda Coalition and Japan: Emergence of a Dynamic Interaction between the Japanese Government and NGOs on Nuclear Disarmament," *Peace Depot Newsletter*, no. 4 (December 1998). See also "Akashi Will Include Recommendation to Control Sub-Critical Tests in Final Report," *Asahi Shimbun*, 20 December 1998.

29. *Editor's note:* Since this chapter was drafted, the Forum's report, *Facing Nuclear Dangers: An Action Plan for the 21st Century*, has been published by the Japan Institute of International Affairs (1999). Its key strengths include an analysis of the prevailing arms control climate that makes explicit the linkage between damaged relations among states and lack of progress on arms control; its attempt to reaffirm and revitalize the Nuclear Non-Proliferation Treaty; presentation of a set of concrete measures that could be taken immediately to promote non-proliferation; and its specific requests to individual states to undertake the restoration of good relations in order to advance nuclear non-proliferation and disarmament.

30. This in turn has implications for the continuation of an international system in which all states feel that their security concerns have been acknowledged. Early writings by Hedley Bull on the links between arms control and the evolution of "international society" are relevant here. Bull warned of a revolt against a security order seen as unsympathetic to the views of smaller and non-nuclear states. See Hedley Bull, "Arms Control and World Order," in Robert O'Neill and David N. Schwartz, eds., *Hedley Bull on Arms Control* (London: Macmillan, 1987), pp. 191–206. It could be argued that, increasingly, this dissatisfaction with a security order dominated by the nuclear powers is evident not just in the preferences of many states but also in the discussions and conclusions of non-state groupings such as the Canberra Commission and the Tokyo Forum.

31. A typical assessment along such lines is found in the Research Institute for Peace and Security, Tokyo, *Asian Security 1992–93* (London: Brasseys, 1993), pp. 219–220.

32. Background is provided by Michael C. Pugh, *The ANZUS Crisis, Nuclear Visiting and Deterrence* (Cambridge: Cambridge University Press, 1989), pp. 106–118.

33. A text of the treaty is located on the Internet at http://www.nuclearfiles.org/docs/1995/951215-bangkok.html.

34. Nutsara Sawatsawang and Phanrawi Tansuphaphon, "ASEAN to Sign Pact Despite U.S. Concerns," *Bangkok Post*, 8 December 1995, p. 9, as reprinted in Foreign Broadcast Information Service, East Asia (Daily Report) [FBIS-EAS], 95-236, 8 December 1995.

35. See a *Yonhap* report reprinted in FBIS-EAS-98-240, 28 August 1998.

36. Cited in Young Whan Kihl, "Seoul's Engagement Policy and US–DPRK Relations," *Korean Journal of Defence Analysis* 10, no. 1 (Summer 1998), p. 30.

37. See John E. Endicott and Alan G. Gorowitz, "Track-II Cooperative Regional Security Efforts: Lessons from the Limited Nuclear Weapons-Free Zone for Northeast Asia," *Pacifica Review* 11, no. 3 (1999).

Part 4

Institutionalizing human security in the Asia-Pacific

14

Human security regimes

Ramesh Thakur

Asia is rife with potential for conflict. There is a concentration of states with the world's largest military establishments, some of them nuclear-armed. It has historic rivalries and ethnic tensions that persist, and it has a diversity of social and economic systems and levels of economic development. Key nations in the region are also undergoing fundamental political, social and economic transitions.[1]

As the global order has transformed over the last half century ... so too has the meaning of peace and security ... security has been transformed to encompass the broad notion of human security [which requires] a much greater stress on people's security, from security through armaments to security through human development, from territorial security to food, employment, and environmental security.[2]

The two contrasting quotations, the first from a US politician-ambassador and the second from the United Nations Secretary-General, represent the poles of traditional and human security. In a book chapter written in 1997, I argued for a shift from "national security" to "human security."[3] Developments across the Asia-Pacific in the period since then have brought home its validity with much greater force and clarity than anyone could have anticipated, from nuclear tests in India and Pakistan to forest fires and regime[4] collapse in Indonesia, floods in China and India, and economic meltdown right across the region. Traditional security threats proved quite unnecessary to destroy the lives and livelihoods of very large numbers of people. When rape is used quite deliberately as an instrument of war and ethnic "impurification," or when thousands are killed by floods resulting from the countryside being ravaged, or when citizens are killed by their own security and paramilitary forces – in these circumstances, the concept of national security is immaterial, irrelevant, and of zero utility in dealing with phenomena causing insecurity at its most extreme limits. By contrast, human security can embrace such diverse phenomena. To insist on national security at the expense of human security would be to trivialize the concept of security in many real-world circumstances to the point of sterility, bereft of any practical meaning.

At the level of institutions, the policy response to the concept of human security is good governance. All contemporary regimes must be based on notions of good governance. Even the crisis in Russia is increasingly being interpreted as a broader crisis of governance, caused by the absence of institutions capable of coping with a globalized world of fast-paced economic and political changes. "Good governance" refers to such factors as the rule of law regulating public and private conduct, power that derives its legitimacy from the consent of the governed and is responsible to the people through periodic elections, accountable and responsive administration, and the observance of human rights in law and through administrative and judicial machinery. At the 1998 meeting of the foreign ministers of the Association of South East Asian Nations (ASEAN), Thailand proposed the establishment of a regional Caucus on Human Security to help people suffering from the economic crisis. Even though the nomenclature was changed to the Caucus on Social Safety Nets,[5] it represents an interesting conceptual development.

In this chapter, I shall begin by recapitulating the principal argument from my article of 1997, and then address the question of regional regime creation as a means of managing the heightened manifestations of human insecurity in the intervening period. By "regime" I mean regular patterns of behaviour, whether desirable or otherwise, and whether embedded in formal organizational structures or cumulative reciprocal learning, around which actor expectations converge.

Review

Following Buzan,[6] I defined "military security" as the defence of a state's citizens, territory, and resources against external enemies. "Political security" involves protecting the organizational stability of states, systems of government, and their legitimating ideologies. "Economic security" entails the maintenance of given levels of welfare and state power through access to resources, finance, and markets. "Societal security" concerns the maintenance of traditional patterns of language, culture, religion, social order, and communal identity within the context of evolutionary change. And by "environmental security" we mean the sustainability of natural ecosystems.

Moreover, the several dimensions were treated not mechanistically but holistically, with many linkages and some tension between them. The border between the domestic and the international becomes increasingly irrelevant with such a holistic approach. Analysts of the security problematique are likely to be grappling simultaneously with problems of internal social cohesion, regime capacity and brittleness, failed states, economic development, structural adjustment, gender relations, ethnic identity, external threats, and transnational and global problems such as AIDS, environmental degradation, drug trafficking, terrorism, and so on. What is increasingly crucial is not how to secure the state against military threats from without, but the optimal mode of articulation between the domestic and international economic, political, and security orders.

A radical conceptual shift, or so it seemed at the time, was from "national security," with its focus on military defence of the state, to "human security," with its emphasis on the individual's welfare. That is, the security referent (the object of security, or that which is to be secured) shifts from the state to the individual. This has a double connotation. Negatively, it refers to freedom *from* – from want, hunger, attack, torture, imprisonment without a free and fair trial, discrimination on spurious grounds, and so on. Positively, it means freedom *to* – the capacity and opportunity that allows each human being to enjoy life to the fullest without imposing constraints upon others engaged in the same pursuit. Putting the two together, human security refers to the quality of life of the people of a society or polity. Anything that degrades their quality of life – demographic pressures, diminished access to or stock of resources, etc. – is a security concern. Conversely, anything that can upgrade their quality of life – economic growth, improved access to resources, social and political empowerment, etc. – is an enhancement of human security.

Human security directs our attention to the rationale, forms, techniques, and measures of state and societal coercion – from the holocaust and the gulags to the death squads of and disappearances in Latin America, the killing fields of Cambodia, the plight of Aborigines in Australia, and the oppression of women everywhere. The threats posed by the administrative, judicial, police, paramilitary, and military structures to individual and group rights are central, not incidental, to human security studies. They are very real, but totally incomprehensible within the analytical framework of national security. Similarly, the social order provides stability and identity, but also embodies and encapsulates caste, class, gender, and other inequalities. Although human rights are principally claims against governments, their reference point can also be the dominant social structure. For example, with regard to the caste system in

India, the government tries to act as the champion of human rights against the dead weight of centuries of social tradition.

The intensional–extensional debate

The definition of any concept involves a trade-off between its intensional and extensional meaning, that is, between precision and broadening. The multidimensional approach to security sacrifices precision for inclusiveness. Realists could legitimately argue that only a "lean" conception of security can provide an honest and effective policy tool to cope with the "mean" enemies of the international jungle.

One possible solution to the dilemma, I argued, is to focus on security policy in relation to crisis, short of which it is more accurate to assess welfare gains and losses rather than increased security and insecurity. Security policy can then be posited as crisis prevention and crisis management, with regard to both institutional capacity and material capability. Moreover, because we cannot be confident of accurate risk assessment and forecasts, we need to develop robust yet flexible "coping capability," including interventions designed at crisis mitigation.[7]

Even if we limit "security" to anything that threatens the core integrity of our units of analysis (namely their very life), many non-traditional concerns merit the gravity of the security label and require exceptional policy measures in response: environmental threats of total inundation, as in the South Pacific and Bangladesh, or total desertification; political threats of the complete collapse of state structures; population flows so large as to destroy the basic identity of host societies and cultures; structural coercion so severe as to turn human beings into de facto chattels; and such like. For example, only a few thousand Indians died in the last war that their country was involved in back in 1971. Millions have died since through structural violence. The annual mortality correlates of poverty – low levels of life expectancy, high levels of maternal and infant mortality – run into several million. Of 23 million babies born each year in India in the 1980s, 4 million died in childbirth, 9 million had serious physical and mental disabilities caused by malnutrition, 7 million suffered from less debilitating forms of malnutrition, and only 3 million grew into healthy adults.[8] Annual deaths – preventable killings – even on this scale cannot be accommodated within the analytical framework of "national security"; they can in "human security."

The narrow definition of security is not just environmentally, societally, and globally negligent. It also presents a falsified image of the policy process. Governments are multi-purpose organizations. The military is only one of several competing interest groups vying for a larger share of the collective goods being allocated authoritatively by the government.

Environmental and social groups also compete for the allocation of scarce resources. There is, therefore, competition, tension, and conflict among major value clusters. Organizations tend to suppress and deny value conflicts in the decision process. The concept of military security as a subset of the national interest serves to disguise the reality of inter-value competition. By contrast, a multidimensional concept of security highlights the need for integrative strategies that resolve or transcend value conflicts.

For example, in a recent article David Baldwin examines and rejects the "prime value" approach to security.[9] The primacy of the goal of security does not withstand rigorous scrutiny, for it does not have privileged claim over such other needs for human beings as food, water, and air. The "core value" approach lessens but does not eliminate the logical and empirical difficulties associated with elevating security over other values. Instead, it is more satisfactory to conceptualize security in terms of the "marginal value" approach: "security is only one of many policy objectives competing for scarce resources and subject to the law of diminishing returns ... Rational policy-makers will allocate resources to security only so long as the marginal return is greater for security than for other uses of the resources."[10] An extra 1 per cent of GDP transferred from the military to the primary health care budget may save a few hundred thousand lives in a country such as India or Pakistan. In such circumstances, the marginal gain to human security is considerably greater than the marginal loss of military capability, unless the latter is sufficient by itself to trigger a full-scale enemy attack.

State security

As noted in the introductory section, the non-traditional sectors of security erupted into crises all across Asia in 1997–98. Indeed the armed forces of Indonesia found themselves at the coalface of the tension between traditional state security and the new human security. Mercifully, in the end they sided with the latter. Since then, we have been confronted by the spectre of a political, social, and economic meltdown in Russia, described as "Indonesia with nukes." And, as an international community, we are yet to devise satisfactory policy responses to the threat of international terrorism using weapons of mass destruction.

The state is an abstract yet powerful notion embracing the total network of authoritative institutions that make and enforce collective decisions throughout the country. In the European conception, the modern state exhibits three principal virtues: political power is depersonalized, standardized, and integrated into the greater social whole.[11] The state embodies the political mission of a society, and its institutions and officials express the proper array of tools that are used in efforts to accomplish the mission.

There are problems with applying the postulated ideal-type state beyond the West. In development theory, a strong state would ensure order, look after national security, and intervene actively in the management of the national economy. In reality, in many developing countries the state is a tool of a narrow family, clique, or sect that is fully preoccupied with fighting off internal and external challenges to its closed privileges. The consolidation of state power can be used in the name of national security and law and order to suppress individual, group, or even majority demands on the government and to plunder the resources of a society. The internal security bureaucracies of many countries are dedicated to the protection of the state against dissident threats from within and can pose a major threat to the human security of the citizens of that state.

Once a state is appropriately disaggregated, security threats can be seen to be sector specific. Ethnic minorities may perceive threats differently from majority communities. The Sinhalese and the Hindus of Kashmir look to the state to provide them with security against Tamil and Islamic fighters in Sri Lanka and India, respectively. To the Tamils and the Kashmiri Muslims, by contrast, the state is itself the principal source of threat to security.

The state is losing its centrality also with regard to large-scale organized violence. War has been a principal source of historical change. Virtually all the states of Europe are the outcomes of war and violence: war made the state before the state made war. The state acquired monopoly over the legitimate use of force and coercion in a historical move to limit violence in anarchical society. Security came to be viewed as the most basic of all the public goods that a state can provide.

In reality, fewer and fewer states do so today. The majority of today's conflicts are internal, over government (civil wars) or territory (state formation). In many armed conflicts there is a situation of hostile coexistence: the state lacks the capacity to crush insurgency, but the challengers lack the capacity to overthrow the regime. Wars, defined in relation to battlefield casualties (whether between or within states), are the exception and armed conflicts are the norm. The increased frequency and intensity of challenges to state authority mean that the point of departure for security studies of developing countries must be the frailty or resilience of state institutions, including the danger of failed states.[12]

Ethno-nationalism is the assertion of rights to sovereignty by ethnic nationalities and, by implication, a reconstruction of the international order on the basis of a system of nations. This is why, at least in the short term, the right to self-determination would be fundamentally destabilizing. That is, "nationalism" is a key threat to state security. But this is just another way of saying that the sanctity of state sovereignty and its accompanying tenet of territorial integrity are the key threats to "national" security.

Ethno-nationalism is a potent rallying cry for political mobilization *within* states. Ethnic conflict may be *rooted* in ancient enmities and hatreds; but it is often *caused* by élites consciously playing upon historical myths and collective memories of past traumas for self-serving power-political ends. Identity politics is simultaneously a rallying point for social coherence and civic pride for "self," and a battle cry for vilifying and cleansing out the "other." For most of the twentieth century the search for national security through self-determination was promoted, at least in rhetoric. Has the time come to look for security from self-determination?[13] Nationalist movements – nations in search of statehood – raise first-order questions about how the demands can be accommodated without massive dislocation, suffering, and the prospect of major conflict; all in all a recipe for massive human insecurity.

Regional security

The end of the Cold War and the triumph of liberal capitalism could lead to a new polarization between the dominant centre and the subordinate periphery. Whereas the centre inhabits a Lockean world, I argued, the periphery is condemned to the world of Hobbes, with life often being nasty, brutish, and short. The polarization has become even starker since then. Common security arrangements on a global scale are almost certainly too ambitious in the foreseeable future. But might they be contemplated as realistic regional arrangements?

A "region" can be defined solely in geographic terms. "Regionalism," in the sense of the sentiment or consciousness of a common identity, is culturally or politically constructed. The difference becomes clear if we think of South and South-East Asia respectively. Physically, the former is one of the most sharply defined regions in the world whereas the latter is a far more loose area. Yet the South Asian Association for Regional Cooperation (SAARC) has failed really to take off, whereas ASEAN has been among the more successful regional associations. As the pre-eminent regional organization in South-East Asia, ASEAN in turn took a leading role in the formation and management of other region-wide institutions such as the ASEAN Regional Forum (ARF), the Asia-Pacific Economic Cooperation (APEC), and the Asia–Europe Meetings (ASEM). Regional organizations would have the advantages of closeness to the conflicts, deeper familiarity with the issues underlying the conflict and the social and political contexts encasing them, and awareness of the urgency to deal with the crisis to hand. The handicaps under which regional arrangements operate include local rivalries, partisanship, the tendency to replicate local power imbalances within the regional organizations, and the fear of establishing precedents for intervention in the internal affairs of member countries.[14]

In order to take on a security role, regional organizations would need to overcome an obstacle and resolve a paradox. They would need to possess the requisite financial, institutional, and military capacity to play a regional conflict management role. They would also need to be synchronous with the regional security complexes, which emphasize the "interdependence of rivalry as well as that of shared interests."[15] That is, all the parties that are central to a regional security complex must be included within the regional arrangements for the latter to have real meaning. Thus, subregional organizations such as ASEAN cannot play regional conflict management roles because they do not coincide with the regional security complex. But if all relevant regional actors are included, then the regional arrangements are rendered impotent because of the refusal of the parties to permit security discussions for fear of derailing regional cooperation on non-security issues,[16] as is the case with SAARC. The question of China–Taiwan relations could play a similar spoiling role in North-East Asia.

Asia-Pacific has only one region-wide Track I framework, namely the ARF. The Forum is unusual in that those in charge of its establishment, agenda, and management are not the major powers. The ARF is unusual also in that, although the driving seat is occupied by ASEAN, the primary focus of security concerns is North-East Asia. Because South-East Asia could not be insulated from a breakdown of peace and order to its north-east, nesting North-East Asia security discussions in ARF provides detached concern without vested interests. In combination with the Council for Security Cooperation in the Asia Pacific (CSCAP) and the regional network of Institutes of Strategic and International Studies, this places ASEAN at the hub of Asia-Pacific's governmental and second-track security dialogue, confidence-building, and preventive diplomacy activities.

The quasi-diplomatic second-track channel of dialogue and discussion is a striking feature of contemporary Asia-Pacific activity. The formula of allowing officials to participate in their private and personal capacity gives them the latitude to deal with pressing issues a little more creatively than would be possible entirely within the constraints of official positions. While officials try to shed some inhibitions about free dialogue, academics try to address problems with a greater sense of awareness of the real world of the policy choices facing decision-makers. Track II is the medium for the dialectic between cutting-edge thought and best-practice diplomacy.

The ARF is still in its infancy. It is ideally well placed to serve as the consolidating and legitimating instrument for regional security initiatives and confidence-building measures. Like Track I, Track II activities too are subject to the law of diminishing returns. Consolidation of existing frameworks and forums may be more pressing a need than multiplying them still further. Otherwise we risk stretching resources and attention spans to beyond the point of sustainability or sensible returns.

Should Australia and New Zealand, which are members of the ARF and APEC and do participate in most Track II activities, count as regional actors? Their involvement with the Asia-Pacific region is inevitable, irreversible, and probably even desirable.[17] But the completion of the transition from a narrowly Eurocentric outlook to a more balanced and nuanced world-view will be neither uncontroversial nor smooth. One of the obstacles is the attitudinal resistance of some Asian leaders to the notion of closer Australasian identification with Asia-Pacific. Self-evidently, Australasians are not Asians in the racial sense and not likely to be even in the distant future. Mutual adjustments and accommodation will be required. Given the asymmetries, the burden of adjustment will fall more heavily on Australians and New Zealanders.

It is equally self-evident that both Australia and New Zealand are Asian in the geopolitical sense. Yet both have been excluded from ASEM. Even though Europe is no longer an option for Australia and New Zealand as their primary area of identification, Asia refuses to embrace them. Their exclusion from ASEM because of the entrenched views of one or two countries or leaders is as damaging to Asia as it is to them. Rather than being neither Western nor Asian, they successfully straddle both worlds. They could act as linchpins between Asia and the West. A self-consciously middle power, Australia has key economic and security interests in the region, and is in a position to exert modest influence. Instead of rejecting Australia and New Zealand from the region and casting stones at international financiers and Jewish conspirators, Asian countries might do better to use Australasian professional expertise in managing large, complex, modern economies.

Nuclear security

A relative shift occurred in the 1990s in the balance between nuclear weapons acquisition and non-proliferation. In the old security agenda, many states were interested in seeking security *through* nuclear weapons. Now, most seek security *from* nuclear weapons. Most analysts had expected the biggest challenge to the anti-nuclear norm to come from North Korea. Instead, it was India and Pakistan that put themselves on the wrong side of history by conducting "in your face" nuclear tests in May 1998. Why, following the French and Chinese examples of 1995–96, are they marching to the drumbeat of a nuclear tune that no one wants to hear any more?

From one point of view, and in particular in the context of the legitimacy given to nuclear weapons by their continued possession and deployment by all five countries that had them when the Nuclear Non-Proliferation Treaty (NPT) was signed in 1968, the subcontinent's nuclearization was quite understandable. But it was nevertheless wrong, and it made the two countries and the world a more dangerous place in consequence. After the fading of the initial euphoria for blasting their way into the nuclear club, more and more people in both India and Pakistan have slowly but surely come to realize that their net national security has been degraded ('twas ever so and ever will be with the balance of terror), their economies have suffered setbacks, and their international prestige has actually diminished.[18]

Anti-nuclear regimes can range from the NPT at the global level to nuclear-weapon-free zones (NWFZs) in regional security arrangements and the infrastructure of stable deterrence in bilateral relations. As part of the strengthening non-proliferation norm, there was a revival of interest in the idea of regional NWFZs.[19] Latin America and the South Pacific anticipated the post–Cold War strategic developments in concluding regional NWFZs in 1967 and 1985, respectively. Zonal agreements for South-East Asia and Africa were concluded in the 1990s. All fit my definition of regimes.

By maintaining the momentum for the continued stigmatization of this weapon of mass destruction, NWFZs sustain the structure of normative restraints on the acquisition, multiplication, deployment, and use of nuclear weapons. Critics and supporters alike agree that, for reasons of international security, NWFZs contribute to the marginalization of nuclear weapons as tools of national security. They institutionalize non-proliferation norms, consolidate non-proliferation successes, and maintain the momentum to denuclearization ahead of the willingness of the nuclear weapons states (NWS) to renounce their own nuclear arsenals.[20]

The NPT embodies the global non-proliferation agenda. There is an intrinsic imbalance of obligations between the nuclear and non-nuclear states. From the perspective of the nuclear powers, NWFZs are non-proliferation measures only, with no relevance for nuclear disarmament, nuclear weapons deployment, or strategic doctrines. They merely assist in ensuring higher levels of compliance with the non-proliferation regime. From a regional perspective, NWFZs also express in-theatre efforts to disengage from the nuclear weapons, deployment policies, and strategic doctrines of the NWS. Sometimes an NWFZ may prove its value as an alternative to the NPT in achieving non-proliferation. For example, Brazil's non-proliferation status was codified within the Tlatelolco arrangements before it signed the NPT. In other contexts, a regional NWFZ can offer additional benefits in helping to reduce the risks of nuclear conflict within a nuclear-charged local rivalry. Non-nuclear NPT parties are legally committed to their non-nuclear status. An NWFZ adds no further legal obstacle to their acquisition of nuclear weapons; it does construct a legal barrier to the introduction of the nuclear weapons of other states into the region. Most importantly, it takes away nuclear weapons from any future security architecture being drafted for the region.

As with arms control in general, some commentators argue that NWFZ arrangements can come only after a general improvement in the security atmosphere in currently volatile and conflict-riven regions. Nations do not distrust each other because they are armed; they are armed because they distrust each other. Therefore, as with the relationship between arms control and conflict, an NWFZ in regions of high conflict intensity may have to follow rather than cause the end of conflicts. On the other hand, others insist that NWFZs can themselves comprise confidence-building measures on the road to peace. The confidence built among regional states through an NWFZ can spill over into other areas of regional interactions. In other words, the vicious cycle of fear, mistrust, and hostility sustaining open or ambiguous nuclear weapons programmes and postures can be replaced by the virtuous cycle of unequivocal non-nuclear status through NWFZ regimes that underpin cooperation and sustain mutual confidence.

The geographical point of intersection of the Pacific balance of power is North-East Asia. The geopolitical balance was fluid and unsettled throughout the twentieth century. Three of the world's five nuclear weapons states are involved in the North-East Asian power equation. Peace and security cannot be consolidated in North-East Asia without the prior resolution of nuclear issues. The search for an NWFZ for North-East Asia can be justified on the grounds of the risks that attend the rivalry between the nuclear powers, the proliferation propensity of regional actors, and the dynamics of interaction between local and international actors. The *unification* of the Korean peninsula may be a purely internal decision for the people of Korea and a product of negotiations between the two parallel sets of authorities north and south of the Demilitarized Zone. The *stability* of the peninsula will be a function of the interaction between local dynamics and major-power relations. The North Pacific remains a potentially unstable zone of confrontation, subject to the pulls and pressures of relations between China, Japan, Russia, and the United States.

It would be prudent to recognize the very real difficulties on the road to establishing an NWFZ in North-East Asia. There is no existing sub-regional organization to initiate and guide negotiations, nor a sub-regional dialogue process that could form the backdrop to an NWFZ negotiation. The North Korean nuclear status must somehow be resolved before any meaningful discussion can begin on NWFZ. There is the politically sensitive issue of how China and Taiwan might be integrated into a regional NWFZ. As for South Asia, the legal fiction of the NPT notwithstanding, in reality there are two more NWS. The pressing task now is to prevent the marriage of warheads and delivery systems. For the foreseeable future, therefore, the South Pacific and South-East Asian NWFZs are likely to remain the only two regimes in the Asia-Pacific for assuaging nuclear anxieties.

At the same time, the Korean Peninsula Energy Development Organization (KEDO) can properly be viewed as a regime for managing North Korea's transition from proliferation-sensitive to proliferation-resistant nuclear reactors with financial and technological assistance from a number of other countries. Its membership comprises South Korea, Japan, the United States, and Indonesia. Its purpose is to enable North Korea to eschew the nuclear weapons option in return for help in developing nuclear energy for peaceful use; hence its description as a "regional security framework."[21] Other than this, however, North Korea has been notably and frustratingly resistant to taking part in regional forums, even those under ASEAN auspices. Unlike South-East Asia, there is no comfort level with multilateral discussion, no habit and practice of intensive consultations among the security élites (policy-makers and intellectuals) based on personalized relationships and underpinned by a language such as English used as the common medium of dialogue by the élites.

The ex-colonial language does unite the élites of South Asia. India and Pakistan could borrow from the Cold War model and adapt its lessons to their own unique environment in putting in place a stability-enhancing nuclear controls regime with crisis-dampening features that construct buffers between erupting tensions and the decision to use nuclear weapons.

Environmental security

Previously we sought security from the environment, trying to tame and control the environment through technology in order to increase net human welfare. Now we seek security in harmony with the environment.

We worry about the threats posed to delicately balanced ecosystems by human activity, and the consequential threat to human welfare. Policy responses include statutory requirements for environmental impact assessments within countries, and international talkfests, negotiations, regimes, and conventions to manage shared environmental problems.

Scarce or strategic resources can be causes, tools, or targets of warfare. They can be the source of political disputes that degenerate into violent conflicts within states as well as between them.[22] The proposition that environmental degradation and resource competition can cause war is not uncontested. Environmental factors, whether rooted in scarcity or in degradation, do not generally cause wars directly. Rather, they are catalysts for war. Whether or not countries resort to violence over threatened resources will depend in part on their capacity to adapt to change. Developing countries have fewer technical, financial, and institutional resources to ameliorate the adverse consequences of environmental damage, and may be correspondingly more vulnerable to social, economic, and political dislocation leading to disturbances to the traditional balances of economic and political authority.[23]

In August 1998, after devastating floods had killed over 3,000 people, the Chinese authorities finally began to admit that land-use mistakes were partly to blame for the scale, if not the outbreak, of the "natural disaster," and announced sweeping policy changes.[24] The contribution of people and government was noted also by the Worldwatch Institute.[25] At about the same time, deforestation, soil erosion, and heavy rain caused landslips and major floods in northern India, leading to the deaths of over 1,000 people there as well.[26]

We need to formulate and implement preventive action in the midst of scientific uncertainty and accompanying residual scepticism about the direct and opportunity costs of such action. The problem is that the opportunity costs of inaction will be even greater. This also shows why the standard static model of international agreements – "years of negotiations leading to a final product" – needs to be replaced by a fluid and dynamic model – "a rolling process of intermediate or self-adjusting agreements that respond quickly to growing scientific understanding."[27]

There have been occasional suggestions about the need for a UN Environment Council. Instead of that, it might make more sense to explore the feasibility, practicality, and modalities of regional environmental management regimes. Regions, by definition, tend to be more physically integrated than their political divisions: nature is not quite as sharply compartmentalized as political entities. The mountain and river systems of South Asia, or the Mekong River in East Asia, are good examples of natural ecosystems that traverse many different countries and political systems. Moreover, the network of practices causing environmental degradation can also be integrated across political frontiers. In an important book, Peter Dauvergne underpins his analysis of deforestation in South-East Asia with the concept of Japan's "shadow ecology," which unites Japanese foreign aid and corporate and consumer practices in the exploitation of resources outside Japan's territorial limits.[28]

Thus environmental problems such as deforestation, air and water pollution, scarcity of drinking water because of falling water tables, depletion of fish stocks through over-fishing, and so on are interlinked across many countries.[29] By their very nature, resources shared by countries require cooperative husbanding, use, and conservation. They also need to rest on reasonably firm foundations of stable and predictable behaviour; that is, on regimes. As food, water, and energy scarcities become more acute, the need for regional environmental regimes will become correspondingly more urgent.

Economic security

Economic security can be described in human terms as the satisfaction of the economic needs and wants of the people. That is, on the broad definition of security, economic growth is a security goal in its own right, for only thus can societal welfare be assured.

Many countries, especially developing countries, are worried that the forces of globalization are going to impinge adversely on their economic sovereignty, cultural integrity, and social stability. "Interdependence" among unequals amounts to the dependence of some on international markets that function under the dominance of others. The United States is perceived as being interested in the creation of rules-based regimes for managing all international transactions, provided that Washington can set, interpret, and enforce the rules. Globalization and liberalization in the absence of effective regulatory institutions to underpin them have led to weak civil society being overwhelmed by rampant transnational forces. Although much of the impact of globalization is beneficial, much is not. For the forces of globalization have also unleashed the infrastructure of uncivil society and accelerated the transnational flows of terrorism, drug trafficking, organized crime, and diseases such as AIDS.

For three decades, the defining characteristic of Asian-Pacific salience in world affairs was economic dynamism. In the quarter century between 1970 and 1995, the East Asian economies produced the fastest rise in incomes for the biggest number of peoples in human history. Their economic success was attributed to several factors: sound economic management by relatively stable political regimes that ushered in rapid structural change, an industrious and increasingly well-educated workforce, high rates of savings and investment by instinctively thrifty peoples, and the adoption of a managed-market strategy of economic development that struck a balance between the interventionist and the free-market state. The state was prepared to assist industries so long as industrial performance was responsive to international market signals.

Flushed with the economic success of their countries and the region as a whole, the long-serving leaders of Indonesia, Malaysia, and Singapore (Suharto, Mahathir bin Mohamad, and Lee Kuan Yew) grew in self-confidence and stature to the point where they and their followers openly lectured the West on decaying values, political institutions, and social cohesion. The International Monetary Fund (IMF), the World Bank, and most of the leading ratings agencies were still bullish about East Asia at the start of 1997. As late as 2 July 1997, the United Nations' *World Economic and Social Survey* forecast growth rates of 7.5, 6.5, and 5.5 per cent, respectively, for Indonesia, Thailand, and South Korea.[30] *The Economist* did warn of the dangers of "primitive, inefficient financial systems smothered by tight regulation" in East Asia outside of Hong Kong and Singapore; of corruption, autocracy, and inadequate infrastructure; of the "object lesson" provided by Japan in "the dangers of delaying structural reform"; and that "over-regulation, inadequate competition and capital-market rigidities could choke growth."[31] In an article that has gained retrospective respectability, confounding the harsh criticisms it attracted at the time, Paul Krugman argued that the "Asian miracle" had no clothes: it was based on massive inputs of capital and labour, not on efficiency gains. Once these were exhausted, the rate of growth would decelerate sharply.[32]

But no one predicted the ferocity of the market reaction to Thailand's problems or the severity and spread of contagion to the rest of the region. Analysts drew comparisons with the great depression of the 1930s: excess capacity, competitive devaluations, collapses in property and equity markets, banking crises, and, of course, policy paralysis. The bubble burst with a currency crisis that began in Thailand. By January 1998, compared with their values a year earlier, stock markets had tumbled to between one-half and one-fifth across the region (fig. 14.1). As one after another economy contracted, the Asian miracle became the Asian malaise. In one year, the economic devastation in Indonesia seemingly wiped out the gains of one generation. For, although the poverty rate had plummeted from 64 per cent in 1975 to 11 per cent in 1995, half the population still lived close to the poverty line.[33]

The point to note for us is the human impact of the economic crisis. People who had a tenuous hold on middle-class ambitions have been pushed back into poverty, hunger, and misery by the millions. According to the International Labour Organization, more than 5 million workers

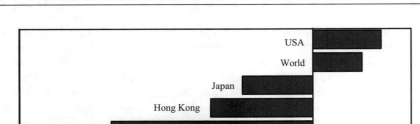

Fig. 14.1 The collapse in Asian stock markets, 1997–98 (percentage change at 21 January 1998 on 31 December 1997) (Source: *The Economist*, 24 January 1998, pp. 109–110)

became unemployed in Indonesia as a direct result of the economic crisis; about 40 per cent of Indonesia's 200 million people fell below the poverty line in 1998; and the figure was forecast to climb to 70 per cent in 1999. The government estimate of poverty in 1998 was 22 per cent; reports commissioned by the World Bank concluded that the level was only 14 per cent.[34] Although the crisis had devastated the formal economy in the cities, Indonesia's flexible labour market made it easier to find work in the informal economy in the countryside. Nevertheless, in addition to the fall in employment there were four further consequences. First, new entrants into the labour market faced bleak job prospects. Secondly, the collapse in jobs, output, and consumption, together with high inflation, produced a sharp fall in real wages and earnings in both the formal and informal sectors of the economy. Thirdly, the lack of a system of unemployment benefits and adequate levels of social assistance produced an increased level of poverty. Finally, three decades of economic growth and modernization had weakened traditional welfare mechanisms such as the extended family or a closely knit village community for mitigating the effects of poverty.[35]

Governance

The combination of the currency freefall and the policy paralysis in the face of the Indonesian forest fires indicated that the affliction to have hit South-East Asia was multidimensional. It was a crisis of governance reflecting institutionalized patronage and corruption, weak central banks, and lack of transparency, accountability, and teeth in regulatory arrangements. It was born of policy failures in managing national economies amidst worsening current account deficits combined with high debt levels and weak and protected domestic financial sectors; major deficiencies in prudential financial management systems; and the political denial of reality. As well as vividly illustrating the costs of "crony capitalism" – where profits are made not through the free interplay of market forces but as a result of access to credit lines and purchasing orders through political patronage – the Asian crisis reinforced the benefits of competitive markets, transparent and effective regulatory institutions, an efficient and corruption-free bureaucracy, and the rule of law. Most analysts concluded that Asia's banks and finance companies had operated with implicit government guarantees. Together with inadequate regulatory arrangements, this seriously distorted investment and lending decisions. Banks were ready to finance risky projects because they could reap any quick profits to be made, while the governments would cover the losses.[36]

Nowhere was this more apparent than in Indonesia's initial responses to the forest fires raging out of control across it, as well as to the subsequent currency crisis. Indonesia's private sector borrowed heavily from foreign banks without hedging against the risk of the rupiah falling sharply. With weak financial governance in the public and private sectors, business was done more on political connections than commercial competence. When the rupiah did collapse, businesses were unable to service their overseas dollar-denominated debts. Because of the history of the political–commercial nexus, the stigma of failure flowed back to the political establishment. In both Indonesia and Thailand, corruption inflated major project costs and made locally made products uncompetitive.

In South Korea, the family conglomerates – the *chaebol* – were overextended, with average debt-to-equity ratios of 4:1. Encouraged and supported by the government, banks provided more credit than was prudent to help the conglomerates diversify and open more export markets. The timing of the presidential election proved fortuitous. Newly elected Kim Dae Jung benefited from having led the opposition to the corrupt business–politics nexus for decades. His election helped to defuse the political anger resulting from the economic crisis and to channel it constructively into implementing painful reforms. The key to economic recovery in all badly affected countries was the credibility of the commitment to reforms. The installation of a new government in Thailand helped to bring about such credibility; the persistence of the old order in Indonesia delayed the return of domestic and international confidence there.

The outbreak of the crisis reflected failures of policy and governance at the national level. Its continuance for a prolonged period was an indictment of regional institutions and great power economic leadership. Created to be the chief vehicle for regional economic cooperation, APEC made no contribution at all to the solution of Asia's first economic crisis since its birth. ASEAN's contribution to the growth and influence of South-East Asia and the management of the security order in the region has been enormous. The hundreds of coordinating meetings held each year under its rubric have added greatly to the texture and institutional complexity of East Asia. Yet ASEAN too was afflicted by policy paralysis when confronted by the multiple crises of 1997: currency and stock market freefalls; forest fires in Indonesia whose damaging environmental effects were felt in Brunei, Malaysia, Singapore, and Thailand; the obduracy of the military regime in Myanmar (Burma); the slide back towards chaos, disorder, and killings after the coup in Cambodia; and the crisis of confidence and legitimacy of the Suharto regime in Indonesia. When the crunch came, the institutional identity of APEC and ASEAN proved to be far too embryonic and fragile, much too dependent still on the personal preferences and policies of the leaders at the top; that is, captive of "crony regionalism."

The architecture of international financial management

The Asian economic meltdown also highlighted deficiencies in the architecture of the global financial order.[37] IMF prescriptions turned out to be a bail-out of international creditors rather than of afflicted countries. They were excessively contractionary. The doctrinaire squeeze on central bank credit and budget deficits was based on the diagnosis of the ailment that had afflicted Latin America a decade earlier – government profligacy. The main problems in Asia were private, not public, sector debt;[38] misallocated investment, not excessive consumption or inadequate saving; and a crisis of confidence. IMF policies were also seen as an attack on economic sovereignty, with a matching fear that Asian pain was being exploited for US gain as local institutions were bought by overseas interests at firesale prices. When Russia faced yet another prospect of economic meltdown in August 1998, the IMF finally began to soften some of its stringent conditions, elevating economic revival, relative to financial stability, to a higher priority than hitherto.[39]

Globalization threatens the ability of states to govern markets and currency transactions. Policy sovereignty lost at the national level can be recouped in the wider setting of regional institutions. Floating exchange rate movements are so heavily influenced by short-term capital movements that they bear little relation to fundamental cost comparisons. Nor do they provide a stable basis for developing international trade, since industry cannot plan output or capacity rationally without knowing or being able to predict comparative costs and prices from one month to the next. Current policy choices are restricted to a free-floating exchange rate, on the one hand, and fixed rates or a currency union, on the other. But the last requires a high and sustained degree of economic convergence, which has proven difficult even for the European Union (EU). The levels of economic development across the Asia-Pacific are far more uneven than in the EU. Nevertheless, regional currency arrangements may prove necessary, and the idea of a three-currency bloc based on the dollar, euro, and yen may have to be revived. It should be easier to manage rates between countries within a region than on a worldwide basis. Any threat to agreed parities or bands should trigger intervention by regional instruments,[40] underpinned by international arrangements such as an IMF Stabilization Fund.

Economic integration can also be postulated as an institutional means of conflict amelioration. A principal original impulse to West European integration was the political motive of avoiding another major war in Europe.[41] Regional organizations help to create webs of functional links, which then improve relations between the member states, and they do help to control some types of conflicts between their member states and prevent them from spreading. They produce these results because functional interdependence promotes a sense of common identity or community among members, raises the threshold of tolerance of irritating behaviour by other members because perceived benefits exceed perceived challenges, increases the cost of violent conflict to all members, and provides mechanisms, experience, and expectations of "integrative solutions." But the more general relationship between the dependent variable of conflict and the independent variable of integration is curvilinear rather than linear. Initially, conflicts seem to increase as countries come into greater contact, but then, beyond an unspecified threshold of integration, conflicts peak and begin to decline.

Human rights

All conflicts have humanitarian consequences. The doctrine of national security has been deeply corrosive of human rights. It is used frequently by governments, which are charged with the main responsibility for the welfare of their citizens, to diminish the security of their peoples by subjecting them to gross human rights abuses.

Democratic governance might provide one answer to the dilemma of reconciling state security with group and human security. Some now advocate democracy as a legal entitlement.[42] Even as a "concession" by the élites to popular demands, it helps to defuse the crisis of legitimacy for the regimes. A refusal to accommodate democratic demands, by contrast, as in Myanmar, disaggregates regime security from state security, heightens the crisis of legitimacy, and creates a crisis in relations with an international community increasingly willing to impose conditionality on its engagement with sovereign states.

The core element of human security is human rights. Civil and political rights are claims by citizens on governments. They can be abused most systematically, pervasively, and widely by governments. So the relationship between governments and human rights organizations is principally adversarial. Yet social and economic rights, for example affirmative action programmes for systematically disadvantaged sectors of society, can be promoted through government action. Once again, therefore, there is a tension between those who would seek security through the state and those who would seek security from it.

Most developing countries have lost strategic leverage. They are neither political prizes to be won nor strategic assets to be harnessed to bloc rivalry. The lifting of the Cold War shadow shows up some hitherto concealed unpleasant aspects of many regimes. In particular, one-party regimes have been substantially delegitimized in many countries of the periphery. At the same time, as the era of European colonialism recedes into historical memory, neither Western leaders nor developing country peoples are willing to accept continuing material deprivation as being the fault of the wicked West. Third World élites who were privileged by competitive bloc rivalry suddenly find themselves under unaccustomed accountability to domestic and international audiences. Reactions to the resulting regime insecurity have varied.

The placing of gender on the security agenda can easily be justified by recalling the role of comfort women for Japanese troops during World War II, and by the use of rape as a weapon of war in former Yugoslavia in the 1990s. Women can confront insecurity that is direct (for example killing) or rooted in structural violence (indirect exploitation) and cultural violence (which legitimizes direct or structural violence).[43] The situation of women in the developing world can be summed up in five words: poor, overworked, unpaid, ill, and illiterate. Traditionally, women have depended for their security on men as protectors and providers in the primordial sexual contract. As developments in technology and the evolving principles of economic, social, and political organization free women from this dependence, some women have come to view men as a source of threat to their gendered security.

With regard to both human rights in general and gender-specific rights in particular, regional regimes can help to reconcile the relativism–universalism debate. Social and cultural practices are less sharply differentiated between countries in the same region. At the same time, human rights claims tend in the first instance to be claims by citizens against their own governments. The adversarial relationship with the state-centric definition of national security is therefore intrinsic to a conception of human security rooted in individual human rights. Instead of posing a false dichotomy between the doctrine of national sovereignty and the philosophy of cultural relativism, on the one hand, and that of international concern and universalism, on the other, it might be better to mediate between them through regional arrangements. National human rights and women's commissions in South, South-East and North-East Asia, for example, can compare notes, draw philosophical, political, and material sustenance from one another, use global legal and normative instruments, and yet credibly reject – and therefore effectively rebut – charges of cultural imperialism. Regional regimes could play the lead roles while international instruments and actors plus transnational non-governmental organizations (NGOs) provide the supporting props. Once again, institutions from Europe, such as the European Commission on Human Rights, provide suitable examples that can be appropriately adapted to regional mores and traditions. In East Asia, Thailand and the Philippines are the only two ASEAN members prepared to argue that the organization needs to confront the issue. The sad fact remains that at the 1998 foreign ministers' meeting, the Thai proposal for "constructive intervention" in crises such as that in Myanmar was modified into the gentler "flexible engagement" before being watered down into the totally innocuous "enhanced interaction."[44]

Of regimes and realism

The primacy of national security over alternative versions, for all actors and in all situations, is logically flawed and empirically false. The logical fallacy lies in the inability to justify collapsing "security" into national security when there is no overarching concept of security that aggregates all dimensions into one, and when absolute security is unattainable. The empirical falsehood lies in the clash with the reality of people feeling degrees of threat to their security from a variety of sources, including the state itself. The concept of national security restricted to threats to the state fails to capture the complexities, dilemmas, and nuances of the contemporary security problematique. It is one-dimensional and too simplistic, and does not provide conceptual ballast and texture to the multi-faceted nature of security. From within the perspective of national security, the state can never be the source of threat to citizens' security, although, in the opposite direction, citizens have often been seen as an "internal security" threat to their own country. In the real world, more people are threatened by the "security agents" of their own state than by the soldiers of enemy states. The number of battle deaths for *all interna-*

tional and civil wars in the twentieth century was 30 and 7 million, respectively; the total number of civilians killed by governments (excluding wars) was 170 million.[45] This is why "human security" offers a more satisfactory analytical and policy template than "national security" for the challenge of humanitarian intervention in today's world.

The realist paradigm rejects the possibility of anything but power-as-might as the basic determinant of international relations. The overriding characteristic of the global diplomatic milieu is anarchy. The lawlessness resulting from the absence of effective international government is rescued from chaos by a system of balance of power. The only effective check on the overly powerful is countervailing power. Regional institutions, far from being aloof, are integral elements of the ubiquitous struggle for power. The task of regional organizations and forums is to enhance the stability of the balance of power, to improve the mechanisms for calibrating and adjusting the shifting power relationships, perhaps to check runaway military growth through multilaterally negotiated arms control agreements, and to underpin the exercise of power in ways that preserve the delicate fabric of regional and world order. In the realist perspective on US foreign policy, therefore, an organization such as NATO becomes the vehicle for multilateralizing US national interest, serving both as a conduit for US power projection to transatlantic troublespots and as a moral framework for legitimating the exercise of US power. The 1999 Kosovo war is a good example of this.

This may contain a clue to why the Southeast Asia Treaty Organization (SEATO) failed. The realist assumptions do not sit comfortably with the Asian methods of regional diplomacy. On the one hand, there is no "Asian way." The phrase is a convenient label used by politicians to short-circuit serious debate, mobilize emotional support, and delegitimize dissent. Asia is far too big and diverse geographically, socially, religiously, culturally, politically, and economically for there to be much coherence or content in the concept. Even East Asia has major cultural dividing lines between Confucians, Muslims, and Buddhists.

On the other hand, there is an ASEAN way. It is process, not outcome, driven. It stresses informality, organizational minimalism, inclusiveness, intensive consultations leading to consensus, and sensitivity to sovereignty concerns. It is suspicious of outside solutions to regional problems. Its core comprises personal relationships, carefully nurtured over several years, among the heads of governments. Élite socialization is more important than formal institutions. Because of the importance attached to consensus, progress can be slow so that all members are comfortable with the pace. This contrasts with the EU way of formal institutions with the power to make decisions that are legally binding on member states, even on those that may have opposed the measures.

The establishment of regional and international organizations is made necessary by the problems created by power politics. But between the realist paradigm, which denies the possibility of regional organizations as autonomous actors, and a revolutionary paradigm, which seeks to replace state actors with a moral community embracing all states within one universally accepted conception of human welfare, lies the ASEAN vision of a moral order based on states' compliance with regional norms. Unlike the revolutionist, the ASEAN preference is to repair, not rebuild, regional and world order. Unlike the realist, the ASEAN approach does believe in the efficacy of regional institutions in moderating and taming the unrelenting struggle for power. Regional institutions are the means for circumventing conflict and mobilizing the collective will of an incipient Asia-Pacific community. In sum, they aim to ameliorate tension without resolving the conflict.

Europe is the font of the modern states system as we know it. Supranational institutions first emerged in Europe too, but only some three centuries after the inauguration of the Westphalian system. By contrast, most of the Asian countries came into independent statehood only at about the time that the pillars of the supranational European community were being established by the former colonial powers in their home continent. It is hardly surprising then that the Asian nations should be far more jealous of their sovereignty. In these circumstances, confronting sensitive issues of sovereignty through formal institution-building is more likely to divide than to unite the inchoate and incipient Asia-Pacific community. The search for common principles, frameworks, and values to underpin a community will be elusive and could prove divisive.[46]

Another problem is how best to involve China in regional forums and dialogue. Its preferred approach seems to be to make unilateral statements of principle to complement bilateral channels for negotiation. The contrasting prescriptions for dealing with China reflect the ambivalent interpretations of its emergence as a major power. They range from appeasement and containment at the two extremes, to enmeshment, engagement, and constrainment in between.[47]

Two sets of paired observations form the basis of this divergence. First, China has no history of territorial expansion and forcible conquest of foreign people. But nor is it ever prepared to renounce existing territorial claims; it is ready to use force to defend them. Secondly, for the first time in two hundred years the world has to cope with a united and powerful China. But so too does China have to come to terms with its status as the emerging superpower. Unfortunately, China has no historical, philosophical, or literary tradition of diplomatic intercourse as a great power in a system of great powers. Its inheritance is that of the Middle Kingdom.

Peace cannot be maintained in Asia without accommodating China's interests. But nor will it be durable if based on appeasement. The trick is to strike the right balance between containment and appeasement. The policy of constructive engagement has exposed the people of China to international influences and facilitated the development of a large market-oriented sector in parts of China's economy. Asian-Pacific governments remain keen to integrate China more fully into open regional and global trading arrangements, to "domesticate" it into the Asian family of nations. Can the dissonance be resolved between ASEAN's habit of private dialogue and China's outbreaks of public action? Regional economic, political, and military regimes might once again provide the answer to the dilemma.

The rational actor model falsifies and distorts the empirical reality of decision-making by states. States are not unitary and cohesive actors pursuing a clearly defined hierarchy of goals through a rational calculation of means and costs. Rather, state actors comprise individuals motivated by personal and bureaucratic ambitions and habits of inertia as much as by notions of the national interest. Nevertheless, for analytical purposes, the rational actor model of state behaviour can still be useful in certain contexts, for example to explain continuity of patterns of behaviour over long periods of time spanning several rounds of turnover in the policy-makers.

Similarly, rather than a wholesale replacement of one security concept by another, it may be more profitable to accept a pluralistic coexistence.[48] In certain contexts, "national security" may still prove more durable and satisfying as the analytical prism through which to view security threats and responses. In other contexts, the security problematique may be better framed in terms of human security. That is, security may be an essentially contested concept, so laden with value that no amount of evidence or argument will persuade analysts and policy-makers to agree on a single version as the correct definition. Perhaps, in the end, "[e]conomic security, environmental security, identity security, social security, and military security are different forms of security, not fundamentally different concepts."[49] The best policy response might be to forge broader security coalitions between states, intergovernmental organizations, and civil society NGOs. The Ottawa Convention on anti-personnel landmines[50] and the newly established permanent International Criminal Court may be important portents of issue-based networks of convenience and convergence of values, instead of the older alliances of convenience based on conjunctions of interests.

The multitude of contemporary international *actors* includes states, intergovernmental organizations, and non-governmental organizations. Acting together, they can form partnerships among civil society stakeholders. The *interaction* between them – the patterns and expectations of behaviour – can convert newly emergent norms into normal or usual international behaviour. The end result or *outcome* will be greatly enhanced human security and traditional national and international security. The three together – actors, interaction, and outcomes – add up to new *regimes*, so that collective patterns of behaviour, and expectations thereof, change, for example with regard to anti-personnel landmines and humanitarian intervention.

Notes

1. Thomas Foley (US Ambassador to Japan), "The U.S.–Japan Link," *International Herald Tribune* (hereafter *IHT*), 28 August 1998.
2. UN Secretary-General Kofi Annan, "The Quiet Revolution," *Global Governance*, no. 4 (April–June 1998), p. 132.
3. Ramesh Thakur, "From National to Human Security," in Stuart Harris and Andrew Mack, eds., *Asia-Pacific Security: The Economics–Politics Nexus* (Sydney: Allen & Unwin, 1997), pp. 52–80.
4. The word "regime" has several different meanings. Here it refers to the complex of ruling authorities and arrangements. But it still encapsulates patterns of behaviour around which actor expectations converge, the main sense in which "regime" is used in this chapter. Its specific meaning – patterns of behaviour or structures of authority – should be quite clear from the context throughout the chapter.
5. Peter Eng, "ASEAN Divided by Stirrings of Democracy," *Japan Times*, 17 August 1998.
6. Barry Buzan, "New Patterns of Global Security in the Twenty-first Century," *International Affairs* 67, no. 3 (July 1991), p. 433. For other attempts at redefining security, see Lester Brown, *Redefining National Security* (Washington DC: Worldwatch Paper no. 14, 1977); Jessica Tuchman Matthews, "Redefining Security," *Foreign Affairs* 68, no. 2 (Spring 1989); J. Ann Tickner, "Re-visioning Security," in Ken Booth and Steve Smith, eds., *International Relations Theory Today* (University Park: Pennsylvania State University Press, 1995), pp. 175–197; and Richard H. Ullman, "Redefining Security," *International Security* 8, no. 1 (Summer 1983), pp. 129–153.
7. Eric K. Stern, "Bringing the Environment in: The Case for Comprehensive Security," *Cooperation and Conflict* 30, no. 3 (September 1995), pp. 225–226.
8. *The Economist* 286, no. 7281 (19 March 1983), p. 54.
9. David Baldwin, "The Concept of Security," *Review of International Studies* 23, no. 1 (January 1997), pp. 5–26. Incidentally, in my original article I had commented on the dominance of Western analysts in the closed circle of international security scholarship; Thakur, "From National to Human Security," pp. 54–55. Of the 90 footnotes in Baldwin's article, not one cites an author with a recognizably non-Western name.
10. Baldwin, "The Concept of Security," pp. 19–20.
11. Gianfranco Poggi, *The State: Its Nature, Development and Prospects* (Palo Alto: Stanford University Press, 1990).
12. See Gerald B. Helman and Steven R. Ratner, "Saving Failed States," *Foreign Policy*, no. 89 (Winter 1992–1993), pp. 3–20.
13. See, for example, Amitai Etzioni, "The Evils of Self-Determination," *Foreign Policy*, no. 89 (Winter 1992–1993), pp. 21–35; Gidon Gottleib, *Nation against State: A New*

Approach to Ethnic Conflicts and the Decline of Sovereignty (New York: Council on Foreign Relations Press, 1993); William Pfaff, "Invitation to War," *Foreign Affairs* 72, no. 3 (Summer 1993), pp. 97–109.

14. See S. Neil McFarlane and Thomas G. Weiss, "Regional Organizations and Regional Security," *Security Studies* 2, no. 1 (Autumn 1992), pp. 7, 11, 31.

15. Barry Buzan, *People, States and Fear: An Agenda for International Security Studies in the Post-Cold War Era*, 2nd edn (Boulder, CO: Lynne Rienner, 1991), p. 190.

16. Mohammed Ayoob, *The Third World Security Predicament: State Making, Regional Conflict, and the International System* (Boulder, CO: Lynne Rienner, 1995), p. 156.

17. See Ramesh Thakur, "Australia's Regional Engagement," *Contemporary Southeast Asia* 20, no. 1 (April 1998), pp. 1–21.

18. I have developed these arguments in four newspaper articles: Ramesh Thakur, "India Was Wrong to Test, but What Can the World Do?" *IHT*, 19 May 1998; "Britain, India and Pakistan Could Start a Disarmament Club," *IHT*, 11 July 1998 (with Ralph Cossa); "Next to Subcontinent Face-off, the Cold War Looks Safe," *IHT*, 20 July 1998; and "Six Lessons from South Asia," *Japan Times*, 27 July 1998.

19. For a fuller discussion, see Ramesh Thakur, ed., *Nuclear Weapons-Free Zones* (London: Macmillan, 1998).

20. Zachary S. Davis, "The Spread of Nuclear-Weapon-Free Zones: Building a New Nuclear Bargain," *Arms Control Today* 26, no. 1 (February 1996), pp. 16, 18.

21. Donald K. Emmerson, "Building Frameworks for Regional Security in the Asia Pacific: Questions and Answers," in Mohamed Jawhar Hassan and Sheikh Ahmad Raffie, eds., *Bringing Peace to the Pacific* (Kuala Lumpur: Institute of Strategic and International Studies, 1997), p. 67.

22. For accounts of the internationalization of environmental concerns, see Peter M. Haas, Robert O. Keohane, and Marc A. Levy, eds., *Institutions for the Earth: Sources of Effective International Environmental Protection* (Cambridge, MA: MIT Press, 1993).

23. Thomas Homer-Dixon, "On the Threshold: Environmental Changes as Causes of Acute Conflict," *International Security* 16, no. 2 (Fall 1991), pp. 88–98.

24. Erik Eckholm, "China Admits to Flood Mismanagement," *IHT*, 27 August 1998.

25. Lester R. Brown and Brian Halweil, "A Human Hand in the Yangtze Flooding," *IHT*, 17 August 1998.

26. R. P. Nailwal, "Heavy Rain, Deforestation Caused Landslip," *Times of India*, 21 August 1998.

27. Matthews, "Redefining Security," p. 176.

28. Peter Dauvergne, *Shadows in the Forest: Japan and the Politics of Timber in Southeast Asia* (Cambridge, MA: MIT Press, 1997).

29. For an exploration of the interdependence of problems and solutions, see, for example, James Shinn, ed., *Fires across the Water: Transnational Problems in Asia* (New York: Council on Foreign Relations, 1998).

30. *Australian*, 3 July 1997.

31. *The Economist* 342, no. 8066 (1 March 1997), p. 15.

32. Paul Krugman, "The Myth of the Asian Miracle," *Foreign Affairs* 73, no. 6 (November/December 1994).

33. *Mitigating the Human Impact of the Asian Crisis: The Role of the UNDP* (New York: UN Development Programme, September 1999), p. 26.

34. The contrasting estimates were reported in the *Japan Times*, 26 January 1999. A study by the United Nations Development Programme concluded that the number of poor in Indonesia in December 1998 was 50 million, or 24 per cent of the population; *Mitigating the Human Impact of the Asian Crisis*, p. 26.

35. Eddy Lee, *The Asian Financial Crisis: The Challenge for Social Policy* (Geneva: International Labour Office, 1998), p. 46.
36. Paul Krugman, "What Happened to Asia?" (January 1998), available on the Internet at http://web.mit.edu/krugman/www/DISINTER.html.
37. This is drawn from Ramesh Thakur, "How East Asians Are Finding Fault with the IMF," *IHT*, 13 August 1998.
38. Official figures showed that Indonesia, South Korea, and Thailand had total external debts of US$379 billion – of which US$294 billion was private sector debt; Michael Richardson, "Applying the Brakes to 'Crony Capitalism,'" *IHT*, 7 January 1998.
39. Louis Uchitelle, "Turmoil Forces the Fund to Soften Its Regulations," *IHT*, 27 August 1998.
40. In August, Hong Kong effectively took the fight to international currency and stock market speculators by intervening aggressively in its own market; see Tom Plate, "Hong Kong Declares War on Speculators," *Japan Times*, 30 August 1998. But not all countries have Hong Kong's deep pockets, and even Hong Kong has limits. In two weeks, the government spent US$12.5 billion, or 13 per cent of the world's third-largest currency reserves, to buy about 6 per cent of the territory's stock market; *IHT*, 31 August 1998.
41. J. S. Nye, *Peace in Parts: Integration and Conflict in Regional Organizations* (Boston: Little, Brown, 1971), p. 117.
42. Thomas M. Franck, "The Emerging Right to Democratic Governance," *American Journal of International Law* 86, no. 1 (1992), pp. 46–91.
43. See Johan Galtung, "Cultural Violence," *Journal of Peace Research* 27, no. 3 (August 1990), pp. 291–305.
44. Peter Eng, "ASEAN Divided by Stirrings of Democracy," *Japan Times*, 17 August 1998.
45. *The Economist*, 11 September 1999, Survey on "Freedom's Journey," p. 7.
46. Paul M. Evans, "Towards a Pacific Concord," in Hassan and Raffie, *Bringing Peace to the Pacific*, p. 6.
47. See Gerald Segal, "East Asia and the 'Constrainment' of China," *International Security* 20, no. 4 (Spring 1996), pp. 107–135.
48. I sometimes wonder whether people from monotheistic backgrounds have a relatively greater difficulty in adjusting to pluralistic reality. The Christian tradition emphasizes a fundamental dichotomy between man and nature and insists on the one correct path to salvation. Hinduism emphasizes a fundamental unity of the universe as a whole and accepts several different gods. As a Hindu, as well as as a migrant, I am quite comfortable with multiple identity and reality.
49. Baldwin, "The Concept of Security," p. 23.
50. See John English, "The Ottawa Process: Paths Followed, Paths Ahead," *Australian Journal of International Affairs* 52, no. 2 (July 1998), pp. 121–132; Ramesh Thakur, "Anti-Personnel Landmines," *Pacifica Review* 10, no. 1 (February 1998), pp. 61–68; and Carl Ungerer's chapter in this volume.

15

Human security and the ASEAN Regional Forum: Time for a rethink about regionalism?

Chandran Jeshurun

The *fin de siècle* is always a time for much pondering over what has been experienced for almost a hundred years as well as for a feeling of anticipation and even trepidation about the likely course of events in the new century. It is also a time when each person tends to reflect about her or his own role and destiny in a changing environment – to ponder how she or he might fit into the broader landscape of "human security." For the people of East Asia in particular, disturbing and challenging questions pertaining to their future livelihood and, indeed, their very survival were looming as we approached the new millennium.

The last decade of the twentieth century certainly provided drama and excitement *par excellence*. First, with the end of the Cold War (in a not necessarily predictable way) the meaning and direction of regional and international security are unclear. Secondly, the whole complex process that is generally known as "globalization" has produced such a fundamentally new world economic situation that the relevance of existing institutions and accepted norms in international trade and commerce is being questioned. East Asia, which experienced the most unprecedented and rapid economic growth of the century, has become the most severely affected by the unexpected recession and ensuing financial turmoil precipitated in mid-1997. The economic crisis that countries in the region are battling undoubtedly provides as appropriate a time as any to re-examine some of the logic as well as the practicality of various forms of regional cooperation in the Asia-Pacific that have been attempted so far.

This chapter will briefly examine one of the direct results of the end of the Cold War in security terms in the subregion of South East Asia, namely the formation of the ASEAN Regional Forum (the ARF) in 1994 by the Association of South East Asian Nations (ASEAN). It intends to focus particularly on the downside of efforts to develop regional security cooperation through the ASEAN format and to relate this to the broader question of the future security architecture of the East Asian region as a whole. An underlying premise of the chapter is that structural questions such as these *do* matter in how the politics of human security will unfold over the next few generations. A more stable regional security architecture would release policy-makers to devote greater attention and energy to addressing fundamental "quality of life" issues than would otherwise be the case.

It must be emphasized that an assessment of the ARF's difficulties is not merely an exercise in listing the inevitable weaknesses of an organization such as ASEAN in a highly heterogeneous region. Rather it is a conscious effort to evaluate the potential for a more truly representative structure of East Asian cooperation. Inevitably, the emergence of other forms of regionalism over the past decade or so have put a less than proactive organization such as ASEAN in a rather defensive posture. Most notably, the formation of the Asia-Pacific Economic Cooperation (APEC) forum posed a direct challenge to the somewhat laid-back approach that had hitherto typified the ASEAN economic model. Since then, however, it can be argued that APEC's existence has resulted in a somewhat diminished role for ASEAN in bringing about more meaningful and structured changes in regional economic cooperation within South-East Asia.

It is in this context that the prospects for a new look at the potential evolution of regionalism in East Asia and its broader Pacific rim environment should be examined. Particular emphasis should be assigned to both the security and economic imperatives that are increasingly determining the national priorities of countries in this region. By the late 1980s, as the "core" ASEAN states of Indonesia, Malaysia, the Philippines, Singapore, and Thailand showed clear signs of recovering quickly from the economic recession that they had just experienced shortly before, the more ambitious among the region's leaders were already looking around for some form of regional cooperation well beyond the subregion of South-East Asia. This was in fact a revival of the much earlier search for building ties with the major economic powerhouse that Japan had become in the 1960s and 1970s as well as with budding newly industrializing economies such as South Korea, Taiwan, and Hong Kong. The idea of some form of cooperative framework among the key countries of North-East Asia and South-East Asia was also undoubtedly motivated by the security imperative. The approaching end of the Viet Nam war and the establishment of formal relations between China and the United States reinforced this by presaging major strategic realignments in the region. Thus, we find a number of embryonic attempts during the period of the Cold War (mostly initiated by staunchly anti-communist political forces) to forge some sort of regional caucus that would provide for greater solidarity among South-East Asia's non-communist governments. A sense of common security was cultivated in the face of changing regional geopolitical circumstances.

ASEAN's downside

The birth of the ARF, on the other hand, was as much an ASEAN-inspired initiative to pre-empt other forums that would focus on regional security as it was a vague revival of efforts within the region to contain and manage the power and influence of major external forces. That its progress, or lack of such, so far reflects rather accurately the state of disarray regarding strategic matters and fundamental economic policies within the inner circles of ASEAN itself, especially among the core member states, is telling. Although various efforts have been made to give substance to its stated goals of achieving a more constructive regional security dialogue, the ARF has been severely constrained by two contentious organizational problems. The first has had to do with the nature of its membership formula. At the outset, this was forced rather haphazardly, with only the main regional parties in East Asia apart from the ASEAN members themselves and those external powers that had been participants in the Post-Ministerial Conferences (PMC) process invited to join the new forum. There were subsequent accessions by other countries, notably Russia and India, and there is now still pending a waiting list of disparate states ranging from France and the United Kingdom, on the one hand, to North Korea on the other. It would appear that part of the reluctance of the core ASEAN member states to admit all and sundry into the ARF is due to the fear of having too many conflicting interests that would in effect slow down its functioning as a meaningful security dialogue.[1]

Fundamental to the evolution of the ARF process has been the extent to which the ASEAN initiators of the whole idea would surrender their control of its agenda and, therefore, its main direction. Led by the Australians at the start but apparently gaining support from the other non-ASEAN states as well, there is now significant disagreement between the ASEAN member states, and the others, over the management of the ARF's dialogue process and in setting its overall agendas and priorities. Clearly, if the ARF were to be overwhelmed by some of the more powerful members, then the whole purpose of having set it up in the first place – to serve the primary security concerns of the ASEAN member states – would be defeated. At the same time, without the cordial and friendly support of dialogue partners such as the United States and Australia it would be a tedious and unpredictable exercise for ASEAN to try and nurture the ARF process in such a way as to fulfil ASEAN's own security goals. Faced with this dilemma, the whole future of the ARF as the credible and effective security dialogue apparatus for the larger region of East and South-East Asia is in some doubt and any perceived delaying of its evolution will only give rise to alternative channels of regional security cooperation.[2]

ASEAN has also become well known for what its own members have come to regard as the "ASEAN way" of conducting their affairs both among themselves and in their relations with others. In the days when everything was going well for the organization and particularly during its successful campaign for a resolution of the Cambodian problem through UN intervention, no one took much note of its methods and there was some general appreciation of a peculiarly South-East Asian diplomatic work ethic. But once the transformation had been made from the PMC level of regional interaction and the ARF had been convened as a purposeful mechanism for regional security dialogue, many of the non-ASEAN states came to view this "ASEAN way" approach to vital strategic and military issues as somewhat inappropriate. Besides, there is also a common perception among the external powers that ASEAN's way of conducting business has not really shown any ostensibly impressive achievements, even in the area of economic cooperation. Indeed, the whole exercise by ASEAN to combat the economic and financial crisis has been described as "business as usual" without appearing to demonstrate any real appreciation of the social and political dangers it poses to the region. Thus, the adoption of an "ASEAN way" in handling as difficult and complex an issue as the future regional security architecture of the region is unlikely to find much favour with most of the non-ASEAN members of the ARF.[3]

Quite apart from the ARF itself not having much of an institutional format more than five years after its formation, it is even more disturbing that the member states of ASEAN have been unable to reach agreement on the role and character of the ASEAN Secretariat based in Jakarta. As late as February 1999 there had been discussions among officials of the member states that the Secretariat ought to be revamped and its role more clearly defined. The task was farmed out to a private management company, Pricewaterhouse Coopers, which subsequently came up with some recommendations. The fact that, in the end, ASEAN preferred to carry on with the Secretariat playing a coordinating role, however, speaks volumes about any mood for change. One of the consultant's proposals actually envisaged a much more proactive function for the central coordinating body of ASEAN (although nowhere near the institutional supremacy of the European Union's headquarters in Brussels), but this was apparently deemed to be premature.[4] Given the prevalence of such conservative attitudes within the organization, then, it should come as no surprise that any interest among the partners in the ARF in moving forward to more institutional arrangements will be actively opposed by ASEAN as a bloc. Thus, the prospects for ARF getting to grips with the key security concerns of the region and progressing in fairly concrete directions towards more meaningful regional cooperation cannot be considered to be very great.

The pressures on regional security

Moving on from the structural and political problems related to the functioning of ARF as an essentially ASEAN-led initiative, a more pressing concern for its future in the rearranging of the regional security architecture is the pace of change in the strategic and geopolitical situation. One might have imagined that a major priority for ARF at the moment would be to anticipate as much as possible the likely realignments in the power balance of the Asia-Pacific theatre as a consequence of ongoing developments in other regions, more especially where it involves the commitment of US forces. However, there has been relative inertia in East and South-East Asia compared with the dynamism of players in the European theatre, as exemplified by the recent expansion of NATO's membership. In this respect, France has been remarkably astute and intrepid in moving into the Asia-Pacific with some bold proposals for creating a new security-based alignment of forces in East and South-East Asia. Its defence minister's tour of the region in 1999, visiting Japan, Korea, Brunei, Singapore, and Thailand, suggests a direct link between the stabilization of the security framework in Europe and the need for some fresh thinking about the future of the Asia-Pacific. The European interest in engaging parties from that region in security dialogue and strategic thinking is linked to the Asia–Europe Meeting (ASEM) format and is in no small way concerned with the potential roles of Russia and China in the evolution of the regional balance of power. The French defence minister's talks with officials in the region did not stop simply at the level of establishing a high-powered security dialogue but actually held out the potential of a contribution by France of its military forces for any Asian eventuality.[5]

It cannot be denied that the doubts at the back of most people's minds in thinking about the security of the region are invariably associated with the potential roles of major powers such as China, Russia, and Japan. There is already an unspoken feeling that China, in particular, is greatly benefiting from the disarray among ASEAN members and its other external partners in the aftermath of the social and political turbulence that the recent economic downturn has caused in the region. Indeed, it would not be too far-fetched to say that it is this perception of a resurgent China emerging as a more influential and decisive factor in the regional security scenario that primarily drives the quiet activity among various local and external players for a "quick-fix" solution should the ARF, for instance, be unable to rise to the occasion. Consequently, we find that the spontaneous response of some of the regional states is to fall back on the tried and tested remedies of the past, with expectations necessarily being pinned on the continued forward deployment of US forces for the foreseeable future. As late as in February 1999, for example, both Australia and Singapore were openly declaring their belief that only a US presence would guarantee the peace and security of the region in the absence of other strategic realignments in the future.[6] At the same time, there have been calls among Japanese opposition groups for a revision of the guidelines for elements of the Self-Defence Forces (SDF) being sent on overseas missions either to take part in peace-keeping operations or in defence of Japanese nationals.[7] On the other side of this trend is the unequivocal commitment of Thailand to keeping itself in the good books of its great northern neighbour (China), as witnessed by the signing of an all-encompassing Sino-Thai bilateral agreement in February 1999.[8] All this obviously demonstrates an urgent need for a more determined and clear-headed approach to the task of building the future security architecture of the region, something that the ARF is still very far from being able to handle, much less initiate.

There are at least two important conditions that have to be borne in mind when the question of how the future of regional security in East and South-East Asia can best be managed by the parties with vested interests in it. One is generating collective approaches and solutions for modifying and, eventually, resolving the Asian financial crisis. This is absolutely imperative if the region is to avoid the sort of social upheaval that has already been presaged by the ugly ethnic and religious disturbances in Indonesia for over a year. The other is to reconcile a sustained and credible US strategic presence in the region with a relatively stable and benign regional balance of power.

The first concern is undoubtedly the more critical at the moment in view of the devastating effects of the economic crisis and the growing realization by all affected parties that a realistic review of the existing state of the global financial order is needed. Because this issue involves Japan and the United States, and their respective policy approaches are often seen to be in conflict, many Asian nations have been caught in the dilemma of demoting some of their real security concerns in favour of economic priorities. Japan has responded to the Asian crisis by coming forward with generous contributions to the various rescue packages led by the International Monetary Fund for countries such as South Korea, Thailand, and Indonesia. Even though Japan has come under some criticism for not playing enough of a leadership role in this effort to move the recovery process forward, it has also distanced itself from the United States by boldly proposing an Asian Monetary Fund for future contingencies.[9] It is, however, implicit in the demands being made of Japan to be more proactive in the economic sphere that it would conceivably contemplate a political quid pro quo whereby it could, for example, play a more seminal part in the work of the ARF. It is in this sort of tricky equation that the place of China becomes critical to the ASEAN states. Thailand is a particularly good example of an ASEAN member state that has recognized the potential impact of growing Chinese influence in South-East Asia by intensifying bilateral ties.[10]

The inevitable corollary to dealing with both China and Japan in framing the parameters of closer economic cooperation in the region is the continued strategic involvement of the United States in East Asia. From the purely economic standpoint, the United States has been roundly condemned by the regional states for its propensity, as the critics allege, to dispense advice and theoretical remedies during their troubles while not being very forthcoming with the dollars and cents that they are in need of so badly. On the other hand, the high moral ground that the Clinton administration has held on to in such matters as the democratization process and human rights has led the United States into direct conflict not only with China but with much of the rest of South-East Asia as well. This has in turn greatly embarrassed those who are staunchly in favour of a continued US security commitment to the region for as long as there is no other alternative mechanism for maintaining the peace and stability of East and South-East Asia. Thus, it is this juxtaposition between the economic imperatives of greater regional interaction and the unavoidable security implications of a region without the US presence that has characterized the paradigm shift in the regional geopolitical scene for the past decade or so.[11]

The new regionalism: An EARF?

One of the unexpected outcomes of the ferocity of the economic maelstrom that swept through the entire region, especially during 1997–1998, is the much more realistic appreciation of what constitutes regional interests and, particularly, of how closely intertwined they are. As was pointed out at the outset of this chapter, there had been a growing appreciation among the more robust economies of the region for some time that the rigid notion of East Asia being somehow detached from South-East Asia was increasingly irrelevant. Various economic interlinkages had been developing even before the coming into being of APEC and there was, therefore, a much better sense of being part of a single region by the early 1990s. Nowhere was this as vividly demonstrated as the attempt in the mid-1990s to forge a regional quadrangle of growth encompassing northern Thailand, the Shan States in Myanmar, Yunnan in south-west China, and Laos with the support of the Asian Development Bank, Japan, and ASEAN. Less noticeable was the increasing integration of Australia and New Zealand into this booming economic portion of the Asia-Pacific. This could be attributed partly to certain unfortunate political differences, especially between the leaders of Malaysia and Australia. There is, however, an interesting contrast between then and the post-1997 period in so far as the apparent link between the economic prospects of the region and its security imperatives was concerned.

It is a testimony of the degree to which the geopolitical situation has changed that security can no longer be divorced from the fundamental economic problems that countries such as Japan, South Korea, Indonesia, and Thailand are experiencing. In the most severely affected states, such as Indonesia, the very cohesion of the nation itself is being threatened, and the breakdown in law and order portends major political change that would have an unavoidable ripple effect on its neighbours. In the pre-crisis period, such potential for a geopolitical rearrangement of the regional map had never been thought likely although the very size of Indonesia as the world's fifth-largest nation was a constant reminder to the rest of the region of the incalculable impact that destabilization in that country would have on others around it. In strictly security-related terms, too, the sudden loss of hitherto ample government revenues, which had enabled many of the regional states to embark upon what is euphemistically called "force modernization," produced the effect of a rundown in military expenditures. It has been estimated that the consequence of this change in the defence profile of most of the regional armed forces, with the notable and worrying exception of Singapore, which is building up relentlessly, will be severely felt in future regional security arrangements because some of them can hardly support even modest joint military exercises with their treaty partners.[12]

Although one would have thought that the onset of a major destabilizing event such as the economic downturn might have induced states that had been hitherto less than cooperative in various regional efforts for economic solidarity to be more receptive, all the evidence so far points to the reverse being true. Not only have practically all the much-touted growth triangles for economic cooperation projects more or less ground to a halt, even the core ASEAN states have been engaged in bitter rivalries and quarrels among themselves over fundamental fiscal and monetary policies. All this naturally does not augur well for any move in the direction of achieving closer and fuller integration of economic and security cooperation within the ASEAN region. There are, therefore, some grounds for scepticism as to the willingness of these South-East Asian states, embroiled as they are in their own intra-regional disputes, to contemplate the establishment of a much broader based Asia-Pacific-wide framework of economic and security understanding. By the same token, however, it can also be argued that because of the very realization of just how much momentum ASEAN has lost, particularly since it brought Viet Nam, Myanmar, and Laos into its fold, interest may now actually be growing in an alternative forum with a more meaningful and substantive agenda. Such a concept, to be attractive to countries in both East and South-East Asia, must necessarily incorporate, from the outset, the twin goals of maintaining economic stability and buttressing regional security.

Faced with these stark economic and security realities there is obviously a need for the regional states to indulge in a certain amount of constructive rethinking as to the ideal form of regional cooperation where their vital interests would be more securely protected. It is in this context that the comment by the erstwhile prime minister of Malaysia, Mahathir bin Mohamad, that the APEC forum has become increasingly ineffective and has degenerated into nothing more than a talkfest should be taken seriously.[13] He is, of course, best remembered for the then controversial proposal in 1989 that the countries of East and South-East Asia should get together in a thinly disguised trade forum to be known as the East Asian Economic Grouping. The idea never had much chance of gaining popular acceptance, however, in the face of the refusal of the United States to countenance any such exclusive arrangement. Even after it had been changed to the East Asian Economic Caucus (EAEC) there was not much support within ASEAN itself. At that time, the objections by the United States were presumably based purely on economic grounds but, just as there has been some discussion of the APEC forum looking at security matters, it cannot be ruled out that some possibility of EAEC taking on a political role might have been considered too.

Today the whole scenario has been dramatically altered as a result of global shifts in the deployment of *force majeure*, as evidenced by what is happening in Europe and in its relations with Russia. Moreover, economic goals and security imperatives have become even more inseparable, as is becoming increasingly clear in the disagreements over the need to review the existing world economic order and the transitory nature of existing security arrangements in East and South-East Asia. Most importantly, there is now a perceptible ground-swell of popular feeling in the region for clearly defined aspects of human security to be prioritized in any future multilateral exercise in regional cooperation. This has been more than borne out by the embarrassingly public differences among ASEAN leaders over fundamental questions of natural justice and human rights in connection with the treatment of the former Malaysian deputy prime minister, Anwar Ibrahim. The time may, thus, be ripe for taking another look at the prospects for a regional organization that would handle not just the obvious economic and security issues in the first instance but also the equally vital elements of human security before they are brought to an international forum. Having noted that the present ARF would be unable to rise to the occasion in view of its internal difficulties and its lack of leadership, the new body should have a much more specific mandate on its membership and working principles. Clearly, the question of who should be qualified to join the organization will lead to endless debate, although a discussion in Australia to redefine the region as an "Eastern Hemisphere" may hold the key to a possible solution.[14] By including Australia and New Zealand in the gathering on both economic and political grounds, it might conceivably be possible to determine the rest of the membership on the basis of the East and South-East Asia format. We would end up, in effect, with an ARF minus its extra-regional partners, thereby comprising the 10 South-East Asian states, Japan, South Korea, China, Taiwan, Australia, and New Zealand. It would, therefore, be entitled to be known as the East Asian Regional Forum (EARF) and work essentially within the bounds of that geographical definition.

Such a proposition naturally begs the question of the current status of the more important external partners of some of the regional states, notably the United States, which is still underwriting much of the region's de facto security. Although the definition of the EARF's membership may appear to be unrealistic for that reason, it could be easily resolved by providing for the organization's functional structure to be inclusive of any other non-member parties that have a vital interest in its well-being. The involvement of such countries or even the EARF's relations with them could very sensibly be determined by the temporary exigencies of ongoing defence pacts, treaty arrangements, and such-like diplomatic conventions that are of a multilateral nature – in other words, those ongoing security arrangements in which more than one of the EARF's members is a signatory. In effect this would provide for the continued presence of US forces under existing arrangements but with the clear proviso that they will be phased out over time. This is somewhat similar to the convention used by Malaysia when it joined the Non-Aligned Movement in the 1960s to explain away the presence of Commonwealth forces on its territory.

In any case, the main argument of this chapter rests on the premise that in the long term the United States is, if not a transitory power in the region, at least one that intends to achieve a more equitable sharing of the defence burden with as many of the regional states as possible. Its other major presumption is that any future cooperative security effort on a regional basis is most likely to be effective and longer lasting if it does not exclude China.

Perhaps most importantly, the region's future security orientation must not be premised solely and blatantly on a potential threat from China. Not only would such an outcome have unpleasant ramifications for policy-makers who view security primarily from a "state-centric" vantagepoint. It would also augur ill for the Asia-Pacific region's individual inhabitants who desire greater opportunities for addressing and overcoming more fundamental human security problems related to their own "quality of life." Any future regional security order, then, must be geared toward a general quest to achieve the higher levels of regional stability and prosperity needed for all Asia-Pacific polities to have a reasonable chance of pursuing such a quest.

Notes

1. See Kavi Chongkitavorn, "Asean Can Learn about Security from Nato," *The Nation* (Bangkok), 15 March 1999.
2. Kavi Chongkitavorn, "ARF Faces Dilemma over Future", *The Nation* (Bangkok), 22 February 1999.
3. Michael Richardson, "ASEAN Struggles to Change its Reputation as Weak, Helpless and Divided," *International Herald Tribune*, 22 April 1999; and Beth Duff-Brown, "ASEAN Policy Put to the Test," *Los Angeles Times*, 9 December 1998.
4. "Asean Group Reviews Role of Secretariat," *The Nation* (Bangkok), 19 February 1999.
5. "The French Connection: Interview with French Defence Minister Alain Richard," *The Straits Times* (Singapore), 24 February 1999; "France Calls for Europe–Asia Security Dialogue," *The New Straits Times* (Kuala Lumpur), 25 February 1999.
6. "Australia, Singapore for U.S. Presence in Region," *The Hindu* (New Delhi), 24 February 1999.
7. "Japanese Factions Accept Expanded Role for Military," *Global Intelligence Update*, 26 February 1999. This report can be retrieved on the Internet at http://www.stratfor.com/services/giu/022699.asp.
8. A text of this "Plan of Action" was issued by *Xinhua*, 30 April 1999, and reprinted in FBIS-CHI-1999-0503.
9. Andrew Cornell, "Japan Pushes for Asian Version of IMF," *Australian Financial Review*, 24 February 1999.
10. "Regional Perspective: Thai Policy Meets China Challenge," *The Nation* (Bangkok), 2 February 1999.
11. Cameron W. Barr, "US Bullies from a Pulpit That Asia May Not Heed," *Christian Science Monitor*, 14 February 1999.
12. Peggy Hu, "Economic Crisis Has Affected S.E. Asia's Security Priorities," United States Information Agency, 5 February 1999.
13. "Mahathir Rejects APEC as Talkfest," *The Age* (Melbourne), 14 January 1999.
14. Kavi Chongkitavorn, "Stamping a New Label for East Asia," *The Nation* (Bangkok), 29 September 1998.

16

Pursuing "informal" human security: A "Track II" status report

Toshiya Hoshino

Introduction

"Security" is an overarching concept that codifies the self-preservation of an actor when faced with external threats. It can be defined in terms both of its referents as well as of its instruments. In terms of referents, security can be viewed in either general or more issue-specific terms, for example environmental degradation (environmental security), food shortages (food security), and energy shortfalls (energy security). With respect to its instruments, security can manifest itself as an act of defence protecting against both military (military security) as well as non-military (i.e. economic security and social security) threats.

When examining security issues, another approach that can be taken is to look at the actors whose security interests are thought to be at stake. This type of analysis can be conducted at three levels: (1) the security of the international system; (2) the state; and (3) the individual. In the modern world, the security of sovereign states (or "national security") has often dominated the field of security studies. International security has generally been equated with keeping the peace among states. Similarly, the security of individuals has primarily been seen as a task of government.

Peace, as an absolute social condition, is theoretically the most desirable prerequisite to enhancing international security. However, the pursuit of security by individual state actors, essentially a self-centred con-

267

cept, has not always promoted peace but has frequently led to war. Peace, in this sense, is a compartmentalized concept that applies only at the "state" level. History is replete with examples of wars breaking out when one state has sought to pursue its security interests at the expense of another state. The outcomes of such conflicts have often been far from peaceful. In fact, they have frequently been costly exercises in themselves and less than "self-preserving" (for both the victors and the defeated) in the long run.

It is noteworthy that the peace and security interests of individual human beings – "human security" – have often been sacrificed in the process. This is a lesson that we learnt the hard way during the twentieth century. The two "world wars" followed by the prolonged period of "Cold War" (not to mention the multitude of large and small "hot" wars in between) changed the course of countless lives. It should be remembered, as well, that ideological factors played a major role in promoting these conflicts. We witnessed a succession of contests between states adhering to fascism and those supporting freedom, or between those promoting socialism and those upholding democracy. Although it can be argued that many of these conflicts revolved around issues of social justice, it must be kept in mind that they also promoted the pursuit of national security at the expense of individual security. Essentially, the modern history of international relations has been dominated by the understanding that security is achieved through competition or a "power struggle" (to use another expression) between state actors. It has been argued that the thinking behind this type of behaviour reflects a zero-sum perception of international relations.

The concept of "human security" runs counter to this line of thought because it seeks to refocus attention on the importance of the individual. The focus on human security offers two advantages to policy-makers. First, it suggests that the security of individual human beings *within* states will be given the attention that it deserves. Second, it champions the pursuit of security agendas that *transcend* state boundaries positively to affect the lives of many people of differing nationalities. It can be argued, therefore, that the pursuit of human security offers to create "win–win" scenarios in opposition to old-fashioned zero-sum outcomes.

Human security seeks to address threats that may be both military and non-military in nature. Although the possibilities of war are as real as they have been in the past, it must also be acknowledged that the fundamental dynamic driving the security equation in international relations changed dramatically during the last decade of the twentieth century. The end of the Cold War, which followed on from the collapse of the Soviet Union, heralded the end of a period of prolonged ideological confrontation. It has led to the integration of the former socialist states into a now broader international society and global marketplace. This movement towards integration has been reinforced by a growing trend towards economic interdependence. Economic integration pre-dated the end of the Cold War and it has facilitated the creation of ties between states with different political, social, and historical backgrounds. Collectively, these two developments – the end of ideological confrontation and intensified economic integration – have created an atmosphere that has supported the successful promotion of a number of security initiatives. These have been pursued at both the Track I (formal/governmental) and Track II (informal/non-governmental) level.

In keeping with this trend, multilateral and comparative security initiatives have become increasingly evident in East Asia (including both North-East and South-East Asia). Theoretically these two approaches reflect what has been described by Jusuf Wanandi as the "new thinking" in international relations.[1] They have been utilized in a number of Track II programmes in order to enhance and supplement more conventional Track I diplomacy. This chapter will report on the progress of the informal Track II activities in the context of Asia-Pacific security cooperation.

Security cooperation in East Asia

Before discussing the role of informal Track II diplomacy, it is necessary to review the multiplicity of formal security schemes based on cooperation that are operating in the Asia-Pacific region.

Various forms of security cooperation have been evident throughout history, but perhaps the most ambitious mechanism – that of "collective security" – was conceived in the twentieth century. Collective security is a type of multilateral security cooperation that expects the collective enforcement of military sanctions against a member state if that state pursues military aggression. The concept was first included in the Covenant of the League of Nations. It was subsequently incorporated into Chapter VII of the United Nations Charter. This universal mechanism of collective security has never been fully put into practice. Instead, a host of more limited, less multilateral, forms of security cooperation – characterized as collective self-defence – have been pursued. Indeed, Chapter VIII of the UN Charter does not preclude "the existence of regional arrangements or agencies for dealing with such matters as are appropriate for regional action, provided that such arrangements or agencies and their activities are consistent with the Purposes and Principles of the United Nations" (Article 52). Ironically, it was the proliferation of bilateral and mutilateral alliance mechanisms conforming to this "regional arrangements" concept that added greatly to confrontation between the two main ideological "blocs" during the Cold War, and this, in turn, made the pursuit of collective security virtually impossible. There is no question that the additional codification of a member's "inherent right of individual or collective self-defence" in Article 51 of the UN Charter further encouraged this development.

East Asia currently lacks anything resembling a basic framework that could encourage the development of a collective security mechanism (or even a limited regional version). Consequently, regional security cooperation has developed into three primary schemes or types of arrangement.

First, there is a set of bilateral military alliances (collective self-defence schemes as mentioned above) that are all linked to Washington – the so-called "hub and spokes" mechanism that incorporates the US–Japan, US–Korea, US–Philippines, US–Thailand, and Australia–New Zealand–United States (ANZUS) alliances.[2] They were all established at the height of the Cold War in an effort to "contain" Soviet expansionism (although none of the treaties openly stated this). However, as part of the general post–Cold War period of adjustment, their importance has been reaffirmed and they continue to serve the broader purpose of enhancing regional security and stability. This was seen when President Clinton visited Tokyo and Seoul in April 1996 to strengthen US alliances in North-East Asia. It was further promoted when he returned to the region to visit Canberra, Bangkok, and Manila in July of the same year. Additionally, Washington has fostered greater bilateral ties in the region by signing a memorandum of understanding on security cooperation with most of the countries of the Association of South East Asian Nations (ASEAN) (the notable exceptions being the Philippines and Thailand). The United States has also put into place a military cooperation agreement with Singapore. This provides for a very limited number of US military logistical personnel to be based in Singapore and incorporates a facilitation of US air and naval movements according to the "places not bases" strategy.[3] The United States and its partners do not, however, have a monopoly on alliances or alignments in the region. Both China and Russia maintain mutual cooperation and assistance relations with North Korea (although crucial articles stipulating defence commitments have recently been re-formulated). It is also worth noting that the two socialist powers once had an alliance between themselves, although it did collapse in the late 1950s and it has not been revived.

The second type of arrangement is codified by the mechanisms of the ASEAN Regional Forum (ARF), which pursues the logic of engagement by cutting across political, economic, ideological, and geographic divides. The ARF's Concept Paper clearly identifies its role as being to promote regional confidence-building, preventive diplomacy, and conflict-avoidance strategies.[4] This role has been pursued by ARF through inter-sessional meetings that take up specific issues such as confidence-building, search and rescue, disaster relief, and peace-keeping operations. The ARF approach has been described as representing a "cooperative security" approach. Unlike collective security or collective self-defence, "cooperative security" aims at stabilizing relations among states that are neither adversaries nor friends, by means of dialogue.[5] In other words, the cooperative security approach embraces inclusiveness in terms of membership and does not require a military response in those cases where individual member states defy the community of states.

The third and final approach can be labelled a type of strategic partnership. Indeed, the term "strategic partnership" has often been utilized in recent years to describe the improved bilateral relationships that now exist between major powers – between the United States and Russia, between the United States and China, and between China and Russia. In the post–Cold War world, the "strategic partners" are neither adversaries nor allies. (One obvious exception is the bilateral major power relationship between Japan and the United States, which is indeed an "alliance.") The choice of the term "partner" signifies this intermediary relationship. While maintaining some reservations regarding levels of security cooperation, these major powers have recognized that they need to stabilize their relations with each other. Japan's approach to improving its relationship with Russia and China is similarly motivated, although its bilateral relationship with the United States complicates its diplomatic initiatives relative to the other two great powers.

In general these major power relationships have a broad scope and they are not limited to addressing security concerns. A key element in all of them is, however, a common interest in pursuing security cooperation. Although the security cooperation being pursued does not encompass joint military action against outside foes, "strategic partnerships" have been successful in laying the foundations on which have been built a series of confidence-building measures and specific agreements covering economic as well as security matters. The mutual agreements between the United States and Russia and the United States and China to de-target their nuclear missiles, however symbolic, have helped in a very practical way to enhance levels of trust. The development of military to military contacts between these states has reinforced this trend.

The four types of security cooperation that have been reviewed can be characterized theoretically by looking at their scope and function. If they are classified according to factors of membership (exclusive or not) and capability (enforcement capable or not), these four approaches will fit in the matrix comprising table 16.1.

These four schemes are not mutually exclusive. There should also be no misunderstanding that any one scheme can hope to satisfy the full

Table 16.1 Schemes of security cooperation in East Asia

Functions	Membership	
	Non-exclusive	Exclusive
Enforcement capable	(1) Collective security (e.g. UN Chapter VII)	(2) Collective self-defence (e.g. US–Japan alliance)
Enforcement not capable (dialogue/prevention)	(3) Cooperative security (e.g. ARF)	(4) Strategic partnership (e.g. US–Russia, US–China)

range of security concerns. It is important, therefore, to acknowledge their functional differences but also to recognize that, if they could be successfully combined, they would be mutually reinforcing and would serve to enhance the overall security environment in East Asia. This is not to suggest that problems of coordination and mutual understanding will not have to be confronted. China's negative reaction when the Japanese and the US governments announced their intention to "reaffirm" the role of their bilateral alliance for the twenty-first century provides a useful example of these potential problems. China believed that the newly reaffirmed alliance might target China and that it could possibly be used to intervene in China's dealings with Taiwan. The agreement was generally welcomed in Washington and Tokyo because it promised significantly to improve the levels of defence cooperation between their defence forces (not just in normal situations but also in the event of contingencies covered by a revision in 1997 of the US–Japan "Guidelines for Defense Cooperation"). This bilateral (i.e. exclusive) move would have better served its purpose, however, if Japan and the United States had more effectively communicated their intentions to China. In the end, Chinese alarm was somewhat dissipated through bilateral "strategic" dialogues with the United States and Japan. Discussion of the issue at the cooperative security level, through the ARF (a Track I forum) and through the Council for Security Cooperation in the Asia Pacific (CSCAP – a Track II organization), also served to reduce tensions.

Many would argue that it is improbable that collective-security-type action will be pursued in East Asia. But the region is not immune from potential crises and contingencies. US officials frequently recall just how close the region could have come to the brink of war if the North Korean government had not agreed to suspend its alleged nuclear weapons programme in June 1994.[6] As the Gulf War and other more recent episodes in Bosnia and Iraq have graphically demonstrated, enforcement actions backed by the United Nations Security Council under Chapter VII of the Charter can be a viable policy option even if they are not a complete manifestation of collective security. All of the states in the region would, therefore, do well to utilize every available means for pursuing security cooperation in order to avoid the situation where future crises might escalate into armed conflict.

Symbiosis of Track I and Track II experiences

If, in spite of the scepticism shown by "realist" thinkers, the idea of security cooperation is gaining more currency today, then the role played by Track II activities should be given greater attention. The term "Track II" covers the activities of scholars and experts (including officials acting in a private capacity) that help to promote and advance official Track I policy agendas. One well-known example of a Track II activity working in the context of Asia-Pacific economic development is the Pacific Economic Cooperation Council (PECC). PECC is an international network of scholars, officials, and industry representatives that has informally promoted regional economic concerns. The activities of PECC contributed greatly to the founding of the Asia-Pacific Economic Cooperation (APEC) forum. This symbiotic relationship between PECC and APEC stands as a classic demonstration of Track II activities successfully reinforcing Track I endeavours.

With respect to security in East Asia, or in the broader Asia-Pacific region, the activities of CSCAP are gaining widespread recognition. The CSCAP grew out of four workshops called Security Cooperation in the Asia Pacific, the first of which was held in October 1991. Ten research organizations in the region from Australia, Canada, Japan, the Republic of Korea, the United States, and five ASEAN member states (Indonesia, Malaysia, the Philippines, Singapore, and Thailand) initiated this round of meetings so as to encourage regional dialogue on security issues. By the time its 1993 meeting was held, the group had forged a consensual agenda. This sought, first, to encourage security dialogue at the official ASEAN Post-Ministerial Conferences, and, secondly, to establish an international non-governmental organization to support the security dialogue occurring through official channels. After ASEAN had established its Regional Forum in July 1994, CSCAP was formally launched in June of that year, identifying itself as the principal Track II organization for pursuing ARF initiatives.

Significantly, however, the idea of establishing a multilateral dialogue on security issues did not begin to gain favour in East Asia until the early 1990s. In fact, Washington had traditionally been sceptical of Moscow's repeated proposals to establish an overall security architecture in the Asia-Pacific region similar to the Conference on Security and Co-operation in Europe (CSCE). They were seen as a deliberate plan to undermine the American alliance network in Asia and the Pacific. However, the end of the Cold War encouraged the movement towards multilateralism. It coincided with a rising level of self-confidence in many East Asian countries (as represented by the Philippines' 1991 decision to withdraw US basing rights) and a wave of US force withdrawals as part of the overall post–Cold War adjustment made by the Bush administration. Such developments were met in the region with mixed feelings of relief and anxiety. Those mixed emotions extended to the issue of whether or not a US forward presence in the region should still be supported. It was feared that a US withdrawal would create a political vacuum and an opportunity for regional powers to project unwanted influence beyond their borders.

Collectively, these developments created an atmosphere conducive to the emergence of multilateral security dialogues. These were designed not to replace America's bilateral alliances in East Asia but more to engage regional powers in a network of cooperation. Fortuitously, continuous engagement also served the overall interests of the United States. President Clinton and his foreign policy team clearly recognized this when coming into office.[7] The President put forward his vision for a "New Pacific Community" in his speech to the Korean National Assembly in July 1993. In that speech, he identified four priorities in the region: (1) a continued US military presence; (2) stronger efforts to combat the proliferation of weapons of mass destruction; (3) support for democracy; and (4) the promotion of new multilateral regional dialogues on a full range of common security challenges.[8] This policy line was subsequently reflected in the Pentagon's 1994 "Bottom-Up Review" and in the 1995 report on "The United States Security Strategy for the East Asia-Pacific Region" (commonly known as the East Asia Strategy Report or EASR). Both of these documents made it clear that the United States would keep approximately 100,000 troops in the region. It was a signal to the regional states that any US strategic withdrawal would be limited and that no further troop reductions would follow.

It was against this background that the security environment in East Asia transformed itself from being one dominated primarily by bilateral relations to one more fully embracing multilateral directions. This transition has marked a parallel shift away from the traditional mode of pursuing security interests through confrontation to one that values cooperation.

Cooperative security in the Asia-Pacific region

Cooperative security is an approach that encompasses activities such as confidence-building, promotion of transparency, and preventive diplomacy.[9] It can be pursued at both the Track I and Track II levels. In order to establish a better understanding of cooperative security it is worth stating what cooperative security is *not*:

- cooperative security is *not* a type of arrangement that identifies sources of threats outside of its forum;
- cooperative security is *not* a type of security cooperation that is usually backed by an enforcement mechanism;
- cooperative security is *not* a type of activity that produces visible and immediate outcomes.

It is easy to recognize that this approach is qualitatively different from the traditional approaches of alliance (collective self-defence) and collective security. In other words, cooperative security is founded on important characteristics that include the principles of non-exclusionary membership and of "internalization" of the sources of threat. Consequently, the approach is most fitted to maintaining a constant channel of communication among parties even when they are in conflict.

There are some weaknesses in the cooperative security approach. For example, it may not be suitable in a crisis management type situation that requires rapid and massive responses (including military enforcement actions) because both consensus among and the consent of relevant parties are required before joint action can be taken. This general requirement normally precludes cooperative security from being utilized as a tool of intervention in internal affairs, regardless of how useful such an approach may appear to be. One may therefore conclude that cooperative security is an approach that is inherently limited. Compared with the alliance security mode, which utilizes a combination of mechanisms including deterrence in peacetime and crisis response in wartime, cooperative security is based only on a range of strictly peacetime mechanisms such as dialogue, confidence-building, and preventive diplomacy.

Naturally this raises questions about the relative value and utility of the cooperative security approach. One critic has argued, for example, that the ARF process is a mechanism that is "built on sand" and warned that ASEAN countries have no power to mediate in the major powers' relationships. Worse, ASEAN members have provided an opportunity for China to pressure ASEAN and turn their unity into disarray in the case of the South China Sea disputes.[10]

It is true that the idea of cooperative security is more in tune with the thinking of liberal institutionalists who explore the possibility of institution-building through "cooperation" however anarchic the international society may be. Realists who, following Hans Morgenthau's famous dictum, stress the "struggle of power" defined "in terms of national interest" are more suspicious about cooperation. However, it would be far from correct for liberal institutionalists to believe that cooperation is easily attainable even if states wholeheartedly adopt a cooperative security approach. A naive sense of optimism is the last thing that we can expect in the complicated strategic environment in East Asia.

The strategic environment of East Asia and cooperative security

Whether by divine providence or simply by coincidence, East Asia is a strategic crossroads. Throughout history, the region has been a cauldron for conflicts between contending empires and civilizations. Indeed, Samuel Huntington has identified six civilizations in Asia.[11] Four major powers representing four of these civilizations – Japan, Russia, China, and India – now largely shape the fate of this region along with one "out-of-area" power, the United States. It is profoundly important to recognize that the region is characterized by a complex of realities rooted in civilization-level differences. Furthermore, all of the major powers that have extended their influence across North-East Asia have done so by pursuing the path of imperialism. Typically, empire-building is based upon political domination where a core people dominate peripheral peoples with dissimilar cultural identities. As a result, empires have no lack of diversity in cultural and tribal background.

The extent of civilizational, cultural, and tribal diversity in East Asia (unlike the situation in Europe) largely explains why the conflicts in the region did not simply converge into the East–West rivalry during the Cold War period. The division of the Korean peninsula and the de facto split between Beijing and Taipei are clear exceptions. But the ending of the Cold War did not solve the majority of problems in East Asia, apart from these two obvious flashpoints.

Besides the legacies of the Cold War, three other types of issues are also dominant in the region. First, there are issues that pre-date the Cold War. Whereas Western analysts debate the "end of history," the peoples of North-East Asia have maintained a focus on the animosities entrenched in their "history" (in other words, "past issues" dating back to the colonial days rather than the Marxist–Hegelian sense of history as a "broad evolution of human societies advancing toward a final goal").[12] In fact, the depth of mistrust fostered by an attention to historical legacies cannot be underestimated. For example, the final resolution of territorial disputes that arose in relation to the end of World War II is currently the most pressing challenge alienating Japan and Russia. Also illustrative is the historically based animosity that China often directs toward Japan.

Secondly, there are a number of non-traditional security challenges that cover a wide range of issues, including the environment, economics, food, energy, terrorism, and drug trafficking. The violent impact of the Asian financial crisis has reinforced the hard lesson that the globalization of the market economy, unless it is properly managed, can quickly undermine the fundamental stability of national governments and any region's political order.

Thirdly, there is a list of immediate military security issues that constitute "clear and present dangers." The possibility of a military confrontation between the two Koreas or between China and Taiwan cannot be ruled out. The nuclear arms race between India and Pakistan has challenged the very core of the international nuclear non-proliferation regime. The unannounced firing by North Korea of a long-range, multiple-stage *Taepodong* "missile," which penetrated Japanese territorial air space, and recent news reports that the Stalinist regime in Pyongyang has deployed its *Nodong* missiles, have been sharp wake-up calls for Japan. They have also served to generate a far more realistic debate about national defence. The infiltration of North Korean submarines and battleships into South Korean territorial waters and the pervasive suspicion that North Korea is seriously attempting to become a nuclear power have reminded all of the stark reality of military stand-off across Korea's Demilitarized Zone. Although the level of trilateral cooperation between Japan, the United States, and the Republic of Korea is stronger than ever, the increasing volume of anti-coalition propaganda coming out of North Korea is worrisome to say the least.

As long as such military threats continue to dominate the security landscape in East Asia, it is impossible to imagine the abrogation of alliance relationships like that binding the United States and Japan. Nor can a credible US military presence that supports these alliances be done away with in the absence of a workable alternative. However, when assessing the region and its multiple sources of instability, where civilization, culture, and history complicate international relations, it is also correct to recognize that measures of deterrence and response *alone* cannot ensure regional stability and state security. For this reason it is argued that the cooperative security approach can be utilized to *enhance* security in the region and for the individuals who inhabit it.

Formal and informal practice of cooperative security in East Asia

As has been mentioned earlier, it is worth keeping in mind that cooperative security primarily represents a set of peacetime measures based mainly on the voluntary activities of confidence-building and preventive diplomacy. These are cooperative measures and their effectiveness is disputed by realists. The actuality is, however, more encouraging than the realists' interpretation. Five distinct levels of activity can be ascertained.

First, the ARF has made a substantial amount of progress since its inception in 1994, through both ministerial and inter-sessional meetings, towards addressing specific areas such as confidence-building, peace-keeping operations, non-proliferation, and search and rescue. China's willingness to participate actively in this forum is noteworthy. Of course, this could be interpreted as China stressing "multilateralism" in order to criticize the "outdated" role of bilateral alliances (such as the US–Japan alliance) that impede China's national interests. But participation entails obligation and responsibility. In this regard, it is significant that China volunteered to chair a recent ARF inter-sessional meeting on confidence-building and then released its own defence policy paper. This would never have taken place if the idea of cooperative security had not led to the creation of a suitable institutional framework such as the ARF. It can also be argued that multilateral forums can provide useful opportunities for additional bilateral dialogues and meetings that can help dissipate misunderstandings and tension. For example, US Secretary of State Warren Christopher and Chinese Foreign Minister Qian Qichen had a *tête-à-tête* meeting during the ARF session in Jakarta in 1996 and this served as a valuable opportunity to pursue understanding through dialogue in the aftermath of the Taiwan Strait crisis of March of that year.

Secondly, unofficial Track II meetings can provide useful forums for promoting cooperative security. The activities of CSCAP have served as an example of how this can have a positive effect. CSCAP has organized a working group to promote security cooperation in the North Pacific and this is now the only body whose membership includes representatives from all of the relevant parties concerned with security in North-East Asia (namely, the United States, Japan, China, Russia, North Korea, South Korea, Canada, and Mongolia, along with security experts from South-East Asia, the South Pacific, and Taiwan). The workshop has been particularly useful because it has counterbalanced the activities of the ARF, which tend to focus on security concerns in South-East Asia. CSCAP has been visibly successful in discussing peace and security issues, including the situation on the Korean peninsula. This has been possible only because CSCAP successfully involved both North Korea and Mongolia, which have not yet participated in an official-level regional multilateral security dialogue of the ARF. CSCAP is also engaged in issues such as the elaboration of guidelines related to maritime security cooperation and an initiative to develop a regional framework for the peaceful use of nuclear energy and non-proliferation (known as the PACATOM initiative).

Thirdly, we can recognize the ongoing Four Party Talks in Geneva as a form of cooperative security. They are specifically designed to promote dialogue among the parties to the Armistice Agreement of the Korean war in an effort to replace it with a lasting peace regime. The forum originated with an idea to create a channel of dialogue between North and South Korea, with the United States and China participating as intermediaries. The actual process of consultation has been far from smooth over the delicate issues of a withdrawal of the US forces in South Korea and the dissolution of the United Nations Command. Nonetheless, the forum has played an invaluable role in encouraging direct communication between the two Koreas, a development that might not otherwise have been possible.

Fourthly, recent active summit-level diplomacy involving the major powers in North-East Asia has shown a strong affiliation with the cooperative security approach. There have been examples of states seeking to enhance the security environment through dialogue and communication by making allowances for different political and economic beliefs and by acknowledging deep-rooted historical animosities. The declaration of a "mature and strategic partnership" between the United States and Russia in January 1994 was one such example, as was the announcement heralding the beginnings of a "constructive strategic partnership" between China and Russia in September of that same year. "Partnership" relations similar to these two examples have since been developed between the United States and China, Japan and China, and Japan and Russia. They have helped to broaden the scope of the security dialogue in the region and, along with the exchange of military and civilian defence personnel, this has all helped to enhance stability.

Ideally, cooperative security is more multilateral in form and more inclusive in substance than these bilateral "partnerships." However, given the indivisible nature of the values of "international peace and security" and the fact that stability among the major powers has a much broader impact on the interests of other states, the net effect of these developments may not differ that much, in a qualitative sense, from the outcomes expected in the case of a multilateral approach.[13] This logic can be applied to the US–Japan alliance. Despite its bilateral "exclusionary" form, it generates a multilateral "public good." This assessment is derived from the fact that the alliance, although it was originally intended to protect Japan and to counter the threat posed by the former Soviet Union, can also be expected to play a major role in maintaining peace and stability in the region by facilitating the effective forward deployment of US military forces. On the other hand, there are those (the Chinese for example) who question the utility of the US–Japan alliance in the new post–Cold War world by stressing its Cold War origins.

Finally, it is important to recognize that individual countries can make, and have made, unilateral steps to try and generate an atmosphere that is conducive to cooperative security. Many governments in the region are becoming more active in hosting, and cooperating with, these activities. In doing so they are recognizing the advantages to be gained through supporting confidence-building and seeking to avoid misunderstandings through direct exposure and direct human-security-oriented networking.

Dilemmas of cooperative security in East Asia

The previous section has outlined some of the major cooperative security activities occurring in East Asia at the unilateral, bilateral, subregional, and regional levels. Although all of these are generally positive developments, there are some remaining challenges for cooperative security in the region. How well they are met, however, may affect the region's opportunity to focus on more "quality of life" or human security concerns. Three of these deserve further attention.

The first and foremost imperative is active engagement with North Korea, probably the most isolated and thus the least transparent state in the world, so as to bring Pyongyang into the network of regional dialogues. It is a daunting challenge because the Pyongyang government's *juche* (self-reliance) ideology rejects the ideas of mutual communication and dialogue that are so fundamental to the process of confidence-building. For North Korean élites, power defined in terms of military strength may be the only common language for understanding. It is why the North Korean government has put a greater priority on consultations with the United States than with Japan or South Korea. The Four Party Talks forum that Washington and Seoul proposed jointly was a measure designed to overcome this absence of communication between North and South Korea. It is generally acknowledged that a direct North–South dialogue is the most fundamental requisite for the future settlement of the division of the peninsula. Having said that, however, it is poor policy to bargain with Pyongyang when it solicits dialogue with the international community through systematic violations of international norms. The international community's willingness to engage with North Korea over its suspected development of weapons of mass destruction and its suspicious activities at underground facilities are two examples of this.

The stability of East Asia is an interest shared by the four major powers of Japan, the United States, China, and Russia. As far as the long-term security of the region is concerned, nothing is more important than cooperation and coordination between them. In relation to the Korean issue, the idea has been floated of organizing a six-party forum to discuss matters of common concern by adding Japan and Russia to the list of states currently involved in the Four Party Talks.[14] This idea may well prove to be premature and even counterproductive if the six-party grouping is intended to replace the current four-party mechanism, because it would, in all probability, be vigorously opposed by China and North Korea. Nonetheless, it would be a workable and useful mechanism for promoting positive engagement if the agenda was directed more towards including transboundary challenges in the subregion such as those involving the environment and the supply of energy. In North-East Asia, there are precedents of more functional and issue-oriented cooperation in the Korean Peninsula Energy Development Organization (KEDO) and the Tumen River Development project sponsored by the United Nations Development Programme (UNDP). These may have a beneficial effect in the future if they are given the opportunity to "open up" and reform North Korean society, but they both require broad-based international support and this has been difficult to achieve in the face of the Pyongyang government's repeated demonstrations of uncompromising behaviour.

The second challenge revolves around whether or not the predominantly bilateral major power "partnerships" can be engineered to work in a complementary fashion. Trilateral relations among major powers can be unstable but, at the same time, it is important to find out whether the three sets of bilateral "partnerships" – Japan–US, US–China, and Japan–China – can be directed towards "concerted bilateralism" as opposed to "competitive bilateralism." The Japan–US alliance relationship differs qualitatively from the US–China and Japan–China relationships. On the one hand, China is extremely cautious about the development of bilateral Japan–US defence cooperation, particularly as it affects its interests "in the areas surrounding Japan." On the other hand, it has also been suggested that any improvement in the relationship between Washington and Beijing can be made only at the expense of the relationship between Washington and Tokyo. Indeed there are some indications that this has been the case. For example, it has been claimed that President Clinton pointedly planned to visit China without stopping over in Japan, an episode that was called "Japan passing." Although guiding these three sets of bilateral relations in a more cooperative direction is no easy task, attempts have already been made to promote the stability of trilateral Japan–US–China relations (mainly at Track II level) and these may well have an enduring and positive effect in the region.

The third challenge is to separate engagement from intervention. This challenge relates to situations in which it is hoped to assist reform and problem-solving through various engagement measures but the same activities could also be considered to be a serious intervention in domestic affairs. In regard to trilateral Japan–US–China relations, any developments that relate to Taiwan fall into this category. In the case of ASEAN, in this period of economic crisis and interdependence as well as membership expansion, it has become more possible to take up some matters that would previously have been quarantined as "domestic affairs." Some members adamantly oppose the idea, but others, most notably Thailand and the Philippines, have argued that a policy of "flexible engagement" should replace ASEAN's existing adherence to the principle of "non-intervention." The dilemma can be difficult to reconcile because co-operative security presupposes consensus and consent from the parties directly concerned, but the candid dialogue that is needed to achieve such an understanding will necessarily touch the sensitive core of a state's domestic concerns. A review of the boundary between engagement and intervention that stresses the "cooperative" element in the ASEAN security dialogue may be the best way forward.

CSCAP as an informal human security activity

The symbiotic relationship between Track I and II efforts has both a positive and a negative side to it. On the positive side, the development of additional communication and personal networks has made it possible for new ideas and initiatives to be tested at the Track II level before they are put onto the official negotiating table. On the other hand, the close linkage between two levels of negotiation can easily lead to Track I politics being transmitted into supposedly informal Track II forums. CSCAP has experienced both sides of the equation.

A distinctively positive outcome for CSCAP, particularly from an East Asian perspective, is that it has been able to include North Korea as a formal member and Taiwanese scholars as participants at working group meetings. This level of "inclusiveness" would have been extremely difficult to achieve at the Track I level. It should be noted, however, that with respect to South-East Asia the Track I efforts of the ARF are somewhat more advanced as far as the membership of Cambodia, Myanmar, and Laos is concerned. CSCAP has been successful in engaging North Korea, probably the most closed country in the world, in the regional security dialogue. CSCAP and its North Pacific Working Group can claim success owing to the fact they have established a forum where experts, including officials acting in a private capacity, from all the key relevant countries with regard to peace and stability in North-East Asia – such as Canada, China, Japan, Mongolia, North Korea, South Korea, Russia, and the United States – can interact with experts from the ASEAN countries of Australia, New Zealand, India, and Taiwan. While this generates a broader discussion than that sponsored by the official Four Party Talks, there can be no doubt that CSCAP is making a significant contribution to enhancing regional dialogue. At one public symposium held in Tokyo in December 1997, CSCAP successfully organized the first ever candid discussion on security issues in North-East Asia that was attended by representatives from China, Indonesia, Japan, Malaysia, North Korea, South Korea, Russia, and the United States.

CSCAP is also innovative in the sense that it allows discussion on a broader security agenda than would normally be permitted by any Track I initiative. For example, one of CSCAP's principal working groups has devoted its efforts to defining what is meant by the terms "cooperative" and "comprehensive" security. This has led to exchanges covering a new generation of regional security issues that take into consideration the environment, access to energy and food resources, and economic stability. The "Asian financial crisis" and its implications for regional security have similarly become the current focus for a working group established under the auspices of CSCAP. Overall, these developments demonstrate that the concept of security cooperation being engaged through CSCAP is far more ambitious than that normally discussed through official channels.

Although these positive developments are encouraging, their limited scope must still be recognized. The ability of organizations such as CSCAP to affect the security agenda remains subject to the harsh realities of international politics. In particular, the primacy of national sovereignty, in terms both of external autonomy and of internal jurisdiction, still dominates the regional security agenda. Politics affects the way that state actors allocate their scarce resources among themselves and it influences the way that they defend what they consider to be their core interests. For this reason, politics can also be as influential at times in Track II discourse as it is in Track I activities. This was illustrated when the question of Chinese membership of CSCAP was stalled for two and half years over a dispute relating to the inclusion of Taiwanese representatives. The matter was finally resolved in December 1996 when CSCAP agreed to exclude "internal cross-strait issues" from CSCAP's agenda and China acquiesced to Taiwanese participation in the working groups.

The symbiotic relationship between the ARF and CSCAP can be analysed from various theoretical perspectives. One useful approach would be to characterize CSCAP–ARF linkage as the process of both the internalization and the institutionalization of ideas developed by what Peter Haas has called the "epistemic community."[15] The epistemic community represents a network of professionals with valuable scientific knowledge and expertise in a given issue area. Many CSCAP activities are intended to bridge the gap between professional ideas and policy recommendations. Those ideas are related to subjects such as military transparency and confidence-building, the principles of regional maritime cooperation, the peaceful use of nuclear energy and the promotion of non-proliferation, preventive diplomacy, and transnational crimes. Not all Track II discussions will quickly be taken up by officials involved in Track I talks. But there is no denying that parallel efforts at both Track I and II levels would mutually reinforce the development of new consensus among members of the common – East Asia and Pacific – community.

Conclusion

If, then, the cooperative approach to security has become not just desirable but also workable, how can we maintain the momentum? A key requirement would be to deepen the mutual consciousness of "community" in Asia in general and in North-East Asia in particular as we embark on the voyage through the twenty-first century. Contrary to common concerns expressed about the regionalist approach, which would be highly relevant if we were to fall into the trap of exclusionary regional bloc-building, an open and constructive regional community has more to contribute to the overall stability of the international order.[16]

Moreover, this positive "community" consciousness would be greatly enhanced if it were backed by certain guiding principles. One of these should be the participation of *all* of the relevant parties. This ideal of "non-exclusion" is a fundamental principle of security cooperation. In this connection, the conspicuous absence of North Korea in many of the region-wide forums, including the ARF, is a significant challenge that must be overcome. CSCAP has partially succeeded in engaging Pyongyang officials, but additional avenues should also be pursued. Although an early acceptance of North Korea into the ARF will be a short-term goal, Japan could also pursue constructive engagement with Pyongyang. This may not be possible at an official level owing to the backlash created by North Korea's recent destabilizing actions (missile launches, etc.), but it should at least be pursued through credible unofficial channels.

A second guiding principle is to establish a commonly accepted code of conduct governing international relations in the region. In a nutshell, this "code of conduct" would be based on the expectation that the member states would adhere to a commitment to pursue the peaceful settlement of conflicts, arms control and disarmament, non-proliferation of weapons of mass destruction, and preventive diplomacy. In relation to this, Japan's basic commitment to "exclusively defensive defence" serves as a model that could be internationalized because it reflects an attitude that does not intend to threaten others or intervene in their sovereign affairs.

Practically, however, "intervention" and "non-intervention" may not always have to be a dichotomy if all the members of the community maintain a genuine commitment to the previously outlined codes of conduct in the event of conflict. This is because intervention will not be necessary if the parties to the conflict show restraint and demonstrate an aptitude for resolving their differences solely by peaceful means. On the other hand, those who resist any intervention from outside should also recognize that they bear responsibilities as well as rights in this regard. They must acknowledge that in this period of globalization and growing interdependence their domestic affairs can easily have international repercussions.

True regional and international cooperation is indeed difficult to achieve, as both realists and liberal institutionalists would agree. This is particularly so in the highly sensitive field of security. But, just like many things in life, difficulty alone does not discourage people from trying to achieve their goals. Fortunately, past legacies and historical animosities have gradually been balanced with more future-oriented visions. The traditional conception of security, which stresses a competitive struggle of power and interests, has been diversified to incorporate a cooperative aspect. Strategies of deterrence and containment are no longer the only policy options to be pursued in international relations. And a sense of community is developing. This is, in essence, a "community of values," based on a consciousness that cooperation is not necessarily an exception but a desirable rule.

Any security order in East Asia would have to be based on a sense of one community. However, it is worth noting that the growing sense of community in East Asia and in the Asia-Pacific region is certainly shared by the people and the relevant governments. The formal mechanisms of APEC and ARF are strongly backed by the realities of economic and informational interdependence in the region. There is also a tangible demand for region-wide security dialogues and confidence-building to be pursued. Even in North-East Asia, where the complexity of inter-state politics permits no easy compromises, KEDO has led to an emerging sense that there will be grounds for further subregional community-building and collaboration. Behind, and along with, this growth in community-mindedness one can identify the symbiotic intellectual role played by non-governmental actors. CSCAP is one such organization. Involving experts from all of the relevant parties, CSCAP working groups are exploring key areas of concern – comprehensive and cooperative security; confidence- and security-building measures; maritime cooperation; North Pacific security and transnational crime – and they are producing a host of new ideas and initiatives to inspire further cooperative action at the official governmental level.

If a consensus on the utility of multilateral security cooperation is emerging, it is possible that more stable security architectures in the region will emerge. These are most likely to assume complex and multi-layered dimensions. Each of the four types of security cooperation discussed in this chapter – collective security, collective self-defence, co-operative security, and strategic partnership – constitutes a potential component of such a regional order. Deterrence and enforcement would be applied against potential threats, but such strategies would be balanced by confidence-building and the stabilization of major power relations.

The building of a new regional security order in East Asia, however worthy a task it may be, will also need to meet two other significant challenges. One of these is the wave of globalization that is sweeping across the economic, environmental, and telecommunications areas. There is a need to reappraise how effective and relevant existing regional collaborative efforts will be in facing these issues that inherently have global implications. The second major challenge is to address the rise of parochial nationalism in the region. We are faced with a growing conflict of interest between regional demands for greater security cooperation and national claims to domestic sovereignty. East Asia and the Asia-Pacific region as a whole are geographically a vast expanse in which the priorities of each government's security interests may differ naturally, between North-East and South-East Asia, and between the Western and Eastern Pacific. Although peace may be precarious, one thing that all the states share is a common destiny. If we come back to the original premise of interpreting security as a manifestation of the actor's interest in self-preservation, multilateral cooperation through Track I and II diplomacy is well suited to the task of identifying issues and consolidating ideas and resources that can help to preserve the interests of the "collective self."

Building an institutional framework to support a human security agenda is intrinsically time consuming. A clear preference would be to adopt an evolutionary, step-by-step approach based on consensus, and this is particularly the case when it comes to security issues. For any institutional framework to be effective in pursuing a human security agenda, the following five elements would have to be in place: (1) a scheme for information sharing; (2) rule/norm-setting; (3) networking; (4) development cooperation; and (5) constructive cooperation with civil society.

The idea of security based on human interests, or human security, rests to a large extent on new thinking that deserves further elaboration. The holistic approach to the concept of human security, which makes it inclusive in terms of its membership, is fundamentally sound. It is also important to consider the paradigm of human security in terms of both the rights that can be claimed *as well as* shared obligations and responsibilities.

It is concluded here that security interests in the context of human security should be seen as indivisible and non-exclusionary. In other words, one individual's or one state's security gain will not necessarily be achieved by reducing the security interests of another. Quite the opposite is expected. The human security agenda, with its focus on cooperation rather than competition, holds the key to enhancing total (i.e. indivisible and non-exclusionary) security en route to achieving common interests against common threats. In ideal circumstances the pursuit of human security may overcome the traditional realist notion of the "security dilemma," which stresses the trade-off and zero-sum nature of international relations. In empirical society, however, power struggles, political calculation, and give-and-take usually intervene in the various stages of decision-making. Nonetheless, it is incumbent on us to strive to create regimes that can overcome such impediments and promote human security interests. If all five elements mentioned earlier are successfully incorporated, the prospects of realizing human security in a more holistic and indivisible manner brighten immeasurably.

In the conceptual pursuit and practical application of human security, it can thus be assumed that Track II forums will play a major role. The emerging human security agenda is no less pressing than traditional security concerns but it is more compatible with the maxims and instruments of cooperative security discussed in this chapter. Ultimately, the security and welfare of individuals must be served by the state, regimes, or other existing agents in international relations if they are to sustain their relevance in our time. In this context, human security is an indispensable element linking individual wants and needs to those processes and mechanisms most conducive to serving them.

Notes

1. Jusuf Wanandi, "The ARF: Objectives, Processes and Programmes," in Thangam Ranath, ed., *The Emerging Regional Security Architecture in the Asia-Pacific Region* (Kuala Lumpur: ISIS-Malaysia, 1996), p. 41.
2. See William Tow, Russell Trood, and Toshiya Hoshino, eds., *Bilateral Alliances in a Multipolar Region: Future of San Francisco System in the Asia-Pacific* (Brisbane and Tokyo: Griffith University and the Japan Institute of International Affairs, 1997).
3. Daniel Okimoto et al., *A United States Policy for the Changing Realities of East Asia: Toward a New Consensus* (Stanford, CA: Asia/Pacific Research Center, 1996), pp. 28–29.
4. The ASEAN Regional Forum, "A Concept Paper," 18 March 1995.

5. Matake Kamiya, "The US–Japan Alliance and Regional Security Cooperation: Toward a Double-Layered Security System," in Ralph A. Cossa, ed., *Restructuring the US– Japan Alliance: Toward a More Equal Partnership* (Washington DC: Center for Strategic and International Studies, 1997).

6. For background, see Don Oberdorfer, *Two Koreas: A Contemporary History* (Reading, MA: Addison-Wesley, 1997), chap. 12.

7. One of the first indications of the new administration's interest in multilateral cooperation in the Asia-Pacific region came in a confirmation statement by soon-to-be Assistant Secretary of State for East Asia and Pacific Affairs Winston Lord in April 1993, in which he said: "Today, no region in the world is more important for the United States than Asia and the Pacific. Tomorrow, in the 21st century, no region will be as important."

8. See Ralph A. Cossa, *The Major Powers in Northeast Asian Security* (Washington DC: Institute for National Strategic Studies, 1996), p. 46.

9. For a schematic comparison of the four types of security cooperation in the Asia-Pacific region – collective security, collective self-defence, cooperative security, and security cooperation dialogues (including "strategic cooperation") – see Toshiya Hoshino, "Ajia-Taiheiyo Chiiki ni okeru Kokusai Anzen Hosho no Shinario: Domei no Ronri to Taiwa no Ronri [A Scenario of International Security in the Asia-Pacific Region: On the Logic of Alliance and Dialogue]," *Human Security* no. 2 (Strategic Peace and International Affairs Research Institute, Tokai University, 1997), pp. 17–28 (in Japanese).

10. Robyn Lim, "The ASEAN Regional Forum: Building on Sand," *Contemporary Southeast Asia* 20, no. 2 (August 1998), p. 115.

11. Samuel P. Huntington, *The Clash of Civilizations and the Remaking of World Order* (New York: Simon & Schuster, 1996).

12. See Francis Fukuyama, *The End of History and the Last Man* (New York: Free Press, 1992).

13. For a qualitative definition of multilateralism, see John Gerald Ruggie, "Multilateralism: The Anatomy of an Institution," in John Gerald Ruggie, ed., *Multilateralism Matters* (New York: Columbia University Press, 1993), chap. 1.

14. For Japan, Prime Minister Obuchi first mentioned the idea on the occasion of his summit meeting with US President Clinton in Washington DC in 1998.

15. Peter Haas, "Introduction: Epistemic Communities and International Policy Coordination," *International Organization* 46, no. 1 (Winter 1992). The author has benefited in developing his views on this point from Dr. Sung-Han Kim's pioneering work applying the epistemic community concept specifically to Asian security problems. See, for example, his comments on this concept in chapter 17 of this volume.

16. On the relationship between regional order and global order, see Akio Watanabe and Toshiya Hoshino, "Kokuren to Ajia-Taiheiyo no Anzen Hosho: Shudan-teki Anzen Hosho to Shudan-teki Jiei no Aida [The United Nations and the Security of Asia-Pacific Region: Between Collective Security and Collective Self-Defence]," *Kokusai Seiji (International Relations)* 114 (March 1997), pp. 57–71 (in Japanese). Charles Kupchan predicts "the emergence of regional unipolarity in each of the world's three areas of industrial and military power – North America, Europe, and East Asia" after "the inevitable decline" of the Pax Americana, noting that "securing peace within regions is an essential first step toward securing peace globally." See Charles Kupchan, "After Pax Americana: Benign Power, Regional Integration, and the Sources of a Stable Multipolarity," *International Security* 23, no. 2 (Fall 1998), p. 42.

17

Human security and regional cooperation: Preparing for the twenty-first century

Sung-Han Kim

Many countries have derived enormous economic benefits from the end of the Cold War. Yet the income gap between the industrialized and developing worlds has continued to widen. This trend has been compounded in some countries by internal conflict and state failure. At the same time, new security threats have emerged, including an increase in transnational crime and the proliferation of weapons of mass destruction. Armed conflict has taken on a different shape and is often rooted in religious or ethnic discord.

Growing international recognition of the human cost of conflict, in addition to other post–Cold War developments, has led the international community to re-examine the whole concept of security. Countries such as Australia, Canada, Sweden, Norway, and the Netherlands have been at the forefront of this effort. This evolution of an increasingly comprehensive pursuit of international security has led to a greater recognition of just how important "human security" has become. Focusing on the individual's most basic freedoms and needs, human security is more and more viewed as being as important to global peace and stability as are more traditional, "state-centric" components of strategic policy such as arms control and disarmament.

In December 1996, the Organization for Security and Co-operation in Europe (OSCE) summit in Lisbon agreed that a comprehensive system of security for Europe must cover more than simply military security. It also recognized that security includes economic dimensions, social and environmental issues, human rights, and freedom of the press and media. Moreover, as the Lisbon Declaration on a Common and Comprehensive Security Model for Europe noted, "[t]he OSCE comprehensive approach to security requires improvement in the implementation of all commit-ments in the human dimension, in particular with respect to human rights and fundamental freedoms. This will further anchor the common values of a free and democratic society in all participating societies."[1]

Human security is much more than the absence of military threat. It includes security against economic privation, an acceptable quality of life, and a guarantee of fundamental human rights. At a minimum, human security requires that basic human needs are met, but it also acknow-ledges that sustained economic development, human rights and funda-mental freedoms, the rule of law, good governance, sustainable develop-ment, and social equity are important so that lasting peace and stability can be achieved.[2]

It can be strongly argued that the core of human security is human rights. All of these points are concerned with linking values to interests. One recent example of this trend – marrying normative enquiries to strategic studies – is the recently revived interest in the "democratic peace" proposition that democracies do not go to war against one an-other.[3]

The Asian financial crisis and human security

By mid-1997, the whole of Asia – with the exception of Cambodia, Laos, Myanmar, and North Korea – had become a showplace for economic success, political stability, and, generally, social cohesion. But Asia's economic confidence was suddenly undermined by an unexpected and explosive financial crisis. The crisis had a profound effect on the political and social cohesion of key Asian states. This period of economic stress aggravated conditions that precipitated human security transgressions. Human rights violations in East Asia, for instance, intensified, democra-tization was gagged, and threats to independent media increased. Elec-toral fraud, aggressive nationalism, racism, and involuntary migration all became more evident. Various issue areas in human security emerged as paramount as the economic crisis in Asia came to dominate Asia during the last years of the twentieth century.

Political and socio-economic insecurity

The ability of each Asian country to cope with the effects of the economic crisis clearly rested on the affected states' domestic political leaderships –

specifically, the ability of each government to convince its people to accept the prescribed International Monetary Fund reforms despite the widespread privation that accompanied the economic downturn. An important element of a politically effective response was a realization that Asian states would need to share the costs of reform and that an equitable restructuring would need to occur across all sectors of these societies. Catastrophic economic crises are particularly damaging to one-party regimes that have built their reputation not on democracy or human rights but almost entirely on delivering economic growth year after year, decade after decade.[4] Political leaders in many parts of Asia cannot promise to deliver continued material benefits to the people as a trade-off for depriving them of fundamental human and political rights.

Indeed, Asian populaces have come to believe that one of the fundamental causes of the Asian financial crisis was the collusion between politics and business, which lowered the competitiveness of their countries' domestic markets and increased their vulnerability to external financial forces. Hence, the demand for democratic governance is increasing. This trend, however, is also intertwined with rising anti-Western and anti-capitalist sentiments among those people who are suffering the most from painful structural readjustment processes.

Therefore, if the current Asian economic crisis is prolonged, it could seriously disrupt the societies of Asia. Throughout the region, the status of the middle class is being eroded, particularly in Indonesia, Thailand, and South Korea, which means the gap between the rich and the poor is widening. The weaker status of the middle class is leading to the breakdown of the family, in which husbands who have lost their job are forced to be separated from their wives and children are being abandoned. Guaranteed employment is one of the most important aspects of economic security. As job lay-offs intensify, on the other hand, female workers are experiencing added discrimination, being asked to leave their workplaces. This is exacerbating gender discrimination, which is still rampant in every sector of Asian society. All of these developments may well lead to popular revolt, and thus could become a threat to regional political stability.

Intra-state ethnic conflict and involuntary migration

The orchestrated rape and murder of ethnic Chinese in Indonesia's riots in 1999 were a grim enough reminder of the lingering dangers of ethnic and religious antipathies as economic hardships worsen. Indonesia's economic and political crisis raised serious concerns in neighbouring countries about its potential to spread to them, particularly through the involuntary migration of ethnic Chinese. If refugees swarmed to the coasts of Singapore, Malaysia, and Australia, for example, they would become a serious political as well as economic burden for the countries concerned. Such a development could create international disputes or conflicts over how to handle the refugees from a human security perspective.

Moreoever, sophisticated criminal organizations earn billions of dollars every year by smuggling hundreds of thousands of migrants across national boundaries. Human smuggling has become one of the most profitable enterprises today, affecting nearly every region of the world. In East Asia, Japan has been the favoured target for smuggling syndicates. Chinese migrants are being smuggled first to Thailand and then to Japan. Population growth, unemployment, and poverty in East Asia, exacerbated by the economic crisis, are spurring millions to seek a better life outside of their home country.

The lack of a consistent and concerted international response has aided the smugglers' success. Fearing political repercussions, some governments have refrained from discussing the topic openly and only recently have international organizations begun to address the issue. For many gangs, human smuggling – with its almost unlimited profit potential – has replaced drug trafficking as the enterprise of choice, since laws in most countries penalize drug smuggling far more severely than its human counterpart. Human smuggling is likely to grow, presenting challenges to the sovereignty and security of all affected countries.

Drug trafficking and transnational crime

The drug threat, in spite of its severe national security implications, is not inherently a military threat. It is a criminal activity. Thus, the straightforward application of military firepower to this problem is not likely to be effective.[5] The idea of a "war on drugs" is based on the assumption that a reduced supply of drugs would have the effect of reducing consumption by individuals. However, the profitability of the current system in Asia and Latin America is so great that even dramatically improved success in supply-side enforcement will only marginally offset the incentives for generating new sources.

Prolonged economic crisis in Asia will increase both the demand for and the supply of drugs. Weak democratic institutions, corruption, and the lack of hard currencies provide criminal organizations with a favourable environment for drug trafficking. As a result, drug-related crimes and violence will increase the health and social costs to the public of illegal drug use.

International organized crime undermines fragile new democracies as well as developing nations in Asia. When a society loses order and discipline owing to economic hardship, it is exposed to organized crime, thereby raising a security problem to the neighbouring countries and to the region as a whole. In parts of the former Soviet Union, for instance, organized crime poses a threat to regional as well as global security because of the potential for theft and smuggling of nuclear materials remaining in those countries.

International crime syndicates target nations whose law enforcement agencies lack the capacity and experience to stop them. Money laundering and other criminal activities in and around the major offshore financial centres are rapidly increasing. These include such financial crimes as counterfeiting, large-scale international fraud and embezzlement, and computer intrusion of banks and cellular phones.

Environmental degradation

Environmental security issues can be divided into two categories: (1) transnational environmental problems that threaten a nation's security, broadly defined (i.e. problems such as global warming, which "threaten to significantly degrade the quality of life for the inhabitants of a state"); and (2) transnational environmental or resource problems that threaten a nation's security, traditionally defined (for example, those that affect territorial integrity or political stability, such as disputes over scarce water supplies in the Middle East or the question of what to do with refugees fleeing a degraded environment). The interdependent nature of environmental problems, however, means that these categories are not completely distinct.[6]

Environmental threats do not heed national borders and can pose long-term dangers to security and well-being. Natural resource scarcities often trigger and exacerbate conflict. Climate change, ozone depletion, and the transnational movement of dangerous chemicals directly threaten public health.

Economic crisis in Asia will further degrade environmental conditions. Each country suffering from economic hardship will tend to shift budget items allocated for environment-related policies to other areas more directly linked to economic recovery. This is particularly problematic since the advent of severe budget constraints in many Asian states aggravated by the economic crisis. Interest in the environment can be better maintained, paradoxically, when economic growth is sustained.

Threat to Asian values

The concept of "Asian values" or the "Asian way" began to gain more political attention around 1992–1993. Some influential Asian leaders and opinion-makers have called for a return to the traditional core values of

Asia because Western societies were experiencing intensified economic and social problems.[7] Backed by the rapid economic development of a few Asian countries of the region, the then prime minister of Singapore, Lee Kuan Yew, and Prime Minister Mahathir bin Mohamad of Malaysia were two of the most vocal proponents of Asian values.

Asian values have been touted as the driving force behind Asia's rapid and remarkable economic strides during the past several decades. According to Kishore Mahbubani, a Singaporean diplomat and writer, Asian values include non-interference in internal affairs, saving face, and accepting hierarchy.[8] Francis Fukuyama's short list of Asian values is "a combination of the work ethic, respect for community and authority, and a tradition of paternalistic government."[9] This list is not exhaustive, however. Indeed, Asians are also said to prize consensus over confrontation, and to emphasize the importance of education. Put together, these values are held to justify regimes that, to the West, look illiberal. Invoking Asian values, authoritarian governments are said only to be providing their people with what they want. While they delivered unprecedented economic success, the claim was taken seriously.

The direst threat to Asia under the economic crisis may well be the discrediting of "Asian values." Indeed, some of the sins laid at the door of the region's economic systems look suspiciously like Asian values gone wrong. The attachment to the family becomes nepotism. The importance of personal relationships rather than formal legality becomes cronyism. Consensus becomes wheel-greasing and corrupt politics. Conservatism and respect for authority become rigidity and an inability to innovate. Much-vaunted educational achievements become rote-learning and a refusal to question those in authority.[10]

In short, "Asian values" are dynamic and evolving rather than a "proven" commodity. Clearly, regional leaders and citizens should not be over-confident and complacent about the power of Asian values as a sole route to Asia's economic prosperity. Values are needed in Asia, of course, in order to create regional prosperity and identity. But this should not be perceived as a requirement that automatically entails zero-sum relations with the West.[11]

Challenges for US leadership

Human security cannot be attained without durable traditional security. The financial crisis highlights the need for a sustained US security presence in East Asia, both to protect against the renewal of old tensions and to respond to the potential outbreak of new sources of instability. However, the recent financial crisis has placed new limitations on Japan's and

Korea's host-nation support for the US security presence in those countries and on opportunities for joint exercises necessary to sustain strong military cooperation with key allies and friends.[12]

The challenges for US leadership in response to the region's financial crisis are to contain the damage so that it does not cause a round of global economic deflation and domestic instability, which could harm regional security as well as human security, and to sustain confidence in US leadership. Despite the limits of its own fiscal capabilities, the United States is expected to help ease the impact of the crisis on impoverished populations in Asia as a way of demonstrating US leadership.

From the US viewpoint, therefore, it is necessary to manage the political and socio-economic repercussions of the Asian economic crisis in the short term as well to develop mid- to long-term strategies. The United States must engage more actively in the discussion of human security issues because dissatisfaction and bitterness within Asian societies over globalization and reduced leverage within the international marketplace could develop into anti-Americanism.

In this sense, US support for regional cooperation mechanisms such as the Asia-Pacific Economic Cooperation forum and the Regional Forum of the Association of South East Asian Nations (ASEAN) is likely to be even more important as regional cooperation is challenged by stresses stemming from the financial crisis. These multilateral organizations are the places where human security issues will be discussed as a way of preparing for the time when Asia will make another take-off with democracy and sustainable development.

Regional cooperation for human security: An evolutionary approach

Forming an "epistemic community"

Anxiety in Asia as a whole is now likely to focus much more on domestic political and social issues than on external issues (such as the future of US military commitment to the region and regional security cooperation). As highlighted above, human security encompasses a wide array of complex issues that are interconnected with each other and thus require a wide base of knowledge and information for policy-makers to identify their state interests and recognize the latitude of action deemed appropriate in specific issue areas of human security. Control over knowledge and information is an important dimension of power and the diffusion of new ideas and information can lead to new patterns of behaviour. It can also be an important determinant of international policy coordination. Thus, an international epistemic community needs to be formed to deal with newly emerging human security issues in the Asia-Pacific.

An "epistemic community" is a network of professionals with recognized expertise and competence in a particular domain, and an authoritative claim to epistemic community may consist of professionals from a variety of disciplines and backgrounds.[13] The Council for Security Cooperation in the Asia Pacific is an example of such a network. An epistemic or epistemic-like community composed of experts sharing beliefs can help decision-makers gain a sense of who the "winners" and "losers" would be as the result of a particular action or event. Most human security issues such as the environment and involuntary migration are difficult for a body of experts and policy-makers from just one country to assess. Hence, epistemic communities are needed at the initial stage of dealing with human security issues to broaden the range of expertise and options in confronting these problems.

There exist serious normative variations or differences among the countries or parties concerning how to prioritize human security issues. Some countries put more emphasis on democratic or humanitarian values, others stress technical issues. The values debate emerges once again over what "universal" values are and whether many Asian countries are ready to accept them by rejecting their own traditions.[14] Therefore, epistemic communities can shed light on the nature of interlinkages between issues and on the chain of events that might proceed either from failure to take action or from instituting a particular policy. If an epistemic community can adopt what might be called "Guiding Principles on Human Security," this would contribute to gradually resolving the normative conflicts inherent within human security issues among the countries.

Coalition-building among like-minded countries

If epistemic communities on human security help define the self-interests of a state, then a coalition among like-minded countries can be built. Realistically, a number of countries will realize that power can be obtained from networking and coalition-building. It is most likely that government officials will try to establish issue-based coalitions with other countries in many fields of human security.

Such coalitions would function best by identifying and collaborating on specific functions and tasks. Rapid information exchange could be used to strengthen such activities as addressing human rights abuses or international crime, areas where the timely exchange of information across borders is essential. Inter-regional epistemic communities could also play a role in helping to establish free media and to counter hate propaganda, and so bolster democracy and reduce the likelihood of conflict in troubled areas. Tackling the problem of food security is another area that could benefit from enhanced information networks because experts and information sources could be accessed quickly, facilitating the delivery of advice and knowledge.

At the moment, democratic countries such as the United States, Japan, Australia, Canada, New Zealand, and South Korea have the best chance of forging coalitions to tackle human security issues. In particular, if Japan were to assume a leadership role on human security issues together with the United States, it would come to possess greater scope for conducting its much-vaunted "soft-power diplomacy" in very worthwhile ways. But it is difficult for the Japanese to act assertively in Asia when they have not resolved the "problem of the past." If Japan were to face its past wartime legacy in a genuine way, it would become more morally qualified to talk about human security issues.[15]

"Preventive" regional cooperation

One of the stated aims of the inaugural meeting of the ASEAN Regional Forum (ARF) in 1994 was "the enhancement of political and security cooperation within the region as a means of ensuring a lasting peace, stability and prosperity for the region and its peoples."[16] However, the financial crisis in Asia has demonstrated that regional security arrangements, as presently constituted, are not well organized to handle a prolonged socio-economic shock. Would it be possible for the ARF to deal with human security issues in the Asia-Pacific region? If it succeeds in facilitating epistemic communities and/or coalition-building among likeminded countries, the answer is probably "yes." The ARF's immediate task is to prevent the socio-economic effects of the financial crisis in Asia from developing into threats to human security. The ARF should identify the risks to the security of the region's peoples arising from economic, social, and environmental problems and discuss their causes and potential consequences. Under a revised ARF, epistemic communities could bring fresh air into the ARF to upgrade its legitimacy.

Human security, most of all, is rooted in the protection of human rights. Human rights and regional security issues are inextricably linked. The security of nation-states begins with the security of the civil society of which they are composed. The security problems that beset the region – notably in Cambodia, North Korea, East Timor, and Myanmar – are the projected shadow of human rights violations. Conflicts cannot be resolved, confidence cannot be built, and multilateral cooperation cannot be strengthened unless the root cause of regional security issues is addressed – violations of human rights.[17] Human rights violations therefore need to be prevented.

It is noteworthy that the fourth Ministerial Meeting of the ARF in 1997 agreed to accelerate "preventive diplomacy" – the second stage of its regional confidence-building strategy – particularly as ARF members, including China, were initially sceptical of ARF moving rapidly toward preventive diplomacy. As former UN Secretary-General Boutros Boutros-Ghali aptly defined it, preventive diplomacy is an "action to prevent disputes from arising between parties, to prevent existing disputes from escalating into conflicts, and to limit the spread of the latter when they occur."[18] With respect to implementation or practical modalities, there may be several operational measures: confidence-building, fact-finding, early warning, preventive deployment, and demilitarized zones. Institution-building and preventive humanitarian action can also be added to the category of preventive diplomatic measures. All these modalities embody human security issues and it can thus be argued that human security adds legitimacy and momentum to the cooperative security strategy.

Preventive diplomacy's newly acquired meaning is due to the emergence of a concept of "cooperative security," which has replaced the old concept of collective security of the Cold War period.[19] In addition, there is growing interest in non-traditional security threats, such as economic conflict, population movements, drug trafficking, transnational environmental problems, and religious and ethnic nationalism. If these threats cannot be met effectively with traditional forms of readiness and deterrence, then more constructive and sophisticated forms of influence and intervention are required. This is the *raison d'être* of cooperative security in the post–Cold War era. Human security can be understood in the same context.

However, the real problem seems to lie not in a clear-cut definition of preventive diplomacy, but in the implementation of the fundamental measures of preventive diplomacy. This is the ultimate challenge for the ARF. The ARF has sought the promotion of confidence-building measures (CBMs), which are a part of preventive diplomacy, and is trying to expand its role by providing the ARF chair with a "good offices" role.[20] If this is made possible, the ARF will be able to progress towards becoming an organization of conflict prevention, although it will still be far from being an instrument of conflict resolution.

Proposals by various ARF member states for enacting CBMs were simply suggestions that arose out of the talking shop, and they were not legally binding. The ARF is a discussion forum; it is not yet a negotiating body. Even so, CBMs have become the fastest-growing preoccupations in the ARF, although most such CBM proposals are not even half as good as is claimed. Indeed, the ARF needs to avoid becoming obsessed with "establishing" CBMs. Rather it should look to confidence-building "processes" such as formal and informal dialogues encompassing traditional and human security issues. As suggested earlier, epistemic communities could facilitate the CBM process, thereby removing the increasing suspicions among the regional countries.

Against this backdrop, it is realistic for the ARF to have decided to move forward to the second stage of consideration of preventive diplomacy rather than being obsessed with "discovering" confidence-building measures.[21] Widening the scope of deliberations by "pushing the wagon to roll on the rocky road" will be more helpful for the ARF to upgrade its status over the long term. Preventive diplomacy *can* coexist with confidence-building.

In addition, as an initial step in implementing human security, the views or suggestions on specific issues of human security agreed upon by the ARF members need to be transmitted by the ARF chair to the countries or parties concerned.[22] In this way, the ARF could be gradually transformed from a talking shop into a genuine body of security cooperation in both the traditional and human security areas.

Monitoring human security

When the ARF develops into a genuine cooperative security mechanism, it will be necessary for it to assume a monitoring role in order to attain enduring human security. The heads of government of each member state will need to appoint a special coordinator for human security issues. Perhaps emulating the OSCE summit proposals for Europe, the ARF could also consider appointing an ombudsperson with responsibility for freedom of the media. A mandate for the ombudsperson's activities should be submitted annually to the chair of the ARF. At present, however, the prospects for the ARF reaching the stage where it can monitor the human security situation in the Asia-Pacific region are still distant.

Conclusion

The concepts of "human security" and "global governance" can raise perplexing but intriguing questions. Whereas human security is concerned primarily with individual welfare conditions, global governance focuses on generalized rules of international regimes. To juxtapose these two concepts in a single thematic sweep may be considered at best too ambitious or at worst foolhardy. But we are at a critical juncture in human history: the forces of globalization could tip us toward either more human forms of governance or growing global disparities that will turn the world into small islands of riches among oceans of structural poverty, resentment, and violence.[23] Globalization of the world economy and society is increasingly demanding that "security" – including such components of humans rights as political, socio-economic, cultural, and environmental security – be more broadly considered.

The opening of a new century has always served as a symbolic turning point in the history of human civilization. When greater security cooperation is achieved at the regional level, the vision of global governance becomes more reasonable. The Asia-Pacific region stands at a crossroads between self-destruction and self-renewal. Despite the financial crisis, the region will have renewed opportunities for another take-off if it deals effectively with the root causes and effects of that event. This is the mission for epistemic communities intent on shaping and realizing human security.

Notes

1. The Lisbon Declaration can be found on the Internet at http://www.osceprag.cz/indexeda.htm.
2. Lloyd Axworthy, "Human Security: Safety for People in a Changing World," a concept paper (April 1999), on the Internet at http://www.dfait-maeci.gc.ca/foreignp/Human Security/secur-e.htm, #3.
3. Ramesh Thakur, "From National Security to Human Security," in Stuart Harris and Andrew Mack, eds., *Asia-Pacific Security: The Economics–Politics Nexus* (Sydney: Allen & Unwin, 1997), p. 73.
4. Paul Dibb, David D. Hale, and Peter Prince, "The Strategic Implications of Asia's Economic Crisis," *Survival* 40, no. 2 (Summer 1998), p. 15.
5. Michael J. Dziedzic, "The Transnational Drug Trade and Regional Security," *Survival* 31, no. 6 (November/December 1989), p. 544.
6. Joseph J. Romm, *Defining National Security: The Nonmilitary Aspects* (New York: Council on Foreign Relations Press, 1993), p. 15.
7. Alan Dupont, "Is There an 'Asian Way'?" *Survival* 38, no. 2 (Summer 1996), pp. 13–33.
8. Kishore Mahbubani, "The Pacific Impulse," *Survival* 37, no. 1 (Spring 1995), pp. 116–117. Also see his "The Pacific Way," *Foreign Affairs* 74, no. 1 (January/February 1993), pp. 100–111.
9. Francis Fukuyama, "Asian Values and the Asian Crisis," *Commentary* 109, no. 2 (February 1998), p. 25.
10. "Asian Values Revisited: What Would Confucius Say Now?" *The Economist* 348, no. 8078 (25 July 1998), p. 23.
11. As noted by Geun Lee, "The New Asianism and Its Implications for ASEM," paper presented at the 1st Yonsei-Warwick Conference on ASEM, 9–10 November 1998, Seoul, Korea, p. 9.

12. Scott Snyder and Richard Solomon, "Beyond the Asian Financial Crisis: Challenges and Opportunities for U.S. Leadership," a Special Report of the United States Institute of Peace, April 1998, p. 18.
13. Peter M. Haas, "Introduction: Epistemic Communities and International Policy Coordination," *International Organization* 46, no. 1 (Winter 1992), pp. 2–3.
14. Concerning the potential dominance of specific Asian values, see Han Sung-Joo, "Asian Values: Asset or Liability," in JCIE, ed., *Globalization, Governance, and Civil Society* (Tokyo: JCIE, 1998), pp. 63–71.
15. Sung-Han Kim, "The Role of Japan and the United States in Asia: A Korean Perspective," paper presented at the Pacific Symposium on "U.S. Engagement Policy in a Changing Asia: A Time for Reassessment," 1–2 March 1999, Honolulu, Hawaii, pp. 10–11.
16. Point 8 of "Chairman's Statement – The First ASEAN Regional Forum," Bangkok, 25 July 1994. This can be accessed on the Internet at http://www.dfat.gov.au/arf/arfl.html.
17. Rory Mungoven, Asia-Pacific Director, Amnesty International, "Human Rights and Regional Security: A Challenge for the ASEAN Regional Forum," Kuala Lumpur, 26 July 1997.
18. Boutros Boutros-Ghali, *An Agenda for Peace: Preventive Diplomacy, Peace-Making and Peace-Keeping* (New York: United Nations, 1992), p. 5. Boutros-Ghali made an excellent attempt to define preventive diplomacy as a concept and activity since preventive diplomacy had remained largely undefined since the end of the Cold War. During the Cold War, the goal of preventive diplomacy was advanced simply to keep local conflicts from becoming entangled in superpower rivalry.
19. Janne E. Nolan et al., "The Concept of Cooperative Security," in Janne E. Nolan, ed., *Global Engagement: Cooperation & Security in the 21st Century* (Washington DC: Brookings Institution, 1994), pp. 5–6.
20. The ARF "Concept Paper" (18 March 1995) identified several activities as examples of preventive diplomacy, for example using good offices to resolve conflicts, third-party mediation, fact-finding, and moral suasion.
21. Sung-Han Kim, "The Role of the ARF and the Korean Peninsula," *Journal of East Asian Affairs* 12, no. 2 (1998), pp. 506–528. This paper was originally presented at the Third CSCAP North Pacific Working Group Meeting in Makuhari, Japan, 15–16 December 1997.
22. This perspective was shared by Australian Foreign Minister Alexander Downer in the 1997 fourth ARF Ministerial Meeting.
23. Majid Tehranian, "Human Security and Global Governance: Power Shifts and Emerging Security Regimes," on the Internet at http://www.toda.org/hugg_hon_papers/tehranian.htm, p. 3.

Conclusion

18

The security dilemma revisited: Implications for the Asia-Pacific

Joseph A. Camilleri

Security analysis is in a state of flux, indeed profound contestation, a proposition for which the very title of this volume, not to mention the diverse perspectives it encompasses, offers ample and eloquent testimony. The field is now one in which competing ideas and approaches vie for the attention of theorists and practitioners alike. National and military security are now juxtaposed with common and comprehensive security, traditional security studies with critical security studies.

The realist/neo-realist paradigm, with its emphasis on the centrality of the state, force, and the structural anarchy of the international system, is the principal, though by no means only, casualty of this prolonged period of intellectual ferment. Liberal and neoliberal institutionalism and various forms of constructivism have no doubt widened the debate, but they too are vulnerable to criticism. These more recent contributions often suffer from a lack of definitional clarity or analytical rigour. They do not on balance appear to have been any more successful than their realist counterparts in resolving the structure–agency dilemma, or adequately grappling with the consequences of regionalization and globalization. Although they have made a compelling case for a wider notion of security, they have tended to fudge the normative and institutional implications of that widening. There is, then, a case for engaging yet again with the meaning of security before considering the internationalization of the security dilemma, the scope and limitations of widening the security discourse, and the evolving role of multilateral institutions. Having cleared a few conceptual cobwebs, it may then be possible to shed more light on the emerging security architecture of the Asia-Pacific region.

Reconceptualizing security

Much confusion still surrounds both the meaning of "security" – what is it to be secure? – and the subject of security – who or what is to be secured? The traditional view has tended to equate security with the protection of boundaries, or, to be more precise, with the territorial integrity of the state. Such a formulation is less than satisfactory. Though its boundaries may remain intact, a society (e.g. South Africa, Algeria, India, Fiji) may experience traumatic disruption as a result of racial, religious, or ethnic conflict. Indeed, the protection of boundaries in the face of either internal or external threats, even when successful, may itself have profoundly adverse consequences for security, whether as a result of economic hardship, social dislocation, or political instability (e.g. Indonesia, Myanmar, Papua New Guinea). To make the integrity or sovereignty of the state central to the definition of security is to confuse ends and means, and to obscure what exactly is to be secured.

The state is not the ultimate subject of security. It is at best the institutional response to the search for security. The purpose of the state, or at least its promise, is to deliver the kind of social and political order within which the subject or citizen can feel relatively secure. This proposition underpins most social contract theories. Yet a considerable gap may separate promise and performance. States are not always effective providers of security. It is arguable that over the course of the twentieth century the state's instrumental role in the provision of security was one of diminishing efficacy. Several contributing factors readily come to mind, notably the increasing potency and precision of offensive weapon systems and the increasing porosity of state boundaries. Economic warfare, urban terrorism, aerial piracy, large population movements, and transnational crime have all exposed the vulnerability of states and visibly circumscribed their protective capabilities. As the Kosovo example has so graphically illustrated, the power to hurt has vastly outdistanced the power to defend. It was not only the Serbian state which was unable to secure its population against the incessant pounding of NATO air raids; the United States itself, try as it might, could not ensure the security of Albanian Kosovars.

The state's instrumental role, and the limitations to which it is subject, are equally apparent in the economic sphere. As Leong Liew observes in this volume, to enhance the economic security of its citizens the state may pursue any number of trade and foreign policies: it may seek secure access to raw materials, protect its own markets, or attempt to penetrate foreign markets (p. 200). These policies, however, are not ends in themselves, nor are they assured of success. They are at best instruments of varying degrees of effectiveness, and the only measure by which to evaluate that effectiveness is the degree to which any given policy achieves the economic welfare of society as a whole. On occasions, policies, far from achieving their stated objectives, may prove altogether counterproductive. Protectionist measures, for example, may lead to counterprotection or even to military conflict. Nor can security be viewed exclusively as external policy. Leong Liew rightly draws attention to the complexities that surround the internal dimension of security policy. At one level the state may be said to enhance the security of its citizens to the extent that it safeguards their property rights. At another level the violation of property rights, whether by organized workers or landless peasants, may positively enhance the economic security of the most underprivileged sections of society (p. 202).

How, then, are the diverse and multidimensional facets of security to be reconciled or synthesized? Barry Buzan attempts to do this, but not altogether successfully, by making survival the centrepiece of his conception of security.[1] A key question remains unanswered: *whose survival?* To argue that security refers to "existential threats requiring emergency measures" is not terribly helpful. Who, after all, is entitled to survive? Who can make a significant statement, or speech-act, about survival? Is it states, the leaders of states, citizens, social organizations, political movements, ethnic communities, banks, transnational corporations, the International Monetary Fund, or the International Olympic Committee? What, in any case, is meant by survival? Does it refer primarily to physical survival? Is such survival the unavoidable priority in any hierarchy of human needs? Without physical survival, it is true, individual human beings lack the capacity to achieve most of their social, economic or political objectives. In this sense, self-preservation appears as the *sine qua non* of security. Reduced to this formulation, however, the relationship between survival and security becomes mere tautology.

The more interesting question to ask would be: is the survival of the state a precondition of individual security? Here the answer is problematic. How the question is answered will depend on time and circumstance. There are numerous historical examples of individual human beings continuing to maximize their security interests even when one or more of the collectivities – social, political, religious institutions, indeed the state itself – to which they belonged ceased to exist. The dissolution of the Soviet and East German states is a case in point. Though physical survival, whether of the individual or the collectivity, is undoubtedly part of the equation, security involves the satisfaction of a great many other needs. Nor can it be assumed that the hierarchy of needs is uniform across time and space – different cultural and political settings are likely to produce different perceptions of need and different policy responses.

Security, we wish to argue, is not primarily a physical but a psycho-social experience. After all, the fear of physical attack is itself a psycho-social phenomenon. Indeed, a strong case can be made for treating *insecurity*, rather than security, as the conceptual point of departure. That, in a sense, is the deeper meaning of *human security*. Many proponents of the notion of human security, including Ramesh Thakur, In-Taek Hyun, and Woosang Kim, equate it with "quality of life." This approach, although it has the obvious advantage of highlighting the concept's multi-dimensional character, in practice deprives it of its explanatory power. If, on the other hand, the stress is placed on the psycho-social dimensions of insecurity, it matters less whether or not the concept is consciously reflected in the discursive practices of states. More important are the analytical insights it offers us.

Lorraine Elliott cites approvingly the UNDP's conception of human security as something "universal, interdependent, and people centred" (p. 158). All this is helpful, but goes nowhere near far enough. Analytically, what is critical to human security is not sustainable development, human rights and fundamental freedoms, the rule of law, good governance, protection of the environment, or social equity per se. These are all highly desirable outcomes, and no doubt integral to human welfare, but their relationship to security is far more complex. What is critical to security is the maintenance of a social order that has enough pattern and regularity to it to inspire in the self a degree of confidence in the future. This is precisely what we mean by *psycho-social security*, or what McSweeney calls *ontological security*.[2] Conversely, insecurity relates to the experience of social disruption, the fragility of social relationships, the absence of cognitive control over, or affective empathy with, various forms of human interaction (which obviously include the ecological implications of such interaction). Like McSweeney, we see psycho-social insecurity as the perceived disruption – actual or potential – of the social order. We may speak of a cleavage or dissonance in the patterns of mutual knowledge, as well as in the fabric of common norms and shared loyalties. To this extent, insecurity is inextricably linked with the problem of *collective identity*.

The awakening of national consciousness in late eighteenth-century Europe and the subsequent development of notions of nationhood and national identity may be understood as the peculiarly modern and politically far-reaching response to the experience of insecurity. The individual's feelings of insecurity may be accentuated by the realization that this is a social rather than purely personal experience. In periods of acute collective anxiety and insecurity, the tendency will be to search for new unifying symbols or to revive long-established ones. This is precisely the function of national culture, national honour, and national glory, and the collective memories of the past and collective expectations of the future that they imply. National identity does not, however, operate in a vacuum. The principle of self-determination has been repeatedly used to establish a fusion between nation and state.[3] Over time, a form of bureaucratic nationalism has emerged whose function has been to appeal to – some would say manipulate – national symbols and loyalties as a means of strengthening the unity and legitimacy of the state.[4] Withaya Sucharithanarugse makes the intriguing but valid observation that the state in developing countries is more often than not at odds with the nation (p. 53), to which might be added that the phenomenon is by no means confined to the Third World. Nation-building has become inseparable from, and in many instances the legitimating principle for, state-building, and national security but a codeword for state security.

The notion of psycho-social insecurity takes us, then, well beyond Buzan and Waever's simplistic duality of "state security" and "societal security,"[5] in which society and identity are postulated as objective realities, with little sense, it would seem, of how subjective and multidimensional are the values that are susceptible to threat. Security is thereby reduced to a commodity and people to mere consumers, with the state as the only producer. Such a conception runs the risk of conveniently removing both human agency and interests from the consumption and production of security. In this context the contribution of constructivists, notably Alexander Wendt,[6] is especially helpful. By placing the emphasis on intersubjective understandings and expectations, collective identity is seen as a variable which can itself change over time, and at the same time induce change in the definition of state interests, hence in state behaviour.

Enough has been said to indicate that security and insecurity are fundamentally subjective and relational. The construction of the image of self and other is replete with moral choices. To identify the needs which security policy must address is to make moral judgements about competing priorities, loyalties, and identities. This applies as much to issues of environmental security as to military security, as much to the question of NATO's enlargement as it does to the Korean conflict or the East Timor dispute. Human security discourse may therefore be considered in part an attempt to develop the policy implications of this normative perspective. It is, in fact, part of a larger project which takes issue with the positivist reading of social order and points to the essentially unstable, fluid, contested, and normative character of security.

There is, however, more to security than its subjective quality. To treat it as purely subjective is to fall into the trap of critical security studies which assume that reality is mere perception. The analysis of security policies and priorities must therefore elucidate their structural underpinning. To illustrate, American identity – the image that the United States has of itself and of its place in the world, and the security policies to which it gives rise – is not a given. It is the product of a complex and evolving set of interests, many of them enjoying a powerful domestic base, although more often than not their structure and mode of operation are essentially transnational. Here, one has in mind a wide range of business groups, defence-industrial pressures, media conglomerates, and numerous other organized lobbies. Other countries, be it China, Japan, or Indonesia, will have their own distinctive configuration of interests, but the same principle will apply. As Ramesh Thakur observes, the state in many developing countries is often a tool in the hands of a dominant family, clique, or sect whose primary aim is to fend off internal or external challenges to its privileged position (p. 234). The East Timor dispute is not merely the product of collective symbols and attachments, of potent memories and myths which are the essential ingredients of identity politics. In Indonesia, the United States, Australia, and East Timor itself, interests combine in ways that help to explain the nature of the conflict and the changing prospects of conflict resolution. Identity cannot be separated from interests, the subjective from the material.

The internationalization of security

Probably more than any other recent development, the internationalization of security has helped to shape the evolution of security discourse and practice. In this context the term "security" is used loosely to cover not only the security policies of states or other actors, but the range of insecurities that have guided their policies and priorities. Internationalization is not a new phenomenon, but it has gathered enormous pace and intensity over the past hundred years, and may now be said to characterize the contemporary interplay of interests and identities, of structure and agency. Internationalization refers not just to the sum total of transactions between states, or even to the wider process of interaction across state boundaries. The term is used here to denote the increasing interconnectedness of the international system, that is the increasing sensitivity of one geographical area to developments in another, and of one sector (be it military, economic, or environmental) to another. For our purposes, internationalization encompasses the twin processes of globalization and regionalization. Interdependence theories have rightly emphasized the impact of the growing number of linkages in production, communication, and transportation on economic activity, but have largely neglected the interconnectedness that permeates the field of security relations. It is not possible within the scope of this chapter to do justice to the multiple forms of interconnectedness to have emerged in recent decades, but four dimensions of the trend are worth identifying.

The first involves the *internationalization of conflict*, that is the deepening interconnection of different regions and between regions and the global system. This trend has found its most striking expression in two world wars, but also in the Cold War, in which ideological and strategic bipolarity assumed global proportions. The global spread of ideologies was mirrored and reinforced by the global contest for spheres of influence, the global projection of military power, and the global reach of weapons of mass destruction and the intercontinental means of delivering them.

A second and closely related dimension is the emergence of a *global military order*. The global alliance systems of the Cold War period entailed integrated command structures and common military doctrines supported by large troop deployments, military bases, command, control, and communications facilities, joint military exercises, and joint procurement policies. The end of the Cold War has done little to reverse this trend, as demonstrated by the revamping and enlargement of NATO and the peace-keeping/peace-enforcement roles it assumed in Bosnia and Kosovo, by the extension of the Japan–US security arrangements, and by the establishment of ad hoc global military coalitions, notably in the Iraq–Kuwait crisis. Equally significant has been the internationalization of military production and distribution networks involving a range of licensed production, co-production, and offsets, joint R&D, and subcontracting arrangements. As a consequence, the development of military technology, arms transfers, and even strategic doctrine has come to depend on a web of interlocking public–private arrangements increasingly dominated by transnational industrial, financial, and political interests, some operating legally and others not.

The two preceding aspects of internationalization are inextricably linked with a third tendency, that is *global military intervention*. During the Cold War period it manifested itself primarily in the expansionist policies of the two superpowers. Being a continental power, the Soviet Union tended to limit its interventionist tendencies to its immediate sphere of influence (e.g. Eastern Europe, Afghanistan), whereas the United States, given its much greater capacity to project power across the seas, was able to pursue a policy of global intervention (from Germany to Japan, Korea, Viet Nam, the Middle East, not to mention various parts of Central and South America). This is not to say that intervention was uniformly successful, as America's humiliating defeat in Viet Nam and

Russia's debacle in Afghanistan clearly demonstrated. The disintegration of the Soviet state left the United States as the only power capable of pursuing interventionist policies on a global scale, although the equally significant trend has been the increasingly active role of the United Nations, made possible in part by the end of strategic and ideological bipolarity which had in effect curtailed the Security Council's ability to act. Many have argued that in the post–Cold War period the UN Security Council has functioned largely as an arm of US geopolitical interests. Though this proposition is amply supported by the available evidence, there is no denying that, regardless of humanitarian justification, only the United Nations is now seen as capable of conferring legitimacy on any given operation. Hence Washington's sustained efforts to clothe its policies with the mantle of respectability by seeking UN support for, and wherever possible formal authorization of, a number of military operations (e.g. the Gulf war, Bosnia, Kosovo). At the very least, it has sought to operate under the umbrella of an alliance, usually NATO, or an ad hoc coalition (e.g. the Gulf war), for purposes of legitimation and burden-sharing. As a broad generalization, it would seem that globalized intervention is increasingly assuming a multilateral profile, although, as one would expect, many of these operations still reflect what may best be described as "residual American hegemony."[7]

Multilateral arrangements have assumed increasing importance since World War II, and should be treated as another defining characteristic of the internationalization of security. The alliances created during the Cold War on either side of the ideological divide had as their primary justification the collective security of their members. The ensuing legal and military structures were explicitly premised on the principle of collective action, that is on the readiness of all members to come to each other's assistance should any one of them be the victim of aggression. It is worth remembering, however, that the construction of alliances, which reflected and sustained the polarization and insecurities of international politics for the best part of 40 years, was itself an afterthought intended to complement the collective security provisions of the UN Charter. Alliances were considered a necessary but less than ideal response to the perception of insecurity – necessary because the UN Security Council was, by virtue of the Cold War, in effect paralysed, and less than ideal because they endowed the international system with much higher levels of polarization and militarization. Detente and the decline of the Cold War raised expectations of a reinvigorated UN system, but also led to increasing interest in the development of both old and new regional institutions. These security organizations (e.g. the Organization for Security and Co-operation in Europe, the Organization of African Unity, the Association of

South East Asian Nations, the ASEAN Regional Forum) were, by virtue of their inclusive membership, thought likely to foster a more consensual approach to conflict management and a more viable relationship between a given region and the global security system. To put it simply, multilateralism – and the institutional growth it implied – was designed to remedy the deficiencies of international diplomacy and create an international framework more conducive to the promotion of international security.

The wider security agenda: Normative and institutional implications

It is now commonplace to refer to the various sectors of security relations. In addition to military security, reference is often made to economic, environmental, societal, and political security. This much wider notion of security has come to be accepted by a great many scholars, and at least rhetorically by a good many governments. Trade rivalries, international debt, destabilizing financial flows, transborder pollution, drug trafficking, large population movements, and even human rights abuses are now said to form part of the security agenda. Advocates of human security see the wider agenda as a necessary response to the multiple challenges confronting security policy, or, to put it differently, as recognition of the multiple insecurities that are part and parcel of everyday life in a rapidly globalizing world. Those wedded to a more traditional security perspective remain generally sceptical of more comprehensive notions of security because they risk undermining the centrality of force in security calculations, and indirectly at least the primacy of the state in the formulation and execution of security policy.

The traditional view can no doubt be severely criticized for its failure to come to terms with the interconnectedness of the international system. Yet the frequently made case for comprehensive security also leaves much to be desired. To argue for a wider security agenda is one thing; to explain how it is to be widened and how that widening would affect the theory and practice of security is quite another. Proponents of human, comprehensive, or unconventional security have generally evaded or inadequately addressed a number of key questions. If the security discourse is to be widened, if the use and threat of force are no longer to be considered the core of the security dilemma, what is to take their place? What is the inner logic of the new discourse, and how are its diverse threads to be connected? What are the principal agents or agencies in identity formation, in the shaping of security policy? If the understanding and practice of security are undergoing profound change, what is the dynamic of this evolutionary process? What, in other words, are the structures and interests that guide and constrain the process?

To widen the concept so that it embraces all that contributes to human well-being, as well as the perceived threat to it, is indeed comprehensive and no doubt well intentioned, but per se analytically useless. As William Tow and Russell Trood rightly point out in chapter 1 of this volume, the challenge for the advocates of human security is to clarify the concept and develop a framework which can command the attention of scholars and policy-makers alike (p. 14). To express the sentiment a little differently, the concept must be formulated in such a way that comprehensiveness does not detract from coherence, and good intentions do not prejudice analytical rigour. This is not an impossible task. The first step is to return to our initial observation, and make insecurity rather than security our point of departure. To operationalize the concept, insecurity may be treated as a codeword for the complex set of images and identities that inject much higher levels of polarization into the international system, both within and between states, and as a consequence increase the likely frequency and intensity of violent conflict.

The above formulation is preferable to Buzan's vague notion of securitization (and desecuritization),[8] in that it identifies with greater clarity how and at what point insecurity forms the basis for security policy. The pitfalls of Buzan's approach become readily apparent when he attempts to connect economic and military security. He characterizes the global liberal order as the "desecuritization of economics," by which he presumably has in mind the pacifying impact of trade liberalization, financial deregulation, and economic interdependence more generally. However, this way of conceptualizing the linkage between the economic and strategic dimensions of security, especially when it speaks of the "desecuritizing achievements of liberalism," is to adopt an unnecessarily limiting perspective, not to say extraordinarily West-centric view of the world. Major liberal economies may not be at war with each other, but they are – especially the United States – committed to high levels of military spending (even in the post–Cold War period) and to the development of ever more sophisticated military technologies (most strikingly reflected in the so-called "revolution in military affairs"). They remain committed not only to global deterrence strategies and global military deployments but to the actual application of large-scale force whenever economic or strategic interests are at stake. In the Gulf war and the Kosovo conflict we have a graphic illustration of the complex relationship between insecurities and military conflict. These insecurities refer not only to the experience of lesser players, be they ethnic communities or the ruling regimes in Iraq or Serbia, but to NATO and the United States and their respective concerns about identity, purpose, leadership, and, at least in the case of the Gulf war, energy security.

What emerges from this brief discussion is that notions of common, comprehensive, human, or democratic security can be useful analytical tools, but only to the extent that they make explicit the subjective, relational, and normative dimensions of security relations and elucidate the polarizing implications of identity politics. Peter Chalk's emphasis on "grey area phenomena" is instructive in that it points to the salience of a range of old and new insecurities, but also to the transnational structures and interests that fuel and even mould them. This is as true of transnational organized crime as it is of religious and ethnic identities. Thakur is right to stress the crisis of governance implicit in the East Asian financial crisis (pp. 244–246), but inextricably intertwined with the failure of domestic institutions was the equally deleterious impact of money markets and the International Monetary Fund. Similarly, Elliott is right to focus on the shortcomings of the traditional security approach to environmental degradation (pp. 162–163), given its preoccupation with threats to state security, its neglect of the complex sources of insecurity, and its tendency to privilege military solutions.

None of this, however, is to suggest that the widening of the security agenda should be treated as a licence for endlessly expanding the field of enquiry or intruding an ever-growing number of variables into the equation. Security discourse can legitimately and profitably subject to critical scrutiny a number of boundaries, notably those between states, between insiders and outsiders, between government and non-government institutions, state and civil society, internal and external security. But the point of such analysis must be to generate richer insights into the sources of insecurity and the structures, agencies, and relationships needed to sustain a viable security system.

This brief re-examination of the security dilemma reveals the centrality of the institutional context. Institutional analysis is needed to establish how insecurities are perceived and interpreted, how security decisions are made, how security functions are performed, in short how political space is organized at the national and international but also subnational, supranational, and transnational levels. Security discourse must, in other words, illuminate the relationship between the balance of interests and shifting patterns of identity, between norms and the distribution of power.

As already intimated, the growth of regional and global institutions is in large measure a response to the internationalization of conflict. An equally close correlation exists between institution-building and more comprehensive notions of security. This will come as no surprise given that the widening of the security agenda is itself both cause and effect of the process of internationalization. The formation of new multilateral institutions – and the revamping of existing ones – stems directly from the perceived inadequacies of established institutions and the emergence of new insecurities. As William Maley so graphically illustrates in his discussion of refugee flows, the geographical scope and complexity of the issues involved have greatly exceeded the problem-solving capacities of territorially bound states. This is not to say that states do not still perform key functions, or that multilateral institutions do not, at least in part, depend for their effectiveness on the skills, resources, and infrastructure available to states. Multilateralism is not in any case a uniform or monolithic trend, nor does it hold the solution to every problem. It takes different forms and serves different purposes in different places at different times. Multilateralism can operate globally, but also regionally and subregionally, both formally and informally, as a Track I, Track II, or even Track III process, in relation to one or several dimensions of security policy.

There are, however, certain functions common to most multilateral institutions, which have assumed particular importance during the post–Cold War period, reflecting in part two converging yet contradictory trends: increasing interdependence and multipolarity. Three of these functions are worth highlighting.

Setting norms

Institutions validate the experience of insecurity, give meaning and legitimacy to new concepts of security, and enshrine the values or principles which guide public expectations and define acceptable behaviour, whether in relation to conduct in war, humanitarian intervention, global warming, or treatment of refugees. Institutions provide the framework within which collective identities can emerge and mature, but also within which interests can be articulated and reconciled.

Managing conflict

Institutions provide an umbrella for discussion and negotiation across the policy and conflict spectrum (this is as much the case for international institutions as it is for the state itself). Institutions can be broad-ranging and of indefinite duration (e.g. the ASEAN Regional Forum), but they can also be conflict specific (i.e. formed to deal with a particular conflict, as in the South China Sea Workshops), function specific (i.e. concerned with a particular issue or set of issues, e.g. the United Nations High Commissioner for Refugees), or time specific (e.g. the United Nations Transitional Authority in Cambodia).

Harmonizing decision-making processes

Institutional arrangements are needed to coordinate between different levels of decision-making, for example between the approaches of different states, between bilateral and multilateral regimes, between different regions, and between the regional and the global. In the case of regional organizations, the effectiveness with which these various functions will be performed will depend on a number of key variables, not least the inclusiveness and cohesiveness of their membership, the resources available to them, and the degree of support they can reasonably expect from relevant actors.

The Asia-Pacific context

In the Asia-Pacific region, it is not so much human as comprehensive security that has commanded attention. Quite apart from the prominence which the term acquired in Japanese security policy after the mid-1970s, comprehensive security has been most extensively developed in South-East Asia. In 1984, Malaysian Deputy Prime Minister Musa Hitan advanced the following formulation:

> Reduced to basics, there are three pillars in Malaysia's doctrine of comprehensive security. The first is the need to ensure a secure Southeast Asia. The second is to ensure a strong and effective ASEAN community. The third, and most basic, is the necessity to ensure that Malaysia is *sound, secure and strong within.*[9]

Economic growth, he went on to argue, was a necessary component of comprehensive security, for it made possible a viable programme of social justice, contributed to inter-ethnic harmony, hence social cohesion and national unity, and allowed for the modernization of Malaysia's armed forces. Central, in fact, to the way ASEAN as a whole – not just Malaysia – has understood comprehensive security and the related notion of national resilience is the emphasis on threats to internal security and, with it, a preoccupation with the wide-ranging tasks of nation-building.[10] Here it is worth adding that in many cases both internal security and nation-building have had as much to do with the survival of the state, if not the ruling élite, as with any wider notion of human security.

With the European experience partly in mind, but more specifically with the aim of devising a formula better suited to the region's circumstances, the Council for Security Cooperation in the Asia Pacific (CSCAP) established a working group to examine the concepts of comprehensive and cooperative security. In this context it is worth recalling Toshiya Hoshino's portrayal of CSCAP as one of the more innovative yet influential attempts at Track II dialogue (p. 278). The results of the working group's deliberations were published in a memorandum setting out an "overarching organizing concept for the management of security in the region." Comprehensive security was defined as "sustainable security" in all fields (personal, political, economic, social, cultural, military, environmental) in both a domestic and external context, essentially through collaborative means.[11] Under economic issues were listed a number of macro-economic indicators of national strength (e.g. competitive capability, food and energy sufficiency) but also economic factors impacting directly on everyday life (e.g. poverty, unemployment, dislocations caused by structural reform). A long list of other threats to security followed, including drug abuse, epidemics, corruption, insurgency, ethnic and religious extremism, threats to life and personal liberties, and a range of environmental challenges. Finally, the paper drew attention to several underlying principles: the interdependence of various dimensions of security, the perception of security as a cooperative enterprise, acknowledgement of the possible benefits of self-reliance in defence, the value of inclusive processes and institutions, a preference for non-military solutions to conflict, and support for the accepted norms of responsible international behaviour.

The CSCAP paper did not explicitly grapple with the issue of psycho-social insecurity, nor did it offer an analytically rigorous definition of security, or for that matter any clear policy guidelines. Ambiguities surrounding the subject of security and the interconnections between different dimensions of (in)security were not adequately considered, let alone resolved. The paper did, however, succeed in highlighting the multi-faceted and multidimensional character of comprehensive security, and created a potentially useful bridge between traditional and less conventional forms of security discourse.

Prospective agenda and institutional requirements

Shifting the focus of attention from concepts to practice in Asia-Pacific, the picture of security relations that emerges is one of considerable progress at many levels and with respect to several conflicts. These unmistakable signs of progress, some of which became apparent even before the end of the Cold War, were made possible by a timely combination of factors. These may be briefly characterized as follows:

- The emergence of an increasingly interdependent trading and investment region, which includes East Asia, North America, and Oceania, but whose precise boundaries are susceptible to change in the face of shifting patterns of economic activity. This region is best understood as a "production alliance" rather than a trading bloc, whose dynamism rests in part on a unique but shifting division of labour, access to a large US market, and continued Japanese penetration of Asian supplier networks.[12]

- A gradual shift in US attitudes, culminating in President Clinton's embrace of the concept of multilateral security dialogue as one of the four pillars of the "new Pacific Community."
- A comparable shift in Japanese and Chinese attitudes, attributable in part to Japan's and China's interest in raising their international profile in ways that are less likely to stir regional anxieties and might make their growing economic or political dominance more palatable.
- The leadership role of ASEAN, and the unique contributions of a number of small and middle powers, in particular Indonesia, Malaysia, Australia, and Canada.
- The particular diplomatic style favoured by a number of Asian governments, and most closely associated with ASEAN's practice, with its emphasis on longer time-horizons and policy perspectives, informal structures and processes, consensual approaches to decision-making, multidimensional or comprehensive notions of security, and the principle of non-interference in the internal affairs of other countries[13] – all of which have helped to make multilateralism both more enticing and less threatening than might otherwise be the case.
- The rising influence exerted by important elements of the business and academic communities and by a growing number of networks of non-governmental organizations, all with a vested interest in regional co-operation.

These and other factors have certainly eased the path of multilateral security dialogue, but they have not made it irreversible. The region has yet to develop an institutional framework able to deliver anything resembling comprehensive security. Neither economic dynamism nor complex interdependence offers a sufficient guarantee of success. Indeed, their combined effect is a contradictory one, on the one hand providing the glue holding the emerging Pacific community together, and on the other generating competitive pressures driving societies and economies apart. Equally problematic are the alliances and strategic partnerships dating back to the Cold War period, which, precisely because they no longer enjoy the legitimating function conferred by the East–West conflict, are likely to seek new and potentially destabilizing sources of legitimation, or alternatively return to the containment strategies of an earlier period. There are in reality a great many economic, geopolitical, and cultural forces at work, which, if not properly addressed, could endanger continued progress towards a multilateral framework of comprehensive security. The following list, which is by no means exhaustive, is nevertheless indicative of the many actual and potential sources of insecurity:

- The negative possibilities inherent in rapid industrialization and economic and financial networking, including rising military expenditures and acquisition of potentially destabilizing offensive weapons systems and platforms;[14] the proliferation of nuclear capabilities; rapid environmental degradation, with far-reaching transboundary implications; disparities of wealth and income within and between states; financial instability (strikingly illustrated in the East Asian crisis of the late 1990s); and the consequent suspicions and fears harboured by the less prosperous and successful vis-à-vis those exercising economic dominance[15] (recent events in Indonesia could easily gain further momentum and be replicated elsewhere).
- Latent or overt bilateral tensions, many of them pre-dating the Cold War (e.g. Sino-Japanese rivalry, Japan–Korea tensions, Indo-Pakistan conflict, competing territorial claims in relation to the Spratlys, the Kuril Islands or Northern Territories, and the Senkaku [Daioyutai] Islands).
- Unresolved separatist claims (e.g. Tibet, Kashmir, East Timor), issues of divided sovereignty (China–Taiwan, the Korean peninsula), and internal instability reflected in illegitimate political institutions (e.g. Myanmar, Cambodia, Indonesia).
- A rapidly changing balance of interests associated with the relative decline of US dominance and the corresponding rise of China and perhaps Japan as major centres of power, with all that this implies for possible mistrust and misunderstanding during the period of transition.
- The steep learning curve that the Asia-Pacific region must necessarily experience when building a multilateral security system, given the general lack of familiarity with, or even confidence in, such processes, and the cultural, political, and economic heterogeneity of the region.[16]

Enough has been said to indicate that the creation of a new security framework in the Asia-Pacific will not be the handiwork of an existing or aspiring hegemon. It will not, in other words, emerge under conditions of "hegemonic stability." Rather, it will arise in slow and tortuous fashion in the context of a still unfolding historical process, in which power is diffuse and decisions depend for their legitimacy on consensus rather than diktat. It does not, however, follow from this evolutionary perspective that the process need be at the mercy of ad hoc improvisation. A measure of politically prudent yet conceptually inventive planning, at least on the part of certain actors, would seem both feasible and desirable.

A few steps on the road to a "Pacific house"

For a *Pacific house*[17] to be both durable and comfortable, its design and construction will need to be conscious of the multiple and interacting insecurities that still afflict many of the states and communities of the region. Expressed a little differently, the *Pacific house* will need to be sensitive to diverse needs, levels of economic development, and cultural and political traditions. It will need to reflect a pluralist, cosmopolitan architecture, incorporating a great many styles (formal and informal) and a range of structures (bilateral and multilateral, governmental and non-governmental), each performing its own function, and none overwhelming the other. It is perhaps appropriate that this all too brief discussion of the security prospects of the Asia-Pacific region should therefore conclude with some sense of the tasks that lie ahead. Here particular attention must be drawn to the institutional requirements of such a project. Without adequate institutional foundations, using the resources and capabilities of both states and non-state actors, it is difficult to imagine how the house will withstand the internal and external buffeting that will surely come its way.

Listed below are a few proposals, some more ambitious than others, but all of which are deserving of serious consideration:

- A *Regional Declaration of Principles* (similar to the proposed Pacific Concord),[18] with an emphasis on common security, economic cooperation, multicultural tolerance and harmony, and respect for comprehensive human rights and freedoms; consistent with the case advanced by Hyun-Seok Yu, such a declaration should facilitate rather than obstruct a process of inclusive and ongoing negotiation and review.
- *An Asia-Pacific Annual or Biennial Leaders Meeting*, to act as the roof or umbrella for the *Pacific house*, and to consider a wide range of economic, security, and related issues.
- Asia-Pacific Economic Cooperation (APEC) and the ASEAN Regional Forum (ARF) would constitute the two main pillars of the regional architecture, but with each pillar over time giving more attention to the interconnection between economy and security. APEC could begin by giving more systematic attention to a number of unconventional security issues, in particular those relating to energy security, food security, labour migration, and drug trafficking.
- More regular and efficient communication flows between APEC and ARF, particularly at the level of senior officials, with the focus at least initially on overlapping interest in such areas as transnational economic crime and the marine environment.
- A more direct and methodical CSCAP contribution to ARF's future

development, with particular reference to preventive diplomacy and conflict resolution (this to include detailed studies, policy recommendations, and transitional strategies).

- The establishment of forums giving a voice to other epistemic communities, including environmental and medical scientists, lawyers and judges, parliamentarians and civil servants; such forums may, for example, provide, at least initially, a more congenial environment for the promotion of a regional human rights dialogue.[19]
- A more concerted effort to improve communication and cooperation between subregional institutions (such as ASEAN and the South Pacific Forum), and to inject their concerns into the wider regional framework.
- Continued encouragement for the development of conflict-specific, informal mechanisms, as was the case with the Cambodian peace process, and as might happen with the South China Sea Workshops.
- An informal Track I or Track II working group to prepare a detailed inventory of current regional dialogue mechanisms operating across the range of issues relevant to the comprehensive security agenda.
- Another working group to be asked to prepare an annual report to the ARF Senior Officials Meeting setting out action taken in response to ARF decisions and recommendations.
- The developing Asia–Europe dialogue to give serious attention to issues of comprehensive security, including global environmental change, transnational crime, human rights, peace-keeping, and UN reform.
- More effective links between regional Track I and Track II institutions and the UN system, around such issues as nuclear non-proliferation, a UN arms register, the Law of the Sea, peace-keeping, conflict prevention, and conflict resolution.

These proposals may not all be immediately feasible or universally acceptable. But if the merger of human security and comprehensive security is to progress from conceptual abstraction to policy relevance, the time may well have come for serious and detailed discussion of a number of practical initiatives and for more sustained interaction between policymaker, citizen, and scholar.

Notes

1. See Barry Buzan, "Rethinking Security after the Cold War," *Cooperation and Conflict* 32, no. 1 (March 1997), p. 115.
2. Bill McSweeney, *Security, Identity and Interests* (Cambridge: Cambridge University Press, forthcoming).

3. See J. A. Camilleri and Jim Falk, *The End of Sovereignty? The Politics of a Shrinking and Fragmenting World* (Aldershot, UK: Edward Elgar, 1992), pp. 203–204.
4. See A. D. Smith, "Ethnie and Nation in the Modern World," *Millennium* 14, no. 2 (Summer 1985), pp. 131–132.
5. Barry Buzan and Ole Waever, "Slippery, Contradictory? Sociologically Untenable? The Copenhagen School Replies," *Review of International Studies* 23, no. 2 (1997), pp. 241–250.
6. See Alexander Wendt, "Collective Identity Formation and the International State," *American Political Science Review* 88, no. 2 (June 1994), pp. 384–396.
7. See Joseph A. Camilleri, "The Asia-Pacific in the Post-Hegemonic World," in Andrew Mack and John Ravenhill, eds., *Pacific Co-operation: Building Economic and Security Regimes in the Asia-Pacific Region* (Boulder, CO: Westview Press, 1995), pp. 193–196.
8. Buzan, "Rethinking Security after the Cold War," p. 24.
9. Speech given in Singapore on 2 March 1984 and reprinted as "Malaysia's Doctrine of Comprehensive Security," in *Foreign Affairs (Malaysia)* 17, no. 1 (March 1984), pp. 94–99, at p. 94, emphasis added.
10. See Muthiah Alagappa, "Comprehensive Security: Interpretations in ASEAN Countries," in Robert Scalapino et al., eds., *Asian Security Issues: Regional and Global* (Berkeley: Institute of Asian Studies, University of California, 1988), pp. 50–78, and Alan Dupont, "Concepts of Security," in James Rolfe, ed., *Unsolved Futures: Comprehensive Security in Asia-Pacific* (Wellington: Centre for Strategic Studies, 1995), p. 7.
11. *The Concepts of Comprehensive Security and Cooperative Security*, CSCAP Memorandum no. 3 (1995), p. 2.
12. Peter Katzenstein, "Regionalism in Comparative Perspective," *Co-operation and Conflict* 31, no. 2 (1996), pp. 134–139.
13. See Des Ball, "Strategic Culture in the Asia-Pacific Region," *Security Studies* 13, no. 1 (Autumn 1993), pp. 44–74; also Mohamed Jawhar Hassan, "The Concept of Comprehensive Security," paper presented at the second meeting of the CSCAP Working Group on Concepts of Comprehensive Security and Cooperative Security, Kuala Lumpur, 27–29 August 1995, pp. 12–13.
14. J. N. Mak and B. A. Hamzah, "The External Maritime Dimension of ASEAN Security," *Journal of Strategic Studies* 18, no. 3 (September 1995), pp. 133–136.
15. See Mohamed Jawhar Hassan, "Economic Pragmatism and Its Implications for Security and Confidence Building among States in the Asia-Pacific Region," in *Disarmament: Topical Papers*, no. 13 (New York: UN Department of Political Affairs, 1993), p. 74.
16. See Edward A. Olsen and David Winterford, "Multilateral Arms Control Regimes in Asia: Prospects and Options," *Asia Perspectives* 18, no. 1 (Spring–Summer 1994), p. 21.
17. This highly suggestive term was first used by Peter Polomka, "Asia-Pacific Security: Towards a 'Pacific House'," *Australian Journal of International Affairs* 33, no. 2 (December 1990), pp. 269–279.
18. See Paul Evans, "Towards a Pacific Concord," paper presented at the ASEAN-ISIS 10th Round Table, Kuala Lumpur, 5–8 June 1996.
19. See Joseph A. Camilleri, "Regional Human Rights Dialogue in Asia Pacific: Prospects and Proposals," *Pacifica Review: Peace, Security and Global Change* 10, no. 3 (October 1998), pp. 178–179.

Contributors

Anthony Bergin is an Associate Professor in the Australian Defence Force Academy's School of Politics and Director of the Australian Defence Studies Centre in Canberra, Australia.

Ikrar Nusa Bhakti is an analyst with the Centre for Political and Regional Studies at the Indonesia Institute for Sciences, Jakarta, Indonesia.

Joseph A. Camilleri is Professor of International Relations at LaTrobe University, Bundooora, Victoria, Australia.

Peter A. Chalk was an international relations lecturer in the Department of Government, University of Queensland, Brisbane, Australia, and is currently a policy analyst with the RAND Corporation in Washington DC.

Lorraine Elliott lectures in environmental politics at the Australian National University's Department of International Relations, Canberra, Australia.

Marianne Hanson is a Senior Lecturer in International Relations with the University of Queensland's Department of Government, Brisbane, Australia.

Toshiya Hoshino is an Associate Professor at the Osaka School of International Public Policy, Osaka University, Osaka, Japan.

In-Taek Hyun is an Associate Professor of Political Science at Korea University, Seoul, Republic of Korea, and Research Director of that university's Ilmin International Relations Institute.

Chandran Jeshurun is an independent analyst of Asian politics and international relations and formerly affiliated with the Institute of Southeast Asian Studies in Singapore.

Sung-Han Kim is an Associate Professor at the Institute of Foreign Affairs and Trade in Seoul, Republic of Korea.

Woosang Kim is an Associate Professor of Political Science, Yonsei University, Seoul, Republic of Korea.

Leong Liew is a Senior Lecturer in International Economics in the Faculty of International Business and Politics at Griffith University, Brisbane, Australia.

William Maley is a Senior Lecturer in the School of Politics, Australian Defence Force Academy, Canberra, Australia.

Jin-Hyun Paik is a Professor of Politics at the Graduate Institute for International and Area Studies, Seoul National University, Seoul, Republic of Korea.

Withaya Sucharithanarugse is a past Director, Institute of Asian Studies, Chulalongkorn University, Bangkok, Thailand.

Ramesh Thakur is Professor and Vice Rector at the United Nations University, Tokyo, Japan.

William T. Tow is an Associate Professor of International Relations at the University of Queensland's Department of Government and Director of the International Relations and Asia-Politics Research Institute, Brisbane, Australia.

Russell Trood is Associate Professor and Director of the Centre for the Study of Australia–Asia Relations at Griffith University's School of Asian and International Studies, Brisbane, Australia.

Carl Ungerer is with Australia's Office of National Assessments. He previously was with the Department of Foreign Affairs and Trade and is a Ph.D. candidate with the University of Queensland's Department of Government, Brisbane, Australia.

Wilfrido V. Villacorta is Professor and President of the Yuchengco Institute for East Asia, De La Salle University, Manila, the Philippines.

Hyun-Seok Yu is Assistant Professor in ChoongAng University's Department of International Relations, Ansung, Kyunggi-Do, Republic of Korea.

Index

326